DESIGN JURIES ON TRIAL
THE RENAISSANCE OF THE DESIGN STUDIO

20th *Anniversary Edition*

KATHRYN H. ANTHONY

Originally published by Van Nostrand Reinhold, New York, NY, USA 1991
Reprinted by the author, Champaign, IL, USA 1999, 2012
kanthony@illinois.edu

Design Juries on Trial, 20th Anniversary Edition
Copyright © 1999, 2012 by Kathryn H. Anthony

Reprinted by the author, Champaign, Illinois, 1999, 2012 kanthony@illinois.edu

All rights reserved. No part of this work covered by the copyright hereon
may be reproduced or used in any form or by any means-graphic, electronic,
or mechanical, including photocopying, recording, taping, or information storage
and retrieval systems-without written permission of the author.

ISBN 10: 974845019
ISBN 13: 9780974845012

Copyright ©1991 by Van Nostrand Reinhold, since transferred to the author.
Library of Congress Catalog Card Number 91-723

Manufactured in the United States of America

Cover Design by Gloria M. Colom

Published by Van Nostrand Reinhold
115 Fifth Avenue
New York, NY, USA 10003

Chapman and Hall
2-6 Boundary Row
London, SE l8HN, England

Thomas Nelson Australia
102 Dodds Street
South Melbourne 3205
Victoria, Australia

Nelson Canada
1120 Birchmount Road
Scarborough, Ontario M 1 K 504, Canada

16 IS 14 13 12 11 10 9 8 7 6 5 4 3 2 I
Library of Congress Cataloging-ill-Publication Data
Anthony, Kathryn H.

Design juries on trial: the renaissance of the design studio I Kathryn H. Anthony.
p. em.
Includes index.
ISBN 0-442-00235-1

1. Architectural design-Evaluation. 2. Architectural design-
Awards. 3. Communication in architectural design. 4. Jury-Biography-History
and criticism. I. Title.
NA2750.A64 1991
729'079-dc20

91-723
CIP

I'm always interested in readers' comments and reactions to Design Juries on Trial. Feel free to e-mail me at kanthony@illinois.edu.

From Students:

"*Design Juries on Trial* is a terrific source of guidance. It reveals some of the mysteries of architectural education that I had to find out the hard way." – Amy J. Isenburg, Former Vice President, The American Institute of Architecture Students (AIAS)

"I would recommend this book to every student and educator who is concerned about the quality of his or her personal experiences in architectural education." – Christine A. Malecki, Former Vice President, The American Institute of Architecture Students (AIAS)

"*Design Juries on Trial* is the first research endeavor that collectively represents the students' perspective of traditional design juries and how ineffective, habitual techniques may be transformed into effective teaching methods." – Brian Bayer, Former Editor of *CRIT*, Journal of the American Institute of Architecture Students (AIAS)

From faculty:

"Frank Lloyd Wright, Gropius, Corbusier, Kahn, Gehry and other great architects have viewed themselves as contributors to the built environment, and as agents of social change. The profession itself has articulated often-inflated commitments to changing our physical and social environments. Yet it has been Kathryn Anthony who, through her quietly consistent and thoroughly researched admonishments to the profession and to design schools, has brought to architecture a true sense of how far short we have fallen in opening the profession to all…" – Theodore C. Landsmark, M. Ev.D., J.D., D.F.A. (hon.), Ph.D., President, Boston Architectural College; Former President, Association of Collegiate Schools of Architecture

"She has dared to ask questions that have challenged the status quo… Professor Anthony's research, scholarly publications, and public presentations have been catalysts for significant changes in academia and the profession… Kathryn Anthony has inspired generations of students, teachers and practitioners through her teaching and scholarship." – Georgia Bizios, FAIA, ACSA Distinguished Professor, North Carolina State University

"There had always been a lot of talk in private conversations—occasionally a public one—about so and so's studio practices that reflected frontier-cowboy training, practices and antics. Generally these were understood as idiosyncratic, individual incidents. But Professor Anthony brought to public, academic and professional light the much-needed empirical, in-depth examination of the nature of the pedagogical processes that limited diverse teaching practices and undermined the fundamental goals of architecture as a social art. Her book, *Design Juries on Trial*, is an insightful, informative and delightful read even today." – Sherry Ahrentzen, Ph.D., ACSA Distinguished Professor, Associate Director of Research, Arizona State University Stardust Center for Affordable Homes and the Family

"Kathryn Anthony fearlessly took on the sacred cows within architectural education and practice, the design jury and studio culture. Her book *Design Juries on Trial* was a catalyst for a national discussion and movement that resulted in the AIAS Studio Culture Task Force and ultimately the NAAB requirement that every accredited architecture program develop a Studio Culture Policy that has vastly improved our student's learning environment." – Geraldine Forbes Isais, ACSA Distinguished Professor, Dean, School of Architecture and Planning, University of New Mexico

"It is a book that should be read by every single faculty member or potential juror in architecture schools, and by students as well… This book is a significant milestone in architectural education." – Diane Ghirardo, Ph.D., Former Executive Editor, *Journal of Architectural Education,* Professor, School of Architecture, University of Southern California

"We should all read it and re-read it… It is timely, it is clear, it is provocative and it is invaluable at this stage in the evolution of architectural education." – Patrick J. Quinn, FAIA, FAAR, FRSA, Former President, Association of Collegiate Schools of Architecture (ACSA), Institute Professor of Architecture, Rensselaer Polytechnic Institute

"It strikes at the very heart of what all of us as academics are occupied with every semester of every academic year. It should be…compulsory reading for all faculty in schools of architecture throughout the country." – R. Alan Forrester, Former Director, School of Architecture, University of Illinois at Urbana-Champaign

"**Design Juries on Trial** brings together the most experienced professionals with the instructors and the students… It addresses a range of concerns, from providing advice to students who must endure the studio review to suggesting measures for the instructor to be a more effective teacher. The very essence of design, architecture and education is dissected and reconsidered to create a … users manual for the design studio." – Marvin Malecha, Former President, Association of Collegiate Schools of Architecture (ACSA), Dean, North Carolina State University

From practitioners:

"Kathryn Anthony has written two books that have been the moral compass for an architecture industry that resists change and needs freshness…she is not only a scholar, but a pioneer." – Nicholas Watkins, Ph.D., Principal, Director of Health Care Research, HOK

"It's been an honor to be part of what will undoubtedly be the handbook on 'constructive juries' for students and design professionals!" – Ronette King, Gensler and Associates Architects

"Reading it and thinking about it challenges design educators to question their methods and assumptions, invites design students to examine the studio subculture as well as change their behavior in it, demands professional designers to evaluate the relationships between design education and current practice patterns, and requires design researchers to ask: Why has so little research been done on this important area before?" – Min Kantrowitz, Min Kantrowitz & Associates, in *Environment & Behavior*

"Ms. Anthony makes her case with superb research, expert witnesses both for and against the jury system, thought provoking questions on topics like 'hidden agendas' and 'stars' and 'gender discrimination' in design education, and detailed promises for a better future. The readers of this valuable work, who become the jury, should represent great numbers of our profession." – Charles Sappenfield, FAIA in *Competitions*

DEDICATION

To Barry

To Harry, Anne, and Mary Anne

To design students of the past, present, and future

CREDITS

Every effort has been made to make the information in this book as complete and accurate as possible, but the author and publisher are not responsible for any errors or omissions, and no warranty or fitness is implied. If any credit lines here inadvertently have been omitted, please contact the publisher and we will correct them in our next reprint.

This book is sold with the understanding that the author and publisher are not engaged in rendering professional advice or services to the reader. Neither author nor publisher shall bear liability or responsibility to any person or entity with respect to any loss or damage arising from information contained in this book.

DRAWING CREDITS: Figs. 1-1, 1-2, 2-1, 2-2, 2-3, 2-5, 2-6, 2-7, 3-1, 3-2, 3-3, 3-4, 3-6, 3-7, 3-8, 4-1, 4-2, 4-3, 4-4, 5-1, 5-2, 5-3, 5-4, 5-5, 5-6, 6-1, 6-2, 6-3, 6-4, 6-5, 6-6, 6-7, 6-8, 6-9, 6-10, 6-11, 6-12, 6-13, 6-16, 7-1, 7-2, 7-3, 8-1, 8-2, 8-3, 8-4, 8-5, 9-2, 9-4, 9-8, 9-9, 9-10, 9-11, 10-1, 10-3, 10-4, 10-5, 10-6, 11-3, 11-4, 11-5, 11-6, 11-7, 12-1, 12-2, 12-3, 12-4, 12-5—drawn by Ray Lytle; Figs. 2-4, 6-17 (courtesy of Roger Fisher and William Ury), 11-1, A-1, A-2, A-3, A-4, A-5, A-6, A-7, B-1, B-2, B-3, B-4, B-5, B-6, C-1 (courtesy of Robert I. Selby), C-2 (courtesy of Arthur L. Kaha), C-3, C-5—drawn by Mary Shiffer; Figs. 4-5, 5-7, 6-14, 6-15, 6-18, 7-4, 8-6, 9-3, 9-5, 9-6, 9-7, 10-2 (courtesy of Ronald Beckman and Edward R. Ostrander), 11-2 (courtesy of the National Council of Architectural Registration Boards), C-4 (courtesy of Stefani Ledewitz)—drawn by the author; Fig. 9-1—drawn by Clayton Haldeman; Tables B-1, B-2—drawn by the author.

STATEMENT CREDITS: pp. 1, 157—courtesy of The Architectural Press [in Gowan, James (ed.), *A Continuing Experiment: Learning and Teaching at the Architectural Association*, London: Architectural Press, pp. 23, 17]; pp. 8, 67, 85, 93, 205-207—courtesy of Cesar Pelli; pp. 8, 46, 75, 94, 96, 107, 148, 183-184—courtesy of Joseph Esherick; pp. 8, 96, 139, 147, 193-197—courtesy of John F. Hartray, Jr.; pp. 8, 65, 83, 107, 140, 207-209—courtesy of Lawrence B. Perkins; pp. 8, 20, 84, 85, 203-205—courtesy of Charles W. Moore; pp. 8, 211-212—courtesy of Robert A. M. Stern; pp. 15, 30, 85, 140, 149, 197-199—courtesy of Steven Izenour; pp. 30, 50, 215-216—courtesy of John C. Walker; pp. 31, 38, 46, 65, 74, 84, 107, 175-176—courtesy of William Callaway; pp. 31, 65, 84, 107, 176-177—courtesy of Christopher Degenhardt; pp. 31, 84, 95, 144, 178-179—courtesy of the late Norman R. DeHaan; pp. 31, 85, 140, 189-191—courtesy of Charles Gwathmey; pp. 31, 107, 139, 148, 149, 191-193—courtesy of Donald J. Hackl; p. 39—courtesy of Victoria J. Ellis; pp. 46, 140, 212-213—courtesy of Minoru Takeyama; pp. 46, 186-189—courtesy of Michael Graves; pp. 46, 71, 84, 173-175—courtesy of Laurence Booth; pp. 50, 83, 148, 209-211—courtesy of Martha Schwartz; pp. 52, 171-173—courtesy of Carol Ross Barney; pp. 65, 74, 84, 140, 173—courtesy of Joan Blutter; pp. 67, 83, 140, 179-182—courtesy of Larry N. Deutsch; pp. 67, 85, 95, 107, 112, 140, 200-202—courtesy of Ronette J. King; pp. 67, 84, 85, 95, 220-221—courtesy of Jeffrey Werner; pp. 75, 129—courtesy of Robert Selby; pp. 75-78—courtesy of Roger Fisher and William Ury; pp. 76, 84, 182-183—courtesy of Peter Eisenman; pp. 80, 147, 184-186—courtesy of Rodney F. Friedman; pp. 107, 118, 129—courtesy of Thomas Dutton; pp. 116, 117, 124, 125—courtesy of Stefani Ledewitz; p. 127—courtesy of Anthony C. Antoniades; p. 128—courtesy of Robert Levy; p. 128—courtesy of Arthur E. Stamps, III; p. 128—courtesy of Howard Ray Lawrence; p. 128— courtesy of Juan C. Bertotto; p. 129—courtesy of Peter Prangnell; pp. 129, 217-219—courtesy of Cynthia Weese; pp. 129, 130—courtesy of Ronald Beckman and Edward R. Ostrander; pp. 131, 132—courtesy of M. Joe Numbers; p. 135n.11—courtesy of Ruth Parnall; pp. 143, 144, 199-200—courtesy of E. Fay Jones; p. 144—courtesy of *The San Diego Union*; p. 153n.3—courtesy of the National Council of Architectural Registration Boards; p. 157—courtesy of Progressive Architecture; p. 166, 167—courtesy of Robert Gutman; p. 167—courtesy of Maxwell Business Communications; pp. 202-203—courtesy of Richard Meier; pp. 214-215—courtesy of Susana Torre; pp. 216-217—courtesy of Peter Walker.

PHOTO CREDITS: Fig. 13-1—courtesy of Carol Ross Barney; Fig. 13-2—courtesy of Joan Blutter; Fig. 13-3—courtesy of Laurence Booth; Fig. 13-4—courtesy of William Callaway (photo: Dixi Carillo); Fig. 13-5—courtesy of Christopher Degenhardt; Fig. 13-6—courtesy of the late Norman R. DeHaan (photo: Bruce Powell); Fig. 13-7—courtesy of Larry N. Deutsch; Fig. 13-8—courtesy of Peter Eisenman (photo: Dick Frank Studios, Inc.); Fig. 13-9—courtesy of Joseph Esherick; Fig. 13-10—courtesy of Rodney F. Friedman; Fig. 13-11—courtesy of Michael Graves (photo: William Taylor); Fig. 13-12—courtesy of Charles Gwathmey; Fig. 13-13—courtesy of Donald J. Hackl; Fig. 13-4—courtesy of John F. Hartray, Jr. (photo: Bruce Van Inwegen); Fig. 13-15—courtesy of Steven Izenour; Fig. 13-16—courtesy of E. Fay Jones; Fig. 13-17—courtesy of Ronette J. King; Fig. 13-18—courtesy of Richard Meier (photo: Scott Frances/Esto); Fig. 13-19—courtesy of Charles W. Moore; Fig. 13-20—courtesy of Cesar Pelli (photo: Michael Marstand); Fig. 13-21—courtesy of Lawrence B. Perkins; Fig. 13-22—courtesy of Martha Schwartz; Fig. 13-23—courtesy of Robert A. M. Stern (photo: Franz Walderdorff); Fig. 13-24—courtesy of Minoru Takeyama (photo: Kyle Smith); Fig. 13-25—courtesy of Susana Torre (photo: Max Hilaire); Fig. 13-26—courtesy of John C. Walker; Fig. 13-27—courtesy of Peter Walker; Fig. 13-28—courtesy of Cynthia Weese (photo: Norman Phillips of London, Ltd.); Fig. 13-29—courtesy of Jeffrey Werner.

CONTENTS

Preface to the 20th Anniversary Edition xi

Preface xiii

Acknowledgements xvii

Part 1 AN OVERVIEW OF DESIGN JURIES 1

Chapter 1 Introduction: A Hazing Ritual 3
A Multilayered Approach 5
Organization of this Book 6

Chapter 2 What are Design Juries? A Historical and Comparative Analysis 8
A Brief Overview of Juries in Design Education 9
The Design Studio and the Design Jury in a Broader Educational Context 11
The Design Project, the Term Paper, and the Final Exam 13
Design Juries and Comprehensive Exams 15
Design Juries, Athletics, and the Military 15
Design Juries and Their Counterparts in the Fine Arts: Art, Music, and Drama 16
Design Juries and Their Counterparts in Other Professions: Law and Medicine 17
A Social and Psychological Analysis: Juries As "Festivals" or "Bloodbaths"? 20
Notes 23

Part 2 RESEARCH ABOUT DESIGN JURIES 27

Chapter 3 How Do Students, Faculty, and Practitioners View Design Juries? 29
Why Have Juries? Differing Views About the Purposes of Juries 29
Winners and Losers: The Best and Worst of Design Juries 32
Lessons Learned: The Educational Value of Design Juries 34
Dishing It Out and Taking It: Delivering and Responding to Public Criticism 36
The Studio Subculture: The Eating, Sleeping, and Working Habits of Design Students 38
Notes 40

Part 3 WHAT STUDENTS CAN DO 43

Chapter 4 The Preventive Approach: Learning the Art of Time Management 45
Buy a Portable Calendar and Use It 47
Set Priorities 47
Take Small Steps 48
Classic Time Management Tips 49
Avoid Procrastination 50
Summary Checklist 51
Notes 52

Chapter 5 Avoiding Guesswork: Learning How to Research Your Project and Its Users 54
Where Do I Begin? How to Gather Existing Information 55
How Can I Remember What I Read? How to Record and Document Existing Information 56
How to Gather Existing Information 57
How to Present Your Research Findings Effectively 58
How to Apply Your Research Findings to Design 59
Summary Checklist 60
Notes 62

Chapter 6 Quick on Your Feet: Learning the Art of Communication 65
Why Learn to Speak? 65
Become an Effective Speaker 66
Handle Questions Effectively: Learn to Listen 74
Learn How to Negotiate 75
Summary Checklist 79
Notes 80

Chapter 7 Dazzling Drawings: Preparing Effective Graphic Presentations for the Jury 83
Catching the Jury's Eye 84
A Selective Process 85
Communicate Clearly 86
The Visual-Verbal Connection 88
Prepare for Logistical Details 88
Summary Checklist 89
Notes 90

Chapter 8 Burnout on the Boards: How to Handle Studio Stress 91
Overcome the Jury Jitters 92
Reduce Stress Before and After the Jury 94
Broaden Your Horizons 95

x Contents

  Redefine the Studio Subculture: The Role of Sleep and Food 96
  Summary Checklist 99
  Notes 100

Part 4 WHAT FACULTY AND VISITING CRITICS CAN DO 103

Chapter 9 Delivering Constructive Criticism 105
  A Critique of Criticism 105
  Stop, Look, and Listen 109
  Be Specific 111
  Offer Some Guidance 112
  Consider Your Overall Verbal and Nonverbal Communication Style 114
  Helpful Desk Critiques 115
  Workshop and Orientation Sessions for Design Critics 117
  Is Constructive Criticism Enough? 118
  Notes 118

Chapter 10 Alternatives to Traditional Design Juries 120
  A Matter of Semantics 120
  Some Prerequisites 121
  Spell It Out 121
  Master the Mystery 122
  Be Prepared 123
  Keep the Original Cast of Characters 123
  Change the Calendar 124
  Drop the Final Jury 124
  Curfew 124
  Prepare a Schedule 124
  Spotlight a Few 124
  Stage an Opening Night 125
  This Time It's for Real 126
  Postdesign Evaluation 127
  Jury Duty 127
  Gimme Shelter 128
  Do Unto Others... 128
  If at First You Don't Succeed... 128
  Show Me Yours... 128
  Round-Robin 129
  Round-Robin-Standard 129
  Student Review 129
  Jurors on Trial 129
  Professor as Advocate 130
  Closed Seminar/Video Review 130
  You Ought to Be in Pictures 130
  The Buddy System 131
  The Brochure or Portfolio Presentation 131
  Meet Me After Class 131
  Dear John... 131
  Self-Evaluation 131
  Common Themes 132
  Notes 134

Part 5 JURIES IN PRACTICE 137

Chapter 11 How Do Practitioners View Professional Design Juries? 139
  Academic and Professional Design Juries 139
  The Pros and Cons of Design Awards Programs 143
  The Pros and Cons of Design Competitions 145
  Some Alternative Models 149
  Notes 153

Part 6 EPILOGUE 155

Chapter 12 Should Juries Be Jettisoned? A Retrospective Critique of Criticism in Design Education and Practice 157
  Should Juries Be Jettisoned? 158
  Promoting Debate and Dialogue About Design 158
  Professional Ethics and Design Education 161
  Competition and its Effects on Design Education and Practice 163
  Sex, Stars, and Studios 165
  The Ecole des Beaux Arts Model in Retrospect: The Designer as Artist 166
  Notes 168

Chapter 13 Leading Practitioners' Reflections on Design Juries 171
  Carol Ross Barney 171
  Joan Blutter 173
  Laurence Booth 173
  William Callaway 175
  Christopher Degenhardt 176
  The Late Norman R. DeHaan 178
  Larry N. Deutsch 179
  Peter Eisenman 182
  Joseph Esherick 183
  Rodney F. Friedman 184
  Michael Graves 186
  Charles Gwathmey 189
  Donald J. Hackl 191
  John F. Hartray, Jr. 193
  Steven Izenour 197
  E. Fay Jones 199
  Ronette J. King 200
  Richard Meier 202
  Charles W Moore 203
  Cesar Pelli 205
  Lawrence B. Perkins 207
  Martha Schwartz 209
  Robert A. M. Stern 211
  Minoru Takeyama 212
  Susana Torre 214
  John C. Walker 215
  Peter Walker 216
  Cynthia Weese 217
  Jeffrey Werner 220

APPENDIXES 223

Appendix A Methodology 225
  Phase 1 229
  Phase 2 230
  Phases 3-6 231
  Phase 7 232
  Phases 8-9 232
  Phase 10 234
  Phase 11 235
  Notes 235

Appendix B Selected Results 236
  Demographic Data 236
  Key Research Findings 237
  Notes 243

Appendix C Sample Jury Forms 244

Index 251

PREFACE TO THE 20TH ANNIVERSARY EDITION

It's hard to believe that 20 years have passed since the publication of my first book, *Design Juries on Trial*.

On the global stage, the Soviet Union collapsed and the European Union rose. Tsunamis, superstorms and earthquakes have shaken us to the core. The threat of global warming has become a reality. The impact of 9/11 and the Great Recession persist today.

On the technological stage, the Internet, smartphones, iPods, iPads, Facebook, Twitter, YouTube and other social media have transformed our everyday lives. A digital revolution has reshaped the design professions. Architectural movements have ebbed and flowed.

A generation of students has come and gone. Yet the message of this book remains.

Even today, many design students still leave design juries shaken, angry, or in tears. Students continue to pull all-nighters, have problems managing their time, and have difficulty speaking in public. Many place their lives in danger—and those of others—when they get behind the wheel with little or no sleep. They continue to injure themselves while building models, sometimes ending up in the emergency room. And many design faculty members continue to rely on the traditional jury system where students sit listless for hours at a time.

Since its first publication, *Design Juries on Trial* fueled the creation of the American Institute of Architecture Students' (AIAS) Studio Culture Task Force, culminating in their 2002 report on *The Redesign of Studio Culture*. It also helped spark the inclusion of studio culture as a key criterion of the National Architectural Accrediting Board accreditation process for all architectural schools in North America. *Design Juries on Trial* formed the basis of lively discussions at many architecture schools around the world.

I have been invited to speak about *Design Juries on Trial* and its impact at conferences of design students, educators, and practitioners and at many universities in the US and abroad, exposing disturbing conditions in design education that had been hidden for far too long.

Building upon my work on design juries, my research shifted to examine conditions in design practice, leading to the publication of my second book, *Designing for Diversity: Gender, Race and Ethnicity in the Architectural Profession*. Using similar social science research methods of surveys, interviews, and archives, we gave voice to those underrepresented in the design professions.

In recent years students and colleagues who have read *Design Juries on Trial* encouraged me to make it more widely available to a global audience. They believe that its content is timeless and its message still needs to be heard.

My hope is that this book continues to empower students to be in control throughout their design studio experience and especially during design juries. And I wish to continue to inspire design faculty to experiment with more effective ways of evaluating student work.

PREFACE

I first became interested in design juries as an architecture graduate student at the University of California, Berkeley, enrolled in a studio course.[1] Having been an undergraduate student in psychology, I had not been exposed to design juries before. The first time I saw a jury was when I experienced it myself. My own performance aside, I truly felt as if I had arrived from another planet. Never had I witnessed teachers hurling out such vicious words across the room - except perhaps in the movies or on TV. Never had I seen students so publicly embarrassed and humiliated except perhaps in second grade. Never had I sensed such an aftermath of confusion, powerlessness, anger, and rage in a classroom setting. It was as if a tornado had just roared through the building.

Years later my curiosity in the subject was rekindled as the roles were reversed and I made my debut as a juror. Admittedly, my adrenalin level was far lower now that I was no longer on the receiving end, but the overall aura of the jury room was the same. And in a different way, I, too, was on the hot seat as one in a long row of jurors offering my pearls of wisdom.[2]

As the room fell silent and I began to speak, I could see the students-and the other jurors-anxiously awaiting my response. Fully aware that I was surrounded by people only inches away who were hanging on my every word, I felt compelled to say something profound and different, something that would truly educate the students, and something that would make me sound intelligent in front of my colleagues. To my right and left were the same cast of characters who would be writing up my yearly teaching evaluation. Before me were Dorothy, the Tin Man, the Cowardly Lion, and the Scarecrow. Despite the pressure to perform, I also felt supremely powerful. And after my script was over, I thought to myself, "Oz has spoken." It was truly an odd sensation.

That fearful look on those students' faces, especially the whites of their eyes, began to haunt me. What were they so afraid of? How could I, a 5'2" young female, possibly be the target of their fears? Was I truly a tiger ready to attack? That look of terror inspired me to delve into the meaning of this awesome event.

I soon began a library search and found that very little had been written about design juries. A few authors mentioned them in passing, but few had looked in depth at the consequences for design students, faculty, and visiting critics.[3]

One of the most intriguing concepts I came across in the literature was the "mastery-mystery" phenomenon coined by Chris Argyris in an article on teaching and learning in design settings.[4] This refers to the way in which students are taught about architecture. Critics have somehow mastered the art of design, but the process through which they arrived at this mastery remains a puzzling mystery to the student. In my mind, the jury epitomized the mastery-mystery phenomenon, and I couldn't help but wonder: did it have to be so? Donald Schon's work took a more in-depth look at the experiential nature of the design studio, especially how teachers and students interact through a mode he terms "reflection-in action", however it did not specifically examine juries.[5]

The opportunity to teach a seminar course focusing on the subject allowed me, with the assistance of several highly motivated students, to begin to explore this topic.[6] The early phases of this research involved a literature review as well as several different methods of gathering information. The review of literature continued throughout the seven-year process. (See Appendix A and Figures A-I to A-3 for a more complete description of the methodology and specific research phases.)

My class and I interviewed design students immediately after they finished presenting their projects to the jury, and asked them what they learned and how they reacted. We surveyed students in architecture, landscape architecture, and urban planning to try to understand how each group viewed the jury process. What do they like and dislike about it? How much do they learn from it? How much sleep do they usually get before the jury? How much food, and what kinds? To provide a comparison, we asked the same types of questions of students outside the design fields about the ways in which their own work was evaluated. We asked several design students to keep a diary of their daily studio experiences whenever they received criticism from their design critic, another student, or someone else during a desk crit, jury, or casual conversation. We also spent long hours observing jury sessions and recording how students and jurors interacted both verbally and no n verbally. We interviewed design faculty to learn their impressions of juries. We surveyed alumni to find out how they viewed their juries in retrospect, now that school was far behind them.

Later on, I continued a series of surveys of students and faculty at other colleges and universities to find out how their experiences compared with those at the original case study school. Altogether, over 800 students, including 725 design students from 92 schools, responded to surveys. Fifty-three faculty were surveyed from a total of 30 schools. (See Appendix A, Figures A4 and A5 for the locations of the schools included in this study) Although the primary focus of my research was on the educational experience in architecture, much of what was found relates directly to students' experiences in landscape architecture, urban planning, and interior design as well as to industrial and graphic design.

Both while on my home campus and away at professional conferences, I made it a practice to raise the subject during casual conversations and written correspondence with students and colleagues, always curious about what they had to say All the while, I made informal field notes as part of my role as a participant-observer in the jury process. I have drawn heavily on my own experiences and those of colleagues and students throughout this book.

Lastly, I sought to broaden this research by seeking to understand how highly successful design practitioners reacted to design juries. What were their own experiences when they were in school? What did they think of the way their work was evaluated at the time? What do they think of academic juries today? And, by comparison, what are their views of professional design juries? I was especially curious to find out if, as students, they sailed right through design juries and studios, or if they, too, experienced any of the turmoil that students do today Were the" stars" of the design professions shining brightly from the very beginning? Based on their own experiences, what words of wisdom could they offer to students and young practitioners?

Recommendations from faculty and students helped produce a list of leading design practitioners to approach for interviews. The list represented a mixture of architects, landscape architects, and interior designers from various geographic regions. (See Appendix A, Figure A-6, for the location of these practitioners.) Most are household names in their respective fields, while a few are budding young stars who have already received numerous design awards and other professional recognition. Thirty agreed to be interviewed and 29 agreed to have their comments included in this book.

Let me preface my remarks by acknowledging that many professors care deeply about their students, treating them with respect and concern; in many cases, the feelings are mutual. Educators such as these have enabled our schools and our students - to grow and flourish. I want neither to ignore their existence nor to downplay their importance, as their role in design education has been crucial. But too many others have routinely used the jury as an excuse to lash out at students, and students at every school can easily pinpoint the worst offenders. It is just this behavior and its consequences- and the system it represents- that prompted this book. What I have learned about juries, based upon the findings from this research, has been tantalizing, edifying, and, at times, horrifying.

NOTES

1. I should add that my focus in graduate school was not on design practice but rather on social and psychological issues in design. My intention was to become a researcher, scholar, and educator about design. My graduate education concentrated on environmental design research, with an emphasis on the newly emerging field of environment and behavior. As such, my courses generally consisted of research seminars rather than design studios.
2. While I am speaking from my personal experience here, other faculty jurors have candidly admitted undergoing some of these same feelings. Along these lines, the late architecture critic and author, Reyner Banham, has written a fascinating account of his experiences as a juror at the Architectural Association in London. After some especially grueling encounters, he wrote: "1 realized you couldn't be an architect *and* a normal human being. " It was the beginning of the end for me; I served on only a few more juries, and in a mood of terminal unease... After twenty years or so of continuous near-participation in this peculiar discourse, I owe the AA some gratitude for helping me to see ... a great truth, and thus to give up juries with a clear conscience." See Banham, Reyner, "Memoirs of a Reluctant Juryman," in Gowan, James (ed.), *A Continuing Experiment: Learning and Teaching at the Architectural Association,* London: Architectural Press, 1975, pp. 173-175; quote from pp. 174-175.
3. At the time, the most closely related work to be found was Attoe, Wayne, *Architecture and Critical Imagination,* New York: Wiley, 1978; Braaten, Leif J., "A Psychologist Looks at the Teaching of Architecture," *AI A Journal* (June 1964), pp. 91-95; Hassid, Sami, "Development and Application of a System for Recording Critical Evaluations of Architectural Works," unpublished manuscript, Department of Architecture, University of California, Berkeley, 1960; Hassid, Sami, "Interest Distribution in the Evaluation of Architectural Design," paper presented at the Faculty Seminar on Architectural Research, Department of Architecture, University of California, Berkeley, 1960; Porter, W L., and M. Kilbridge (eds.), *Architecture Education Study,* Cambridge, MA: Massachusetts Institute of Technology, Laboratory of Architecture and Planning, 1976. Although these sources began to touch on design juries, none of them constitute substantive empirical research on the subject. Since that time, some additional empirical work on the subject has begun to emerge. Consult: Faramawy, Ali Fouad, *Rites of Passage: The Making of a Professional Architect,* Doctor of Architecture Dissertation, The University of Michigan, 1987; Frederickson, Mark, "Design Juries: A Study in Lines of Communication," *Journal of Architectural Education,* 43: 2 (Winter 1990), pp. 22-27; Anderton, Frances, "Response to Fredrickson," *Journal of Architectural Education,* 43:2 (Winter 1990), p. 28. See also Dinham, Sarah M., "Architecture Education: A Comprehensive Research Review," in Alkin, Marvin, (ed.), *Encyclopedia of Educational Research,* New York: The Macmillan Company in conjunction with the

American Educational Research Association, 1991; Dinham, Sarah M., "Architectural Education: The Possibilities for Research on Architecture Teaching," *Architectural Record:* (April 1987), pp. 41-43; Dinham, Sarah M., "Teaching as design: theory, research and implications for design teaching," *Design Studies, 10:2* (April 1989), pp. 80-88; Dinham, Sarah M., "Architectural education: Is jury criticism a valid teaching technique?" *Architectural Record* (November 1986), pp. 51, 53.

4. Argyris, Chris, "Teaching and Learning in Design Settings," Consortium of East Coast Schools of Architecture, *Architecture Education Study, 1: The Papers,* 1981, pp. 551-660; Argyris, Chris and Schon, Donald A, *Theory in Practice: Increasing Professional Effectiveness,* San Francisco: Jossey-Bass, 1974.

5. Schon, Donald A, *The Reflective Practitioner: How Professionals Think in Action,* New York: Basic Books, 1983; Schon, Donald A, "The Architecture Studio as an Exemplar of Education for Reflection-in-Action," *Journal of Architectural Education,* 38: 1 (Fall 1984), pp. 2-9; Schon, Donald A, *Educating the Reflective Practitioner: Toward a New Design for Teaching and Learning in the Professions,* San Francisco: Jossey-Bass, 1987; Schon, Donald A, *The Design Studio: An Exploration of its Traditions and Potentials,* London: RIBA Publications, RIBA Building Industry Trust, 1985; Argyris and Schon, op cit.

6. I was on the faculty of California State Polytechnic University, Pomona at the time. Cal Poly Pomona was the case study school where this research began.

ACKNOWLEDGEMENTS

Writing this book is literally a dream come true. What began as a flash in graduate school and reemerged as a serious interest in my early years of teaching and research has blossomed into an obsession during the past few years. Now, eight years after this project began, it is finally coming to fruition.

Over the years, many colleagues, students, family members, and friends encouraged me to continue my research and writing on juries, engaging me in countless stimulating discussions, writing umpteen letters of support, reviewing manuscript drafts, and providing me with the moral fortitude required to keep afloat. I have them to thank for this book. Any errors or omissions, however, are my own. My deepest gratitude goes to those whose support helped me through this seemingly interminable project:

To my husband, Barry D. Riccio, who continues to serve as an inspiration in many ways. An unusually supportive spouse as well as a most valuable colleague and best friend, he deserves credit for helping me to broaden the historical, analytical, and literary dimensions of this research.
At the same time he has provided a warm and comfortable home environment within which to work, always filled with amazingly creative culinary concoctions to keep the juices flowing.

To my parents and two of my best friends, Harry A and Anne S. Anthony, who served as long-distance research assistants over the past several years by supplying me with countless newspaper clippings and magazine articles related to this book. As two of the earliest supporters of this project, they helped instill in me a lifelong sense of self-worth and a desire to set lofty goals. For that I am forever grateful. To my sister and brother-in-law, Mary Anne Anthony Smith and John Smith, and my nephew and nieces, Alexander, Annie, and Jeannette, who help my academic career in perspective; and to Felicia Riccio, who shares in my success. To my many aunts, uncles, cousins, and extended family of friends who provided much needed diversions throughout the research and writing process.

To the special spaces and places that refreshed me during the critical stages of research and writing: the coastline of La Jolla, the San Francisco Bay area, the Greek islands, the city of Chicago, the Crystal Lake Swimming Pool and most importantly, our cheerful Dutch colonial house in Urbana.

To the many authors whose books about self-motivation and goal seeking inspired me to simply stick with it. From day one, I envisioned this book on the shelf, and now it is finally there. As a result of this experience, I remain convinced that one of the most valuable virtues in this world is sheer persistence.

To Carter Manny and the Graham Foundation for Advanced Studies in the Fine Arts for providing a generous grant that offered crucial financial support during the final stages of this project.

To Everett Smethurst, former editor at Van Nostrand Reinhold, for having the confidence to commit to this publication. To the editorial staff at Van Nostrand Reinhold for their most valuable support throughout the writing and publication process.

To my colleague, Ray Lytle, who illustrated the line drawings throughout the text and whose artistic

Acknowledgements

talents I truly admire. To Mary Shiffer, who produced the computer graphics throughout the text and whose agility on the computer proved most valuable in my time of need.

To Marvin Malecha for providing the crucial moral support needed to help launch this study, which, at the time, I remotely feared might cost me my job. To Margaret Goglia, who first suggested the use of diaries as a research technique. They proved to be one of the most insightful sources of information.

To my former students, wherever they may be today, who worked so diligently on the earliest phases of this research:

Jose Navarro, Ray Luna, Richard Quirk, Kevin Chan, Philip Davies, Gene M. Directo, Dirk Friend, Donna Guzzetta, Monika Harte, Mai Truong, Rafael Urena, and Henry Woo. To Cynthia Cornfield Zien, Nana Kirk, and Ahmed El-Kholei, who assisted with various phases of complex data analysis.

To R. Alan Forrester and the University of Illinois at Urbana-Champaign School of Architecture for continued financial and moral support of this project over the past several years, enabling me to attend several conferences and discuss my research with colleagues from around the globe. To Robert Katz and the University of Illinois Housing Research and Development Program for key support during the early phases. To Jane Cook, Tracy Hawkins, Carole Couch, Barbara Prahl, Carol Berg, and Debbie Mennenga who repeatedly provided outstanding support services for this research. Ms. Cook and Ms. Hawkins are two of the sharpest typists I know.

To Gary Brown for providing premium office space for me and a room with a view on the University of California, Berkeley, campus during an important period of this research.

To David Bell, former editor of the *Journal of Architectural Education,* who believed that the topic was significant enough to merit publication in the journal back in 1987. Nothing I have written before or since has generated such a high level of interest from colleagues and students.

To the current and former staff of the American Institute of Architecture Students headquarters in Washington, D.C., and to the others I met through them: Lee Waldrep, Kent E. Davidson, Matthew Gilbertson, Irene Dumas-Tyson, Douglas Bailey, Carl Costello, Jeff Otto, Cammie Connell, Jason Young, Tom Haskins, Tom Fowler, and others. Not only did they assist in administering surveys, but they also provided unique opportunities for me to meet with design students from across the country.

To many colleagues who provided key support over the past several years in the forms of letters, phone calls, library references, invitations to professional conferences, and valuable insights from their experiences: James R. Anderson, Anthony C. Antoniades, Ronald Beckman, Juan C. Bertotto, Joseph Bilello, Jane Block, Allison Carll-White, Clare Cooper Marcus, Thomas Dutton, Sharon Irish, Michael Jones, Arthur Kaha, Uve Koehler, Howard Ray Lawrence, Stefani Ledewitz, Robert Levy, Donlyn Lyndon, M. Joe Numbers, Brian Orland, Edward R Ostrander, Peter Prangnell, Christopher Quinn, William Rose, Robert Selby, Robert Sommer, Anne Whiston Spirn, Arthur Stamps, Joel Stein, Fred Stitt, Anthony Ward, Sue Weidemann, and Walter Wendler. My many conversations with William Rose over the past several years helped fine-tune several points in the book.

To Melissa Tessendorf and Michael Kinsella, two of the best research assistants money could buy, who also became my congenial office partners and friends. Melissa's effervescent personality and dedication to this project helped keep me going during the final, critical stages of research, writing, and production.

To those colleagues and students who spent many long hours critically reviewing portions of this manuscript: James R. Anderson, Harry A. Anthony, Dan Bendixon, Douglas W Beauchamp, Kathryn Edmonson, James R Franklin, Karen Grieves, Clayton Haldeman, Arthur Kaha, Albert 1. Kerelis, Jr., Michael Kinsella, Laureen Laskowski, Walter Lewis, Tim McGinty, Jack L. Nasar, William Rose, Robert Selby, Brian Scheuzger, Amita Sinha, and Sue Weidemann.

To all those educators and practitioners who participated in surveys and interviews and corresponded with me over the years. I especially appreciate the efforts of the 29 designers who agreed to be interviewed at length and share their comments with readers: Carol Ross Barney, Joan Blutter, Larry Booth, William Callaway, Christopher Degenhardt, the late Norman DeHaan, Larry Deutsch, Peter Eisenman, Joseph Esherick, Rodney Friedman, Michael Graves, Charles Gwathmey, Donald Hackl, Jack Hartray, Steven Izenour, E. Fay Jones, Ronette King, Richard Meier, Charles Moore, Cesar Pelli, Larry Perkins, Martha Schwartz, Robert A. M. Stern, Minoru Takeyama, Susana Torre, John C. Walker, Peter Walker, Cynthia Weese, and Jeffrey Werner. Your insights are truly enlightening.

Finally, to the countless students, many of whom are now practicing designers, who contributed to this project by completing surveys and interviews,' by willing to be watched and videotaped during their jury presentations, and by sharing their most private thoughts and feelings painful as they sometimes were- in their diaries. By necessity, most will remain nameless, but you know who you are. Your comments are priceless. Your candor adds color and life to this work Better than I could ever hope to do, you paint a vivid portrait of the agonies and the ecstasies of life as a design student. And my hope is that through this book, future designers will benefit from your experiences.

DESIGN JURIES ON TRIAL

**THE RENAISSANCE
OF THE DESIGN STUDIO**

PART 1

AN OVERVIEW OF DESIGN JURIES

"At one crit during my fourth year at the AA [Architectural Association in London] a student collapsed whilst his project was being energetically ridiculed by a visiting critic. The critic did not notice this event until a dreadful silence caused him to turn round some moments later. At Oxford girl students had sometimes burst into tears and locked themselves in the lavatories, under similar circumstances. "Come out, Miss Barrett, please come out!" At the Beaux-Arts some students had committed suicide. My own route, as you have gathered, was to go mad." —Martin Pawley's account of "My Lovely Student Life"

CHAPTER 1

Introduction:

A Hazing Ritual

Listen to design students after a typical jury—one of the classic rituals of design education—and this is what you are likely to hear:

"It was a firing line!"
"We were crucified!"
"We were massacred!"
"We were guillotined!"
"We were led like sheep to slaughter!"
"Our work was ripped to shreds!"
"I felt like scum on the earth!"
"I felt like I was falling down a bottomless pit!"
"I said to myself: 'What on earth am I doing here?'"

Even some faculty liken design juries to the hazing rituals that young men undergo during their induction into fraternities.

Juries have been firmly in place for over a century as the predominant method used to evaluate students' performance in design studio courses. They are routinely used in the disciplines of architecture, landscape architecture, urban planning, and interior design. Most design students have juries at least once or twice per term, and in every design studio throughout their educational career. Although they may be called *reviews* or *critiques*, with few exceptions, the format of design juries is virtually the same in every design school in the English-speaking world. Students present their completed design work one by one in front of a group of faculty, visiting professionals, their classmates, and interested passersby (Figure 1-1). Faculty and critics publicly critique each project spontaneously, and students are asked to defend their work.

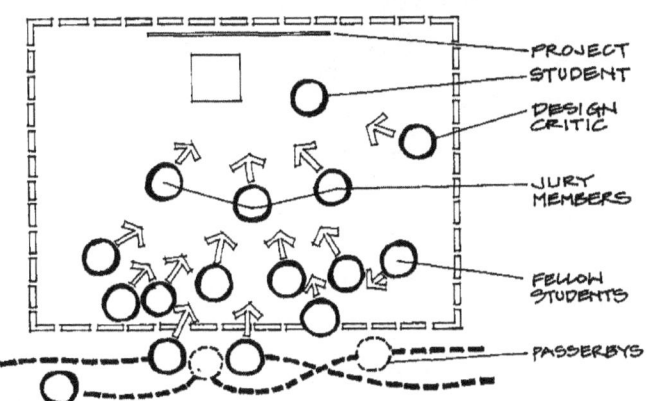

Figure 1-1 The typical opening jury consists of a student presenting a design project, a jury of faculty and visiting critics, the rest of the class, and passersby.

4 Introduction: A Hazing Ritual

What's wrong with this system? The result is often chaos. Although it may work well for some individuals, too many students leave the scene distraught, angry, and humiliated over their own poor performance and loss of control at the jury. After they are out of the "hot seat," many simply tune out other students' presentations, fall asleep, or physically collapse from exhaustion. Some faculty and visiting critics make such brutal remarks that a fistfight might break out in another context. For example, "What do you think you're doing in architecture? Get out of this field, before it's too late!" Or, to a student in his final year, "Have you ever taken freshman design? Then maybe you should retake it!" If comments like these were tape-recorded and sent to students' parents, they might seriously consider withdrawing their sons or daughters from school and asking for their money back. And if elementary and high school teachers and professors of education heard their remarks, they would probably cringe!

On the subject of juries, many design students, faculty, and practitioners have issued an SOS alert. Desperately trying to stay afloat, students attempt to master juries by trial and error. Unfortunately, most keep trying but continue making errors. They receive virtually no systematic information to help them through this grueling emotional experience, and yet their grades in design courses usually depend on their jury performance. Several design faculty admit that the current system is best characterized as "the blind leading the blind."

Faculty and visiting critics receive no formal training in how to conduct juries, and more often than not, they simply rely on the techniques their own professors used when they were in school, however good or bad they may have been. Some junior design faculty are more concerned about how their senior colleagues, rather than the students, will respond to their jury comments.

To many practitioners, juries in practice remain a mystery too. Practicing designers spend hundreds of person-hours and thousands of dollars on professional awards and competition submissions, often without the slightest clue as to how their work will be judged. When the results are in, they often feel discouraged, depressed, bitter, and abused. While the chosen few win, everyone else loses.

Juries have rarely been seriously questioned, studied, and evaluated. They remain the taboo topic of design education and practice, that sacred turf upon which one dare not walk. As a result, some critical issues have long been ignored: What are the goals of design juries? What do students, faculty, and practicing designers think of design juries? How much do students learn from juries? When are juries of greatest educational value? What are students' private reactions to public criticism? What can students, faculty, administrators, and practitioners do to help improve the status quo?

More specifically, for students: How can you better learn to handle stress in the design studio, culminating in the jury experience itself? How can you avoid burnout? How can you avoid falling for the classic "all-nighter" syndrome (Figure 1-2)? How can you begin to master time management, public speaking, listening, negotiating, and other skills that are usually ignored in design education, but that can greatly improve your performance at the design jury? How can you avoid getting stuck on a design concept—or not being able to come up with one at all? How can you use relevant research findings to help provide a basis for some of your important design decisions—

Figure 1-2 The classic "all-nighter" syndrome has become a ritual of design education. Most jurors can easily identify those students who have been up around the clock.

so you no longer have to answer to the jury, "I designed it just because I liked it that way"? How can you best prepare for juries and present your project in the most favorable light? How can you begin to understand why some jury presentations "win" while others "lose"? How can you present your project graphically in the most favorable light? How can you help yourself learn from the jury experience so that next time you won't repeat the same mistakes?

For design faculty and visiting practitioners: How can you become more effective as a juror? How can you learn to improve the way you deliver criticism—so that students remember and learn from what you say? How can you avoid the adversarial relationships between critics and students, so typical in design juries and studios? How can you help create a learning environment that inspires cooperation rather than fierce competition among students?

What types of alternatives to traditional design juries might be used? What innovative ways of evaluating design student performance have been tried, how have students reacted, and what are their costs and benefits? *Should we abandon juries altogether, or can a few minor changes make a big difference?*

What do leading designers think of juries in practice, that is, in professional design awards and competitions? When they serve as jurors, what do they look for? How can you improve your chances for a winning entry? Should your entry "fit in" or "stand out"? What can we do to help improve the way juries are used in design practice?

This book addresses these issues and more. Based on a seven-year-long series of studies of design students, faculty, and some of today's most accomplished design practitioners, it represents a comprehensive body of empirical research on design juries. Systematic observations and videotape recordings of juries, diaries of design students, interviews, and surveys have been used to gather information. Over 900 individuals, including 725 design students, scores of educators, and several award-winning architects, landscape architects, and interior designers, have participated in this research. This book represents the largest such study of this topic. Its results are provocative and call for some sweeping changes in design education and practice.

A MULTILAYERED APPROACH

Design Juries on Trial has several purposes that should be clarified at the very outset. It provides a historical overview and comparative analysis of design juries within the broader contexts of design studios, education, and professional practice.

Second, it presents a sensitive portrait of juries both from the top down and from the bottom up. Relying on both quantitative and qualitative information gathered from students, faculty, and some of today's most talented design practitioners, as well as my own experiences over the past several years as a juror and design faculty member, it attempts to provide a realistic account of what it feels like to experience design juries, both as a critic and as a recipient of criticism. Where information is derived from surveys, diaries, interviews, and observations, it is identified as such; other passages are based on my own reflections upon having completed the research. An attempt is made to develop empathy for the different actors who play a role in the design jury scenario.

Third, the book is a scholarly polemic, challenging some of the fundamental assumptions behind design juries as well as the methods typically employed. It vividly depicts the all-too-often deleterious consequences both upon the judges and those being judged. *As several design practitioners have attested, lifelong work habits, attitudes towards clients, and behavior among coworkers found in professional design studios can often be traced back to experiences with juries in school.* The book exposes and unravels some of the jury's hidden agendas that can impact one's subsequent professional life. However, it also argues that at present it is utopian to believe that juries will be altogether eliminated from design education and practice.

Fourth, it serves as a practical, hands-on guidebook on how to survive within the current system as well as how to transform and improve that system in order to maximize its potential. By demystifying the jury process, it helps place students, faculty, and practitioners in greater control of not only the jury but also the design studio experience as a whole. As a result, both the jury and studio can be free of intimidation, confrontation, and frustration.

Fifth, as a follow-up to the research on juries in design education, one chapter specifically addresses design juries in professional practice. Based on research findings about professional design juries, techniques are suggested for improving the ways in which professional design awards and competitions are submitted and evaluated. This section also offers guidance to those submitting entries, based on the reflections of experienced jurors.

As a result of this multilayered approach, the tone of voice shifts accordingly. In some places the book sounds like the objective scholarly research on which it is based; elsewhere it sounds unabashedly opinionated. It ranges along a continuum of theoretical to practical. In parts it swings from a sharply critical stance toward juries on the one hand to a mildly sympathetic position on the other; the intention is to present many different viewpoints. It oscillates between a serious tone and one that is sprinkled with humor. Wherever it appears, the humor is well intended and not meant to mock the jury system, design education, or the design professions. However, it is sometimes only through the use of humor that those who are deeply entrenched within any subculture can begin to step outside and see it differently. And that is a healthy beginning.

Note as well that the terms *he* and *she* are used interchangeably throughout the book rather than the more awkward *s/he*. This is intentional. All too often, even in this hi-tech era of personal computers, compact discs, FAX machines, and car phones, designers are still stereotypically referred to only as men. It is my hope that through this small but significant gesture design students, educators, and practitioners will recognize both women and men as vital players in the design world.

ORGANIZATION OF THIS BOOK

Part One, An Overview of Design Juries, contains an analysis of juries and design studios from a historical, comparative, and social and psychological perspective. It traces the origins of juries from the Ecole des Beaux Arts in Paris to its present-day form. Part Two, Research About Design Juries, explains how students, faculty, and practitioners respond to juries in educational settings. It presents highlights from the results of interviews, surveys, diaries, observations, my own participant-observation, and other research techniques. Specifically, it looks at why we have juries, students' best and worst jury experiences, what students learn from them, and how professors deliver and how students respond to jury criticism. It also examines the studio subculture, a world unique unto itself.

Part Three, What Students Can Do, responds to many of the problems raised in Part Two as well as others by offering a survival guide. This guide is intended to help the reader prepare for the jury or client presentation as well as to cope more effectively with the design studio experience. While much of it is aimed directly at students, the suggestions offered can also be helpful to design practitioners and faculty. Chapter 4 discusses various approaches to time management that can help the reader work more efficiently and effectively in the studio, thus preventing the last-minute rush before the jury deadline. Chapter 5 addresses how research can be incorporated effectively into the design process and jury or client presentations. It opens the key to a rarely discovered treasure of information: the burgeoning field of environment and behavior—how people respond to the physical environment. It provides a brief overview of key resources and relatively simple research techniques that can be of great aid throughout the design process, and especially at jury or client presentations.

Chapter 6 covers the art of communication, so crucial to a successful jury and design practice. It offers an array of speaking, listening, and negotiating skills that can help the reader deal effectively with professors, critics, coworkers, employers, clients, subcontractors, and others. By applying these techniques, juries and client presentations can become less adversarial and more cooperative in spirit. Students, faculty, and practitioners can walk away from the scene feeling that their concerns have been expressed and heard, and that something good has been accomplished. Chapter 7 suggests ways to help graphic presentations attract the attention of jurors. Based on the experiences of well-known designers who have served as jurors themselves, it takes a serious look at what catches the jury's eye—and what doesn't. Chapter 8 discusses stress in the studio and how to cope with it. It suggests different techniques to help overcome the jury jitters, reduce stress before and after the jury, and place design activities in perspective with other aspects of life. It offers routes to a healthy life-style that can help make the studio subculture more satisfying.

Part Four addresses what faculty and visiting critics can do to improve design juries and the studio experience. Students, too, will find these chapters useful as the information provided here will help them more accurately critique both the criticism they give and receive. Chapter 9 examines the phenomenon of criticism and suggests ways of delivering constructive, as opposed to destructive, criticism in juries, informal desk critiques, and other settings. Chapter 10 presents an array of innovative alternatives to traditional design juries. Based on the experiences of a handful of brave faculty members who have been willing to experiment, this chapter describes what has been tried and how students, faculty, and visitors have reacted.

In Part Five, Juries in Practice, Chapter 11 extends the discussion of academic juries into the professional realm. It compares academic and professional design juries, and suggests ways by which one can help the other. Based on the experiences of leading designers who have been on both sides of the fence, as submitters and jurors, it provides a critique of professional awards programs and design competitions. It also presents some innovative alternatives that help remedy some of their deficiencies.

In Part Six, Epilogue, Chapter 12 concludes with a retrospective critique of juries in light of the research findings and implications of prior chapters. It addresses just how much juries must change in order to significantly improve the status quo, and it suggests ways that the best aspects of juries can be retained and the worst aspects jettisoned. It offers alternative ways to promote debate and dialogue about design in the schools, so that educators need not rely exclusively on juries. Professional ethics, competition and its effects, sexism and the star system, and the designer as artist are examined in light of the research findings, and a strong case is made for a new and improved model of design education.

Chapter 13 presents excerpts from interviews with 29 leading designers offering their personal reflections on design juries. A brief description of the designer, followed by highlights from each interview, is provided. The reader may want to refer to Chapter 13 at the outset in order to become acquainted with the designers whose quotes are interspersed throughout the text.

In sum, the recommendations posed in *Design Juries on Trial* go beyond design juries themselves and extend into the realm of the design studio, the heart of design education and practice. Ultimately, the book aims to improve the quality of the studio experience both in school and in the office, and to inject greater sensitivity and objectivity into this emotionally charged process. More broadly, it speculates about how the improvement of design juries might, in the process, help improve the image of the design professions to society at large.

CHAPTER 2
What are Design Juries?
A Historical and Comparative Analysis

"The jury problem will always be with us." —Peyton Boswell's assessment in 1942[1]

"Design education today is still virtually the same as when I was in school. Students do a design with a common program and common directions; you receive criticism, helpful or unhelpful, as you develop it; and then you come to a point where you present it to a larger group of professors who may comment on it verbally as part of the jury system. And that process has not really changed in any substantial way."—Cesar Pelli

"When I was in design school, juries were private. The students sat around outside the exhibition hall. After the jury was over, the students were called in and one junior faculty member was usually left behind to explain the decisions. He wandered around the room and commented on different projects. It was a big mob scene." —Joseph Esherick

"Design juries were closed when I was in school. The drawings were hung in the jury room, and when we next saw them they were marked up and graded. You could sometimes reconstruct the jury's critical method by studying the marginal notes on the drawings. The Beaux Arts grading system was used....

"In evaluating designs great emphasis was placed on presentation. Colored renderings and models were expected, and some students became very good delineators. Clarity in the plan was considered important. The traffic patterns for vehicles and pedestrians got serious attention. The goal was that persons moving through the building would always remain oriented; I don't think any of us objected to that. But, that was where the crit ended....

"I would have preferred open juries. The only time these were held was when visiting critics came to the school."—John F. Hartray, Jr.

"When I was in school, the jury process was 100% private. We finished each problem at 6:00 on Saturday afternoon whether there was a football game or not. Not 6:01, but 6:00. We picked it up and handed in whatever there was and it went into a pile. Then you hung around outside the door and bit your fingernails."—Lawrence B. Perkins

"I recall lots of waiting around outside while the jurors debated and wrote things on the project. At the time I thought it was too bad to be excluded from the deliberations, but that's an opinion I think I've reversed by now. But what seemed good about it is that it made the drawings have to speak for themselves, and there was no dependence on glib talking to get through it. It seems to me that in the schools I've taught in for the past several decades, as closed juries are less and less in evidence, the amount of emphasis on the glib presentation has escalated. And that seems a shame."—Charles W. Moore

"As I recall at Yale the visiting critics could cast their votes as well as the faculty on the successes of the projects. The juries were highly dramatic occasions. Many students would come to see any given jury. They were a principal teaching tool. They prepared those of us who could deal with them to deal with clients, boards, and public groups. I think it was a very exciting and realistic process. The discussions of architecture were very good on the jury. I remember them, not necessarily all with fondness, but I remember them."—Robert A. M. Stern

A BRIEF HISTORICAL OVERVIEW OF JURIES IN DESIGN EDUCATION

Early Design Education at the Ecole des Beaux Arts

Newcomers to the design professions may wonder where the term *jury* originated and why the legalistic analogy. Oddly enough, the literature provides no clear answer. It seems to have started in France. The original link between design juries and courtroom juries remains a mystery. Nonetheless, the term *jury* conjures up images of a hierarchical relationship where an individual is on trial in front of others who stand in judgment. By today's standards, this is indeed a questionable image for an educational exchange.

The jury system in design education can be traced back to its roots in the nineteenth-century Ecole des Beaux Arts (School of Fine Arts) in Paris. At the Ecole, the design problem superseded the lecture as the primary method of teaching architecture.[2] Learning by doing was stressed almost exclusively. The process of educating students in design studio typically included a fixed curriculum where design study began upon entering school, students being divided into *ateliers*, or studios, led by a *patron*, or master; the use of the *esquisse*, an initial sketch solution to a problem that would be further developed; the tradition of older students, or *anciens*, helping younger ones; the teaching of design by practicing architects; and the evaluation of projects by a jury.[3] The students' fate ultimately rested "in the hands of the gods" — that is, jury members— who decided whether they passed or failed.

Students' completed design work was evaluated behind closed doors by a jury of design faculty (Figure 2-1). After the jury was over, students retrieved their work and noted their marks, usually with little or no comment from their instructors (Figure 2-2).[4]

The Ecole introduced the design *charrette*, a practice still used in many schools today. The term literally means "a cart." Many of the *ateliers* were located at a considerable distance from the central building of the school, sometimes even in far away neighborhoods. On the project due date, freshmen architecture students pulled a cart from one studio to another, collecting the older students' illustration boards and rushing them to the huge gallery where school employees hung them up for the jury to judge just a few hours later. As soon as they saw the cart approaching, other freshmen would stand outside the studio and shout *"La Charrette! La Charrette!"* as loudly as they could, warning the students inside the studio to quickly finish up the final touches on their work. In today's parlance, the term has come to mean a design competition or exercise under extremely tight time constraints, and the last few days and sleepless nights of intense drafting activity just before the project is presented to a jury or to a client.

The Influence of the Ecole des Beaux Arts Across the Atlantic and the Role of the Beaux-Arts Institute of Design

The architectural jury was introduced to North America around the turn of the century.[5] Prior to this period in many

Figure 2-1 At the Ecole des Beaux Arts in Paris, juries evaluated students' design work behind closed doors.

Figure 2-2 Until the late 1940s, early 1950s, and in some schools, early 1960s, juries were held in private. Students' projects were returned only with a grade and a few stray notes in the margins.

American schools, exercises in design were included only at the end of the fourth year of study. With each passing decade, as the design studio became an increasingly important component of the architectural curriculum, the jury achieved greater prominence. The influence of American architects trained at the Ecole des Beaux Arts, as well as several French critics teaching in American design schools, were both major forces in this evolution.[6] In the early part of this century, most architecture schools had at least one Paris-trained professor. Over 500 Americans attended the Ecole des Beaux Arts between 1850 and 1968, when it closed. The French influence on Canadian architectural education was also strong. In addition, Canadian architectural programs were under a strong British and Scottish influence.[7] By the 1930s, the studio and design jury had become firmly established, attaining the popularity they maintain today.

In 1932, two educators, Francke Huntington Bosworth, Jr., and Roy Child Jones, authored a fascinating book entitled *A Study of Architectural Schools* based on their visits to almost 50 North American schools of architecture.[8] They concluded that "both quantitatively and qualitatively practice in design has gone from last to first place in the curriculum. Moreover, it might be said that the entire educational approach, not only in design but in the whole field of architecture, has swung as in law from a lecture system to a case system of teaching."[9] Or, as architect Joseph Esherick describes, "One of the most highly developed aspects of architectural education before the Second [World] War was the degree to which all course work, both academic and technical, was coordinated to support the studio effort in design. The program was essentially single-minded, focused, and continuous. It was hard-boiled and demanding, frankly a matter of training in a well-established way of doing things."[10]

The original American version of design juries was much like that of the Ecole des Beaux Arts. Many American architectural schools, independent studios (*ateliers*), and architectural clubs were affiliates of the Beaux-Arts Institute of Design (BAID) in New York, now the National Institute of Architectural Education.[11]

Several schools used the BAID as an administrative body to issue the writing of design programs and conduct judgments in New York; the extent to which the services of the BAID were used varied from school to school.[12] For those that employed its services fully, both the project assignment and its evaluation were administered elsewhere. The BAID itself did not educate, but merely issued programs and provided the machinery for exhibiting and judging student work. The education itself was supplied by both the critic and fellow students.[13] Competition not only within each school but among different schools was extremely fierce. Some scholars writing in the early 1930s have cleverly referred to this competitive air among students and faculty—who vied for awards for their students—as "architectural football."[14]

The stimulating effect of healthy competition has thus become perverted by practices and attitudes that have their analogies in certain phases of intercollegiate football. Nor can the design critics be blamed entirely, any more than can football coaches. Architectural school authorities have been known to base promotion and salaries on the number of awards critics "pulled down" for their students in Beaux Arts judgments.[15]

Depending on the extent to which the school relied upon the BAID, the role of the studio instructors varied accordingly. At the University of Pennsylvania in the 1930s, for instance, studio instructors generally did not participate in juries of their students' work. Their role, instead, was to offer students a sounding board for a different approach or perspective on their designs.[16]

F. H. Bosworth, Jr., and Roy Childs Jones, the two scholars who visited a wide array of architecture schools in the early 1930s, sharply criticized the Beaux Arts programs distributed by the BAID, stating that they often did not fit appropriately into the design curricula and that programs were often simply the "hurried efforts of busy practitioners. In the schools, too many of our critics in this country have shirked this work. They take the Beaux Arts programmes *in toto* not from the conviction that they best fit an educational scheme, for which no one could criticize them, but because they don't think in broad enough terms to write their own."[17] In other words, faculty were taking the easy way out.[18]

Bosworth and Jones also were highly critical of the artificial nature of both the program and the esquisse as inherited from the Ecole des Beaux Arts. They argued that this teaching technique differs dramatically from the realities of design practice.[19] In practice, work often includes writing design programs and investigating and helping formulate clients' needs. In school, however, the student must leap into a solution without enough time to investigate it fully. In addition, they argued, that students have no input in the actual writing of the program, so that it arrives "like a revelation from an architectural heaven, with whose mysterious workings he [the student] has no concern."[20] A number of design faculties in the early 1930s were questioning seriously whether or not the discrepancies between teaching and practice actually weakened the inherent strength of the problem system so universally used in design education. "They wonder if the traditional programme and esquisse have not exaggerated the competitive game of design at the expense of a true notion of architectural realities."[21]

The influence of the French Ecole des Beaux Arts on many North American institutions was later superseded by that of the German Bauhaus school (1919-1933) and the teaching methods of its founder, Walter Gropius, who later headed the architecture department at Harvard (1938-1952) and integrated architecture, landscape architecture, and urban planning into a single school. The Bauhaus sought not to create neoclassical monuments, the preferred style of the Ecole, but rather to create a "modern" architecture that relied on mass production and modern technology. One of the basic tenets of the Bauhaus philosophy was that the machine was the modern medium of design. According to some scholars, the Bauhaus catapulted into international prominence and soon became the single most important force in the design world during the period between the world wars. Every field of design saw its influence: architecture, product design, furniture, fabrics, graphics, typography, painting, advertising, photographies, film, and others.[22]

The concept of the design studio was strengthened by the Bauhaus. In fact, Gropius's design for the school's headquarters, the Bauhaus Building in Dessau, Germany (1925-1926), included a six-story studio building containing 28 live-in studios for the students with baths and a gymnasium in the basement. The Bauhaus became a small world of its own, containing its own environment for living, eating, working, learning, entertainment, sports, and recreation.[23] The separate studio subculture, born out of the Ecole des Beaux Arts and refined by the Bauhaus, was now even more firmly established.

Despite the profound impact of the Bauhaus on design education, the jury system lingered on as the primary means of evaluating student and professional design work.[24] The literature does not reveal that Gropius and his disciples made any substantive changes to the jury system. With regard to design juries specifically, the French influence still reigned supreme.

Just as in the Ecole des Beaux Arts, juries in North American architectural schools were conducted in private. Many of today's older designers, trained in the 1930s and 1940s, recall their student days when they simply submitted their completed projects for review and their professors disappeared behind closed doors. Hours or sometimes days later, their projects were returned with a simple letter grade and, if they were lucky, a few stray marks or comments on their drawings. The reasoning behind the grade was rarely discussed.

A Gradual Evolution from Closed to Open Juries

A critical turning point in the history of juries in design education occurred when juries went public, that is, when they switched from a closed to an open format.[25] It appears that the exact dates of this radical transformation have never been documented, but conversations with designers of different ages indicate that the process was gradual. The major change appears to have occurred during the late 1940s and 1950s, although in some schools juries did not open up until the 1960s. The reasons for this dramatic shift are not crystal clear.

One possibility is that with the end of World War II and the increasing numbers of older veterans returning to the university as adult students, some faculty felt a greater obligation to open up the evaluation process. Perhaps they believed that more mature students deserved more than a cryptic letter grade. Another possibility is that a few bold professors at prestigious design schools started this new trend and instructors elsewhere felt obliged to follow suit. Those professors who continued to rely on the closed system may have felt peer pressure to conform. In fact, the rigor of the open jury—lasting hours at a time and forcing faculty to openly state their opinions before students and colleagues—may have caused the closed jury to seem like a somewhat irresponsible form of teaching by comparison. The shift from closed to open juries may have also reflected general, widespread trends in education and grading in other fields, moving from an emphasis on responsiveness to authority (a mere letter grade) to a greater emphasis on individuality (a grade with comments and discussion and increased interaction between instructors and students).

Soon after the shift from closed to open juries, it seems that juries became somewhat of a status symbol—a barometer by which one could judge the intellectual rigor of a particular school. Some students made it a habit to sit in on juries at different schools in order to help them decide which one to select for graduate school.[26] Individual faculty members and schools began to compete informally with each other to see who could invite the most prestigious practitioners to serve on the jury—a practice that remains to this day.

In sharp contrast to the original Beaux Arts design juries, this new era of juries is perhaps best characterized by their extremely open, public nature. Students orally present their work one by one before a design jury, who then evaluate their work on the spot in front of the rest of the class. Even the casual passerby, a total stranger, can listen to virtually every ounce of criticism delivered to a student in a jury. Juries generally last several hours. While at some schools juries are held over several days, in extreme cases they can extend into marathon sessions of eight hours or more at a time. More typical is a jury about three to four hours long. This process has remained relatively unchanged for decades, albeit with isolated exceptions at a handful of schools.[27]

THE DESIGN STUDIO AND THE DESIGN JURY IN A BROADER EDUCATIONAL CONTEXT

The design studio is unusual on college campuses. It is perhaps most similar to the scientific laboratory where students are in relatively close contact with each other over extended periods of time. Many graduate students in the sciences are expected to monitor operations at the lab day and night, seven days a week. However, many scientific laboratories, especially those at the graduate level, operate on a much smaller scale than do design studios, and laboratory assistants are given far greater amounts of responsibility than are design students. Often an error or oversight in the lab can cause an explosion, fire, or other disaster. A lab assistant who falls asleep can kill people! Alertness and attention to detail is of paramount importance in lab; it is not quite the same in design studio.

The studio subculture bears a closer resemblance to the sororities and fraternities commonly found on university campuses. As early as their inception back in the late 1820s, "fraternities increasingly made it possible for the individual to find both privacy in his lodging and intimacy in a small group—a second family."[28] The same can be said of design studios, where the prolonged, intense interaction across an academic term can result in a familial atmosphere—with the best and the worst aspects of family life manifested on a day-to-day basis.[29] The intense contact with studio-mates often makes it difficult for design students to maintain their friendships with those in other fields. As many students have admitted, the more years they spend in design, the fewer nondesign students they have as friends. Cloistered into the captivity of studio, the studio commands an increasingly greater role as the center of students' social lives, and consequently, the world outside studio becomes less important.

Design juries have often been compared to the hazing rituals required by those newly inducted into the fraternity. Many designers typically refer to the jury as a "rite of passage"—a process designed either to make or to break you.

Design studios also have several features in common with elementary school classrooms. In both instances, students are assigned desks that belong to them for a long period of time, and no one else uses them. Both have an agenda above and beyond what most instructors announce as the basic content of the course. Teaching this "hidden agenda" involves transmitting to students the basic value systems and ethics of the profession—with the faculty as the ultimate role models. Several scholars have called this hidden agenda the "hidden curriculum": the values, virtues, and desirable ways of behaving that are communicated in subtle ways in every field. The hidden curriculum can often be more powerful than the actual content and substantive information conveyed in the classroom.[30] Note the following quote by Philip Jackson, an educational researcher who was among the first to coin the term *the hidden curriculum*, about life in elementary school classrooms. The resemblance between classrooms and design studios is truly striking.

> There is a social intimacy in schools that is unmatched elsewhere in our society. Buses and movie theaters may be more crowded than classrooms, but people rarely stay in such densely populated settings for extended periods of time and while there, they usually are not expected to concentrate on work or to interact with each other. Even factory workers are not clustered as close together as students in a standard classroom. Indeed, imagine what would happen if a factory the size of a typical elementary school contained three or four hundred adult workers. In all likelihood the unions would not allow it. Only in schools do thirty or more people spend several hours each day literally side by side. Once we leave the classroom we seldom again are required to have contact with so many people for so long a time.[31]

Some scholars have pointed out that as members of crowds, as potential recipients of praise or reproof, and as pawns of institutional authorities, students imbibe the hidden curriculum of elementary classroom settings and learn adaptive strategies to cope with situations later in life.[32] A similar dynamic occurs in the studio environment. Students learn that design is first and foremost an artistic endeavor, and that their chances for success are better if they can please their critics.[33]

Criticism in elementary schools can be classified along a continuum with varying degrees of privacy, from the most secret to the most public (Figure 2-3). In elementary school, the *most secret* form of criticism is communicated to parents or to school officials, but not to students themselves. The results of intelligence quotient (IQ) tests are one type of example. A *slightly less secret but still private* form of criticism is that given in the classic form of written evaluation—the comments along the margins of a student's paper. A *mixture of public and private* evaluation occurs when teachers meet privately with students to discuss their work. Sometimes students are called directly to the teacher's desk, while at other times teachers walk around the room and chat with individual students. "Often, however, these seemingly private conferences are secretly attended by eavesdroppers. Thus, it is quite probable, although it might be difficult to prove, that a student's nearest classmates are more intimately aware of the teacher's evaluation of him than are students sitting at a greater distance."[34] Finally, when public comment is made in the presence of other students, we see the *most public* form of evaluation. Perfect papers or drawings are sometimes displayed for the rest of the class to see. Similarly, examples of poor classroom behavior, resulting in scolding, isolation, or removal from the room, are also highly visible. Thus it is quite common in elementary schools to see students praised or admonished in front of their classmates.[35]

The last two forms of evaluation, those that are the most public, typify the way in which criticism is delivered in design studio. The desk crit, where the instructor meets with the student one on one at her individual work station to deliver ongoing feedback, is much like the so-called

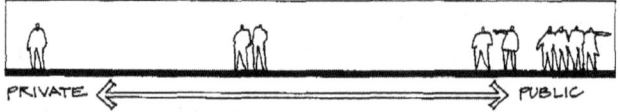

Figure 2-3 Criticism can be viewed along a continuum, from the most private to the most public. Open juries are a most public form of criticism.

private conference at the student's desk. In fact, this one-on-one interaction between student and teacher may be seen as a unique strength of design education, occasionally resulting in lifelong friendships between faculty and students. On the other hand, the jury is most like the public praise or admonishment in front of one's classmates.

Criticism in the studio differs from that in elementary school in a significant way, however. In today's elementary school, teachers generally emphasize praise and downplay punishment. "The dominant viewpoint in education today stresses the pedagogical advantages of success and the disadvantages of failure. In short, our schools are reward-oriented. Thus teachers are instructed to focus on the good aspects of a student's behavior and to overlook the poor."[36] In design schools, just the opposite usually occurs. The research conducted for this book bears this out; students overwhelmingly report that criticism at juries, and to a lesser extent at desk crits, is weighted heavily toward the negative. Referring to design instructors and jurors as critics encapsulates this viewpoint. Both the words *criticism* and *critic* primarily connote a negative evaluation. The strong emphasis on negative criticism—compared to the emphasis on praise in earlier educational settings—can make the new students' introduction to design education all that much harder to take.

THE DESIGN PROJECT, THE TERM PAPER, AND THE FINAL EXAM

Some interesting comparisons can also be drawn between design projects and the term papers and final exams that are used to evaluate student work in other university courses (Figure 2-4).[37] In each case, the intent of feedback is to provide information that can be used to improve subsequent work. Learning from criticism is the key. Some scholars refer to this as "double-loop" learning.[38] Nonetheless, when comparing design with nondesign fields, we can see that *the process, the product, and the method of evaluating student work differ dramatically*. The implication here is not that either system is inherently superior to the other, but rather that they are indeed quite different.

A COMPARISON OF DESIGN PROJECTS, TERM PAPERS AND FINAL EXAMS

	Design project	Term paper	Final exam
Process			
setting	group	solitary	solitary
location	studio	home, library, computer lab	classroom
input from others	faculty, students	optional from faculty and students	none
End Product			
format	oral and graphic (drawings and models)	written	written (essay or multiple choice)
presentation	public	private	private
Method of Evaluation			
feedback	public immediate	private days or weeks later	private days or weeks later
grade	comments from jurors and/or instructor	optional comments from instructor	optional comments from instructor
	letter grade or score	letter grade or score	letter grade or score

Figure 2-4 The end products of most classes on campus are term papers, while the end products of design courses are final design projects. The processes, the products, and the method of feedback differ greatly from one another.

The Process

Preparing a term paper is a solitary activity. Except in the case of a group project, students typically work alone at home, in the library, or in a computer laboratory and only consult with their instructor if they take the initiative. More often than not, they receive little or no input from either their instructor or classmates before their project is due. The procedure for studying for final course examinations is similar. Although in this case, too, panic-stricken students may stay up for all-night cram sessions, they are often alone at home and rarely work as a group except for occasional, informal study group sessions.

By contrast, design students work in a group setting surrounded by classmates, often relying on each other for assistance. They generally complete the bulk of their design work at school in design studio. Students are highly dependent on their design instructors throughout the entire preparation process. Their designs are subject to change almost up until the last minute, depending on the nature of the criticism they receive from their instructor. Faculty often advise students to make substantive changes only a few days before their projects are due. As a result, spending one or two sleepless nights in studio is typical of most design students immediately before the jury, as students frantically work to meet their deadline.

The End Product

Term papers and examinations usually result in some form of expository writing or, in large classes, multiple-choice tests. They are turned in privately. Students rarely see each other's term papers before turning them in, and reading one another's exam can result in punishment for cheating.

The end product of the design process is usually a set of drawings or models mounted on display boards, sometimes accompanied by a brief concept statement. Students supplement their graphic work with an oral presentation at the jury to fellow classmates, faculty, and visiting guests.

The Method of Evaluation

Feedback on term papers and exams usually arrives several days or weeks after students have completed them. Comments are written and received in private and come from only one source—either the professor or the teaching assistant. Rarely is criticism public, and if it is, it may merely be to point out a student who received the highest grade on the exam and to offer congratulations. Feedback is usually in the form of a letter grade, often with written comments. Only the more courageous students dare to confront their instructors individually to challenge their evaluations.[39]

By contrast, feedback on design projects is extremely public. Although the students' grades are not publicized, the criticism they receive is broadcast loudly in the design jury. Jurors provide students with immediate feedback, often even before students have completed their presentation. Criticism is verbal, spontaneous, and free-flowing. Students must digest comments not only from their design instructor, but also from other jurors, visitors, and sometimes classmates. Criticism is often contradictory. Bolder students interact with their critics and defend their projects. Students generally do not learn their grade on their design project until after the jury or the course itself is over.

Students' descriptions of design juries reflect their public nature. They refer to themselves as being "thrown out into the bullring," using the analogy of a bullfight and casting themselves in the role of matador. Others look to sports like baseball, preparing themselves "on deck" while the classmate who precedes them is "batter up" (Figure 2-5). Some design professors use a theatrical metaphor, "bringing down the curtain" on students as they each conclude their presentation before the jury.

In sum, compared with the standard term paper or final exam, certain aspects of the design project—the individual contact with the instructor, the comaraderie that forms among studio-mates, the multiple viewpoints that are offered about individual student work, and the rapidity with which feedback is given—may be somewhat preferable. Each of these characteristics has a downside, however. When they are taken to excess, the student can feel smothered by too much contact with students and instructors, confused by the differences of opinion about his work, and shortchanged by the realization that weeks' worth of work are evaluated in only a few short minutes.

Figure 2-5 Many faculty and students draw upon analogies from the sports world to describe the jury presentation. Here the student is "batter up," while the following student is "on deck," just as in a baseball game.

DESIGN JURIES AND COMPREHENSIVE EXAMS

Juries have more in common with the comprehensive exams given to doctoral students than they do with the term papers and examinations given to undergraduate and masters' level students. Comprehensive exams call for a session where the student defends her work in front of a faculty committee. In this context, again, the student and a group of faculty interact face to face. The questions posed by the committee have been prepared and orchestrated ahead of time. In some cases, students are informed of the questions in advance and work on them as a take-home assignment for a prescribed number of hours or days before the defense. These oral sessions consist of a sole student and his committee, and the public is generally not invited. The stress level at the oral exam is incredibly high, as the test often marks the cutoff point determining whether or not the student is advanced to doctoral candidacy. As Burton Bledstein has put it in his insightful work, *The Culture of Professionalism*, comprehensive exams "tested the larger resources of a candidate, not only the individual's superior intellectual accomplishments but superior emotional control under duress."[40] This "hidden curriculum" sounds remarkably like that of the design jury.

In some countries, this format is typical of design juries; individual students meet with jurors in a closed room with no one present. Some Middle Eastern and Third World students have told me that they made it a regular practice to study the expression on the student's face who exited the jury room in order to mentally prepare themselves for their own face-to-face encounter with the jury. If the student who preceded them looked bright-eyed, they were optimistic that their own jury session would go well. But if that student appeared visibly shaken or sullen, they prepared themselves for impending doom.

DESIGN JURIES, ATHLETICS, AND THE MILITARY

"My first design instructor would just sit there and yell at me and tear my models apart and say, "Don't say it, do it." Architecture school was like boot camp: 12 hours a day seven days a week in basic design....

"In retrospect it was the beginning of a major shift in my education—a totally antiintellectual period in my life. I can honestly say I hardly read a book in my three years of architecture school. It was like going back to kindergarten. All the skills that I learned in 18 years of school were worthless. Every minute, I was being made to feel like a first-grader. So the first couple of years in grad school I didn't do very well. I didn't flunk out, but I didn't get any commends in studio, and I was in the middle to bottom of my class....

"My first design instructor was a bit like a drill sergeant. You're more or less being broken and, as a result, you have this weird relationship with the person. You both hate them and love them because they're forcing you to do these things that are so hard. And you can't help but think: Why am I doing this? Why am I banging my head into the wall for this person? But it did prepare me for what was to come."—Steven Izenour

The design jury and the studio system have much in common with the world of athletics, with the students as the team and the studio instructor in the role of coach.[41] Many students and faculty routinely draw from the sports world when describing juries and studios. The comaraderie or esprit de corps that often forms in studio is somewhat akin to the relationships among members of a football, baseball, or other sports team. Often lifelong friendships can be traced back to studio. The coach's role is to train, lead, and support the team in order to successfully compete and win games. It is also to enforce discipline and rigor. As a result, athletes often have ambivalent feelings towards the coach, just as Steven Izenour's reactions to his first design instructor. Each team member plays a vital role in the success of the team as a whole, such that the whole is greater than the sum of its parts. When the team wins, the coach wins as well, basking in the reflected glory of combined team efforts.

A number of sports psychology researchers have written about the role of *self-efficacy*, or self-confidence, and its relationship to athletes' motivation and performance. Many have demonstrated that if athletes have strong self-confidence, or what researchers have termed "perceived competence" in their abilities, they are more highly motivated and more likely to perform well.[42] In one study of wrestling coaches, results showed that liberal use of reward statements, encouraging positive talk, emphasizing technique improvement, and downplaying outcome were among the strategies rated most effective.[43] In essence, positive rewards seem to work better than punishment. This raises an important question: How does the emphasis on criticism—and primarily on negative criticism—in design education affect student motivation and performance?[44] Chances are that it does more harm than good.

The argument is often made that competitive sports help build character, but increasingly, researchers are demonstrating that this is simply not so. Based on testing administered to approximately 15,000 athletes, researchers have identified general sports personalities. Problem athletes fell into these major syndromes: the con-man athlete, the hyper-anxious athlete, the athlete who resists coaching, the success-phobic athlete, the injury-prone athlete, and the depression-prone athlete.[45] These categories may shed some light on pathological personality types in the design studio: students who try to "pull one over on the jury," trying to make their work look more complete than it really is; students who are chronic worriers; students who resist any advice from design critics, jurors, or classmates; students who fear the limelight of success; students who chronically injure themselves in the heat of the project deadline; and students who are depression-prone, mulling over jurors' negative comments long after the jury is over.

In an extremely insightful analysis of competition that applies not only to sports, but also to many other aspects of life, writer Alfie Kohn has drawn a distinction between *intergroup competition* among groups and *intragroup competition* among individuals within a group.[46] The academic design studio promotes a high degree of intragroup competition, and competition among different schools for design awards promotes a high degree of intergroup competition.[47]

The studio is perhaps most like the Olympic Games, a series of contests between individual actors. In their pure forms, the Olympics are *individual* in both effort and consequence. Athletic contests typically revolve around the demonstration of individual excellence in speed, endurance, mental acuity, accuracy, strength, and coordination.[48] The design studio pivots around the demonstration of individual excellence in the knowledge and skills of design. In the contest as well as the studio, the emphasis is on individual struggle and outcome.

Along these lines, three ways to achieve goals are *competitively,* working against others; *cooperatively,* working with others; and *independently,* working alone without relation to others. In a cooperative model, reward is based on collective performance. As Kohn describes, "Thus a cooperative classroom is not simply one in which students sit together or talk with each other or even share materials. It means that successful completion of a task depends on each student and therefore that each has an incentive to want the other(s) to succeed."[49] With the rare exception of team projects, in design education, the cooperative model is rare. Instead, the competitive model prevails. Although the design studio gives the illusion of a cooperative setting, students' rewards are based on independent rather than collective performance.

Just as athletes are highly competitive, many design students, too, compete fiercely with their studio-mates—in spite of or perhaps because of the comaraderie that builds up in the studio. The "enemy," if there is one, fluctuates from the other students in the class, who are competing for the same grades, to the jurors, who are in the role of devil's advocates. Even though students may occasionally help each other out, they are cautious not to give out too much advice lest, in the process, they damage their own chances for success. In some cases, it may even be in their best interests as a competitor (but certainly not as a friend) to give out the wrong advice. While the design critic may support individual team members during desk crits throughout the design process, in the jury of his own student's work, he generally remains quiet.[50] Worse than that, he may even reinforce some of the negative criticism raised by fellow jurors. He who served as ally has now become an adversary! In this respect, it is as if the coach betrays his team members by going over to the other side of the playing field. A student's first jury is much like a rookie's debut in an actual football game, a true baptism under fire.

At another level, faculty members compete with each other for their students' design awards. The contemporary scene in design education is much like Bosworth and Jones's "architectural football" of the 1930s. In many institutions, design faculty salaries and promotions depend in part on the awards that their students receive. All other things being equal, a design professor whose students have placed routinely in national design competitions is much more likely to rapidly climb up the academic ladder than is her counterpart with less successful students.[51] Just as in the 1930s, competition among schools, too, can be extremely fierce. The preponderance of national student design competitions encourages such competition. A school whose students routinely win competitions often advertises this fact in promotional brochures sent out to prospective students, and lists it as an accomplishment for professional accreditation.

Several individuals interviewed for this book drew analogies between design studio and the military, with the studio as boot camp, the studio instructor as the drill sergeant, and the students as buck privates or entering soldiers. The sergeant's role is to either make or break members of his platoon. Architect Martin Pawley has offered the following description of the design professor: "He is a general! He says to each successive year of freshmen, 'This is our plan of attack.' . . ."[52] Many design instructors routinely refer to themselves as "running a tight ship." The first jury is somewhat akin to a soldier's rite of passage through first combat.

Both the sports and military analogies are heavily slanted toward males. More than females, males have traditionally been involved in organized sports throughout high school and are much more likely to feel comfortable with the so-called competitive team spirit and classic male bonding that occurs in studio. Men, too, are much more likely to feel comfortable with the military comparisons that design instructors often use. Underlying both these analogies is a strong emphasis on competition. More on competition in design education, and the creation of an educational environment that is more hospitable to women, both as students and faculty, will be discussed in greater detail in Chapter 12.

DESIGN JURIES AND THEIR COUNTERPARTS IN THE FINE ARTS: ART, MUSIC, AND DRAMA

Compared to other evaluation techniques, design juries are most similar to the techniques used to evaluate work in the fine arts. The close alliance between environmental design and the art world is probably one reason why this is so. The design of buildings, cities, and the landscape has long been considered primarily an art form.[53] The use of a public review to evaluate student performance is common in art, music, dance, and drama. In the art world, both open and closed juries are routinely used. Design juries are perhaps most like the juries held by painters, sculptors, and photographers. In painting classes, student work is usually evaluated in informal critique sessions where faculty circulate around an exhibit space from one piece to another. In some cases, an outside critic is invited to participate as well. Generally, only a few pieces are discussed in depth. Students sometimes express the ideas behind their artwork. Individual course instructors are responsible for the grade of each student.[54]

Literature on how students and professionals react to juries in the fine arts appears to be minimal.[55] Nonetheless, it does reveal a certain degree of discontent with their public nature. Some of the discussion has centered around the arbitrary nature of professional arts and crafts juries that select art for an exhibition.[56] The act of judging an art exhibition has been labeled by one writer as an unusual combination of "science, art, and gamble," where the weight of each of these factors shifts according to the "experience, intellect, insights, fancies, prejudices, and self-confidence of the various members of the jury."[57]

The public nature of criticism in music education has also been subject to criticism. Apparently, many conductors, caught up in the pressure of public performances, become highly critical of students, often making public comments like "You are the worst third clarinet player I've ever heard!" or "Play it or pack it!" As some educators have argued, comments like these do little to enhance students' self-esteem and desire to improve their performance.[58]

In both the fine arts and environmental design, the presentation of one's creative efforts is viewed as a performance. Tremendous weight is placed on a panel of experts to judge the quality of the work, and these experts are accorded a high status. Jurors are often chosen from a list of "stars" and trendsetters in the field, to whom the masses look for inspiration. Although jurors in both the arts and environmental design share similar criteria in describing their reactions to submitted work—form, balance, and scale, proportion, texture, rhythm, and so on—the specific criteria for judging are rarely made explicit. Instead, expert opinion is what matters most. In many respects, the system resembles the master-apprentice relationship of earlier times. The jury assumes the role of the experienced masters who pass judgment on their underlings. Related to this is the common practice of the apprenticeship, whereby a less experienced artist works alongside one with more experience. In the design professions, this is referred to as a professional internship, a prerequisite to obtaining a professional license to practice on one's own.

The criteria used to select potential job applicants in the fine arts and in design are somewhat comparable. While the performing arts generally rely on a musical or dramatic audition before a panel of judges, the fine arts rely on the portfolio. The portfolio serves as a tangible résumé of one's creative abilities and talents. Budding young artists, photographers, and designers fresh out of school are constantly trying to build up their portfolio in order to advance their professional careers.

DESIGN JURIES AND THEIR COUNTERPARTS IN OTHER PROFESSIONS: LAW AND MEDICINE

The design fields represent a unique blend of the arts, the sciences, and the social sciences. Aesthetic concerns, functional issues, and the psychological characteristics of the environment and the people who use it must be taken into account. In this light, the design professions share much in common with both medicine and law. Rightly or wrongly, the general public often equates the professional status of architects with that of doctors and lawyers. Interestingly, many of the criticisms leveled at medical, legal, and other forms of professional education can also be pointed at design education. Let us first compare the design professions with medical professionals, with a special look at how both are trained and evaluated in school.

Design Education and Medical Education

Like the design disciplines, medicine occupies a special position at the juncture of the sciences and the humanities—a balance of technical prowess and sensitivity to human values. Both these responsibilities have been in conflict for almost a century. In addition, medicine has always mixed theory, practice, and art. A number of scholars have written that universities have a responsibility to provide students with knowledge of the technical fundamentals of the professions, as well as a sensitivity to the impact of technical decisions on individuals and on society.[59] In addition, the need to offer medical students both professional training and a broad-based university education has been stressed. For example, "The university must not only prepare competent professionals, but provide them and the whole of educated men with the critical faculties unique to the educated man . . . the capacity to question, criticize and judge the value issues in fields outside their own."[60] Others have criticized the narrow focus of medical education and students' preoccupation with training in lieu of a more general education. They attribute this largely to the intense competition for admission to medical school.[61]

The studio in the design fields can perhaps best be compared with the internship in a teaching hospital immediately following medical school. While studios begin at the undergraduate level, internships generally begin either during the final year or immediately following medical school. Nonetheless the life-style of both the design student and the medical intern share some important traits.

Both are expected to devote exceptionally long, hard hours toward the pursuit of their goal—most often, ultimately, to obtain a professional license to practice in the field. Working around the clock and pushing oneself to the physical limits of endurance are common to both.

Compared to design students, however, medical interns have much more at stake. While a poor performance at the jury will likely affect students' grades and the way others perceive their design abilities, medical students who err risk human lives. "Pulling all-nighters" seems to be part of the ritual required to train these young professionals, but one that has already been proven to be both unnecessary and dangerous. In fact, a rash of malpractice cases seems to have been related to fatigue, and recent reform efforts have been under way to limit the number of consecutive hours in ordinary, inpatient care and in the emergency room.[62] Some young residents have complained that the typical schedule—at least five days a week with a minimum of 16 hours per day, plus being "on call" in the hospital every third night—is "cruel and unusual punishment." Studies have shown that as many as one-third of medical residents become severely depressed, and that rates of divorce, suicide, drug abuse, and alcoholism are high. The macho explanation that doctors offer for this common practice is, "If I went through it, so can you."[63]

A fascinating look at medical school, largely through the eyes of students, is described in a classic study entitled *Boys in White: Student Culture in Medical School*. The purpose of this research was to present an empathetic view of life as a medical student, and to try to understand "what medical school did to medical students other than giving them a technical education."[64] The study revealed that younger freshman medical students often worked about 77 hours per week, not unlike young design students.[65] It also stressed that medical faculty have diverse responsibilities, including teaching, seeing patients in the hospital or clinic, training residents and interns, and in many cases, research.[66] Similarly, many design faculty are split between teaching and professional practice. Relatively few, however, are actively involved in research and scholarship.

Medical school instructors participating in the study generally suggested a four-way exposure to each topic: reading, attending lecture, doing lab work, and review.[67] By contrast, in design, most instructors consider lab work— that is, studio—to be of first and foremost importance; students are quick to pick up that among all their courses, studio has first priority. Few design studios are accompanied by reading, lectures, or any form of systematic reviews. A walk through the bookstore at any university campus clearly demonstrates the lack of emphasis on required books in design education. If you search the bookshelves for studio course readings, you are likely to find that few books, if any, have been assigned. Usually the studio course simply isn't listed at all. Furthermore, fewer shelves are devoted to architecture and landscape architecture than to most other disciplines.[68] Most books in these fields are required for departmental history courses, introductory lecture classes, and graduate seminars.

The medical internship involves direct contact with patients, learning to examine and diagnose them. Clinical rather than academic work is emphasized, and training is achieved mainly through working with patients rather than lectures and laboratory work. In this case, the intern becomes an apprentice working alongside full-fledged practitioners in the hospital. Here medical training and design training differ dramatically. *While the emphasis in this stage of the medical internship is to maintain a close link between future doctors and patients, design education rarely stresses a close relationship with either the client or the user.* Most design projects in school are for hypothetical clients and users. Connections between future designers and their clients and users are minimal at best—and usually nonexistent. It is only when designers themselves become interns in a professional office that client and user contact is seriously introduced. Some interns in larger design offices, however, still have little client contact, as that is often left to the design principals.

How is student work usually evaluated in the health professions? The techniques are generally quite sophisticated.[69] Multiple methods, including objective tests, paper simulations, computer simulations, simulated patients, videotapes, and direct observation have been routinely used to evaluate student performance. Educational researchers agree that students need information from several sources—peers, clients, instructors, and themselves—in order to compare themselves with a standard. Some have argued that an ideal evaluation system includes (1) a clear purpose; (2) clear performance standards; (3) validity, reliability, and practicality; (4) training for evaluators; and (5) a variety of approaches.[70] Unfortunately, evaluation of student performance in the design professions falls short in just about every one of these areas. These deficiencies, and ways to remedy them, will be discussed in subsequent chapters.

Design Education and Legal Education

How does design education compared with legal education? To a certain extent, both educational systems emphasize public interactions between teachers and students. One of the most commonly used teaching techniques in law is the case or clinical method, where students are presented with the facts of an actual or hypothetical situation as it might arrive at a lawyer's office. This is supplemented with the Socratic method, where public class discussions center around how cases should be decided.[71] These discussions often involve calling on students at random to test their abilities to state their views in public, as portrayed in the 1973 film, *The Paper Chase*. In many respects, the tension experienced by law students involved in the Socratic teaching technique shares much in common with the way in which design students experience design juries. Consider the following quote from a former executive director of the Association of American Law Schools, which sounds much like design education:

> *Articulate students have complained that their teachers tend to "create classroom anxiety," and to "demean and degrade" any students who have the courage to stick their necks out and "get their heads chopped off."... Ever since the modern, standardized law school came into existence, law teachers have described their technique, partly in praise and partly in blame, and pitying the students: "in the first year we scare them to death; in the second year, we work them to death; and in the third year, we bore them to death."*[72]

Others, too, have been highly critical of the "needless destructiveness" of legal education and the fact that it can have the unintended consequence of making its graduates increasingly insensitive and less compassionate toward the needs of others. Some say that techniques used to assess students' performance are partly to blame.[73] The same criticism can be leveled at design education. Some design educators strongly argue the reverse: that such fear and intimidation actually inspire students to work even harder; however, this flies in the face of most findings from educational research.

Some scholars have sharply criticized the monotony of legal education and the strong reliance on the case method, arguing that "... visits to classrooms in every part of the country seemed to present the identical scenery, performers and script ... [it is] too rigid, too uniform, too repetitious and too long."[74] To a certain extent, one could make the same case for design education as well, particularly in light of the almost uniform use of design juries in virtually every design school in the English-speaking world.

The use of the moot court, a simulation of an actual court case, is another common teaching technique. It, too, tests the abilities of students to present and argue their cases in a public setting. It is largely an exercise in public speaking and one that is seen to help prepare law students for the "real world." In this respect, design education differs sharply with legal education. In law school, developing strong rhetorical skills and a sharp command of the language have long been considered key ingredients of success. In design schools, however, these skills are rarely taught.

Another difference between legal and design education is that legal educators seem to place a higher value on the art of good teaching. For instance, as early as the mid-1970s, the Association of American Law Schools was already conducting law-teaching clinics aimed at helping new faculty members become good teachers. Such activities are still relatively rare in the design professions, although they may become more common in the future. Studio instructors usually leap into the world of teaching with no formal preparation whatsoever in learning how to teach. Instead, they are generally selected on the basis of their proven record of design excellence. Once they have begun teaching, they are offered few evaluative measures of their teaching effectiveness, short of the official student course evaluation forms, and little or no guidance about how to improve. While to a certain extent this can be said of higher education in general, the intense contact with students and the public nature of criticism make the preparation of sensitive design teachers all the more important.

Finally, let use compare the standard courtroom jury—that to which most budding young law students aspire—to design juries. A fundamental difference between design juries and courtroom juries is that courtroom juries do not react publicly until presentations by both the prosecution and the defense, as well as subsequent deliberations, are over. In the case of courtroom juries, it is difficult to gauge the jurors' reactions to various presentations because jurors listen to the proceedings in complete silence, giving little or nothing away. And design students do not have a defense attorney on their side.

Some Shared Dilemmas of Professional Education

Among the common traits shared by the education of designers, doctors, and lawyers—and especially the design jury—is a serious ethical dilemma: *To whom does one's primary responsibility lie—the client, the employer, the profession, or the public at large?* This problem seems to span not only these three professions, but also accountancy, engineering, and other professions as well.[75] Confusion about this issue is manifested in the educational system of each of these disciplines. In the environmental design fields, it can be seen in the structure of course curricula, in the selection of required readings, in the nature of design juries—especially in the selection of jurors—and elsewhere. Rarely is the client or user included as a significant component of any of these facets of design education. Rather, the comments of most design instructors in the studio and on the jury imply that the students' primary responsibility is to the profession.

Another issue common to all three: *To what extent is too much stress placed on acquiring competency in school, when in fact the professional's education requires further years of additional training and experience?*[76] Is each field driven primarily by its professional licensing procedures, perhaps at the expense of acquiring a more broad-based education? Within the professional educational curriculum, what is an appropriate balance between acquiring both knowledge and skills, and between delivering education and training?[77] To what extent do the knowledge, skills, and abilities measured by professional registration examinations correspond with what is taught in school?

Yet another question common to all three: *What is the relationship between academic performance and professional performance?* Some educators have expressed fear about what the answer will be. In law, for example, "There is the old adage that the 'A' students become professors; the 'B' students become judges; and the 'C' students make all the money."[78] In design, some have argued that the A students teach, and the B students work for the C students. Or, as Joseph Esherick has put it:

> ... It is unfortunate that no study has as yet been made relating the particular students whom the Beaux-Arts institutions premiated with their later effectiveness in actual practice as architects. Certainly it would seem reasonable to expect, if the system were effective, that those students who did best in school would emerge as the better architects. I have been able to discover no useful correlations.[79]

In fact, published research available to date tends to suggest little correlation between the grades awarded in professional education and achievement in professional practice.[80] More research is needed on this important issue, however.[81]

Related to this is the evaluation of professional education. *What is the nature of evaluations in each profession? Who is best equipped to evaluate? Are the measures for professional accreditation valid indicators of the quality of professional education?* In design education, professional accreditation is the primary vehicle of evaluation. In architectural education, for example, this task is performed by the National Architectural Accrediting Board (NAAB). Internal evaluation procedures conducted within each university provide a different set of measures. Nonetheless, both the professional accreditation process and internal evaluation procedures typically pay little attention to the jury process. The jury is not accountable to any higher body and appears to fall between the cracks, allowing a relative free-for-all to occur.

A SOCIAL AND PSYCHOLOGICAL ANALYSIS: JURIES AS "FESTIVALS" OR "BLOODBATHS"?

"A class is set up with a beginning and an end, and generally a grade at that end. . . . But the students seem to want to have some sort of culminating festivity and they get disappointed if the jury process happens without such a culmination. In practice, the culmination is getting the damn thing built, but that isn't part of the school experience usually. In school, it becomes necessary to have some obviously artificial, but important, festivity. I think festivities and bloodbaths get mixed up in people's minds, and I think the jury sometimes becomes a 'festival' or 'bloodbath,' a trauma, and that students miss it if they don't have it. . . ."—Charles W. Moore

The lenses of sociologists and psychologists can be applied to help paint a more vivid portrait of design juries and studios both in education and in practice. Some key concepts crucial to a deeper understanding of design juries are charisma, the star system, authority, and paternalism.

Charisma and the Star System

What is charisma? Sociologist Max Weber defined charisma as a form of "natural leadership," special gifts of the body and spirit, gifts that are often believed to be supernatural and not accessible to everyone. "In order to do justice to their mission, the holders of charisma, the master as well as his disciples and followers, must stand outside the ties of this world, outside of routine occupations, as well as outside the routine obligations of family life."[82] Weber went on to argue that pure charisma flows from personal strength which is constantly being proved. Historically, charismatic leaders have separated themselves from the world at large in significant ways. Catholic priests, for example, must live in celibacy.

The profound power of charismatic leaders rests in a strong level of recognition and springs from faithful devotion. "It is devotion to the extraordinary and unheard-of, to what is strange to all rule and tradition and which therefore is viewed as divine. It is a devotion born of distress and enthusiasm."[83]

How does the notion of charisma shed light on design juries and the studio scene? Charisma helps explain the control that some design instructors maintain over their students. How else can one explain the devotion with which students labor over their projects in studio? What else can account for students' willingness to meet with their instructor in studio at 2:00 A.M., while elsewhere on campus, most students are fast asleep or otherwise engaged? Fear, desperation, and sheer dedication are other possible explanations, of course, but not surprisingly, these traits often accompany loyal disciples anxious and willing to please their charismatic leaders.

The hero-worshipping of design "gurus" and "cult" figures often resembles the activities that characterize groupies around rock stars, devout followers of religious leaders, and dedicated fans of politicians (Figure 2-6). For instance, at one university that was hosting a distinguished architect, faculty members designed and constructed a large mobile of the celebrated guest's head. The mobile was hung prominently at the entrance to the architecture building, where it dangled in the breeze for an entire semester. While another prestigious architect was in residence, faculty members were offered specially designed, personally autographed posters commemorating the visit. Students could purchase unsigned copies for $5. Replace the poster with an album cover, and the architect with a rock star, and there you have it![84]

Figure 2-6 The star system is firmly in place in the design professions. Many students engage in star-worshipping and model themselves after the stars. At my university, students have formed "The Architects Who Wear Black and/or Round Glasses Club," inspired by their mentor, Frank Lloyd Wright.

The reverence for stellar designers is just as, if not even more, apparent in design practice. Mobs flock around eminent designers following their public appearances at conferences, lectures, and the like. Architects visit the Michael Graves building in Portland or the Helmut Jahn buildings in Chicago, often in the spirit of paying homage to a religious shrine.[85] To have one's work featured on the cover of *Progressive Architecture* or one of the other leading design magazines is yet another tangible symbol of one's status as a star. In an acerbic style, social critic Tom Wolfe has called attention to these and other cultish behavior patterns among architects, generating a wild flurry of controversy among the profession.[86] His book, *From Bauhaus to Our House*, a scathing critique of the star system in architecture, created such a stir that when he was invited to speak at the 1985 American Institute of Architects convention in San Francisco, a movement was under way to boycott the entire conference.

As Wolfe points out, many of these cultish tendencies can be traced to the links between the design professions and the art world. In fact, highly accomplished artists enjoy a fleet of disciples and aspiring artists who view them as heroic role models. The same is true for musicians, dancers, and other performing artists. The opening vignette in Woody Allen's 1989 film, *New York Stories*, about a self-absorbed artist and his devoted followers, could just as easily have been about a designer.

Authority, Paternalism, and the Design Studio

Charismatic figures typically possess an intense aura of authority that allows them to cast an almost magical spell on their followers. According to social critic and professor Richard Sennett, assurance, superior judgment, the ability to impose discipline, and the capacity to inspire fear are key ingredients of authority. "Some [musical] conductors, like Toscanini, create discipline by inspiring terror; he screamed, stamped his foot, even threw his stick at the players. A man possessed of the Truth at each moment, he would brook no falseness from others. To avoid his wrath, you did what he said."[87] The same could be said about Frank Lloyd Wright, one of the most charismatic figures in the history of architecture.

In extreme cases, some studio "masters" evoke a similar sense of fear on the part of their students and colleagues in design studio. Dreading that the studio instructor might appear on the scene any time, day or night, design students labor away in studio around the clock. Fearing humiliation, the possibility of being proven wrong, or simply "making a scene," most students choose not to risk engaging in a dialogue, much less arguing with design critics or jurors. The image sent to student by some jurors is: "I am Oz, the Great and Terrible. Who are you, and why do you seek me?" As a result, many students are discouraged from simply questioning jurors. The fear is not just from teacher to student or from practitioner to student, however. It can also be from teacher to another. Junior faculty often hesitate to disagree with a more senior colleague, especially if that person is a star in the field or in the school. This "Oz"-like aura is not limited to juries in design education, however. It can also be seen on professional design juries where one stellar designer creates an authoritarian air that tends to take over the rest of the jury.[88]

The fear of debating and engaging in a meaningful dialogue is prevalent in design education even outside the studio. Eminent design practitioners deliver public lectures at colleges, universities, and professional conferences that all too often consist of little more than flashy show-and-tell sessions, with hundreds of slides but little or no time for questions and answers. The audience may be reluctant to ask questions, overwhelmed by the stature of the speaker, or the format simply is not set up to encourage a lively discussion (i.e., poor acoustics from the audience and other obstacles). Or else it is simply too late in the evening to bother.

The blame lies not with the presenters, but with those who extend the invitation and organize these gala events. Not having been exposed to other more interactive forms of presentation, they simply lead the audience in a round of applause, return to the microphone, thank the speaker, and bid everyone a "Good night." Such lengthy illustrated monologues that remain unquestioned simply reinforce the role of the expert, superstar designer with ultimate authority. In this sense, design is quite different from other professions and academic disciplines where animated exchanges are a regular part of any public presentation, especially those featuring the more prominent members of the field.

The studio critic often is characterized by other qualities typical of authority figures.[89] Although there are many notable exceptions, self-assurance and unusually large egos are in rich supply among some highly accomplished studio instructors.[90] For example, at one university, a special two-hour evening session was devoted to an illustrated presentation of the studio instructor's autobiography. It opened with a slide of a map of the world highlighted by colorful pushpins to mark where he had lived and when. Next were chronologically arranged slides of the instructor as a baby, toddler, and curious young boy, perhaps in the vein of *Portrait of the Artist* [Architect] *as a Young Man.*

The ability to impose discipline is another feature of authority figures. One might argue how successfully this is achieved in the university design studio. While at first glance the studio might appear like a rather disorderly and undisciplined environment, littered with tracing paper, model cutouts, and the like, the fact that students willingly devote so many hours of the week to the studio is evidence of discipline and dedication to their work.

One of the most powerful forms of authority is paternalism.[91] Paternalism is derived from patrimonialism, a society in which people are connected by their relationship through their fathers. Paternalism is a contemporary version of patrimonialism, in that it legitimizes power *outside* the family by appealing to roles *within* the family. Those in subservient roles are expected to remain loyal, appreciative, and passive. The liberty of one person to judge another, as adult to adult, is eroded. Rather, the process of judging is strictly one-way, from the father figure to the child figure. Paternalism relates to the notion of in loco parentis, or in lieu of the parent. In the nineteenth century many paternalistic principles, including in loco parentis, were at the very core of asylums, workhouses, and prisons, where one purpose was to foster a sense of community among the masses.

Sennett refers to paternalism as "an authority of false love," finding it a false relationship because although the father figure appears at one level to be caring and nurturing, in fact the father only cares about his subjects insofar as it serve his interests. The loyal subjects, however, mistake power for love and nurturance. They magnify the role of the surrogate father to one of supreme importance. Furthermore, Sennett believes that the idea of transferring a relationship from the domain of family onto the domain of work is misguided at the outset; in fact a paternal relationship in the work environment can never truly emulate that of home life.[92]

Although rarely referred to as such, the currents of paternalism run strong throughout both design education and practice (Figure 2-7).[93] Students tend to view their design critic as a surrogate parent or father figure. As one student explained his jury experience, "My professor was a real lifesaver.... He jumped in and bailed us out.... He is like our father and we are his children, and he stands up for us." Or another: "I won't forget the smile of my instructor,

WALTER GROPIUS   MIES VAN DER ROHE

Figure 2-7 The currents of paternalism run strong throughout the design professions. Designers are often introduced by their affiliations with well-known male stars in the field, for example, "He worked with Gropius and Mies Van der Rohe."

his arm around me, and his words, 'You're great!' At that moment, they meant so much to me." Students often experience some of the same feelings they would with their own father: loyalty, trust, and admiration when things are going well, and if that relationship in any way goes awry, pain, anger, and outright betrayal.

In practice, too, paternalism is very much alive and well. Typically a young graduate aspires to work for a well-known designer with strong name recognition. Even if one's work experience for any of these practitioners is brief, he can still always say "I worked with Gehry"—that is, I worked with the mentor, saint, or father figure.[94] Well-known designers themselves are typically introduced at public presentations in terms of their common links to these key figures. For instance, "He worked with Gropius and Mies Van der Rohe." "He trained under Le Corbusier." "He worked at the office of Jose Luis Sert." "He was a disciple of Frank Lloyd Wright." All these relationships with the ultimate father figure, the master builders and icons of the profession, help legitimize one's own place in the design world.

Philosopher Hannah Arendt poses three different representative models to illustrate different forms of political authority: authoritarian, tyrannical, and totalitarian. The authoritarian model is compared to a pyramid, where the focal point is at the top and where authority and power filter successively down to the base. All layers are firmly interrelated like converging rays. The tyrannical model is a pyramid whose intervening layers between top and bottom are destroyed, "so that the top remains suspended, supported only by the proverbial bayonets, over a mass of carefully isolated, disintegrated, and completely equal individuals."[95] The image of totalitarian rule and organization is likened to the structure of an onion, where in the central empty space a leader is located. Whatever a leader does is done from within, not from without or above. The movement of this system provides the fiction of a normal world combined with a consciousness of being different from and more radical than it. "The onion structure makes the system organizationally shock-proof against the factuality of the real world."96

While Arendt's discussion of authority centers primarily around political philosophy, some of her concepts provide useful frameworks from which to view design juries and studios. The argument posed here is not that studios literally represent any one of these three models of authority. In reality, they may reflect an unusual combination of them all. Each provides partial explanations of some otherwise puzzling phenomena: the prominence of a distinct hierarchy in studio with students at the bottom and the jurors at the top; the unusual reverence and placement of the professor or top designer "upon a pedestal"; why jurors' comments usually remain unquestioned; and the sense of isolation that design students experience from the rest of the university. The way in which the design studio is structured—the pervasiveness of the star system, the charismatic nature of the stars, and the unquestioned authority of the studio master—helps shed some light on why the design studio has become a mysterious, curious world all its own.

NOTES

1. Boswell, Peyton, "Peyton Boswell Comments," *Art Digest*, 16:2 (March 15, 1942), p. 3.

2. Bosworth, F. H., Jr., and Roy Childs Jones, *A Study of Architectural Schools*, New York: Scribner, 1932, p. 7.

3. Aguirre, John, "The Ecole des Beaux-Arts: A Light-Hearted View," *AIA Journal* (July 1960), pp. 23-26; Carlhian, Jean Paul, "Beaux-Arts or Bozarts?" *Architectural Record* (January 1976), pp. 131-134; Carlhian, Jean Paul, "The Ecole des Beaux-Arts: Modes and Manners," *Journal of Architectural Education*, 33:2 (November 1979), pp. 7-17; Moore, John C. B., "The Ecole des Beaux Arts: A Serious Study," *AIA Journal* (July 1960), pp. 27-31; Chafee, Richard, "The Teaching of Architecture at the Ecole des Beaux-Arts," in Drexler, Arthur (ed.), *The Architecture of the Ecole des Beaux-Arts*, Cambridge, MA: MIT Press, 1977, pp. 61-109; Draper, Joan, "The Ecole des Beaux-Arts and the Architectural Profession in the United States: The Case of John Galen Howard," in Kostof, Spiro (ed.), *The Architect: Chapters in the History of the Profession*, New York: Oxford University Press, 1977, pp. 209-237.

    The Ecole des Beaux Arts emphasized producing a solution rather than solving a problem; the educational philosophy stressed product rather than process. See Lawson, Bryan, *How Designers Think*, Boston: Butterworth Architecture, 1988, p. 2.

4. The grading system at the Ecole des Beaux Arts was as follows: The top score, equivalent to an A+ today, was a Medal. Next was a 1st Mention, equivalent to an A; followed by a 2nd Mention, like a B; and a Mention, the counterpart of today's C. An HC meant *hors de concours*, or "out of competition," meaning that the terms of the competition had been violated. *Four*, the French term for "oven," signified a failure (i.e., you were baked or burned)! Those students receiving either an HC or *Four* had to repeat the exercise, amounting to about two months' worth of extra work.

    At the start of a project, the student had to prepare a sketch solution in approximately eight hours, while locked up in a cubicle at the Ecole. He prepared his *esquisse* using an enormous carbon paper, submitting the original when eight hours were up and keeping the carbon copy. Two months later, the jury had his original *esquisse* hanging under his final board. If the final solution was not in agreement with the original sketch, the grade was an HC.

    Architect James Gowan has referred to the jury or crit of the Ecole des Beaux Arts as a "crude but entertaining form of assessment." According to Gowan, "In the Beaux Arts system, which is still the model for most architectural teaching, particularly in America, the end of a particular bout of activity is celebrated with a grand display of work, Royal Academy fashion, when the professor directs a monologue of wit and opinion at a mute but no doubt admiring assembly of students." Gowan, James, "Introduction," in Gowan, James, *A Continuing Experiment: Learning and Teaching at the Architectural Association*, London: Architectural Press Ltd., 1975, pp. 13-16, quote from p. 15.

5. Kostof, op. cit.

6. Bosworth and Jones, op. cit., p. 9.

7. The grand prize of most superior fellowships and competitions in the early twentieth-century American schools was to travel to Europe to study examples of the Beaux Arts masters and their successors. See McCommons, Richard E., Gerald Martin Moeller, Jr., Karen L. Eldridge, and Betty J. Fishman (eds.), *Guide to Architecture Schools in North America: Members and Affiliates of the ACSA*, Washington, DC: Association of Collegiate Schools of Architecture (ACSA) Press, 1989, pp. viii-ix.

8. Bosworth went to Yale and the Ecole des Beaux Arts in Paris and was dean at Cornell. Jones studied at Purdue and the University of Pennsylvania and was head at the University of Minnesota. Both Bosworth and Jones served as presidents of the Association of Collegiate Schools of Architecture. See Bosworth, Francke Huntington, Jr., and Roy Childs Jones, "Deja Vu: Excerpts from a Study of Architectural Schools," *Journal of Architectural Education*, 31:1 (Fall 1978), pp. 21-25.

9. Bosworth and Jones, *A Study of Architectural Schools*, p. 6.

10. Esherick, Joseph, "Architectural Education in the Thirties and Seventies: A Personal View," in Kostof, op. cit., pp. 238-279, quote from p. 243.

11. The organization was originally formed in 1894 in New York as the Beaux-Arts Society of Architects and was later known as the Society of Beaux-Arts Architects. In 1916 the functions of the society were taken over by a new organization incorporated under the Regents of the State of New York known as the Beaux-Arts Institute of Design (BAID). The original articles of incorporation stated that one of the goals of the society was "to cultivate and perpetuate the associations

and principles of the Ecole des Beaux-Arts of Paris." See Bosworth and Jones, *A Study of Architectural Schools*, p. 7.

12. Some schools based their entire design program on the assignments of the BAID, issuing virtually every program it sent out and sending it back to New York to be judged. As of the early 1930s, Columbia, Pennsylvania, Carnegie-Mellon, the University of Illinois, Catholic University, and the University of Washington fell into this category. Other schools, such as Washington University in St. Louis, relied on the BAID programs but did not send their finished drawings to New York. Still other schools preferred not to rely on the services of BAID. At the University of Oregon, for example, students worked on their design projects at their own pace, and the completed projects were reviewed and discussed rather than judged, thus sharply reducing the competitive atmosphere. The University of Kansas, Cornell, the University of California, and the University of Minnesota also rarely relied on the BAID, preferring to control their own educational policies in design. The English Canadian schools typically did not rely on the BAID programs, while the French Canadian schools did. See Bosworth and Jones, *A Study of Architectural Schools*, p. 38; Esherick, Joseph, "Architectural Education in the Thirties and Seventies: A Personal View," in Kostof, op. cit., pp. 238-279, quote from pp. 239-240, p. 243.

13. Bosworth and Jones, *A Study of Architectural Schools*, p. 8.

14. Ibid., pp. 42-44.

15. Ibid., pp. 43-44.

16. Esherick, op. cit., pp. 247-248.

17. Bosworth and Jones, *A Study of Architectural Schools*, p. 49.

18. One could argue that the same situation exists today, where a large number of design faculty routinely rely on competition programs written by others rather than writing class assignments themselves.

19. A number of the educators and practitioners interviewed for this book have made the same argument, claiming that the intense rush of the esquisse and charrette are superficial and misleading ways to teach design.

20. Bosworth and Jones, *A Study of Architectural Schools*, p. 49.

21. Ibid., p. 50.

22. See, for example, Fitch, James Marston, *Water Gropius*, New York: Braziller, 1960; Winifried Nerdinger, *Walter Gropius: The Architect Walter Gropius Drawings, Prints and Photographs from Busch-Reisinger Museum, Harvard University Art Museums, Cambridge/Mass. and from Bauhaus-Archiv Berlin. With Complete Project Catalog*, Cambridge, MA: Busch-Reisinger Museum, 1985.

23. Nerdinger, op. cit., p. 70.

24. Critic Tom Wolfe has provided a somewhat cynical view of the strong influence of the Bauhaus school on the design professions. See Wolfe, Tom, *From Bauhaus to Our House*, New York: Farrar, Straus & Giroux, 1981.

25. Closed juries are still typically used in most schools to determine student awards and prizes and to select entries for submission to national design competitions.

26. Architect Michael Graves was one such example. He visited a number of prospective graduate schools and listened in on their juries in order to help him decide which one he wanted most to attend.

27. These exceptions are discussed in further detail in Chapter 10.

28. Bledstein, Burton J., *The Culture of Professionalism: The Middle Class and the Development of Higher Education in America*, New York: Norton, 1976, p. 254.

29. As many students have candidly admitted, they would really rather not get to know their studio neighbors at 3:00 A.M.!

30. Giroux, Henry, and David Purpel (eds.), *The Hidden Curriculum and Moral Education: Deception or Discovery?* Berkeley, CA: McCutchan, 1983; Illich, Ivan, *Deschooling Society*, New York: Harper Collins, 1970, p. 74.

31. Jackson, Philip, "The Daily Grind...," in Giroux and Purpel, op. cit., pp. 28-60, quote from p. 33.

32. Ibid., p. 35.

33. The same argument is made in Dutton, Thomas A., "Design Studio and Pedagogy," *Journal of Architectural Education*, 41:1 (Fall 1987), pp. 16-25; and Ward, Anthony, "Ideology, Culture and the Design Studio," in Hardie, Graeme, Robin Moore, and Henry Sanoff (eds.), *Changing Paradigms: EDRA 20, 1989. Proceedings of the Annual Conference*. Oklahoma City: Environmental Design Research Association, 1989, pp. 95-102.

34. Jackson, op. cit., p. 45.

35. Based on material in ibid.

36. Ibid., p. 48.

37. For those unfamiliar with the nature of design projects typically assigned in design studios, here are just a few examples. For interior designers: the executive suite of a first-class hotel, an interior of a theme restaurant. For architects: a house, an office building, a city hall. For landscape architects: a neighborhood park, a bikeway system, a downtown streetscape system. For urban planners: a residential subdivision, a new town, an urban land use transportation study.

38. Ashby, W. R., *Design for a Brain*, New York: Wiley, 1952; Argyris, Chris, "Theories of Action that Inhibit Individual Learning," *American Psychologist*, 31:9 (September 1976), pp. 638-654.

39. This finding is supported by the results of student diaries and interviews. These methods and others used for this research are described in greater detail in Appendix A.

40. Bledstein, Burton J., *The Culture of Professionalism: The Middle Class and the Development of Higher Education in America*, New York: Norton, 1976, p. 94.

41. In fact, a sizable literature exists on coaching and coach effectiveness training. See, for example, Gould, Daniel, Ken Hodge, Kirsten Peterson, and John Giannini, "An Exploratory Examination of Strategies Used by Elite Coaches to Enhance Self-Efficacy in Athletes," *Journal of Sport & Exercise Psychology*, 11 (1989), pp. 128-140; Roberts, Glyn C., Doug-

las A. Kleiber, and Joan L. Duda, "An Analysis of Motivation in Children's Sport: The Role of Perceived Competence in Participation," *Journal of Sport Psychology*, 3 (1981), pp. 206-216; Smith, Ronald E., Frank L. Smoll, and Bill Curtis, "Coach Effectiveness: A Cognitive-Behavioral Approach to Enhancing Relationship Skills in Youth Sport Coaches," *Journal of Sport Psychology*, 1 (1979), pp. 59-75.

42. See, for example, Roberts, Kleiber, and Duda, op. cit.

43. The results of several of these studies are discussed in Gould et al., op. cit.

44. In Chapter 9 we present various ways in which constructive criticism can be delivered.

45. Ogilvie, Bruce C., and Thomas A. Tutko, "Sport: If You Want to Build Character, Try Something Else," *Psychology Today*, 5 (October 1971), pp. 60-63.

46. Kohn, Alfie, *No Contest: The Case Against Competition*, Boston: Houghton Mifflin Co., 1986, p. 5. Kohn's book received the 1987 National Psychology Award for Excellence in the Media. We will draw on this source extensively in Chapter 12.

47. In the world of practice, intergroup competition, where one firm routinely vies with its competitors, is the norm, and yet when individuals within a firm enter design competitions, intragroup competition is again at work.

48. For some distinctions among the concepts of play, recreation, contest or match, game, and sport, consult Edwards, Harry, *Sociology of Sport*. Homewood, IL: Dorsey, 1973, chap. 3, pp. 43-61.

49. Kohn, op. cit., p. 6.

50. At some schools, studio critics are encouraged to say little at juries of their own students in order to allow other jurors to speak. Also, they often view themselves as "biased sources" of opinions because they have seen their students struggling throughout the design process, while the jurors are only viewing the end product.

51. The role of faculty in student design competitions raises some serious ethical issues that are discussed in Chapter 12.

52. Pawley, Martin, "Demilitarisation of the University," in Gowan, James, *A Continuing Experiment: Learning and Teaching at the Architectural Association*, London: Architectural Press Ltd., 1975, pp. 115-125, quote from p. 121.

53. Many American schools of architecture actually originated in schools of engineering. Over the last century, however, most have shifted to become a part of a school or college of fine and applied arts, or something like it. Art and architecture are often found in the same building on campus or at least are nearby. In some larger campuses, architecture, landscape architecture, and urban planning have bound together as a separate school or college of environmental design. Interior design, on the other hand, has traditionally been linked with colleges of agriculture and the study of home economics, today often termed family and consumer studies. It is rare to find interior design located in the same physical facility as the other fields in environmental design. Given that so many of the concerns of interior designers are similar to those of environmental designers, perhaps we will see these fields more closely linked in the future.

54. Art educator John Michael has outlined the art process and what is happening to the student: motivation; confidence in one's ability to express with art media; knowledge of art and art processes; skill in the use of media; and evaluation. He outlines the evaluation process as follows: (1) Does the work indicate what the student was trying to say, to communicate? (2) Does the work indicate that the student was confident and unrestrained in approaching art? (3) Does the work indicate perceptual awareness and sensitivity? (4) Does the work indicate aesthetic sensitivity, harmonious organization, and knowledge of art? (5) Does the art work indicate creativity, uniqueness, and originality? (6) Does the art work indicate skill in handling media and processes that are appropriate for the expression? Does the art work indicate that the artist was involved, enjoyed the experience, and probably has a good attitude toward art? (See also Michael, John A., "Studio Art Experience: The Heart of Art Education," *Art Education*, *33:2* (February 1980), pp. 15-19.

55. A series of computer literature searches revealed only a small handful of articles, few of which appeared to be based on serious empirical research.

56. Lafofsky, Charles, "Juries, Not So Grand," *Ceramics Monthly*, *24*:5 (May 1976), pp. 15, 55.

57. Brennan, Harold J., "Jurying . . . Science, Art, or Gamble?" *Ceramics Monthly*, *19*:8 (October 1971), pp. 31-32, quote from p. 31. The recent controversy over the National Endowment for the Arts' funding of work that some have called pornography placed the subjectivity of judging art in the public spotlight. It provoked a public discussion of the key question, What is art, and how do we judge it?

58. Hoff, Helen, "Honey Will Get You Farther Than Vinegar," *Music Education Journal*, *71*:2 (October 1984), pp. 24-28, quote from pp. 24-25.

59. Pellegrino, Edmund D., Presentation in Boley, Bruno A. (ed.), *Crossfire in Professional Education: Students, the Professions and Society*, New York: Pergamon Press, 1977, pp. 2-18.

60. Ibid., p. 16.

61. Wallis, W. Allen, in Boley, op. cit., p. 31.

62. See, for example, New York State Department of Health, *Report of the New York State Ad Hoc Advisory Committee on Emergency Services Regarding Supervision and Resident Working Conditions*, New York: New York State Department of Health, 1987; *American Medical Association Directory of Graduate Medical Education Programs: Special Requirements for Residency Training Programs in Internal Medicine*, Chicago: Accreditation Council on Graduate Medical Education, 1989, pp. 43-84.

63. Wallis, Claudia, "Re-Examining the 36-Hour Day: New York State Leads a Movement to Change the Way U.S. Doctors Are Trained," *Time*, *130* (August 31, 1987), pp. 54-55.

64. The research team relied on participant-observation as their chief method for gathering information. They attended University of Kansas Medical School along with the students,

following them from class to lab to the hospital years. They studied a wide range of students in various years of medical training, following them not only in school, but to the fraternity houses and other spots after class. In addition, the team interviewed students and faculty and produced over 5000 pages of field notes upon which their book is based. See Becker, Howard S., Blanche Geer, Everett C. Hughes, and Anselm L. Strauss, *Boys in White: Student Culture in Medical School*, Chicago: University of Chicago Press, 1961.

65. Ibid., p. 96.

66. Ibid., p. 199.

67. Ibid., p. 91. The appropriateness of this model for design education is discussed in Chapter 12.

68. Urban planning courses differ from the others in this regard. The emphasis on reading is much greater in this field; hence you are much more likely to see many books displayed in this section.

69. Dinham, Sarah M., and Frank T. Stritter, "Professional Education," in Wittrock, M. (ed.), *Handbook of Research on Teaching*, 3d ed., New York: Macmillan, 1986.

70. Ibid.

71. Cardozo, Michael H., presentation in Boley, op. cit., pp. 43-45. The heavy reliance on the case method in law school has been the source of severe criticism, however. Law professor James Boyd White argues that the case method can feel like a charade, where students learn not to think like a lawyer but rather to think like a bar exam. See White, James Boyd, "Doctrine in a Vacuum: Reflections On What A Law School Ought (And Ought Not) to Be," *Journal of Legal Education*, 36:2, (June 1986) pp. 155-166. See also Neumann, Richard K., Jr., "A Preliminary Inquiry into the Art of Critique," *Hastings Law Journal*, 40:4 (April 1989), pp. 725-769.

72. Cardozo, op. cit., pp. 47-48.

73. Ayer, John, "The Make Believe World of the Lawyer," *Learning and the Law*, 4:1 (1977), pp. 43-44, 47; Berger, Curtis J., "The Legal Profession's Need for Human Commitment," 3, *Columbia University General Education Seminar Reports*, No. 2 (1975), pp. 13-15; both cited in Dvorkin, Elizabeth, Jack Himmelstein, and Howard Lesnick in collaboration with a group of law school teachers, students, and administrators working with the Project for the Study and Application of Humanistic Education in Law, *Becoming a Lawyer: A Humanistic Perspective on Legal Education and Professional Identity: A Book of Readings*, Project for the Study and Application of Humanistic Education in Law, New York: Columbia University School of Law, 1980. See also Tribe, D. M. R., and A. J. Tribe, "Assessing Law Students," *Law Teacher*, 20:3 (Summer 1986), pp. 160-168.

74. Cardozo, op. cit., p. 45.

75. Boley, op. cit., p. 68.

76. Ibid., p. 91.

77. Jarvis, Peter, *Professional Education*, London: Croom Helm, 1983.

78. Boley, op. cit., p. 98.

79. Esherick, op. cit., p. 279.

80. Berg, I., *Education and Jobs*, Harmonsworth, UK: Penguin, 1973; Taylor, G. W., P. B. Brice, J. H. Richards, and T. L. Jacobsen, "An Investigation of the Criterion Problem for a Group of Medical General Practitioners," *Journal of Applied Psychology*, 49:6 (1965); both sources cited in Jarvis, op. cit., p. 99.

81. The interviews with leading design practitioners conducted as part of this research begin to address this issue.

82. Weber, Max, "The Sociology of Charismatic Authority," in Gerth, H. H., and C. Wright Mills (eds.), *From Max Weber: Essays in Sociology*, New York: Oxford University Press, 1946, pp. 245-252, quote from p. 248.

83. Ibid., p. 249.

84. At my university, students have formed "The Architects Who Wear Black and/or Round Glasses Club" in honor some of their mentors, notably Le Corbusier.

85. In all fairness, many designers visit the work of the stars not merely to engage in star-worshipping but to judge and critique the work more fairly after seeing it in person.

86. Wolfe, op. cit.

87. Sennett, Richard, *Authority*, New York: Vintage Books, 1981, pp. 17-18.

88. Several of the leading designers interviewed for this book revealed this to be a fairly common occurrence.

89. Based on Sennett, op. cit.

90. One can easily make the argument that it is difficult to survive through the trials of design education without strong self-confidence and optimism about one's future design abilities.

91. Based on Sennett, op. cit.

92. Ibid., pp. 50-83.

93. The predominance of the paternalistic trend and the absence of a maternalistic counterpart are discussed in Chapter 12.

94. My point here is not to criticize the notion of professional mentorship per se, as it can often prove to be a great asset in establishing one's professional career. But I am arguing that in the environmental design professions, and especially in architecture, the scales are tipped heavily in favor of males, rather than females, as mentors.

95. Arendt, Hannah, *Between Past and Future: Eight Exercises in Political Thought*, New York: Penguin Books, 1954, chap. 3, "What is Authority?" pp. 91-141, quote from p. 99.

96. Ibid., pp. 99-100.

PART 2

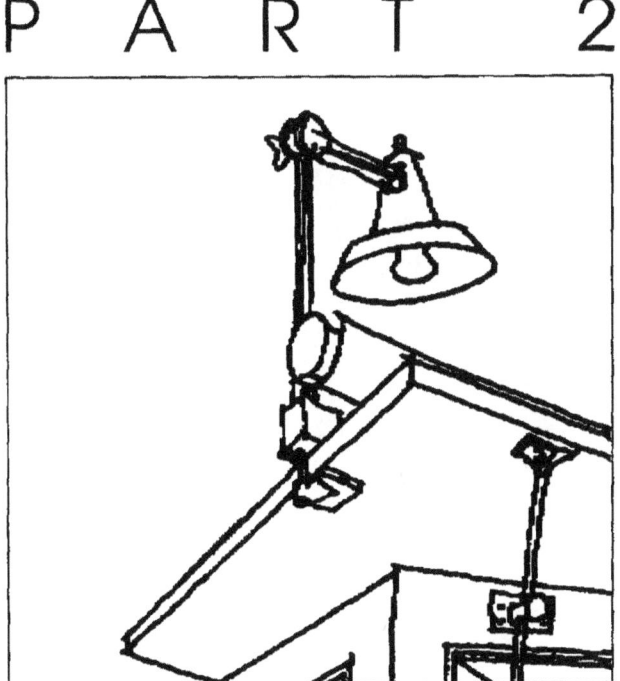

RESEARCH ABOUT DESIGN JURIES

"Adversity causes some men to break, others to break records." — William A. Ward

"What the superior man seeks is in him; what the common man seeks is in others." — Confucius

"The biggest cause of trouble in the world today is that the stupid people are so sure about things and the intelligent folks are so full of doubts." — Bertrand Russell

CHAPTER 3
How Do Students, Faculty, and Practitioners View Design Juries?

"... The jury system nevertheless survives because it achieves results that would be otherwise impossible to obtain: it simulates to some extent the reality of making presentations in practice; it reinforces the importance of meeting deadlines; it provides a forum for students to see each other's work and for faculty to see the work of students other than their own; it encourages graphic quality; and through jury discussion, it raises important issues and promotes new thinking. Like it or not, the architectural jury is probably here to stay and represents one of the unique, recurring experiences in architectural education." —Roger K. Lewis[1]

WHY HAVE JURIES? DIFFERING VIEWS ABOUT THE PURPOSES OF JURIES

Before one can even begin to analyze the design jury system, it is essential to understand why we have them at all. Students experience juries for years on end, but how often is the purpose of the jury ever really explained to them? Perhaps they are mentioned in passing as part of an orientation program upon beginning their design studies. If they are fortunate enough to know some more experienced design students, undoubtedly they will have heard of juries. But rarely are the goals of juries brought out into the open and discussed.

One reason for this is that even design instructors are unclear as to what the goals of juries should be, and they have a plurality of viewpoints on the subject. Here are some comments about the goals of design juries drawn from surveys of design faculty:[2]

"Questions, questions, questions... the search for the best questions."

"Primarily to thicken students' skins and prepare them for public presentation and exchanges. Secondarily: learning from jurors' comments on their projects and relevant generalized discussion; bringing a project to closure with crescendo."

"To serve as a facsimile of an architect/client relationship. Students as designers should learn to express their design to the jury members and at the same time understand their reactions."

Goals of Design Juries According to Faculty

"Aid the student in their own understandings of their own projects: strengths, problems, possibilities, comparisons, placement in time."

"The need to bring the project to a close; a chance to communicate both graphically and verbally; the need to discuss the issues of the project and studio, and extend the discussion with invited critics; the need to share the work; the need to celebrate the work; an aspect of theater, of completion, of marking the place: At this time, this is where I am!!"

"Design juries provide an opportunity for the student to present (communicate) the process and solution to a design problem. The jury should be in the form of a presentation to teachers, professionals, and peers. The criticism should be considered informative and both positive and negative—providing the student with encouragement as well as a stimulus to continue exploration of them."

"To evaluate work and critique student effort and to inform students showing what others have done."

"To expand student awareness of the range of architectural discourse."

"To help students become better designers."

Compare the faculty comments with what students believe to be the goals of design juries:

"To provide an opportunity for students and faculty to discuss the project, what was done, and suggestions to make it better. It should be an informal, positive learning experience, not tense or degrading to the student."

"To evaluate the work done and give students insight as to where they can improve and what strengths they have to develop."

"To build a student's confidence and encourage good design practice."

"To clarify the goals of the project and to generate ideas to improve and expand upon the project."

Figure 3-1 Some have argued that the jury system is much like the mock trial in law school, helping prepare students for stressful situations in the real world.

And how about design practitioners? What do they think the purposes of juries ought to be?

"The jury system is a course in itself in selling. You talk to a jury much the way you talk to a client. You're always trying to sell your ideas. The client relationship is a little different because you're getting a lot of input during the design phase, whereas in a jury, you've had your input from your teacher, and then you're presenting it.

"... I enjoy being on juries.... I think the practicing architect gets as much out of them as the student.... If you're away from the university, it's really nice to have the experience of going back."—John C. Walker

Goals of Design Juries According to Students

"To encourage and provoke thought, exploration, and discussion. To identify successes and encourage further development. To identify weaknesses and offer suggestions for additional study or consideration. To fairly evaluate work on the basis of the program, stated student goals and concepts, and subsequent response, instead of faculty preferences, attitudes, and inflexible beliefs."

"To practice oral delivery, readability of graphics, and marketing of a design for the final jury. Interim juries should be to improve your design and communication skills."

"To be a learning process of not only concept but presentation before a group of people who were not involved in a project's development, in order for students to [learn how to] express themselves both verbally and graphically."

"To discuss the project and design ideas in general, regardless of personal taste (although this may be the hardest thing to exclude). I see it as just a part in the progression towards design excellence. It should open the mind rather than provoke fear. Therefore juries should be more informal to increase participation."

"There's nothing wrong with the jury system. It certainly trains you for the real world. You spend every month of your life having to go out and present in front of faceless people. After you've done that, sitting in front of a bunch of people you know isn't quite so bad. It is a part of architecture.... The system is real-world training. It's the architectural equivalent of the mock trial, I guess, over in law school." [Figure 3-1]—*Steven Izenour*

Juries serve many different purposes, and these comments reflect just the tip of the iceberg. *Design practitioners point out that juries should provide an opportunity to learn how to sell your design work, to present your ideas succinctly and accurately and to convince potential clients to hire your firm.* This requires an ability to speak in public and to be able to respond to questions and criticism. But are these skills usually taught in design studio? Unfortunately, the answer is no. The word *sell* rarely is used in design school, and yet those design firms that stay afloat must have someone in the office who is talented in promoting the firm and selling its ideas. Teaching the ability to sell their work in school can only help students become better prepared for the professional design world.[3]

Design faculty believe that juries should provide an opportunity to evaluate students' design work with the assistance of some outside opinions from their colleagues. Assessing the quality of student work is an important part of any teaching assignment. But how well does this evaluation take place? What kinds of feedback are students given about their work? How often do juries point out not only where a design went wrong, but also what could be done to improve it? How often do students receive any written record of the jury proceedings that they can ponder over after the jury is over? Rarely. And it is indeed ironic that while faculty routinely advise students to identify goals for their design projects, they themselves have rarely identified clear, obtainable goals for the jury process.

Students stress that juries should provide an opportunity to learn how well they solved a design problem and

Goals of Design Juries According to Practitioners

> "The purpose of the exercise is to learn. The jury should realize that and the student should realize that, particularly in the early stages. Just be a sponge. Soak up as much as you can get. Be open and honest about it. If you had problems and you couldn't solve a portion of it, say that. Say, 'I couldn't solve it, but do you have any questions about how I could have approached it?' "—William Callaway
>
> "It is important for students to present their end product; after all, they'll have to do that in real life in front of the planning commission or the public. Students need some simulation of that sense of occasion [and] some training in public speaking [and] thinking on your feet. It should all be part of their training. And I think it is lacking [in design education]."—Christopher Degenhardt
>
> "It would be good if students understood when they go into a jury presentation [that] . . . they're really trying to sell their solution to the jury, and the more they can help the jury understand what their solution is, the better the jury experience."—the late Norman R. DeHaan
>
> "For me, juries [in school] were nerve wracking, but they did actually set the tone for what we do every day. We compete for work and we present our work to clients, to boards, or to city reviews. You have to learn to be able to articulate and explain what you're doing as a designer and why. The jury system tries to establish that ability for you. I actually think juries are essential and integral to the education of a designer."—Charles Gwathmey
>
> "Juries in the educational process can serve a very useful purpose. They first should teach the student that in the world of practice much of the decision making is done in the identical fashion, although less well structured. Every time I meet with a client to explore different design solutions and options, it's a jury. The process is a valuable one. However, it should be offered in such a way that it educates the student about what is important to get across in the jury setting in practice. If I had to stand before a jury of peers or a jury of clients or a committee of clients, what points are most essential? If I was told I could only say six sentences about a design solution, what would they be? I don't think that happens in the jury process."—Donald J. Hackl

how they can improve their design work in the future. *Learning from the jury is a key goal.* But do most students actually learn about design from juries? Unfortunately, again the answer is no.

When asked specifically what they think the goals of juries ought to be, the most frequent response, cited by most of the student respondents, is to learn how to improve design skills.[4] (See Appendix B, Figure B-1). Following closely is to learn how to present their work professionally and to improve their knowledge about design. Next, in order from most to least, is to learn how to respond to criticism, to improve their communication skills in general, to improve their oral presentation skills, to discuss their work with others, to improve their graphic skills, to learn how people with expertise in different areas view their work, and to learn how to negotiate with clients. Take a moment to reflect on the typical jury scenario. Which of these goals are truly accomplished? Which of these goals are even taught in any systematic way? The sad fact is that very few of these goals are addressed either at design juries or throughout the studio experience. What students want and need from juries is not what they are getting.

A fundamental flaw of the traditional jury system, then, is that its goals are rarely explicitly spelled out, and to make matters worse, faculty, practitioners, and students have widely differing opinions about what they believe juries ought to accomplish (Figure 3-2). It is not

Figure 3-2 Surveys and interviews reveal that students, faculty, and practitioners do not agree on what the goals of juries ought to be. Discussions about exactly what juries are supposed to accomplish are extremely rare.

surprising that juries often result in chaos and confusion. For professors, visiting critics, and students alike, the journey through the jury process is like driving cross-country without knowing where your final destination will be. Will you head toward Seattle, San Francisco, or San Diego? How can you possibly choose the right route when you don't even know exactly where you are going?

My argument throughout this book is that perhaps juries are trying to accomplish too much. Each goal may be worthwhile, but juries may not always be the most efficient vehicle by which to attain all of them. Other techniques may be more effective. In fact, the plurality of viewpoints about the goals of juries can become an advantage, provided they are discussed openly and used to help reach a consensus about what juries could and should be.

WINNERS AND LOSERS: THE BEST AND WORST OF DESIGN JURIES

For many design students, the jury can feel like a rollercoaster ride (Figure 3-3). Emotions run the gamut from high to low, from utter elation and ecstasy to profound disappointment and anger. These feelings are clearly reflect in student surveys. In answer to the question, "What's the best jury experience you have ever had or seen?" here is what students had to say.

"One with a good balance of compliments and constructive criticism, and total respect for the student as a person."

"The jury members were brief in their comments but concise enough to say what worked and why. Little side notes were made but not dwelt upon. They talked about design in general, the concept and its validity. Also, they wrote comments down. That's more important than a flat letter grade or some obscure code that appears on comment sheets."

"A multi-disciplinary jury—one landscape architect, one architect, one urban planner."

The best jury experiences seem to be characterized by a number of traits. What seems to be a key in helping create an exceptionally favorable jury experience is one where the students believe they actually learn something that can help them become better designers. *From the students' point of view, the best juries combine a balance between positive and negative criticism; they are not lopsided in either direction.* Also, the criticism they receive is specific and constructive. Jurors pinpoint where their designs are strong or weak and what would help improve them (Figure 3-4).

The best juries are also those where the students become actively involved in the process. They have the opportunity to discuss their work with the critics and with each other and to maintain interest and motivation throughout the jury session. Juries using unusual, innovative techniques, such as the "walk-through," small-scale critiques, and students as critics, also stand out. Including

Figure 3-3 Diaries reveal that some students have compared the jury sensation to a ride on a roller coaster, with a dramatic range of highs and lows. For many, the jury is a manic-depressive experience.

Figure 3-4 Surveys, interviews, and observations reveal that some faculty and practitioners find juries dull, drawn out, and boring. While one student was presenting his project, he saw a juror read a catalog for automobile parts.

Student Survey Responses to "What's the *Best* Jury Experience You Have Ever Had or Seen?"

"Very constructive criticism. Compliments along with critique. Tells you how to help your design, not what's wrong with it."

"The best experience is when the jury both compliments along with giving helpful suggestions. The more dialogue that is generated, the more information you learn."

"In the fall, I worked with another student on the final project. We had a strong project and presentation plus the positive support of our instructor. We went into the jury very up and the jury liked it. It was nice to not get ripped to shreds for once."

"During fall semester of last year, a design jury I had was extremely good. They were good listeners, fair, open to new ideas, perceptive of strengths and weaknesses, and most importantly, maintained a positive overall attitude."

"One professor organized a nontraditional jury for my class last year. Two architects from outside the university walked from project to project, making reasonable and perceptive comments on each one; then they sat down with the class as a whole to discuss their perceptions of the project in general. It was a very worthwhile, enlightening experience."

"A 'walk-around' presentation — informal, allowed conversation instead of forced dialogue. By far the best crit I got was [from] this informal jury."

"Informal pinups. You told the class where you had problems and they helped you solve them. [They] also identified potential problems before they were fully formed. All juries should have this relaxed and helpful atmosphere."

"An intermediate jury with two crits — just me and them. Very informal and informative. A lot of interaction between us all."

"A jury member came to the class session following the juries to follow up and explain comments individually to students that were made during the jury. This cleared up ambiguities and motivated me to further develop my design."

"The jury situation where I learned the most was when my design professor requested that the class write personal opinions about each classmate's design. The professor copied the class' comments and gave them back to us. I learned from organizing my thoughts and by writing them on paper, and I learned from reading the comments of the other people in my design studio."

"My best jury experience was my senior year. It was the first time I used the computer in my presentation and the jurors responded very well, saying that it was clear."

"The design was for a new alumni center. The criticism was not from professors, but from the directors of the alumni association. While they may not know about the formal aspects of design, they do know what works for them."

"There wasn't one — just degrees of less criticism."

"None really. Most juries are very negative."

out-of-the-ordinary jurors, such as those from allied disciplines in environmental design or who represent the clients or users, also contributes to a successful jury. We will discuss some of these ideas as well as others in Chapter 10.

By contrast, when asked, "What's the worst jury experience you have ever had or seen?" these are some representative comments:

"The worst jury was when the professor of the class was arguing with the critic over a project. Finally the professor said that the crit's comments were worthless."

"We brought our models in. The jurors looked at two of them (out of 60 or so) and told us they all sucked! And then went on to tell us that we are the worst group of students that they ever had seen."

"Many people seem to feel raped by vicious juries."

Students' worst jury experiences seem to be typified by strong threads of negativity. The metaphors they use are sharp and pointed. But negative criticism is not the issue per se. Students admit that they need some constructive criticism in order to learn how to improve their work. *Rather it is the heavy-handed nature of the criticism that is offered and the fact that it is delivered in overwhelmingly large doses* (Figure 3-5). Negative criticism is often delivered in an undiplomatic, condescending, and insensitive manner, with harsh words and terrifying possibilities. Consider the devastating effects on students who are advised to abandon their field altogether after investing years in it already. Multiply that difficulty when this bombshell is dropped in front of other authority figures as well as peers.

Student Survey Responses to "What's the *Worst* Jury Experience You Have Ever Had or Seen?"

> "I forgot how to speak."
>
> "I remember during sophomore year a student got nervous and couldn't remember the more important aspects of her design; she was unprepared for the jury's questions."
>
> "All my juries have been equally ugly."
>
> "I have seen faculty essentially 'sleep' through juries."
>
> ". . . The point seemed to be to humiliate the student, his effort, and his ideas. . . ."
>
> "One student was told that he was worthless and that what he had was not worth spending time on, and the professor cut his jury very short."
>
> "I've seen jurors fight with one another."
>
> "When [a juror] told a student to sit down and shut up in the middle of his presentation for final juries. He proceeded to spend 18 minutes tearing him apart."
>
> "The jurors discussed an error on the project and refused to study any other part of the design. They talked to each other but not to me. . . . They didn't care about how I felt."
>
> "The jurors claimed that they didn't like the project 'just because' and had no specific reasoning for it, as though there is only one solution to the project: theirs, with no exceptions."
>
> "The jurors told the student that his project was ugly. They did not offer any suggestion about how to improve it."
>
> "Personal slams at a person's intelligence and taste."
>
> "A girl in class had been having trouble with design and then rather than encouraging her at the jury, the panelists proceeded to tell her all the bad things she did. Later this girl was crying and wanted to quit architecture."
>
> "My project was torn apart without any ways to help improve it."
>
> "The utter demolition of a friend with comments like, 'Have you ever taken freshman design? Maybe you should re-take it!' on a senior year jury."
>
> "I was basically, in a very unprofessional way, told that I was stupid and in the wrong field."
>
> "After six months of staying awake designing and drawing your 'baby'—then when you present the juror tells you to look into shoe sales as a career."
>
> "When the jury questioned my clothing and color choice—why didn't I dress to match my project more closely?"
>
> "I watched a professor pick his nose during a student's entire presentation."
>
> "At times, jurors don't show interest in projects and start daydreaming or balancing checkbooks."
>
> "A professor did not like the design being presented on the computer and refused to analyze the design. The final grades he gave all those who presented on the computer were low (i.e., D's)."
>
> "Vicious, uncalled for ridicule."

Boredom is another characteristic of the worst jury experience. In fact, many students and faculty find juries boring. And some professors admit that they have sometimes seen colleagues nod off and doze through juries.

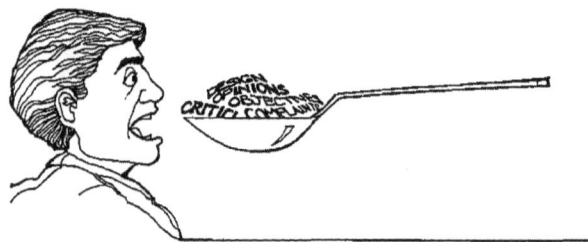

Figure 3-5 Criticism at juries tends to be overwhelmingly negative and offered in large doses. Students need both positive and negative criticism, but at present negative criticism is too heavy-handed to be of much use.

But acting obviously bored by balancing checkbooks or ordering from automobile catalogs during a jury is offensive to students. What can we do to help make juries more interesting?

LESSONS LEARNED: THE EDUCATIONAL VALUE OF DESIGN JURIES

Assuming that one of the key goals of design juries is for students to learn how to become better designers, one of the key questions in assessing them is: How much, if at all, do students learn from them? And, more specifically, exactly what do they learn from them? How satisfied are they with juries and with their design education in general? Questions like these were posed to design students across the country, and the following describes what was found.

How satisfied are students with various aspects of their education? (See Appendix B, Figure B-2.) Surveys

Figure 3-6 Surveys reveal that women students are more dissatisfied with their design education and with design juries than are males. Over the years, the intimidating nature of juries may have driven many talented women away from the design professions altogether. At present they are still grossly underrepresented as design faculty and as licensed design professionals in leadership roles.

show that juries are the greatest source of students' dissatisfaction. Compared to graduate students, undergraduates report slightly lower levels of satisfaction with architectural education, design education, studios, and juries. Compared to their male counterparts, women students are consistently more dissatisfied with every aspect of their architectural education (Figure 3-6). (See Appendix B, Figure B-3.)

In general, compared to final juries, interim juries are a more effective learning technique. While interim juries seem to serve many useful purposes, the educational value of final juries appears to be minimal at best. (See Appendix B, Figure B-4.) These findings reflect a general trend in the results from student surveys, student diaries, and interviews with students, faculty, and design practitioners.

What is even more striking, however, is how the amount learned from juries compares to how much students learn from other sources in the studio. *Students report learning the least from criticism of their own and other students' projects at final juries. By contrast, they report learning the most from informal discussions and desk crits with their instructors.* (See Appendix B, Figure B-4.) Both these learning formats are much less structured than are juries. In general, students learn less from juries than they do from other sources. Note also that *students learn more from positive than from negative criticism, and also, relatively speaking, they learn quite a bit from informal discussions with other students.* The amount learned from visiting critics is less than that learned from their instructor and other students; however, this may be due to the fact that visiting critics usually appear only at juries, and not throughout the duration of the project.

In general, graduate students report learning more from most of these sources than do undergraduates. However, graduate students' ratings of the amount learned from final juries is the same as that of undergraduates. Compared to men, women report higher levels of learning from the final jury.

What do students learn from juries? *More often than not, what students claim to have learned from design juries has more to do with presentation style, or how to "play the game," than with design.* For instance, after the first crit of the term, one student learned "to be patient, modest, courteous, to keep my talking to the bare minimum, not to be 'braggish' or unduly 'meek,' and to dress effectively." And after the final crit, the same student learned "to speak softly but carry a gargantuan stick."

Some other students explained:

"What did I learn? I learned that third year [design] is no more organized than second year was last year. I learned that the teachers don't agree on methodology. The most important thing I learned... is what I need to concentrate on if I want to be a good architect and the separation [between] that and what I need... to be an 'A' student."

"I jumped to one conclusion from the feedback I received: in any pin-up presentation, I should not present too much work. I must move as slowly as the rest of the class is moving."

By contrast, here are a few excerpts from three student diaries explaining what they learned after receiving a desk crit from their instructor.

"I am weak about my parapet design, but confident with my concept and plan. I must pay more attention to the support system. As is, I may have difficulty with working drawings and structural efficiency and stability."

"Today we were supposed to have some ideas developed about our airport project. But I did not have any. So I quickly sketched up some rough diagrams and tried to bounce them off our lab instructor to get some feedback. He reacted by saying nothing and then sketched up quickly (in about 10 minutes) a potential elevation view. It was kind of intimidating because I don't sketch very well. I was having a hard enough time getting my ideas together, let alone sketching them. But I like my instructor and his sketch, anyway. I guess he tried to point out to me that my initial idea was too out of scale with the existing airport operation."

"After my desk crit I learned that my concept was wrong. I had put a lot of wasted time into the model and didn't need all the interior walls. I must pick a new sculpture to design my gallery for because mine is too abstract. I am feeling depressed for wasting all that time."

While students report learning more from desk crits than they do from design juries, the amount they learn from the crit, too, seems somewhat questionable. Feelings of frustration and depression at never having gotten it "just right" may interfere with students' ability to learn from the desk crit as well as the jury (Figure 3-7). In fact, they will never get the project "just right." As one faculty member argues, "Completing a project is an illusion. With experience,

Figure 3-7 Although students prefer desk critiques to juries, many still find over-the-table criticism frustrating and depressing. They feel that they have never gotten it "just right."

we just get better at creating that illusion. In other words, it's never perfect—just a better approximation."

Ironically, students are often most clear about what they have learned when they discuss their projects not with their instructor or a jury, but with other students. For example,

> "I visited a friend's house for a final crit from her. She thinks the project is good but one floor needs a bit more "interaction" (that's my concept). So I added a central den to finish out my design. I helped her with her design. It really helps to have an objective eye look at your work."

The vast majority of students believe that juries and design studios need to be improved (see Appendix B, Figure B-5). Compared to male students, women students are more likely to suggest that design studios need improvement. In general, compared to undergraduates, graduate students report slightly more favorable opinions about juries.

DISHING IT OUT AND TAKING IT: DELIVERING AND RESPONDING TO PUBLIC CRITICISM

Findings from student diaries, interviews, and surveys demonstrate that the overwhelming majority of criticism at most design juries is negative. Furthermore, it is sometimes delivered in a tactless and destructive manner that does little to help students learn. Results from every phase of this research bear this out. In fact, a few design faculty have candidly admitted that some jury scenarios are simply lawsuits waiting to happen! Can you imagine raising children amidst a similar atmosphere, where just about all they hear from their parents is what they've done wrong, rather than what they've done right? Therapists' couches are full of clients who as adults are still trying to rid themselves of such miserable childhood memories.[5] But let us now focus on how students are "taking it."

While students react favorably to positive situations, the data show that because most jurors' comments are negative, students' psychological reactions to design juries are also overwhelmingly negative.[6] In addition, a large number of students experience similarly negative reactions to desk crits and design studio in general. To many students, the pressure to complete an acceptable design project is a constant struggle.

Indeed, students' reactions to public criticism can be highly problematic. Student surveys, interviews, and diaries show that being in a relatively vulnerable position, they usually take jurors' comments at face value. Thus when a juror suggests that they leave the field, they may seriously consider doing so and spend days pondering over the possibility. Students are often perplexed about which comments to believe and which to take with a grain of salt. Accepting whatever they hear as the truth, they find it increasingly confusing to sift and sort out jurors' contradictory comments.

Psychologists sometimes refer to overreacting as "catastrophizing." In fact, many design students tend to catastrophize the jurors' comments in the aftermath of the jury. Terrible premonitions of impending doom start running through their heads: "Will I flunk out of school?" "What will my parents think?" "Will I end up in a homeless shelter?" With such thunderous clouds looming overhead, how can students think objectively about their design work? Students, like the rest of us, have a tendency to dwell on the negative. Even if most of the comments they hear are praiseworthy, they are likely to focus on those that are not.

If they have received negative criticism at a jury, graduate students are more likely than undergraduates to become angry and upset afterwards. Perhaps because they are more experienced than their younger counterparts, they may believe they are more deserving of praise and are thus even more devastated when they are reprimanded. Compared to male students, women are more likely to become angry and upset, trying their best to hold back tears. Several report that they cry soon after the jury is over.[7] For many women, the pressure to maintain emotional control compounds the intense pressure of the jury itself. Anecdotal evidence reveals that some students of color may experience similar emotional difficulties at the jury. In one extreme case, an African-American student, devastated by an extremely harsh set of jury comments, collapsed on the floor in front of the jurors. When his friends took him to the nearby student hospital and the staff opened up his wallet, they discovered that it was his birthday! The fierce public review on what should have otherwise been a happy day was just too much.

Students' Private Reactions to Public Jury Criticism

"The thing that has made my day... is that my instructor came by and said, 'You have a good project here.' I felt that this was the first positive thing he ever said about my work and it made me feel a lot better."

"I was told that my new project is a much better choice [than what I had before]. This gives me the positive input I need to want to work more on the project. I am feeling positive and confident."

"After the final jury: feeling fantastic! I finally have got the idea of designing an entire design around a concept. The guest critic said, 'I'm happy to be here' after looking at my project. He said I possibly went too far and maybe should tone it down a little, but the other juror said that it is better to take it too far than not far enough. I got congratulated by the other students. Well, now I'll go home and sleep for a couple days."

"I was so embarrassed after my presentation that I just walked out of the class. The whole day I felt like scum on the earth. Worse than that, when I came home, the whole night I resented myself."

"On Friday [of the final jury week] my instructor informed me that my drawings were fine but I had concentrated my investigation in the wrong area. I was flabbergasted. Nothing of that sort had been said to anyone else and this confused me."

"Today we had a pin-up review of our design concepts. The 'hot shot' designer from a large office started to make comments about each student's concept. He looked at mine and said... 'You don't have a concept here.' I was kind of upset but then I thought to myself, 'Hey, he always has negative things to say anyway, to me or to anyone else.' Then I didn't [let him] bother [me] and kept on working on my design."

"Before the final jury I was exhausted. I have been up the last two nights until 3:00 A.M. and am really sick of this project. But I am pleased with the final design. I am too tired to present! After the jury: the professors didn't like any of the projects in the class! Then whose fault is it if no project is up to their standards? Something must be wrong with the instruction! I feel disgusted!"

"After class I ran into my instructor. I told him that I felt as if I didn't really get much feedback during my review, and he said that it was because I had a good project."

"I've seen a student verbally humiliated about his concept or drawing abilities, i.e., 'Your drawings are crap. Take that board down and put it around the corner because I don't want to look at it!'"

"A fellow student was told his rationale for a design was bullshit."

"One jury member's comment was: 'How did you fit five pounds of shit into a two pound bag?'"

"'It looks like a big penis.' Description by a juror of another student's theater facade marquee."

"The jury just cut this one project apart.... They said the facade looked like two giant lips."

"I was told that I would be better off 'selling dresses.' (Yes, I am a female)."

Design students' psychological reactions to jurors' criticisms and to desk crits in studio are much like those experienced by doctoral students struggling to complete their dissertations. Students' relationships to their design critics and jurors in many ways parallel those between doctoral students and dissertation committee members. Sociologist David Sternberg has identified various types of anxieties and depressions that result from the dissertation experience: *doubts about the dissertation itself; bewildered and negative feelings about oneself; negative relationships with others; and reification, alienation and the dissertation-as-enemy.*[8] Each of these applies to design students as well.

Doubts About the Design Project Itself

Many students worry that "My concept is no good!" or "I've got designer's block—I can't draw another line!" In a more advanced course where each student selects her own project, like a design thesis studio, many express concerns that "I must have made a mistake in picking this project." They may be plagued by the myth of the perfect design project, that is, the belief that each design project must be the best work they have ever produced, their magnum opus. No design is ever perfect. Students who strive to produce a masterpiece project may find themselves trapped. In their quest for perfection they may become obsessed with minute details that later preclude them from completing their work in time for the jury. This scenario is often especially the case for thesis students who often have an entire term or school year to work on just one major design project.

Bewildered and Negative Feelings About Oneself

Such thoughts as "What am I doing here?" "Should I really continue in design?" "Am I in over my head?" "Why am I torturing myself?" commonly plague design students, particularly after a jury that has gone awry. They may even see themselves as masochists who purposely inflict pain upon themselves, denying all pleasures. This is especially the case when they watch their friends in other disciplines dash off to parties, nights out, and other social engagements while they are toiling away in studio all night long.

Another common thought is, "Everyone else in studio is ahead of me. I must be the dumbest one in the class." Being able to watch neighbors work in studio makes this reaction especially common for design students; students in other disciplines generally lack the opportunity to see how their classmates are doing while a project is either in progress or near completion. Some design students are likely to see themselves as impostors who have somehow eked their way through school and done well only by being at the right place at the right time. Convinced that they are intellectual frauds, deep down they dread the day when they will be "found out," that is, when others realize that they are not really as bright as they appear.[9]

Ruining Relationships with Others

"I have no social life except studio." "I don't have time for a girlfriend." "I'm married to my studio desk." "My career as a design student is coming between me and my spouse." "I'm just kissing up to my design critic." Design students often feel like sacrificial lambs, utterly degraded, questioning whether or not their own ideas even matter. Their sole aim is to please their critic and the jurors. Any other relationship, be it with friends, family, or romantic endeavors, is placed on the back burner. Friendships outside the design studio tend to drift away. Absenteeism from home, family, and social engagements is chronic, and the blame is always placed on one source: "I have to work on my design." As many can attest, living with a design student can be like living with a dissertation student, an alcoholic, or more accurately, a workaholic.[10]

Design-as-Enemy

"My design is torturing me!" "It's gotten totally out of control!" "I've become possessed by my design project!" Some students have a tendency to anthropomorphize their design work, that is, to ascribe to it human qualities, often tending toward the diabolical. Viewing their design as an evil spirit that needs to be exorcised, students fail to realize who created that monster in the first place (Figure 3-8).

In sum, many design students find it extremely taxing to be on the receiving end of public criticism. To outsiders, their emotional roller-coaster ride may sound like a touch of manic-depression, with high highs and low lows. How to help turn the jury and design studio into a positive, more even-keeled experience will be addressed in subsequent chapters.

Figure 3-8 Some students feel that their design is an evil spirit that needs to be exorcised. In this sense, design students share much in common with graduate students, who often feel the same way about their doctoral dissertations.

THE STUDIO SUBCULTURE: THE EATING, SLEEPING, AND WORKING HABITS OF DESIGN STUDENTS

"In not a few of the American universities [the design] student is conceded by outside opinion to be slightly crazy. His ways and habits are hard to understand. He goes back to his drafting room at night, he makes an infernal racket when he works, he rather enjoys having a victrola or radio blaring forth ragtime or 'Amos and Andy' when he attempts to concentrate."—F. H. Bosworth, Jr., and Roy Childs Jones's account of the studio subculture of the 1930s[11]

"In my design studio at the Ecole des Beaux Arts, all our drafting supplies were stored high up on a mezzanine. The upper classmen could reach them by using the stairs, but they made the freshmen climb up a knotted rope hanging from the ceiling. The freshmen were allowed to use the stairs only on the way down."—An emeritus faculty member who studied at the Ecole during the 1940s

"Some people make a career of sleeping in the studio. I saw that in undergraduate school. One guy had his sleeping bag, another had his pet bird, for whatever reasons. And if you got on a team with them, forget it."—William Callaway

From its inception, the design studio has encouraged a subculture all its own, a different world with its own values and behaviors. In a sense, the studio represents a microcosm of the design world. At the university, studios form the very core of design education. They function not only as classroom, but also as office and, as many students can attest, often even as "home." Some psychologists would refer to studios as a "third place"—a place where people meet and socialize that has a character all its own.

Take a look at any nearby design studio. You are likely to see not only all the trappings of the design work at hand—layers upon layers of tracings and leftover scraps from architectural models—but also personalized individual work stations within the studio. The close proximity of studio work stations results in a strong sense of territoriality, where students clearly mark off their own personal space that separates them from others in the room. Students are sometimes encouraged to bring in photographs, posters, postcards, mementos, and other trinkets from home to help them work in a more comfortable atmosphere in school. For many students, their individual work station at studio is in fact a "symbol of self," much like the home itself.[12] In essence, the studio serves as a "secondary territory" with a regular cast of characters who share strong territorial feelings about the place.

In fact, many design students actually spend more time at their design studio on campus than they do in their real home, be it the dorm, a fraternity or sorority, an apartment off campus, or elsewhere. In this sense, they are not all that different from graduate students in lab-oriented science fields, who spend many hours on campus and few hours at home. Working around the clock, especially when a jury date draws near, design students may only venture out of the studio to attend other classes, or to eat or sleep.

Design students' working, sleeping, and eating habits leave much to be desired. Most design students work haphazardly on their projects, often taking their time during the first few weeks of the assignment and rushing madly to finish it off at the end. At the early stages, when they should be gathering information about the experiences of other designers and about the successes and failures of previous designs, they are often simply wasting their time. Survey results indicate that few students attempt to manage their time while working on their design projects.[14] Surveys also reveal that few students prepare in advance for their oral presentation at the jury.[15] The work habits of many students are chaotic at best, resulting in a frenzy before the jury.

Surveys show that the sleeping and eating patterns of design versus nondesign students are dramatically different. Of all students sampled, architecture students are the most likely to stay up all night before a project is due. *The night before a jury, about one-third of the architecture students surveyed do not sleep at all, and another half sleep only for one to four hours.* Less than a quarter sleep for five hours or more. (See Appendix B, Figure B-6).[16] Ironically, when asked if they thought their sleeping patterns before the jury affect their performance, the vast majority said yes, admitting that it worsens.[17] But even though they know these habits can take their toll at the jury, they still persist.

Survey data reveal that just before jury deadlines, compared to their counterparts in other fields, design students eat much more poorly. The week before the jury, their eating habits are better, but not too much. On jury day, design students tend to eat less than usual, often skipping meals altogether. Many students take to eating all their meals from vending machines. Over half the students admit that they eat mainly junk food on the day of the jury, and just under half eat mostly junk food during the week before the jury (See Appendix B).[18] Ironically, over half the students admit that their eating patterns affect their jury performance, with three-quarters of this group believing that it worsens.[19]

A journey through the trash can of any design studio is likely to uncover a pile of plastic wrappers from Hostess Twinkies, Milky Ways, M&M's, potato chips, and pizza delivery cartons. Caffeinated drinks are also consumed in abundance.[20] Struggling to keep themselves wide awake while their bodies are telling them it's time to sleep, design students are often highly dependent on stimulants such as coffee, Coca Cola, or in some cases, amphetamines or cocaine. While many admit that their poor eating habits worsen their performance on the jury, they still continue to wolf down the same fast food.

All this sounds like a prescription for disaster, and it often is. Several successive nights without any sleep can produce intensely high levels of stress and anxiety, and the jury is simply the culminating event. Results of the student surveys show that at over half the schools, instructors almost always hold the jury on the same date that the project is due.[21] This merely exacerbates the problem. As a result,

> *"Why is it we entered (school) with incredibly diverse backgrounds, interests and friends and we leave here with the exact same handwriting, muttering a language that prevents normal communication and exchange with most anyone outside of our future profession—and we like it this way. . . . At parties the architecture students subconsciously form perfect geometric circles and soon the circles expand to fill all vacant space—so that by the end of your second semester of studio work, your normal (non-architecture) friends will no longer have you. . . . I am modestly suggesting: diversity, divestment, dispersal—it is time to branch out, now that we have gone through the full mind and body immersion into the profession of architecture. It is time to open our eyes and minds and expose ourselves to the rest of the universe."*
> —Victoria J. Ellis, Commencement Address[13]

many students report a sense of "burnout," or complete mental and physical exhaustion.[22] One student's account is typical: "Today is our final presentation. I have been up all night and the night before and before.... Now I am too tired even to care. I just want to have it over and done with." A number of students clearly expressed a preference for "ending it all" rather than braving the dreaded jury. Apathy and indifference are all too common.

In fact, *the studio subculture may well be harmful to students' mental and physical health.* Sleep deprivation researchers and nutritionist specialists agree that we do not function at our maximum potential when we have not had enough sleep or when we are on an empty stomach.[23] Imagine taking your driver's license exam without having slept at all the night before, with a random collection of junk food in your stomach. If you had a choice, you would probably prefer to take the test another day. But for design students, there is no other day. And compared to the driving test, the jury may be far more important. To make matters worse, our bodies become more vulnerable to physical and mental illnesses.

Compared to younger design students, returning older students with spouses or children of their own are generally more likely to lead a somewhat more normal life. Accustomed to juggling the responsibilities of a job, school, and family life, these individuals can prove a healthy influence on their studio-mates.

While no one is forcing students to stay up all night, the current studio subculture encourages it. Studios are usually accessible 24 hours a day. Well-meaning professors sometimes offer criticism so late in the process that students have to stay up all night just to address their concerns. And everyone else does it. A certain comaraderie or esprit de corps is created while students work together side by side from sunset to sunrise. For some, it may be a symbol of machismo and a form of male bonding. But is it really a necessary ritual of design education? Hardly.

In sum, *juries are in serious trouble—and so is design education.* Faculty, students, and practitioners do not even remotely agree on what they are supposed to accomplish. Although students occasionally experience a positive jury leaving them exhilarated, more often than not the opposite occurs, leaving them downtrodden and depressed. Students' accounts of their worst jury experiences read much like soap operas, with the jurors cast as cruel villains. In the worst cases, criticism from the jurors is both harsh and vicious. While students appear to retain something from interim juries, they learn relatively little, if anything, from final juries, the culminating events of the academic term. Compared to other methods of learning about design, students learn least from design juries. And ironically, it appears that juries may be partially responsible for driving away many qualified women and people of color—groups already vastly underrepresented in the field—from the environmental design professions. The studio subculture may well be harmful to students' mental and physical health, yet it is psychologically reinforced by current practices commonly in place. A key question remains: With such a bizarre background in school, how do students make a successful leap into practice? *In fact, some never do.* We will address this important question in more detail in Chapter 12.

As part of a recent initiative on design excellence sponsored by the American Institute of Architects, architect Welde Coxe raises serious concerns about the academic design studio, its tradition of criticism, and its consequences for the profession. He argues:

"There is growing awareness that through a flaw in the education process architects may be shooting themselves in the foot—and, in so doing, crippling their chances for career success . . . improper delivery of criticism in architectural schools undermines rather than builds self-worth . . . few will contest the generalization that 90 percent of the graduates of the leading business schools seem to go out into the world confident of their eventual success, while a very high percentage of architectural school graduates come out with doubts about whether they will ever have a chance to succeed . . . If misguided criticism during the studio education process is at fault . . . the tragedy is that it is entirely unnecessary . . . There is growing evidence that overall, a large percentage of architects lack desirable self-confidence and their careers are being limited as a consequence . . . The result is often a demoralized profession that continues to have great doubts about its ability to achieve lofty goals."[24]

The next few chapters address some of these concerns as well as others by offering a survival guide to the jury and to the studio. Students, faculty, and practitioners need not be content with the status quo. As many have argued, there is much room for improvement.

NOTES

1. Lewis, Roger K., *Architect? A Candid Guide to the Profession*, Cambridge, MA: MIT Press, 1985, p. 77.

2. Here and throughout the text, verbatim quotes from faculty and students are identified only in a general manner. While demographic information was collected about the respondents' school, sex, race, age, academic major, and year in the program, it has been purposely omitted here in order to protect their confidentiality and the reputation of the educational institution. Verbatim quotes from design practitioners who were interviewed are attributed and identified by name, as these interviews were not confidential and quotes were obtained with their written permission. In some later chapters discussing how to improve juries, selected quotes from faculty members are attributed. These quotes, too, were not confidential and were included with their written permission. In each case, the selected quotes represent typical responses to these questions, as well as responses at both ends of the spectrum, positive and negative.

3. We will discuss how students can effectively learn to present and "sell" their work in Chapter 6. Chapter 12 addresses the link between education and practice, addressing some of the themes raised here.

4. We can interpret these results to mean specific skills such as drawing, modeling as well as the more general applications of design principles to specific problems.

5. More about how instructors deliver criticism, and how they can improve the way in which they "dish it out" to students, can be found in Chapter 9.

6. It is likely that students express a high degree of dissatisfaction with any measure of evaluation—a final examination, a term paper, or other measure. What is unique about the jury, however, is its lack of predictability compared to these other techniques. If a student studies intensely for an examination, she is likely to do well. Slaving away for hours on end for a design project has no bearing at all on how the jury will go. A student who has received A's in previous design courses can still have a devastating jury. Masters level students often express high levels of frustration with the unpredictable nature of juries, especially because now, upon graduating and entering the job market—more than ever before—they need to feel confident about their design abilities.

7. More on the emotional management that must take place during the jury, and especially the problems that women face, is described in Chapter 12.

8. Sternberg, David, *How to Complete and Survive a Doctoral Dissertation*, New York: St. Martin's Press, 1981, pp. 159-169. Much of the following section is based on my extension of Sternberg's work to the design studio.

9. For more on this fascinating subject, see Clance, Pauline Rose, *The Impostor Phenomenon: Overcoming the Fear that Haunts Your Success*, Atlanta, GA: Peachtree Publishers, 1985. In fact, the impostor phenomenon cuts across all walks of life and seems to especially afflict some of the most talented and creative members of society.

10. Based on her impressive research on workaholics, Marilyn Machlowitz aptly points out that "Living a life of peaceful co-existence with a work addict is certainly not impossible, but that minimum return will require plenty of patience and countless compromises. . . ." In Marilyn Machlowitz, *Workaholics: Living with Them, Working with Them*, New York: Mentor, New American Library, 1980, p. 129. At present, little if any research has specifically examined the family and friendship patterns of design students and practitioners. Given the special difficulties they often experience, this would make a fascinating study.

11. Bosworth, F. H., Jr., and Roy Childs Jones, *A Study of Architectural Schools*, New York: Scribner, 1932, p. 108.

12. Cooper Marcus, Clare, "The House as Symbol of Self," in Jon Lang et al. (ed.), *Designing for Human Behavior*, Stroudsburg, PA: Dowden, Hutchinson and Ross, 1974, pp. 130-146.

13. Ellis, Victoria J., "Commencement Address," University of Illinois at Urbana-Champaign, School of Architecture, May 13, 1990.

14. The student survey administered in Phase 3 to the American Institute of Architecture students asked: "At your school, how often do most students budget their time while working on their design projects?" Over half (53%) said "never," 37% were neutral, and 11% said "always." These percentages reflect collapsed data from a 5-point scale, where one end point was "never" and the other "always."

15. The Phase 3 student survey revealed that when asked: "At your school, how often do most students prepare for the jury by practicing their oral presentation before the class?" 89% responded "never," 9% "sometimes," and 3% "always." When asked what specific aspects of juries needed improvement, over half (55%) believed students should arrive better prepared, and 52% believed the students should brush up on their presentation skills.

16. When asked how many hours of sleep they thought *most students at their school* get the night before a jury, of the 103 respondents to this item, 19% said none, 63% said 1-4 hours, 19% said 5-7 hours. When asked the same question about other students' said sleeping habits during the week before the jury, 4% of the 103 respondents reported none, 56% said 1-4 hours, 34% said 5-7 hours, and 6% said 8-9 hours.

17. To be specific, 80% of 375 respondents agreed that their sleeping patterns before the jury affect their performance at the jury. Of those who agreed, 72% admitted that their performance is worse as a result of little sleep. When asked the same questions about most students at your school, the figures were even more exaggerated: 92% of the 103 respondents believed that jury performances were affected by sleeping habits, and 87% believed that the performance of other students at juries was worse as a result.

18. The data reveal that in answer to the question "About how much food do you eat on the day of a jury?" 74% of the 347 respondents reported "much less than usual," 21% somewhere in the middle, and only 5% "much more than usual." Concerning the week before the jury, 37% of 191 respondents reported that they eat much less than usual, 45% somewhere in the middle, and 16% much more than usual. When asked "About how much food do you think *most students at your school* eat on the day of a jury?" of the 103 respondents, 61% reported much less than usual, 34% average, and 5% much more than usual. In answer to the same question for the week before the jury, of the 103 respondents, 33% thought most students ate much less than usual, 48% average, and 18% much more than usual. These responses reflect the collapsed data across a 5-point scale.

19. Of the 377 respondents to this question, 45% thought their eating patterns on jury day affected their performance. Of this group, 59% of 75 respondents thought their performance at the jury was worse. When asked about whether or not the eating patterns of *most students at your school* affect their performance at juries, the 103 students responding were split right down the middle. For those who thought it was affected, 89% believed the performance of other students was worse. Note that the figures here and elsewhere indicate that students' assessments of poor eating habits are worse when asked about other students rather than about themselves.

20. Fortunately a few of the more environmentally conscious universities have instituted recycling programs in design studios and elsewhere on campus so that aluminum cans, glass, papers, and plastics can be disposed of properly.

21. The survey of 103 American Institute of Architecture Students chapter leaders asked students: "At your school, how often are students' design projects due on the same date as the jury?" Over half (57%) responded "always" or "almost always," 25% "sometimes," and 19% "never" or "almost never." These figures reflect the collapsed data from a 5-point scale where 1 is "never" and 5 is "always."

22. Classic studies on burnout can be found in Pines, Ayalla M., Elliot Aronson, and Ditsa Kafry, *Burnout: From Tedium to Personal Growth*, New York: Free Press, 1981; Freudenberger, Herbert J., and Geraldine Richelson, *Burnout and Anxiety: Causes and Consequences*, New York: Bantam Books, 1981; Freudenberger, Herbert, and Geraldine Richelson, *Burnout: The High Cost of High Achievement*, New York: Anchor Press, 1980; Lauderdale, Michael, *Burnout: Strategies for Professional and Organizational Life: Speculations on Evolving Paradigms*, San Diego, CA: University Associates, 1982.

23. More findings from sleep deprivation and nutrition research are presented in Chapter 8.

24. Coxe, Weld, "Why do Architects so Often see Themselves as Victims?" in Vonier, Thomas (ed.), *In Search of Design Excellence*, Washington, DC: The American Institute of Architects Press, 1989, pp. 111-113, quotes from pp. 111-112.

PART 3

WHAT STUDENTS CAN DO

"The mold of a man's fortune is in his own hands."
—Francis Bacon

"Worry often gives a small thing a big shadow."
—Swedish proverb

"Nothing is so fatiguing as the eternal hanging on of an uncompleted task." —William James

"Grow angry slowly—there's plenty of time." —Ralph Waldo Emerson

CHAPTER 4

The Preventive Approach:

Learning the Art of Time Management

"Go through, of an evening, any university campus containing an architectural school. That school can be spotted without fail. It is the one brilliantly lighted attic." —F. H. Bosworth, Jr., and Roy Childs Jones's description of the night life in architecture schools in the 1930s[1]

After observing and interviewing hundreds of design students over the years, I have become convinced that those students who manage their time well perform much better than do their counterparts at the design jury. Students who are good time managers are much more likely to deliver a more complete graphic presentation and a more convincing oral presentation. They exude self-confidence. Not willing to succumb to the "all-nighter syndrome," they are well rested and relatively relaxed at the jury, and they are better able to truly listen and respond to the jury's comments. Unfortunately, such well-organized design students are few and far between.

Some designers believe that planning their work out on a schedule stifles their creativity. The creative process, they argue, can occur at any moment of the day or night, even while lying in bed or taking a shower. Design defies scheduling. Planning ahead and attempting to manage your time put a definite damper on the design process. After all, we're artists, aren't we? And artists don't punch time clocks. To a certain extent, they are right. Designing is in fact a reflective, iterative process that can never be *fully* anticipated and planned out in advance.[2] The process of continually redefining and refining your ideas precludes any preset schedule. Each designer has her own individual rhythms and some sense of when creative breakthroughs are ready to occur.

Nonetheless, what we typically see in design studio is this argument taken to its logical conclusion. With the exception of occasional sketch problems or mock exams, time management is all but ignored. As a result, lots of time in studio—both when instructors are present and when they are not—is used inefficiently and often just plain wasted.[3] Many design instructors assume you can learn how to manage your time through trial and error, but the reality is that some people never do.

Managing time effectively is of paramount importance under high-pressure situations, such as professional licensing exams. For instance, a portion of the 1990 Architect Registration Examination required that six graphic vignettes on site design be completed in 2 hours and 45 minutes, and one graphic problem in building design be finished in 12 hours.[4]

No design practice would stay afloat if at least someone in the office could not master time management skills. Clients have deadlines and expect them to be met. They do not grant "incomplete" grades or extensions. They do not expect to see their designer making a design presentation after staggering in from an all-nighter. Managing time efficiently is a key component of running a successful practice and maintaining a firm's credibility. And it is one of the most fundamental ingredients of professional behavior. Nonetheless, even in the profession, designers are notoriously poor at managing time. One well-known time management consultant told me that he has given up altogether on working with architects. According to that expert, architects are usually convinced that their own time management system "works" for them, and as a result they tend to be uninterested in learning novel, innovative techniques that can help them improve productivity in the office.

Bookstores are full of many thoughtful, well-written guidebooks to time management.[5] You may want to purchase some to have on your own bookshelf, as they inevitably go into much greater depth than is possible here. One such book, Alan Lakein's *How to Get Control of Your Time and Your Life*, has become a classic, and many of the

> *"When I went back to graduate school at Harvard in 1969, every project was done with a team. As a result, the length of time that it took to do something grew... I had seen the pattern that once you get into a team, you sit around and talk, and it took twice as long to get something done. It drove me crazy....*
>
> *"... In undergraduate school, you'd work 20 hours a day but I decided I didn't want to do that anymore. I made it a rule that I was going to get to the studio at 7:00 in the morning, and I was going to leave at 7:00 at night. Period... I held onto that idea so that when I got in a team, I helped organize it so that I could carve out my portion of it, and so that I didn't have to be at the mercy of others 20 hours a day for weeks on end."—William Callaway*
>
> *"I stayed up all night when I was a student. For my thesis I didn't sleep for more than a week. That's my record. Staying up all night in studio is typical all over the world."—Minoru Takeyama*
>
> *"Did I ever stay up all night in studio? Oh yes. All nighters are part of the student culture and a subject of much controversy. But actually all nighters could be desirable because they force students to make decisions when they are exhausted. They can make students do an outrageous amount of work in a short period of time because students have to make a decision in a hurry."—Joseph Esherick*
>
> *"I don't think the problem in design work is simply management of time. I think it's a complex issue of concentration. This is borne out by my own experience and my own work. I can be distracted just like anybody else. If I have a deadline to meet, I'm old and wise enough now to know how much time it's going to take if everything went well. But I also know that more often than not, everything does not go well. So I try to allow even more time....*
>
> *"... One of the points that students should understand is that whether it's mismanagement of time, or the ability to find another way to skin the cat at 2:00 in the morning and therefore having to redraw everything all over again, it will all continue to occur as long as they keep designing buildings. It's exactly the same way as it was in college....*
>
> *"... Many architects later in life design for a while, and then they become managers; they go out and bring buildings into the office for young turks to design. And if they're good at that, they keep going out and getting more buildings. These people are relieved of all-nighters, and they have to be. They have to be fresh to go meet other business people and act the way business people do. For those of us who continue to design, however, the difficulty still remains in working too late and therefore being less than your best because of exhaustion."—Michael Graves*

> *"One skill that is not taught well in school is organization. The key to doing anything is organizing, getting your effort directed, understanding what you're doing, assembling the task and working with other people, assigning work to do and understanding your role in managing projects. None of these aspects are taught in design school."—Laurence Booth*

following ideas are inspired by his work.[6] However, no one source specifically addresses the time management problems unique to the design studio.

Managing time is very much a part of gaining control of your life in general—what some psychologists call "self-management." Self-management involves planning, organizing, educating, directing, controlling, and evaluating yourself in a number of arenas. Managing information is one of these critical arenas, as is managing time. The ability to determine goals, set priorities and stick to them, maintain concentration and control interruptions, and avoid that most common pitfall, procrastination, are all key ingredients.

Few people anywhere have the luxury of being able to work on only one task at a time. As a student, you take other courses that have deadlines of their own—for exams, term papers, short assignments, and the like. Students often shove the requirements of nondesign courses aside in order to devote themselves more fully to their studios. When these other deadlines pile up along with the design jury, physical collapse from sheer exhaustion can be the result.

Practitioners are usually required to work on different aspects of the same project or on several different projects at the same time. Being able to juggle several different tasks concurrently is an extremely important skill both in school and in the working world. In fact, maintaining this balancing act is probably one of the most important skills needed and one that can ultimately increase your productivity many times over.

One aspect of design studio that makes it especially difficult to manage time effectively is that you are almost constantly subject to interruptions from others—be it your design critic, other coworkers or classmates, or simply friends or colleagues dropping by. You are working in an open office plan with minimal privacy and control of your own space and time—unless you actively take steps to counteract this. Research has demonstrated that unwanted interruptions and a general lack of privacy are among the most common source of complaints from workers in open office plans.[7] Working efficiently in studio means gaining the ability to handle these interruptions effectively and keeping yourself in control of your work environment.

The way in which most studio assignments are handed out to students also exacerbates your ability to manage time effectively. Most assignments are given out in a rather loose, unstructured time framework. You may have the first one or two weeks to come up with a set of concept diagrams, another couple of weeks to come up with some preliminary sketches, yet another period to produce more detailed floor plans, sections, and elevations for an interim jury, and then a final period to refine these earlier ideas and prepare a final presentation, perhaps with an additional model and more sophisticated set of drawings. Exactly how you progress on your design work within and between each of these steps is generally left up to you. This situation makes it all the more difficult to try to plan out the process ahead of time and try to keep yourself on a schedule. Furthermore, even minor, last-minute changes to your design often have spillover or domino effects on other components of your project. This, too, makes managing the time you spend on a project exceedingly frustrating.

In their efforts to encourage students to work on their design projects as long as they need to, many design school buildings remain unlocked at all times. Often architecture design studios produce the few beams of light shining on campus from dusk until dawn. Other schools purposely lock their doors at midnight or some other time for safety reasons. In any case, the relatively easy access to design studio, no matter what the hour, day or night, makes it even more tempting to turn design into a completely open-ended process whose only structure is that arbitrary deadline when the project is due.

How can you begin to take control of this seemingly impossible situation? What follows are some tips that you can try either in isolation or in combination with each other. Keep in mind that no one time management technique is perfect and that your best bet is to adjust any of these guidelines to your own life-style and needs. Or you may use these guidelines to help spark your own ideas. *There simply is no magic formula, but instead, seek to discover whatever works best for you.* My aim here is simply to plant some ideas for you to think about and try. The key is to develop these skills through practice, so that they eventually become automatic habits.

BUY A PORTABLE CALENDAR AND USE IT

Using a portable calendar may sound like the most mundane of suggestions to you, and one that makes you feel less like an artist and more like a bureaucrat, but you will soon see that it can prove to be very effective. Use it as a tool not only to plan out your class schedule as well as various appointments, but also to list various tasks that you must accomplish each day (Figure 4-1). Include as

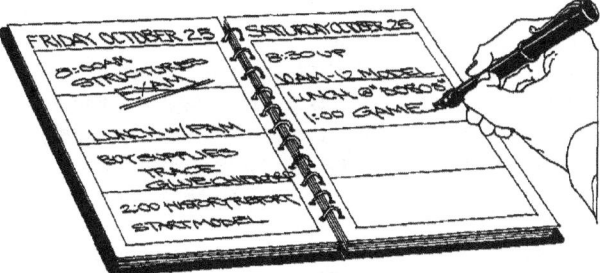

Figure 4-1 Using a portable calendar, preferably one with lots of space on each page, is one of the essential techniques of effective time management. Take it with you everywhere.

much information in your calendar as possible so that you do not have to wade through piles of notes to find what you need. For example, if you have an appointment during the day, write down whom you will meet, exactly where you must go (street address, room number), and the telephone numbers of the people you will be meeting so that in case you are late, you can call and notify them easily. If you need to bring something with you to this appointment, write that down in your calendar as well so that you don't forget and show up without it.

If you have to accomplish several tasks during the next few days, write them all down in your calendar on the day(s) you are most likely to get to them. Avoid carrying around numerous lists of things to do, scratch papers or cocktail napkins with reminders of appointments, phone numbers, and the like. Empty your pockets, purses, and desks right now and begin getting in the habit of keeping it all in one place—your calendar. You will be amazed at how much simpler your life can be, and how much time you will save looking for important information you'll need each day. Just be sure not to lose that calendar!

The best calendars are ones with ample space for each day so that you can fit all you need in one space. Experiment with different formats and find the one that works best for you. One that fits easily in a pocket, purse, backpack or attache case is most likely to be used.

Take the calendar with you everywhere. That way if, say, someone asks if you are free next Wednesday at 5:00 for an informal studio review session, you can check right away and write yourself a reminder. When in doubt, write it down.

SET PRIORITIES

Productivity and *survival* are light-years apart. Most design students are quite capable of survival, but few are truly productive. Ideally, your aim is to be as productive as possible by combining *effectiveness,* or doing the right job, with *efficiency,* or doing the right job "right." Take time every day to set your goals and priorities and to plan out activities. The key to time management "is not to spend more hours on the project but to work more effectively within the time allotted."[8] This may mean occasionally taking legitimate shortcuts to get where you want to go. What you ultimately have to show to your jurors, clients, or employers as a result of your efforts is far more important than the sheer number of hours, days, weeks, or months you have been slaving away.

When you begin to set priorities for yourself, be sure to separate what is *important* from what is *urgent*. We tend to react to what is most urgent, but it may not truly be what is most important in the long run. When dealing with urgent tasks, we lose control by reacting to demands others place upon us. But when dealing with important tasks, we are in the driver's seat. In order to be most productive, keep yourself—not others—in control of your time. Whenever possible, plan to complete tasks well ahead of deadlines so that they do not become urgent, taking your energy away from what is really most important for you.

At the beginning of each week, take some time to tentatively plan out the week as a whole. Decide what you need to accomplish by the end of the week and what specific steps will help you reach your goals. This will help you see the bigger picture and how each week relates to the entire term.

Take about 5 to 10 minutes each evening to plot out what you must accomplish by the end of the next working day. What are your goals? Which of these goals is absolutely critical? Which activities are so important that if you do not finish them, something catastrophic may happen—that is, you will fail a class, get fired, or some other dramatic consequence? First, define each goal, and second, list the activities or tasks you must do to accomplish these goals. Label the most important goal for that day *A*, the second most important *B*, the third most important *C*, and so on.[9]

Based on your past experiences, estimate which of these tasks you are capable of accomplishing during the course of a day. Whatever your schedule for that day, make sure that you accomplish the tasks needed to achieve your *A* goal and try to get to each of the other goals in their order of importance. But *be flexible*. If you do not finish all of them, reassign them for another day or reassess if they were important enough to include in the first place. Even your *A* goal and related tasks may be inappropriate. If need be, simply reorder or eliminate such tasks altogether. Sometimes priorities shift as each task is accomplished. Whatever you do, try not to let your day be consumed by *C* tasks, as they often are. The time and energy spent on *C* tasks can be so exhausting that you don't even feel like getting around to the *A*'s.

You may ask: Isn't the time I spend planning taken out of the time I could spend working on my design project? Yes, it is. However, such planning time can help you work more efficiently and effectively not only on your design,

Figure 4-2 Learn to juggle different aspects of your life along with design studio.

but on other tasks as well. *Being able to juggle many different kinds of activities within the course of a workday is but another key to a successful professional career* (Figure 4-2).

TAKE SMALL STEPS

Don't see your design project as one enormous, dreaded task that must be accomplished. While continuing to work on the big picture, break down the project into smaller tasks. Using the analogy of a young child first learning to walk, many psychologists advise their clients to "take baby steps." Babies don't zoom out of their cribs and immediately walk out the door. They learn to walk slowly, one small step at a time. The completion of each small step makes it easier for them to master the next one. In this respect, design work is not unlike learning to walk or ride a bicycle or sail a boat. It is extremely time consuming and requires much patience.

Design is a cumulative process where one set of decisions affects subsequent ones. Therefore, if one of your goals for the week is to try to build a workable model, think of all the steps you will need to take in order to get there, including producing several different types of crude, working models and selecting the one you like the best. Your *A* goal for the week could be to produce the model.

Your related activities, which could be spaced throughout the week, could be to review and analyze some inspiring, published photographs of actual buildings or models that somehow capture a piece of what you would like to do, to reexamine your prior floor plans to see how they relate to the building model as a whole, to critically examine drafts of your elevations, and to build three rough models to choose from. Each one of these processes takes up quite a bit of time. The key in making this system work is to block out large chunks of time to work on your A activities.

CLASSIC TIME MANAGEMENT TIPS

Build in enough production time to complete your project. Work backwards from the due date and estimate how long it takes you to draw up all your final plans, sections, elevations, perspective drawings, to build your model, or to do whatever else is required—once the design is in final form. And remember that just about every task takes about three or four times as long to actually accomplish as we estimate! This will ensure that you will indeed finish. And when 50% of your time is up, ask yourself: Is my project 50% complete? How will you know?

Give yourself an extra day or two to meet your deadline. What if you come down with the flu the night before the project is due? In fact, illnesses are often brought on by the onset of deadlines. Tell yourself that the project is not really due Tuesday at 5 P.M. but rather Sunday at 5 P.M. Don't let anyone persuade you otherwise.

To avoid being interrupted, place a "Do Not Disturb" sign on your studio desk. Or "Work in Progress. Please come back after 10:00." Or "Designer at Work! Please leave a message." If you choose to do this, stick to it. If someone comes by your desk and wants to talk, simply point to the sign and continue doing your design work (Figure 4-3).

Block out chunks of time when you wish to work undisturbed. Make an appointment with yourself in your calendar and don't let anyone take this time away from you. No matter where you're working, be it in studio or at home, keep this time to yourself and work on your design. You can block out time either horizontally throughout the week, for instance, Monday, Wednesday, and Friday from 10 to 12, or vertically, for instance, Thursday afternoon from 1 to 5 (Figure 4-4).

Throughout the course of each day, keep asking yourself: "What is the best use of my time right now?"[10] Use this technique as a tool to keep checking on yourself. If what you are doing is not the best use of your time, switch to something else. Check yourself against your list of priority goals and activities for each day.

Identify that time during the day or evening when you work best. For some people, this is 7:00 A.M., for others it is 10:00 A.M., for others it is mid-afternoon or even 10 P.M. This optimal time varies greatly from person to person. If at

Figure 4-3 If you wish to work undisturbed at your studio desk, put up a "Do Not Disturb" sign in a prominent location, along with a message pad.

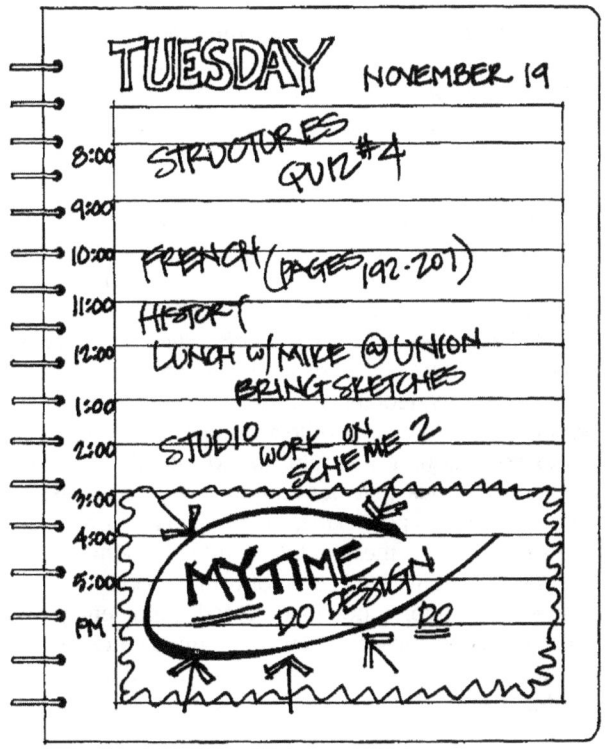

Figure 4-4 Block out large chunks of time when you need to work on your design. Make an appointment with yourself in your calendar, and stick to it.

all possible, schedule at least some of your design work for those times and work on it regularly then. If you have outside employment and are able to select your work hours, reserve at least some of these optimal hours for your own studio work.

> "As you become more mature, you realize that conceiving an idea or concept is almost like laying an egg. It truly is! The analogy of conception is very accurate. You realize that there are different kinds of situations which allow you to work best—to imagine or daydream, or whatever it is that you do in order to come up with an idea. You need to get in touch with how you actually work.... Pete [Peter Walker] and I design very differently. Where we get our ideas and how we work is completely different. His best time to conceive is when he's standing in the shower. He designs in his head. He'll have the whole thing mapped out by the end of a shower. He comes to an idea very quickly all in his head. Then he draws the idea out. I'm very different. I have many ideas swirling around in my head. They're in my subconscious, but they can't be released until I'm actually sitting in front of a piece of paper and drawing. My method is much more slow—it involves drawing." —Martha Schwartz
>
> "I find that your first ideas are usually the best. You refine them, but they are your first reaction and often the strongest idea. Sometimes the first thing you put down on paper is something that you've been thinking about in the shower." —John C. Walker

Reserve at least an hour a day for the unexpected. You may have an overnight assignment due in another course. A friend from out of town may drop in for a surprise visit. Your checking account may be overdrawn.

At least once or twice a week, schedule some free time for yourself to do whatever you wish. Maybe a friend wants to rent a videotape and watch a movie together. You want to go out to your favorite restaurant or organize your photo collection. You would like to attend an exciting event on campus that has nothing to do with design; perhaps a famous politician is in town and giving a speech. The key is to plan these activities ahead of time so that you will have completed some of your important A activities before you go. Above all, don't feel guilty; enjoy yourself. You will be surprised how much more efficiently you can work on your design project the next day after this needed break.

AVOID PROCRASTINATION

Sometimes you truly find yourself staring at the same piece of tracing for what seems like hours on end, failing to make any progress at all. You have procrastinated so long that you simply cannot even take the first step to forge ahead on your design. In this case, a few special techniques may work well for you.

One of the most difficult parts of the design process is simply getting started. As one of my colleagues tells his students, "*Good finishes are frequently the result of good starts. Start anywhere—but start!*"

Keep a log for a week and note whenever you put off working on your design project. Become aware of what draws you away from your design work and why. What's the temptation? What's the price you've paid? After the week is up, review your log and try to discover any patterns that typify how and when you procrastinate. Does one of your best friends routinely lure you away from studio to the local drinking establishment at 11:00 P.M.? Does a short break for dinner turn into a three-hour-long escape from studio, only to find yourself feeling that much farther behind, dreading having to stay up till 2:00 A.M.? Does the student who sits at the studio desk next to yours relish in describing all the intricate details of his love life—for an hour-long monologue? Next week, whenever these same trends begin to surface, nip them in the bud and make sure that you do not let such temptations pull you away from your work.

Stop to estimate the price you will pay for your delay. Often delaying one project simply has domino effects on others. For instance, putting off key tasks in your design work may well have you running into a deadline for a term paper in another class—thereby giving you two big problems to worry about instead of one. Taking an incomplete grade in your design studio may force you to stay on campus during the summer, while your lease expires at the end of the spring term and some summer subletters are moving in the next day. Now, in addition to worrying about your design project, you must worry about finding a roof over your head! Sometimes the length of time required to complete a task actually enlarges the longer you put it off. Stopping to figure this out ahead of time can give you the motivation needed to avoid procrastinating and move forward on your design work.

If you get stuck on one idea in your design, do anything different for only five minutes. Distract your attention from your mental block and get busy doing something else—anything at all—on your design project. Or simply give yourself a five-minute break to buy a soft drink and take a short walk down the hall. You may find that when you return to the thought that has been stumping you, you may have a new burst of energy.

Leave your studio desk, find a chair, and sit in it for 15 minutes. Do not talk to anyone, do not read, do not listen to music. You may need to escape to an extremely private place to do this—a bathroom toilet stall or an empty classroom are possibilities. Just sit there in solitary confinement. After the 15 minutes are up, you may feel so guilty about wasting all that time that you will not think twice about getting back to work. Plus you have given yourself a needed break in concentration that can make it easier to start up again.

LEARNING THE ART OF TIME MANAGEMENT
SUMMARY CHECKLIST

USE A CALENDAR EFFECTIVELY

___ Buy a portable calendar and use it regularly.
___ Record all appointments, phone numbers, and places to meet in your calendar.
___ Empty your pockets and purses of scratch paper, cocktail napkins, and other loose notes.

SET PRIORITIES

___ Set priorities for each week.
___ Set priorities for each day.
___ Separate important from urgent tasks. Concentrate on important ones.
___ Keep yourself, not others, in control of your time.

TAKE SMALL STEPS

___ Break down your design project into a series of smaller tasks.
___ Block out large chunks of time to work on time-consuming tasks.

CLASSIC TIME MANAGEMENT TIPS

___ Build in enough production time to complete your project. Work backwards from the due date.
___ When 50% of your time is up, ask yourself: is my project 50% complete?
___ Give yourself an extra day or two to meet your deadline.
___ To avoid being interrupted, try placing a "Do not Disturb" sign on your studio desk.
___ Block out chunks of time when you wish to work undisturbed. Make an appointment with yourself in your calendar and don't let anyone take this time away from you.
___ Throughout the course of each day, keep asking yourself: "What is the best use of my time right now?"
___ Identify that time during the day or evening when you work best.
___ Reserve at least an hour a day for something unexpected.
___ At least once or twice a week, schedule some free time for yourself to do whatever you wish.

AVOID PROCRASTINATION

___ Start anywhere--but start!
___ Keep a log for a week and note whenever you put off working on your design project.
___ Stop to estimate the price you will pay for your delay.
___ If you get stuck on one idea in your design, do anything different for only five minutes.
___ Leave your studio desk, find a chair, and sit in it for 15 minutes.
___ Move your tracing to a different spot on your desk. Clear off all extraneous material from your desk. Sharpen your pencil.
___ Make a promise that by the end of the hour, afternoon, or evening, you will have accomplished something specific and show it to someone else.
___ Give yourself a short deadline to accomplish even the smallest task on your project.
___ Remember: it doesn't have to be perfect, it just has to be done.
___ Learn from others who are effective time managers.

___ Evaluate which techniques helped you the most and least, and learn from your experiences.

Figure 4-5 Summary checklist of time management skills.

Move your tracing to a different spot on your desk. Clear off all extraneous material from your desk and keep only that paper that you are working on right now. Sharpen your pencil. Or go to the library and begin working on 8½" × 11" format for awhile. These may not seem like the most profound suggestions, but they can help you feel as if you now have a fresh start on your project.

Make a promise that by the end of the hour, afternoon, or evening, you will have accomplished something specific and show it to someone else. Giving yourself an artificial deadline, attached with some accountability to another person, is more likely to yield results than simply telling yourself, "I'll get to it later." Use the buddy system to your advantage in design studio. You can even turn it into a game of sorts, where whoever finishes more quickly gets a reward.

Save and review your work products. Critique yourself for the work in progress, and reward yourself for work well done. Similarly, know how to account for your own failures. *If you don't finish, it's not the end of the world. But then be sure to make up the lost time the next day.*

Give yourself a short deadline to accomplish even the smallest task on your project. Bring in a kitchen timer to your studio desk or use the built-in alarm on your watch. Set it for 30 minutes, check the time periodically, and stop this task when the bell rings. You may be surprised at what you can accomplish in a short time.

You can try this for some bite-sized task that requires even less time. For instance, give yourself five minutes to decide when to meet one of your studio-mates to discuss your project or to assemble all the articles you have collected that relate to your design project and put them all in one place.

Are you falling into the "perfectionist syndrome?" Remember: It doesn't have to be perfect, it just has to be done. No matter what masterpiece you are producing right now, chances are that when you take another look at it six months, a year, or two or three years from now, it will be nowhere near what you are capable of doing at that time. It will never be perfect. It is far more important to be able to complete the project—as good a design as you are capable of doing at that time—in its entirety than to be pondering over the "perfect design" for 10 weeks and have nothing but a few concept diagrams to show at the final jury.

Learn from others who are effective time managers. Many returning students with families, jobs, and other responsibilities have already learned through experience how to become effective jugglers. Watch how these students work throughout the design process and how this impacts their performance at the jury. Ask them what techniques they use.

In any case, *after trying some of these techniques for yourself, evaluate which helped you the most and least, and based on your own self-criticism, learn from your experiences—and from your mistakes* (Figure 4-5). None of these suggestions is foolproof. You may want to try some variations of your own or come up with some new time management techniques. Whatever you choose to do, be sure to experiment with different strategies until you find a system that suits your needs. Most importantly, be persistent in experimenting and evaluating, and don't succumb to premature frustration. Just remember: Don't give up! The more often you try a new time management technique, the more likely it is to work for you. Patience and perseverance in the short run will inevitably pay off in the long run. And not only will your jury performance improve, but you may actually enjoy the experience!

NOTES

1. Bosworth, F. H., Jr., and Roy Childs Jones, *A Study of Architectural Schools*, New York: Scribner, 1932, p. 110.

2. Schon, Donald A., *The Reflective Practitioner*, New York: Basic Books, 1983.

3. Unfortunately, many design instructors themselves may be poor organizers of time, incapable of teaching time management skills to their students.

4. *June 1990 Juror's Manual*, Washington, DC: National Council of Architectural Registration Boards, 1990, Appendix 1, p. 6.

5. Some other useful resources on managing time as well as information include Blanchard, Kenneth H., and Spencer Johnson, *The One Minute Manager*, New York: Berkeley Books, 1983; Drucker, Peter F., *The Effective Executive*, New York: Harper Collins, 1967; Drucker, Peter F., *Management: Tasks, Responsibilities, Practices*, New York: Harper Collins, 1974; Eisenberg, Ronni, with Kate Kelly, *Organize Yourself!* New York: Collier Books, Macmillan, 1986; Mackenzie, R. Alec, *The Time Trap*, New York: Amacom, a Division of American Management Association, 1972; Reynolds, Helen, and Mary E. Tramel, *Executive Time Management: Getting 12 Hours' Work out of an 8-Hour Day*, Englewood Cliffs, NJ: Prentice-Hall, 1979.

"My advice to students is to get your projects done! I had one student when I was teaching who never was ready for a jury, come hell or high water. One time he told me that his mother-in-law died, but he wasn't married yet. I said, 'Wait a minute, you're not married are you?' He said, 'I'm thinking about getting married and her mother died.' And the next time his model fell off his motorcycle in the middle of the Eisenhower Expressway. Something was always wrong."—Carol Ross Barney

6. Lakein, Alan, *How to Get Control of Your Time and Your Life*, New York: Wyden, 1973.

7. Harris, Louis, and associates, *The Steelcase National Study of Office Environments: Do They Work?* Grand Rapids, MI: Steelcase, Inc., 1978; Wineman, Jean, "Office Design and Evaluation: An Overview," *Environment and Behavior, 14*:3 (May 1982), pp. 271-298; Wineman, Jean (ed.), *Behavioral Issues in Office Design*, New York: Van Nostrand Reinhold, 1986; Brill, M., with S. T. Margulis, E. Konar, and BOSTI in association with Westinghouse Furniture Systems, *Using Office Design to Increase Productivity, 1-2*, Buffalo, NY: Workplace Design and Productivity, Inc., 1984.

8. Lakein, op. cit., p. 60.

9. Ibid.

10. Ibid., p. 117.

CHAPTER 5

Avoiding Guesswork:
Learning How to Research Your Project and Its Users

"About a week before a program was to be issued the title alone would be announced, and we would then spend as much time as we could in the library in search of any information related to the subject at hand. This usually meant looking up examples of buildings of a particular type that had actually been built or were projected. At that time there was, in the journals, relatively little analytical work and virtually no research on building types or functions....

"... The urging to study examples of building types was serious, and we were also urged, in fact directed, not only to look at buildings of the kind we were dealing with in the design course but to talk to people who used the buildings or who worked in them. Thus if the problem was a restaurant, we were urged to observe how the restaurant worked from the patron's point of view, and to talk to the owner, the waiters, the cook, the dishwasher, and the janitor. We were to take notes, make measured drawings and sketches, and try as much as possible to be familiar with the functional and operational side of what we were doing." —Joseph Esherick's account of life as an architecture student at the University of Pennsylvania in the 1930s[1]

Experienced faculty, visiting critics, and even casual observers of design juries admit that the rationales that most students present for their design decisions are extremely weak. Few students devote ample time prior to the jury to preparing a credible response to questions like these: "Why did you choose to design the project the way you did?" "What were the bases for your critical design decisions?" Many students simply choose to respond to these types of questions by saying, "Because that's the way I like it," or, even worse, "I really don't know." *On countless occasions, I have seen answers like these ignite a confrontation between students and jurors, perpetuating the mastery-mystery phenomenon.* Such responses send a message to jurors that students have not adequately thought through their design. Other students point to precedents that inspired their own work, but often lack the ability to clearly state *why* those precedents are appropriate for their site. That is simply not enough to convince a jury of the strength of a design proposal.[2]

In practice as well, designers often rely on personal tastes and preferences when they present work to clients and juries. They tend to speak a language that many clients do not understand, and they often have little empirical basis for their design decisions. In response to clients' questions about why they chose a particular design concept or detail, they may respond, "The site seemed to call for this solution," or, "This solution is the one that our design team prefers." To the client, such statements are meaningless and confusing, smacking of arrogance—in some cases, a turnoff from hiring a firm for future work.

Given the wealth of research now available in a myriad of books and design journals, designers no longer need to offer such clumsy responses to questions like these. In fact, the results from numerous research studies offer design guidelines for many different types of spaces and building types. *Being able to point to research results and how they influenced your design decisions can help you build a much more convincing case before jurors or clients. Research in the relatively new field of environment and behavior can be especially useful in this regard. This field offers a treasure of information for designers, yet few designers know what it is and where to look for it. It is truly an untapped resource.*[3]

Environment and behavior addresses how people

perceive and respond to the physical environment, and the applied side of this field addresses user needs in design. The field offers much useful information that applies directly to design projects, for example: how to design hospitals so that visitors and patients can find their way quickly and easily; how to design plazas that people will use and not just admire from a distance; how to design housing environments that encourage chance meetings and that are safe for children to play.

Findings from environment-behavior research must be taken into account *in tandem with* other factors that influence design, such as aesthetics, climate, orientation, topography, and other site considerations; zoning; energy efficiency; function; structural concerns; building or plant materials; contextual issues; life cycle costs; the construction process; and others. Each of these areas has a solid information base that is often drawn upon when designing a project. In school, these areas are typically stressed either through support courses or as part of design studio. Because few design instructors emphasize environment and behavior, few design programs require that it be offered as a separate course, and most practicing designers are unfamiliar with this field, this chapter emphasizes its unique contributions to the design studio and to presentations to juries and clients.[4]

How can you go about finding examples of the spaces you are designing? How can you uncover information from environment-behavior research that you can apply to your design projects? Where do you begin to look? How can you best apply the research findings to your design work? We'll look at some of these issues in this chapter.

WHERE DO I BEGIN? HOW TO GATHER EXISTING INFORMATION

Gathering information on precedents for your design projects is relatively easy. Most colleges or universities where environmental design is taught generally have fairly complete collections of materials in their own libraries (Figure 5-1). Although you may be tempted to simply zoom into specialized sources right away, *start by taking some time to browse through the library shelves.* Browsing is one of the most effective ways to obtain an overview of what literature is available. And often it is only through browsing that you are able to uncover material that may indirectly relate to your work, or material that is simply enlightening and expands your horizons in broader areas.

Once you have browsed through some basic, general sources relating to your design project, begin to search for information on the building or space type you are designing, for parts within that building or space, and for key issues mentioned in the design program by using specialized sources. *Various indices are available to help you locate materials in a systematic way*, rather than simply comb through issue after issue of the journals in the hopes of locating some project remotely close to your assignment. *The Architectural Periodicals Index, Architecture Index, Art Index, Avery Index to Architectural Periodicals,* and the *Vance Bibliographies* are among the most valuable resources. They contain complete listings of materials published in the leading design journals. By looking up the building or space type, the name of the project or designer, or other identifying characteristics, you will be directed to the specific issue of each journal that carries any relevant information. All you need to do is find it on the shelf, turn to the appropriate page, and the article should appear. In addition, *some key reference books are extremely useful*. The comprehensive, five-volume *Encyclopedia of Architecture* is a most valuable resource to any design student or practitioner, as is the classic *Macmillan Encyclopedia of Architects*.[5]

To locate environment-behavior research and its applications to design, visit a campus library and begin by looking for some classic works in the field. Ask campus librarians to help you find information. A brief overview of the environment-behavior field and how its findings have been applied to design is provided in the recently completed *Encyclopedia of Architecture*.[6] Some more general textbooks in the field include Charles J. Holahan's *Environmental Psychology* and Thomas F. Saarinen's *Environmental Planning: Perception and Behavior*, as well as several others.[7]

A myriad of sources is available about user needs in specific spaces and building types.[8] *Many of these offer suggested design guidelines to help create successful spaces from the user's point of view.* Some *key journals* in environment and behavior include the *Journal of Architectural and Planning Research, Environment & Behavior, Children's Environment Quarterly*, and the *Journal of Environmental Psychology*. Another useful source of information is the *proceedings from the annual conferences of the Environmental Design Research Association (EDRA)*, a multidisciplinary professional organization composed of interior designers, graphic designers, space planners, facility managers, architects, landscape architects, urban design-

Figure 5-1 Libraries offer a wealth of information about the successes and failures of completed design work. Take advantage of them to learn from the experiences of others and to avoid reinventing the wheel each time you begin a new project.

ers and planners, as well as psychologists, sociologists, anthropologists, geographers, and others, all of whom share a common interest in how people use the physical environment. Each year this organization holds a conference, and selected papers, symposia, workshops, and poster sessions are published either in full or in a summary abstract in the *EDRA Conference Proceedings.*[9]

Another rich source of information, often overlooked, can be found in magazines and trade journals from other fields. Trade magazines are concerned with offices, schools, banks, hotels, museums, supermarkets, swimming pools, zoos, and almost any building or space you can imagine. Many of these periodicals feature articles on design issues and case studies. Finding these sources usually requires a visit to a general university library or a more specialized library geared to the profession at hand; environmental design libraries typically do not carry these materials. Simply think about what kinds of people are involved with the space you are designing—either as clients, users, managers, visitors, or some other role—and then ask a reference librarian to point you to the kinds of magazines these people are likely to read.

HOW CAN I REMEMBER WHAT I READ? HOW TO RECORD AND DOCUMENT EXISTING INFORMATION

Documenting, analyzing, and synthesizing the information you collect is just as important as collecting it in the first place. Many design students are very good at *collecting* relevant information; however, all too often these so-called research materials end up as impressive-looking stacks of xeroxes or spiral-bound reports that collect dust in the studio. Studio instructors and students often point to these piles at the beginning of design juries, sometimes even passing them around for the jurors to see, all the while realizing that it is virtually impossible for the jurors to really do this work any justice in such a short period of time. Even worse, students rarely refer to this "research" material in any substantive way during the jury, except to mention merely that it was collected.

Design students often "borrow" from the materials prepared by others all too liberally. In other disciplines this practice is often referred to as plagiarism. One can draw a fine line between being inspired by the work of others and simply copying it. Much of design involves both of these skills, and often both are perfectly acceptable. However, *if the work is copied it must be credited.* Otherwise, it appears as if the work shown is only your own. Anything shown to the jury should be carefully credited to its original source.

The key to turning a collection of documents into useful information that can help you at the jury involves several steps. For one, *every source that is consulted must be carefully recorded and documented.* That means maintaining the general rules of scholarship by carefully noting down the bibliographic citation of each and every source you have found, including both written and graphic information (photographs, plans, drawings, etc.). This can be done in various formats but generally should include the full name of all the authors, the exact title of the book, including any subtitle, the city of publication, the name of the publisher, the year of publication, and the specific pages cited. For a journal article you'll need the names of the authors, the exact title of the article, the title of the journal, the volume, number, exact date, and pages of the article itself. Consult the references in this book as a guide. You may also wish to note the call number of the book or magazine issue and the specific library from where it came in case you need to locate it at another date. It is often easiest to write this information directly on the top of the first page of anything you collect, so that it is immediately available for reference.

You should also get in the habit of *keeping track of all your sources in a separate file, either on the computer or in some hard-copy format, as an annotated bibliography.* Preparing an annotated bibliography means that in addition to noting the citation in full, you prepare a brief description about what that source contains. The level of detail you include for each source will vary depending on how useful it is, how closely it parallels the type of building or space you are creating, or the extent to which it addresses issues that are similar to those found in your own design problem.

In preparing your notes on each source, one of the most effective techniques is to *read and study your source carefully, and then put it away and summarize in your own words and graphics* the essence of what the author is trying to say and/or show. Do not copy word for word unless for some reason you need a verbatim quote. Instead, translate the author's ideas into your own words and drawings. It is this process of translation that often helps you remember what you read and saw, instead of having it go in one eye and out the other.

Once you have collected various sources of information and recorded each in note form, *skim through your notes with a specific purpose in mind.* For instance, if you are working on a project that emphasizes day lighting, your purpose may be to ask, "How has each of the design projects I studied made especially effective use of natural light?" Or, if your project is located on a steep, sloping site, your purpose may be to ask, "How has each of these designs maximized the use of the slope, turning it into one of the strengths of the project?" Or, if your purpose is to encourage social interaction, "What specific design features has research shown to be most and least conducive to people meeting each other?" *Summarize the answers to questions like these again in writing, supplementing your test with annotated graphics.* This kind of analysis and synthesis will not only help you retain what you read,

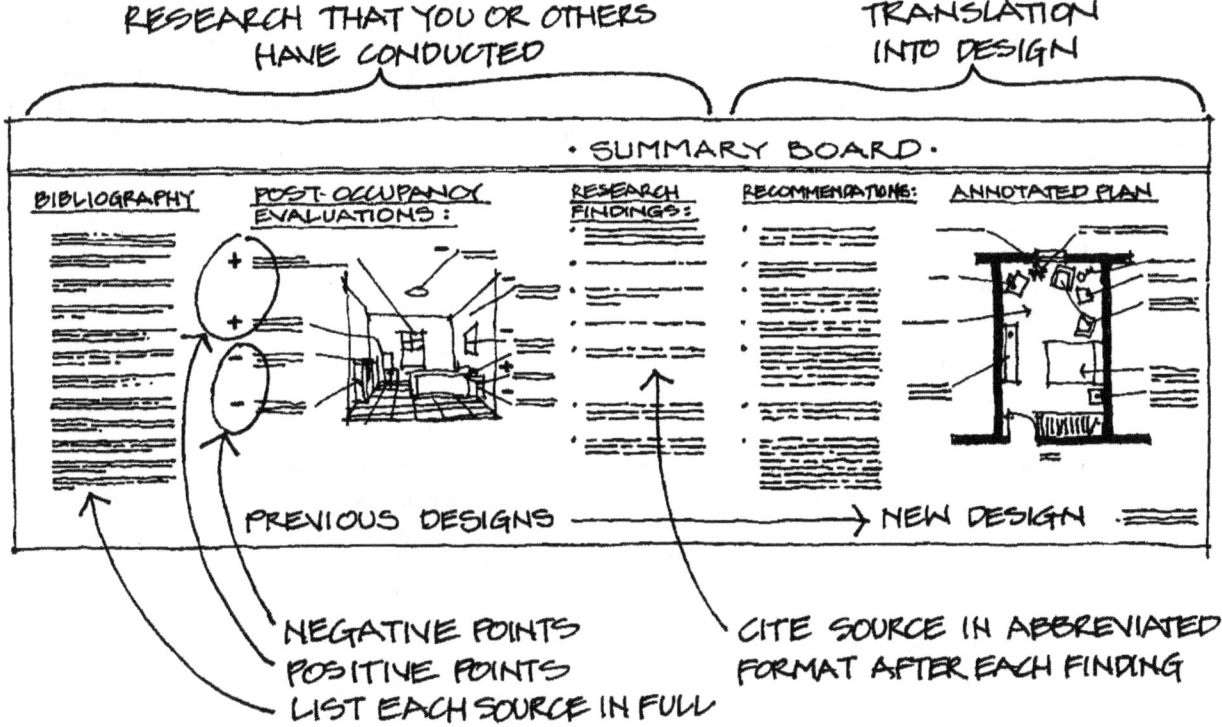

Figure 5-2 Use a summary board to present highlights of the research you or others have conducted. Note key research findings and recommendations, and then show graphically how you have applied them to your current design project.

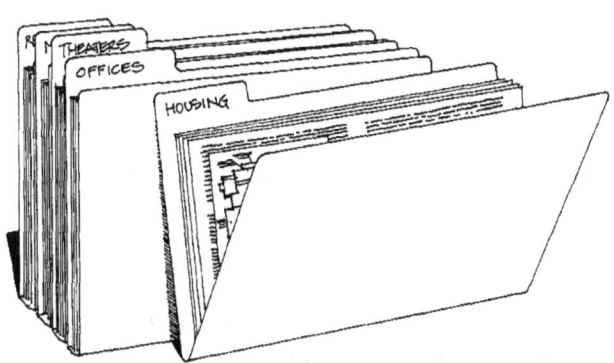

Figure 5-3 Keep all original research materials on file to save for future reference. File them by building or space type (e.g., hospitals, schools, housing), by user type (e.g., elderly, single-parent family, people with physical challenges), or by issues (e.g., way-finding, social interaction, privacy, territoriality). Such materials can make a favorable impression on jurors and future clients by demonstrating a concern for the users' needs.

but more importantly, it will help you pull it all together in a meaningful way, allowing you to not only collect but analyze and synthesize, thus reaching a higher form of learning.[10]

Summarize this end product on a board that you can show to jurors and clients (Figure 5-2). The key is to translate what you have read into a few key graphics, along with short, catchy statements in your own words that highlight what you believe to be most important to your current design problem. A single board packed with relevant information will make your case much more convincing to the jury or client than a mountain of xeroxed articles. Keep all the reference material on hand in case you need to refer to it as a backup in your presentation. Once your own project is complete, organize it by subcategories and file it away so that you can retrieve it easily at a later date, should you be given another assignment on a similar project type, or should some similar issues be raised in a different kind of project (Figure 5-3).

HOW TO GATHER NEW INFORMATION

What if your design project is about a space or building type on which there is little or no existing research? Or what if the research you are able to find is not quite comparable to the project you are undertaking? Or what if the issues raised by this design project are significantly different from those you have come across in the literature? When designing, can you possibly do anything except guess? Not so.

In this case, you may want to gather new information that can help guide your design. Your best bet is to *look for a place that in some way emulates the setting that you are designing*. The space should house similar kinds of uses to the one you will be designing. Conducting an abbreviated postoccupancy evaluation (POE) of this existing space can provide useful information for the new space you are creating. *A POE involves gathering information from people about how they use an existing space, using that information to be able to identify the strong and weak points of an existing design, and then, based on that critique, to incorporate this information into your own design.* It is a process that can be easily adapted to your time frame, be it a month, a week, or even a day.[11] The key is to identify the most pressing issues that you need to know about and then focus your investigation on them.

You can often conduct a highly informative POE by carefully studying the setting where the people you are designing for are currently located. For instance, if you are designing a new home for a family or household, conduct a POE of their current home. Walk through the environment with some typical users, and ask them their opinions about specific spaces as you go along.

In order to be useful, your POE must gather information about people's attitudes toward and behavior in the environment: *what people think about and how they use a place.* This means asking people questions as well as watching them. The tools we use to ask people are generally either interviews, surveys, or questionnaires. Interviews are generally conducted one on one, and are either face to face or over the telephone. They are a useful way to obtain in-depth information from a limited number of people. Surveys and questionnaires are generally conducted in written form. Surveys allow you to obtain information from a large number of people.[12] To understand how people actually use a space, in addition to asking them about it, it is useful to actually observe how they behave. Often what people do and what they say they do are quite different.[13] We also look for physical traces, or ways that people have modified spaces after moving into them, and archives, written documentation about the history of the space and how it has been used over time.

Some excellent source books are available to help you conduct POEs.[14] Many of these books contain easy-to-understand accounts about how to conduct interviews, how to write surveys, how to observe people, how to look for physical traces, and so on. *Conducting and analyzing research is in itself an art form, much like the design process itself, and it takes some effort and preparation to do it well.* Designing any kind of survey research instrument, especially, takes careful planning.

To elicit useful design information, some of the simplest questions to ask in any POE are the following:

What do you like best about this space?
What do you like least about it?
What changes would you make, if at all, to improve it?
What spaces have you seen that work better than this one? Where are they—and why are they better?

To add to this, you may want to ask questions that relate specifically to unresolved issues you may have about your own design project. For instance, suppose you are trying to decide how to encourage employees to mix and mingle in a common space you are designing. Visit an existing work environment in some way similar to the one you are creating, and study any common spaces that do exist on that site. Ask the workers questions like these: "To what extent does this space enable you to meet your coworkers?" "Is there anything about this space that you think *especially helps* people to meet each other?" "Is there anything about this space that you think *discourages* people from meeting each other?" "If you could design a brand new space to *encourage* people to meet each other, what would it be like?"

In conducting any kind of POE, you must carefully record all the information you have collected, and analyze it as best you can by looking for common themes and trends. Naturally, you are unlikely to find agreement on all issues. But by reviewing the kinds of issues that arise and the concerns that people point out, you will be able to design a project that is more responsive to what people actually need—not simply what you think they need. Based on the information you have collected, what kinds of design decisions would you suggest? *Do not be afraid to make the leap from research to design.* It is often easier than you think. It may simply require some extra effort to think creatively about what you have learned.

HOW TO PRESENT YOUR RESEARCH FINDINGS EFFECTIVELY

In presenting some of your research results, keep in mind that jurors, clients, public agencies, and other audiences are likely to pay more attention to certain findings than to others. Psychologist Robert Sommer has systematically evaluated why clients take the results of certain design research studies more seriously than others, and what factors make clients most likely to implement research recommendations.[15] Based on Sommer's research, here are some suggestions:

Present research results with strong visual appeal. Using photographs, drawings, plans, sketches, graphs, or other visual modes of communication, along with short captions, can be a powerful way to convey key research findings. A word of caution, however: be careful not to go overboard here. Concentrate only on those results that are most important. The same principles that apply to oral presentation skills, as described in Chapter 6, apply to the graphic presentation of research as well.

Whenever possible, use "magic numbers"; they can work wonders. Follow-up interviews conducted long after the research was completed revealed that clients often attached great meaning to specific numbers found in research results. For example, from this research we can state that surveys show that over 4 out of 5 students believe juries need improvement. (See Appendix B, Figure B-5.) This is more powerful than simply stating that most students think juries ought to be improved.

Use verbatim comments to help humanize your research results. Sommer's studies showed that "sometimes a single graphic comment in a respondent's own words is more persuasive than a mass of tables and charts."[16] Draw such comments from interviews or from open-ended survey items. Note how the comments from interviews and surveys with students, faculty, and design professionals enliven the research results reported throughout this book. Simply reporting quantitative data would not have the same effect.

Identify at least some recommendations that can be easily and promptly implemented. In such a manner, clients can, if they wish, test out the value of some of these recommendations and feel a sense of accomplishment. For example, some of the innovative jury techniques presented in Chapter 10 can be implemented with little effort. One need not take years to improve juries; quite the contrary. Some of these improvements can be made in simply a few hours.

HOW TO APPLY YOUR RESEARCH FINDINGS TO DESIGN

Applying research findings to design helps complete the idealized design cycle, much like that which occurs in the auto industry when designers use consumer feedback to improve upon last year's model (Figure 5-4). Results from POEs can be used to help produce a design program for a new building or space. POE leads naturally into programming, which in turn leads into design itself. When used together, they can provide a solid intellectual basis for your design decisions.

Two of the most effective tools for communicating your research findings and applying them to design are a findings/recommendations table and an annotated plan. Use a findings/recommendations table to highlight the major findings from your research on one column, and the major design implications, recommendations, or guidelines on the other column (Figure 5-5).

Present highlights from this type of information on a board to show the jury. Then supplement it with an annotated plan, either on the same board or a separate one, indicating key points from your design and showing exactly how they relate back to the research. Producing an annotated plan simply means adding notes onto the plan itself explaining why you chose to design what you did. The rationales for your key design decisions will then be communicated clearly, and you only need to point to them at jury time when asked those all-important questions. Figure 5-6 shows an example of an annotated plan.

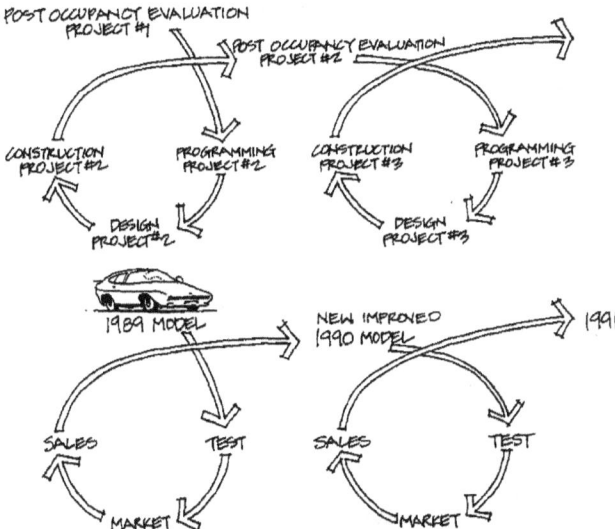

Figure 5-4 Postoccupancy evaluation helps complete the ideal design cycle so that the project at hand benefits from the experiences of people who have previously used similar types of spaces. Serious design mistakes can thus be easily prevented rather than repeated, as they often are.

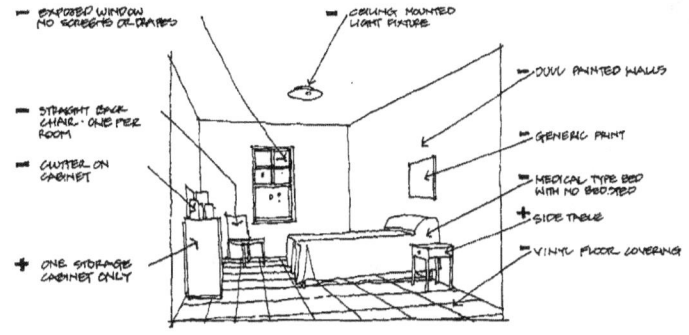

Figure 5-5 A summary table showing research findings along with recommendations is an effective way to present the application of research to design decisions.

In sum, by incorporating the results of environment-behavior research into design projects and into the design jury, *you are able to focus on how people will relate to and understand the spaces you are creating* (Figure 5-7). Instead of simply guessing about what kinds of behavior you expect to occur in a particular space, you are able to draw upon studies that have influenced and supported your design decisions. *With each new project, you are not reinventing the wheel, but rather building upon others' previous experiences — not just your own — with your particular project type. You will demonstrate that you have learned from both the mistakes and successes of previously-built projects. You can present your design decisions in a way that is more objective, based on systematic information. Being familiar with relevant environment-behavior research demonstrates to clients that you are concerned about their needs — not just your own — and the needs of those who will use the spaces you create.* In the process, you

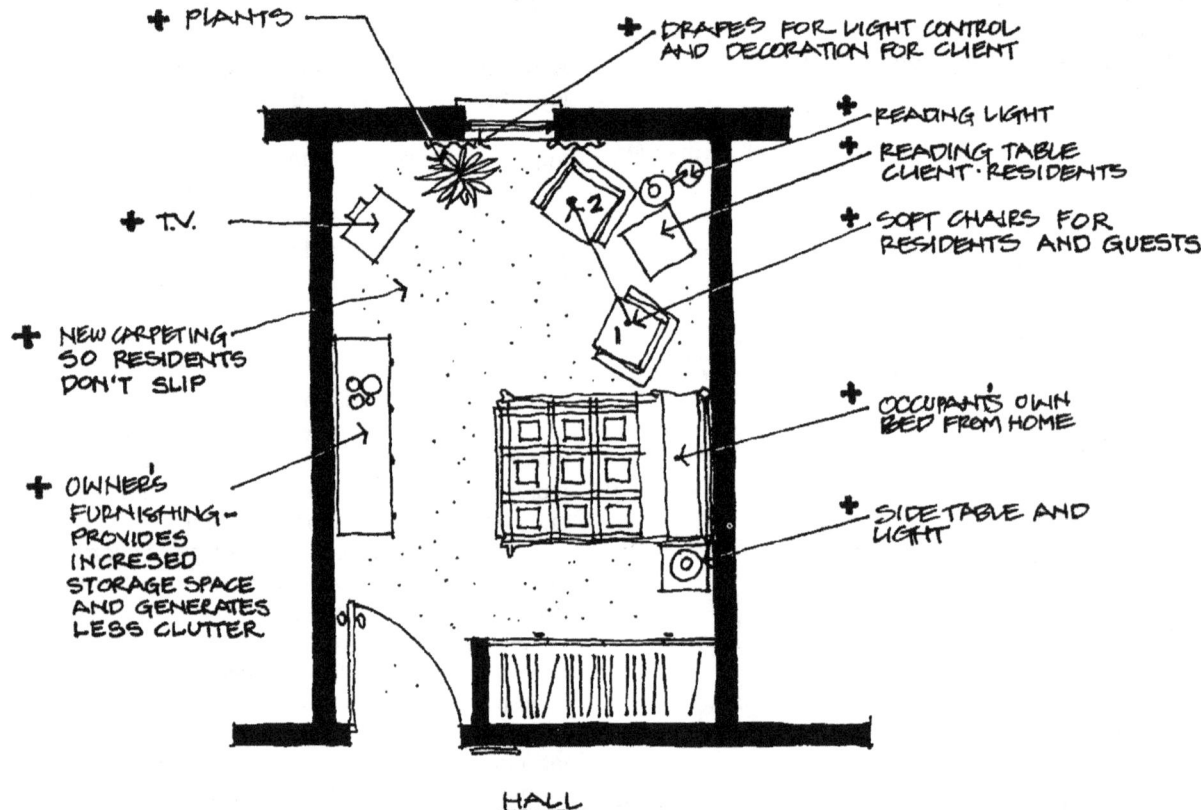

Figure 5-6 An annotated plan is an effective way of showing the jury how research translates into design. Include this as part of your summary research board.

LEARNING HOW TO RESEARCH YOUR PROJECT AND ITS USERS SUMMARY CHECKLIST

GATHERING EXISTING INFORMATION

___ Take some time to browse through the library shelves.
___ Use indices and reference books to help you locate materials in a systematic way.
___ To locate environment-behavior research applications to design, visit a campus library and look for classic works.
___ Seek out key sources that feature design guidelines on user needs in specific spaces and building types.
___ Search through key journals and conference proceedings.
___ Review magazines and trade journals from other fields.

Figure 5-7 Summary checklist of research skills.

RECORDING AND DOCUMENTING EXISTING INFORMATION

___ Document, analyze and synthesize the information you collect.
___ If a work is copied, be sure to credit the source.
  ___ For a book: Note full name of author, title and subtitle, place of publication, publisher, year, and page numbers consulted. Note the library call number for future use.
  ___ For a journal article: Note full name of author, title of article, full name of journal, volume number, year, and page numbers consulted. Note the library call number for future use.
  ___ Consult any published bibliography for proper format.
___ Keep track of all your sources in a separate file as an annotated bibliography.
___ Read and study your sources carefully, and then summarize in your own words and graphics.
___ Skim through your notes with a specific purpose in mind.
___ Pose key questions relating to the project at hand, and summarize your answers in writing and annotated graphics.
___ Summarize your end product on a board that you can show to jurors and clients.

GATHERING NEW INFORMATION

___ Look for a place that emulates the setting that you are designing.
___ Conduct a post-occupancy evaluation (POE) by learning how people use an existing space, using that information to identify its strong and weak design features.
___ Incorporate information from the POE into your own design.
___ Study the setting where the people you are designing for are currently located.
___ Learn what people think about and how they use a place.
___ Consult key source books on conducting POEs.
___ If time is limited, ask some basic questions:
  ___ *What do you like best about this space?*
  ___ *What do you like least about it?*
  ___ *What changes would you make, if at all, to improve it?*
  ___ *What spaces have you seen that work better than this one? Where are they--and why are they better?*
___ Ask about issues that are unresolved in your design.
___ Record all the information you collect.
___ Review your results and distill the implications for your design.

PRESENTING YOUR RESEARCH FINDINGS EFFECTIVELY

___ Use strong visual appeal through photographs, drawings, plans, sketches, graphs and other visuals.
___ Whenever possible, use "magic numbers".
___ Use verbatim comments.
___ Identify some recomendations that can be easily and promptly implemented.

APPLYING YOUR RESEARCH FINDINGS TO DESIGN

___ Prepare a findings/recommendations table.
___ Prepare an annotated plan.
___ Prepare highlights of both on a summary board to show to the jury or clients.
___ Stress how key points from the research relate to your own design.

Figure 5-7 Continued.

can help create a more favorable image of the design professions to the public at large.

NOTES

1. Esherick, Joseph, "Architectural Education in the Thirties and Seventies: A Personal View," in Spiro Kostof (ed.), *The Architect: Chapters in the History of the Profession*, New York: Oxford University Press, 1977, pp. 238-279, quote from pp. 258, 264.

2. The current jury system is heavily weighted toward highly subjective, aesthetic, artistic criteria. In Chapter 10, I suggest alternate forms of juries and methods of evaluating design work that are much less subjective. Art and aesthetics still play an important role, but they are viewed along with other important criteria. As juries begin to change, as the criteria for judging design work continue to broaden, and as the composition of the jury becomes more diverse, including the results of environment-behavior research in presentations to jurors and clients will become increasingly more important.

3. Some faculty may argue that presenting the findings from environment-behavior research may actually detract from students' jury presentations. The problem is that to date, relatively few design instructors who serve as jurors have little more than a passing interest in or knowledge of this field. And to some jurors, admitting the authority of the people who use spaces may appear as a challenge to their own expertise. This need not be the case. In fact, both are useful sources of information about design, and both should be considered; such information is not a zero-sum game. As more students who have been exposed to this material graduate and begin practicing, and as the field continues to grow and become more widely known, this situation will change dramatically.

4. Many universities now offer courses in environment and behavior. The National Architectural Accrediting Board guidelines stipulate that information from the field of environment and behavior must be addressed in the undergraduate architectural curriculum. In some schools, this material is addressed in a separate course, while in others it is included informally as part of a design studio. The field is so rich that the former arrangement is far preferable; without adequate training in this field themselves, few design instructors pay more than lip service to it in studio. Occasionally such courses are also offered to practitioners as part of continuing education programs. Environment-behavior courses can be offered through departments of interior design, architecture, landscape architecture, or in some cases urban planning or urban design, and additionally they are sometimes found in psychology, sociology, anthropology, or geography. The names of such courses vary, including "Social and Behavioral Factors in Design," "Social and Psychological Issues in Environmental Design," "Environment and Behavior," "User Needs in Design," "Design-Behavior," and "Person-Environment Relations."

5. Among the key indices in architecture are the following: *Architectural Periodicals Index*, 1972-current, published quarterly; *Architecture Index*, 1950-current, published annually; *Art Index*, 1929-current, published quarterly; *Avery Index to Architectural Periodicals*, 2d ed., revised and enlarged, 1973-current, annual supplements; *Avery Obituary Index of Architects and Artists*, 1963; *Avery Obituary Index of Architects*, 2d ed., 1980; *Construction Index*, published quarterly. Additional key references include: Colvin, Howard Mantagu, *A Biographical Dictionary of English Architects, 1660-1840*, rev. ed., New York: John Murray Ltd., 1980; Morgan, Ann L., and Colin Naylor (eds.), *Contemporary Architects*, Chicago: St. James Press, 1982; Placzek, Adolf K. (ed.), *Macmillan Encyclopedia of Architects*, 1-4, New York: Free Press, 1982; Vance Bibliographies, *Architecture Series Bibliographies*, Monticello, IL: Vance Bibliographies, 1978-current; Wilkes, Joseph A., and Robert T. Packard (eds.), *Encyclopedia of Architecture: Design, Engineering & Construction*, 1-5, New York: Wiley, 1988-1990; Withey, Henry F., and Elsie Rathburn Withey, *Biographical Dictionary of American Architects (Deceased)*, Los Angeles: New Age, 1956.

6. Anthony, Kathryn H., "Behavior and Architecture," in Wilkes, Joseph A., and Robert T. Packard (eds.), *Encyclopedia of Architecture: Design, Engineering & Construction, 1*, New York: Wiley, 1988, pp. 421-438.

7. Holahan, Charles J., *Environmental Psychology*, New York: Random House, 1982; Saarinen, Thomas F., *Environmental Planning: Perception and Behavior*, Prospect Heights, IL: Waveland Press, 1984; Bell, Paul A., Jeffrey D. Fisher, Andrew Baum, and Thomas E. Greene, *Environmental Psychology*, 3d ed., Chicago: Holt, Rinehart and Winston, Inc., 1990. Downs, Roger M., and David Stea (eds.), *Image and Environment: Cognitive Mapping and Spatial Behavior*, Chicago: Aldine, 1973; Friedmann, Arnold, Craig Zimring, and Erv Zube (eds.), *Environmental Design Evaluation*, New York: Plenum, 1978; Moore, Gary T., and Reginald G. Golledge (eds.), *Environmental Knowing: Theories, Research, and Methods*, Stroudsburg, PA: Dowden, Hutchinson and Ross, 1976; Proshansky, Howard M., William H. Ittelson, and Leanne G. Rivlin (eds.), *Environmental Psychology: People and Their Physical Settings*, New York: Holt, Rinehart and Winston, 1976; Stokols, Daniel, and Irwin Altman (eds.), *Handbook of Environmental Psychology*, 1-2, New York: Wiley, 1987.

8. The environment-behavior field has literally hundreds of valuable references for designers. Here is a sampling of some of the more easily accessible works that focus on the application of user-needs research to design.

   For *interior design and furniture arrangement*, see Kron, Joan, *Home-Psych: The Social Psychology of Home and Decoration*, New York: Clarkson N. Potter, 1983; Hall, Edward T., *The Hidden Dimension*, Garden City, NY: Anchor/Doubleday, 1966; Sommer, Robert, *Personal Space: The Behavioral Basis of Design*, Englewood Cliffs, NJ: Prentice-Hall, 1969.

   For *environments for people with physical disabilities*, see Bednar, M. (ed.), *Barrier-Free Environments*, Stroudsburg, PA: Dowden, Hutchinson and Ross, 1977; Goldsmith, S., *Designing for the Disabled*, 3d ed., London: Royal Institute of British Architects (RIBA) Publications, 1976; Lifchez, Raymond, and Barbara Winslow, *Design for Independent Living: The Environment and Physically Disabled People*, New York: Whitney Library of Design, 1979.

For *housing design, general references*, see Cooper Marcus, Clare and Wendy Sarkissian with Sheena Wilson and Donald Perlgut, *Housing as if People Mattered: Site Design Guidelines for Medium-Density Family Housing*, Berkeley: University of California Press, 1986; Kira, Alexander, *The Bathroom*, New York: Bantam Books, 1976; Norcross, Carl, *Townhouses and Condominiums: Residents' Likes and Dislikes, A Special Report*, Washington, DC: Urban Land Institute, 1973; U.S. Department of Housing and Urban Development, *HUD Condominium/Cooperative Study*, 1-3, Washington, DC: U.S. Government Printing Office, 1975.

For *housing design for nontraditional households and single-parent families*, see Franck, Karen A., and Sherry Ahrentzen, *New Households, New Housing*, New York: Van Nostrand Reinhold, 1989; McCamant, Kathryn, and Charles Durrett, *Cohousing: A Contemporary Approach to Housing Ourselves*, Berkeley, CA: Habitat Press/Ten Speed Press, 1989.

For *housing design for low-income people*, see Cooper Marcus, Clare C., *Easter Hill Village*, New York: Free Press, 1975; Francescato, Guido, Sue Weidemann, James Anderson, and Richard Chenoweth, *Residents' Satisfaction in HUD-Assisted Housing: Design and Management Factors*, Washington, DC: U.S. Department of Housing and Urban Development, 1979; Newman, Oscar, *Defensible Space: Crime Prevention Through Urban Design*, New York: Macmillan, 1972.

For *housing design for the elderly*, see Carstens, Diane Y., *Site Planning and Design for the Elderly: Issues, Guidelines, and Alternatives*, New York: Van Nostrand Reinhold, 1985; Hoglund, J. David, *Housing for the Elderly: Privacy and Independence*, New York: Van Nostrand Reinhold, 1985; Lawton, Mortimer Powell, *Planning and Managing Housing for the Elderly*, New York: Wiley, 1974; Regnier, Victor, and John Pynoos, *Housing the Aged: Design Directives and Policy Considerations*, New York: Elsevier, 1987.

For *office design*, see Brill, M., with S. T. Margulis, E. Konar, and BOSTI in association with Westinghouse Furniture Systems, *Using Office Design to Increase Productivity, 1-2*, Buffalo, NY: Workplace Design and Productivity, Inc., 1984; Harris, Louis, and associates, *The Steelcase National Study of Office Environments: Do They Work?* Grand Rapids, MI: Steelcase, Inc., 1978; Wineman, Jean (ed.), *Behavioral Issues in Office Design*, New York: Van Nostrand Reinhold, 1986.

For *hospital design*, see Carpman, Jan Reizenstein, M. A. Grant, and D. A. Simmons, *Design that Cares: Planning Health Facilities for Patients and Visitors*, Chicago: American Hospital Publishing, 1986.

For *large-scale architecture and urban design*, see Appleyard, Donald, *Livable Streets*, Berkeley: University of California Press, 1981; Lynch, Kevin, *Good City Form*, Cambridge, MA: MIT Press, 1981; Lynch, Kevin, *Managing the Sense of a Region*, Cambridge, MA: MIT Press, 1976; Lynch, Kevin, *Site Planning*, 2d ed., Cambridge, MA: MIT Press, 1981; Lynch, Kevin, *What Time Is This Place?* Cambridge, MA: MIT Press, 1972.

For *plazas and urban open spaces*, see Whyte, William H., *The Social Life of Small Urban Spaces*, Washington, DC: Conservation Foundation, 1980; Whyte, William H., *City: Rediscovering the Center*, New York: Doubleday, 1988; Cooper Marcus, Clare, and Carolyn Francis (eds.), *People Places: Design Guidelines for Urban Open Space*, New York: Van Nostrand Reinhold, 1990.

9. If your library does not have all volumes of the proceedings, which began in 1969, ask your librarian to order them. *Proceedings of the Annual Conferences of the Environmental Design Research Association (EDRA)*, 1969-present, an annual publication, as well as *Design Research News*, a professional newsletter, are both available from Environmental Design Research Association, Inc., P.O. Box 24083, Oklahoma City, OK 73124.

A highly useful document is Wener, Richard, and Francoise Szigeti (eds.), *Cumulative Index to the Proceedings of the Environmental Design Research Association*, Washington, DC: EDRA, 1988. The index provides quick access to thousands of research papers and abstracts included in the first 18 volumes (1969-1987) of the *Proceedings*. Updates are forthcoming. This source provides cross-indexed listings of key works in four categories: *settings, users, topics, and modes of inquiry*. The settings include community facilities, community types, designed public settings, educational, housing, institutions, libraries, natural settings, theaters, transportation, workplaces, and zoos/museums. Among the special user groups covered are children, consumers, disabled, elderly, ethnic minorities, homeless, low income, pedestrians, refugees, single-parent families, students, Third World, women, and workers.

10. Bloom, Benjamin, *Taxonomy of Educational Objectives: Handbook I: Cognitive Domain*, New York: McKay, 1956.

11. Environment-behavior researchers would argue that under ideal conditions, a POE should be conducted over a relatively long time period, especially to allow monitoring of changes in the building or space. Funded research sponsored by federal or state agencies or by outside clients conducted through universities or the private sector sometimes does allow this. To students and design practitioners who lack the luxury of such external financial support, I suggest that even a brief POE is better than no POE at all. If you have only half a day to visit a place similar to the one you are designing, conducting a mini-POE is better than conducting none at all. A brief POE can be conducted along with other forms of structured on-site evaluation, such as site analysis.

12. Surveys are generally considered a more efficient means of collecting information than are interviews, mainly because they are less time consuming. However, one should exercise caution in administering a survey. Writing the survey questions, conducting a practice or "pilot test" to make sure the questions are appropriate and can be easily answered, and collecting and analyzing the results are art forms in themselves. Anyone who attempts to administer a survey should first consult some key references. (See note 14)

13. One of the classic examples used to illustrate this point is the following: If you were to conduct a survey and ask people how often they wash their hands after using the rest room, most people will tell you that they do so just about all the time. In fact, anyone who has spent much time in a public rest room knows that a relatively high percentage of people

leave without ever touching soap or water. This is true despite our emphasis on health and safety, signs, and other visible reminders.

14. Among the most valuable are Babbie, Earl R., *Survey Research Methods*, Belmont, CA: Wadsworth, 1975; Preiser, Wolfgang F. E., Harvey Z. Rabinowitz, and Edward T. White, *Post-Occupancy Evaluation*, New York: Van Nostrand Reinhold, 1988; Preiser, Wolfgang F. E., *Building Evaluation*, New York: Plenum, 1989; Sommer, Robert, and Barbara Sommer, *A Practical Guide for Behavioral Research: Tools and Techniques*, 2d ed., New York: Oxford University Press, 1986; Zeisel, John, *Inquiry by Design: Tools for Environment-Behavior Research*, Monterey, CA: Brooks/Cole, 1981.

15. Sommer, Robert, "Research on Utilization: Did Anyone Use It? Where Did We Lose It?", Keynote Address presented at the 21st annual conference of the Environmental Design Research Association (EDRA), Urbana, Illinois, April 1990.

16. Ibid., p. 16.

CHAPTER 6

Quick on Your Feet:

Learning the Art of Communication

"Brevity is a great charm of eloquence." —Cicero

"[Two] of the things that juries have exposed are the poor English and lack of speech command. Certainly 80% of the students lose points on how they present their own material. The world has changed enough so that most [architecture students] could not graduate from any good high school as of 1925. And I mean most.... Good drafting in your speech and good drafting on a piece of paper is the same state of mind." —Lawrence B. Perkins

WHY LEARN TO SPEAK?

Most design curricula pay little or no attention to acquiring verbal communication skills.[1] Students have repeatedly pointed out this deficiency on survey after survey, asking for help.[2] Interviews with practitioners have stressed the same point. The emphasis is almost exclusively on communicating visually. *A visual emphasis is appropriate for closed juries, museum exhibits, or published projects where the designer is not present to elaborate on the work.* But in open juries in school, just as in professional presentations in practice, your project and you are inseparable. And your visual and verbal presentations should complement each other.

Unfortunately, most design studios are structured so that you are not only allowed but also encouraged to continue working on your visual materials—drawings and models—until the very last minute.[3] As a result, the natural temptation is to complete as much as possible on the visual, ignore the verbal, and simply hope for the best

---

"Even the best ideas need to be sold. And part of selling good products is communicating what's good about them. Students need to learn that both the spoken and the written word are inevitably going to be a terribly important part of his or her communication pattern. And the design will not speak for itself. I don't think the schools spend a lot of time on the development of those skills. I don't think they even spend enough time getting the student to recognize the need for those skills.

"... It has always been my view that the faculty has a responsibility to teach, and a student has a responsibility to learn, and even if the faculty fails to teach, the student can not forego his or her responsibility to learn. Even if you're not taught how to read and write and speak properly in school, you only need to be made aware to take advantage of the opportunity to learn." —Christopher Degenhardt

"I've always thought that there should be some salesmanship [taught in school]. Somebody once said that 'If you have to be born with only one talent, sell.' Because that's what you're doing all the time... and sales is not a dirty word.... If you look at all the hero, icon landscape architects, they're all great salesmen.

"... [What makes great salesmanship?] I think supreme confidence and a bit above average ego. They feel extremely confident that what they're saying is the right way. [Much of their success] is due to not just their presentation but their salesmanship abilities." —William Callaway

"Your own skills of communication are terribly important because if you can't communicate your ideas and your concepts visually or verbally, then you're in trouble." —Joan Blutter

"My words seemed to come out with difficulty, so I tried to speak loudly and clearly to try to intimidate the audience. And it worked." —A design student

Figure 6-1 Public speaking is one of the aspects of life that people fear most. But designers who are terrorized by public presentations are often doomed to a career behind the drafting table.

when you are on center stage. My observations of student jury presentations over the years have shown this to be the typical scenario. *Few students take the time to carefully prepare their verbal presentation once they complete their design project, and it shows.*

Many people believe that the ability to speak in public is inherited and that it cannot be learned—you either have it or you don't. In fact, speaking in front of an audience, whether it be two close friends or 200 distant strangers, is a skill that can be studied, practiced, and perfected. Just as you may have learned to sail, skate, draw, or use a personal computer, you can also learn how to speak clearly and confidently before others. Equally important, you can discover how to overcome your fears and anxieties about public speaking.[4] In fact, speaking before an audience is one of the most dreaded aspects of life; many people fear it even more than death itself!

In design practice, those professionals who are able to rise to positions of management and leadership are often those who possess strong public-speaking skills, among other qualities. By contrast, individuals who are constantly plagued by stage fright and who shudder at the mere thought of presenting design work before a group are likely to be doomed to a career behind the drafting table, taking directions from others and rarely given a chance to present their own ideas. Buried behind rolls of tracing paper or glued to the screen of a computer, the shy, timid designer who is terrorized by public presentations is likely to remain there for years (Figure 6-1). The ability to promote and sell one's ideas is absolutely paramount to a successful design practice, and yet selling is rarely taught in the Ivory Academic Tower.

Gaining public-speaking skills is one of many ways to learn how to communicate effectively. *Speaking is simply one end of the continuum, while listening is the other.* As

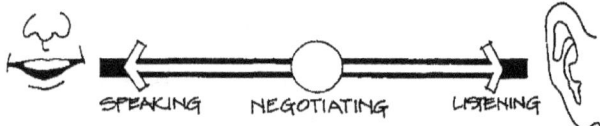

Figure 6-2 Speaking, negotiating, and listening are all part of a continuum.

you present your work before jurors, clients, or any other audience, your speaking skills are critical. When you respond to questions they present to you, your listening skills are equally critical.[5] And when you attempt to arrive at a design solution together with the input of jurors and other class members, you are actually negotiating your ideas. *Negotiating falls somewhere in the middle of this continuum* (Figure 6-2). In this chapter, we will address these three scenarios.

You may ask, Why should I bother learning how to speak in public? After all, I might be perfectly content to live behind the drafting table the rest of my life! In fact, mastering public speaking yields unintended benefits that can help you professionally in a multitude of ways. It can help boost your self-confidence and self-image, qualities that can help you land, keep, and advance in any job. It can help prevent you from becoming embroiled in embarrassing situations where you are caught off guard and proceed to fall flat on your face, wondering if in fact English is truly your native language.[6] It can help you in your professional life as you present your work to coworkers, clients, professional organizations, and even the public at large. It can even come in handy at staff meetings with colleagues and superiors, allowing you to exert a greater influence on important decisions that must be made. It can help you earn the recognition of your peers. And it can help enhance your ability to communicate with colleagues, family, and friends.

BECOME AN EFFECTIVE SPEAKER

So, how can you become a good speaker? *Take the time to practice. The more you keep at it, the better you will become—once you have learned some basic skills.* Practicing does not simply mean the routine method of trial and error, however. In fact, throughout their design studies, students have plenty of opportunities to practice speaking in front of juries. But most continue trying and continue making errors, simply because they have never learned how to communicate effectively in the first place. The habits acquired at the very first jury as a freshman are often seen at the jury of the master's thesis student.

A wealth of information on public speaking is available if you only take the time to look for it. Invest in a few books on the subject and you will soon see that they will pay off many times over.[7] In cultivating public-speaking skills, you can often be your own best critic. Based on the criteria described in the following pages, you can learn how to

> "Students are . . . not always learning the basics. . . . They get out of school unprepared because they haven't been strong in English and classics and math. Instead, they put all their eggs in the basket of design. . . .
>
> ". . . The expression of oneself to a client or potential client is [extremely important]. If you haven't learned that, then all the creativity in the world does no good because you have to be able to sell your work. Therefore you need marketing, you need speech, you need theater, and you need psychology to know how to relate that which you are dreaming up to an application that potential clients can accept comfortably and so that they will transfer their time, energy, and money to you. . . .
>
> ". . . Do you know why I'm able to articulate my ideas? It's not because of my design projects, but because of my speech and theater training. When I got to the University I was able to take speech classes which were a way of presenting myself to the world in a proper manner. You learn debate. You learn opening presentation. You learn how to limit your subject. I think if nothing else, limiting one's subject is the most important factor in life to learn."—Larry N. Deutsch
>
> "As a student, I dreaded formal juries just like most students. It's like going in front of judge and jury. I think that there are two reasons why students become fearful. The first is the natural fear of getting up in front of people. The second is the actual explanation of the work and its possible rejection. I think that getting over fear of speaking in public is one of students' greatest difficulties. You don't get any training whatsoever in school on this topic. It's not part of the design curriculum because the curriculum is already overcrowded. The absence of any training in how to present and communicate your design ideas is one of education's single greatest deficiencies.
>
> ". . . Students really need to be prepared for design juries, and particularly for presenting their work orally. That will help take the edge off the fear. They should understand that showmanship is part of salesmanship. They need to build their self confidence and focus on what they should be: not the fact that they're perspiring under the lights, but that they're talking about a wonderful idea.
>
> ". . . Generally speaking in the design world, you have to be able to sell. My explanation of why there is so much bad work is because there are so many people who can sell well. [A successful practice may] have nothing to do with design skill whatsoever."—Ronette J. King
>
> "Students have to present their ideas and intentions. It is not all in the drawings. They have to complete it with words, and this is very good preparation for real professional life.
>
> ". . . That's exactly what I do every week; I have to present my projects to my clients and to many different groups—boards, advisors, trustees. You have to lead clients with your words into your thoughts and intentions. You have to help them see what is not readily apparent in your drawings or models."—Cesar Pelli
>
> "Personally, I've only had the time to rehearse two or three times in my "jury career," but those were my best presentations, and I knew it."—A design student

benefit from your prior jury experiences and leave your days of trial and error behind you. Here are some tips culled from the public-speaking and communications literature that should prove helpful at presentations to juries, clients, and other audiences.

Prepare in Advance

In order to effectively prepare for oral jury presentation, you must have completed most of your design work. Ideally, you should allow a few days before the presentation to prepare what you plan to say.[8] Few students have this luxury, but those who take even a few hours to carefully prepare and rehearse their presentation are more likely to radiate confidence and enthusiasm about their work. Compared to the rest of the class, they place themselves at a distinct advantage before the jury.

Understand your audience. Consider how much the jurors, clients, and other members of the audience already know or do not know about your project. Try not to speak either above or below their level of knowledge. Anticipate how your own presentation fits in with those of others in the class. If someone else has already given a detailed description of the program assignment, you have no need to repeat this information in your own presentation (Figure 6-3).

Consider exactly who your audience is when you select the words you will say. Suppose, for instance, you have some clients or users on the jury in addition to your design faculty and visiting critics. Not being trained in design, these individuals may not understand everything

> "It's amazing in real life presentations how few times clients really respond to your presentation. Basically they just absorb it for awhile. They really study it before they come back with an opinion."—Jeffrey Werner

Figure 6-3 Understanding your audience is one of the most important keys to a successful presentation.

you say. In these cases, be sure to keep your words simple and *avoid jargon.* When you begin discussing apertures, building envelopes, and building skins, they may be thinking about cameras, stamps, and legs. Before you start to say, "The penetration of the fenestration on the building skin is compatible with the contextual framework of its neighboring structures," translate this into plain language: "The windows on my building resemble those of its neighbors."

Find out how much time you will have to present and plan accordingly. Most jury presentations are of necessity quite brief, about 5 to 10 minutes, depending on the level of study and the number of students in the class; client presentations are more lengthy. In either case, ask whoever is in charge exactly how much time you can count on and prepare your talk to fit within this time limit — and preferably less. Whenever you practice, be sure to have a watch or clock in front of you.

Write a draft of what you plan to say. Then rewrite it again and again. For a short 20-minute speech, experienced speech writers often spend a minimum of about one and a half to two days at 10 hours each; for most designers, this is unrealistic. Nevertheless, writing a short presentation is much more challenging than preparing a long one. Your first version can always be improved. Devote yourself solely to the task of writing your presentation for several hours. Show it to a friend for critique and comment. Rewrite it. Repeat this process as many times as possible.

Start with a simple outline that features a beginning, a middle, and an end. Regard your presentation as a story-telling experience. Think about the order in which you state your points and what logically should come first or last. Make sure that your beginning, middle, and end sections each say something distinct and important. The ending is probably the most important part of any speech, so be sure to rewrite it more than any other part of your presentation.

Write for the spoken, not the written word. Too many students believe that once they write something down, they must suddenly start sounding like Shakespeare. Trying too hard to sound sophisticated in a speech can backfire, since you are less comfortable with what you are saying. Instead of saying, "This designer is presenting you with the following ideas," clearly state, *"What I will try to show you in the next few minutes is... "; "The basic assumptions behind my design project are..."; "Here are the goals I believe to be most important in creating a successful solution to this problem."*

Carefully plan out what points you want to emphasize. Think of what you want the audience to remember most about your presentation. Be sure that these points stand out in your presentation.

Be as specific as possible in anything you say. Avoid generalities. Rather than say, "I was trying to create a welcoming feel in this space," clearly define what you mean by the word "welcoming" and what criteria you are using to establish whether or not a space is in fact welcoming to the people who will use it. Specificity and precision will help make a more persuasive argument for your design ideas.

Experiment with different ways of delivering your speech. Seasoned speech writers often caution against reading your presentation, lest you sound too artificial and robotlike. Instead, many suggest writing out the opening and closing statements, any key transitional phrases, and key quotes or important information that you cannot easily recall, and simply filling in the rest. If this works for you, proceed accordingly. It is probably one of the most effective ways of delivering a speech. However, if you fear that your nerves will get the best of you and that you may even forget your name, much less all the ideas behind your design project, then go ahead and read your presentation. If you choose to read, however, be sure to maintain strong eye contact with the audience and have a firm grasp on your notes (Figure 6-4).

Watch and learn from experienced, entertaining speakers. Reflect on some of the best speeches you have ever heard. Why were they so extraordinary? What lessons can you apply to your own experience? Next time a speaker is on campus, watch her speaking style and method of delivery. See how others rely only occasionally on notes, spending most of their time looking at the audience. You'll be surprised how much you can learn from them.

Study how other visually oriented professionals present their work. For example, the weather forecaster on the television news strongly depends on visuals and uses them effectively to convey information. She refers frequently to the visuals but maintains strong eye contact with the audience. Typically the weather features a "story within a story," moving from general to specific. It has a beginning, a middle, and an end.

Experiment with different ways of preparing notes. You may remember preparing speeches back in high school using the infamous 3″ × 5″ cards. Many experienced speech writers still swear by them today, citing flexibility and increased audience eye contact among their chief

Figure 6-4 Experiment with different ways of delivering your speech. If you choose to read from notes, be sure to maintain strong eye contact with the audience.

virtues. Others vow never to use them again, having witnessed too many presentations turn into absolute disasters when a nervous speaker loses a grip on the cards and instantly scatters them all over the floor. If you choose to use cards, by all means number them so that if disaster does strike at least the damage will be short-lived. (The same rule applies to the use of color slides or photographs.) Or else consider simply stapling the cards together. And do not split one thought or sentence between two cards. This makes for an awkward delivery. Instead, devote some time to the graphic layout of your cards so that you can read them with ease.

Standard 8½" × 11" paper may suffice, provided you use large type so that you can easily read your notes without squinting. To avoid the problem of your sheets flying in the wind, staple all the pages together, place them in a clipboard, or mount each page on a board for easy handling. If the type is large enough to be seen from a distance, you can even add each board to your display once you have finished speaking about it. Or use your sketchbook to record your presentation notes, and later on, add the jurors' comments (Figure 6-5).

Practice your presentation before a mirror, a tape recorder, a videocassette recorder, or another person and critique your performance (Figure 6-6). See yourself as an actor in the speech-making process. Get your points across. Understand how you are projecting and coming across to others. Only you can be the best judge of this. Rehearse your presentation exactly as you plan to say it before the jury, then rewind and play back. This can be a truly eye-opening experience. Critique yourself alone or with a friend and repeat it until you get it just right.[9]

Stage a "dress rehearsal." Actors not only rehearse ahead of time, but they also rehearse in their actual costumes. This technique can work for you, too. Wear your jury "costume" whenever you stage your practice session. As a result, you will feel more comfortable in your presentation garb at the jury, thus allowing you to better concentrate on substance over style.

Zero in on a Few Key Points and Order Them Carefully

Clearly define your goals for this project: What exactly are you trying to accomplish? What are the most important issues you are trying to address? Narrow these down to a total of about three to five and list them on paper. In simple

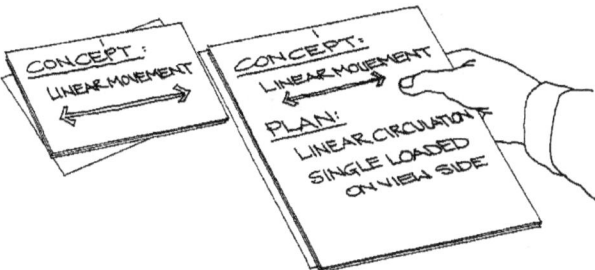

Figure 6-5 Use large type for whatever you read from so that you can see your notes easily.

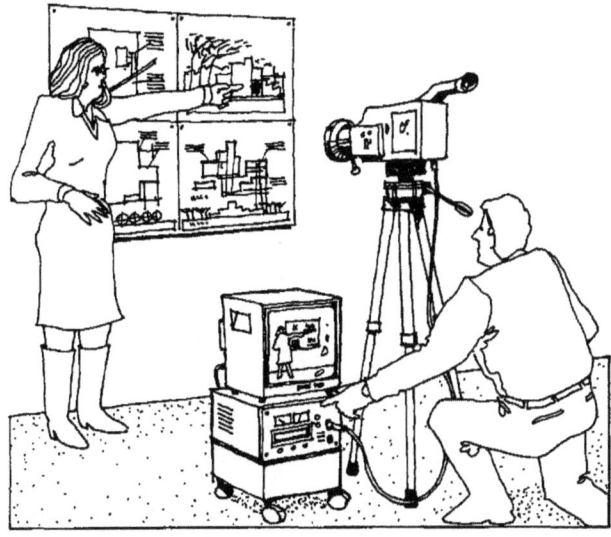

Figure 6-6 Practice your presentation before a mirror, tape recorder, video, or another person and then critique your own performance.

terms, keep in mind the following: *Issues are part of the problem, while goals are part of the solution.* Ideally you should have been pondering over these goals throughout the duration of your project, and not inventing them at the last minute.

One way to help pinpoint these goals is to ask yourself the following questions: *If I can say only a few sentences about this project to try to sell it to a client, what would I say? What is so special about my design? Why should a client be sold on this particular solution to the problem, instead of some other solution?* The trick is to focus your presentation on only a few key points.

Identify specific ways in which you have achieved your goals through your design. For each goal, survey your project carefully and identify exactly where and how you have addressed it. Write this down as well alongside each goal statement. Figure 6-7 shows an example.

Order these goals from most to least important. This is not always easy to do, but it will help strengthen your presentation. Begin with a brief overview of what these goals are all about (simply reading off your list is sufficient),

GOAL	HOW GOAL IS ACHIEVED
One of my goals is to create a strong sense of privacy for each resident.	The goal of privacy is achieved by: 1) providing private entrances to each residence from the street. Even those units that enter on the third floor have a private entrance that can be accessed from the street via an outdoor stairway shared by only two units. 2) providing each unit with private outdoor space, either in the form of a patio or balcony. I made a special effort to study sight lines from these private outdoor spaces, and as a result, designed them in such a way that if you are sitting outside your home, you can not be seen by any of your neighbors. 3) designing each unit to be two stories in height, so that for those units at street level, a minimum area of ceiling space abuts the floor of the unit above it, thus reducing the sense of noise from above. Noise from within your own unit is much easier to tolerate than noise from another apartment. Those units with entrances on the third floor have no one above them, thus ensuring even greater privacy.

Figure 6-7 Present your project to the jury or clients in terms of the goals you have set out to achieve. First state the goal and then show through your drawings and models how that goal has been achieved.

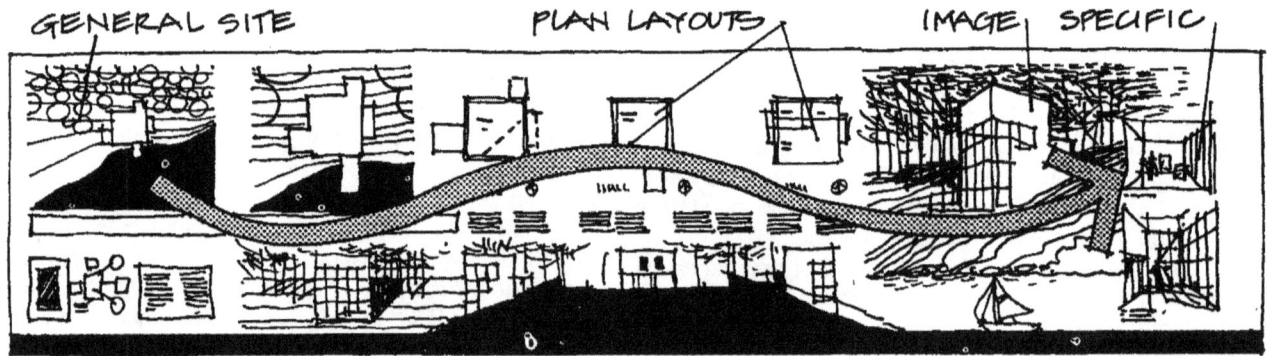

Figure 6-8 Present your work sequentially.

and then discuss each goal and how it has been achieved in greater detail. Show specifically how each issue has been resolved in your drawings and models.

Plan what you present and when. Most students pin up all their boards and place their model before the jury all at once, making it difficult for the audience to quickly absorb everything in front of them. Once you begin to talk, their eyes start wandering all over the place trying to understand what you are showing. Often jurors will jump out of their seats to take a closer look at your boards and model, making it difficult both for you to speak and for them to listen.

To avoid this, one useful strategy is to *present your work sequentially* (Figure 6-8). Simply begin with those

Figure 6-9 Presenting your boards one at a time forces the jurors and the audience to concentrate on only a few points at once, hence minimizing distractions.

> "One thing I learned from a major advertising firm is to start a presentation with a goal board stating what it is you're trying to do. Hold it up and go over it, showing what you're trying to do, and then go on to the next drawing showing how you achieved that goal. Show and explain each board one at a time so your audience doesn't get confused....
>
> "Take, for example, one of our current projects on Lake Shore Drive: a luxury apartment building. Our goal board highlight(s) exclusivity and convenience in function. Then we go into greater detail about how we achieved these goals: easy auto access, plenty of parking for guests, a car wash, errand service, grocery service, and so on. To support these details are the luxury characteristics of the architectural materials and other design elements. And these are ideas that we just keep working over with our client. They're not fixed. Together we add and subtract but we can always go back to this as a base."—Laurence Booth

boards that best tie in to the beginning of your verbal presentation, and then add the others as you progress through your speech (Figure 6-9). Logistically, you'll need at least two people to help you set up while you are speaking. They must know exactly what you are doing and when (i.e., you must rehearse with them ahead of time). This technique forces the jurors and the rest of the audience to concentrate on only a few items at one time. They are less likely to be distracted or jump way ahead of your oral presentation. You and they can proceed together at the same pace. Chicago architect Laurence Booth routinely uses this technique when presenting his work to clients.

For a Dramatic Delivery

Emphasize key points. Stress whatever is most important by changing your tone of voice, pausing, speaking more loudly, slowing down, or repeating what you have just said. Use your body for emphasis by leaning forward, using your hands, or pointing out specific parts of your graphic presentation.

Connect with your audience. To the extent possible, act as if you are having a one-on-one conversation with each member of the audience. Begin by talking to one person who appears visually responsive—that is, is looking right at you, perhaps nods or smiles on occasion, and appears interested in what you are saying. Once you establish rapport with that person, then try the same technique with someone else. If you end up focusing in on someone who looks uninterested, bored, or even hostile, overlook this person and move on to someone else.

Highlight whatever strengths your voice may have. All pitches and timbres are acceptable, and don't try to remake yourself into someone you are not. However, by listening to yourself on tape you can discover those pitches and tones where you sound your best. If you are able to do this, try to accentuate these sounds in your speech.

Listen carefully to how you deliver every sentence. Are you raising your voice at the end of each sentence, even if you're not asking a question? Speech researchers have found that women, especially, have a tendency to do so. Such speech patterns can result in our sounding uncertain and less likely to be taken seriously.

Coordinate your modes of communication as much as possible. Your body, face, eyes, hands, and voice should all act in concert with each other. If you have access to a video camera, practice your presentation and observe whether or not all your components are in sync with each other. If your voice exudes confidence, but your hands are nervously twitching about, your modes of communication are not in harmony. Send consistent messages (Figure 6-10).

Avoid Strategic Errors

Don't begin by apologizing. I have heard these excuses countless times in jury presentations: "I'm sorry this is not finished but..."; "You probably can't read this but..."; "I know you've already seen ten projects just like this but..."; "I know you must all be tired by now but...." Catch yourself before you fall into this trap. Such declarations

72 Quick on Your Feet: Learning the Art of Communication

Figure 6-10 Coordinate your modes of communication as much as possible.

merely tend to discredit the rest of what you have to say, and the jury tends to run rapidly downhill.

Don't dress like you are just getting out of—or into—bed. Just as your project conveys information, your clothing conveys messages to the jury as well. At times it can be distracting, taking the focus off the project and onto you, personally. I have seen design students present their work in almost any outfit imaginable short of a bathing suit (Figure 6-11). From the jurors' point of view, some of the most distracting outfits on both men and women are jeans with holes in strategic locations.

Some women students seem to purposely dress in a provocative or seductive manner at juries, with extremely low-cut shirts and very form-fitting outfits. In today's era, when women must still work especially hard to be taken seriously as professionals, appearing as a sex symbol before the jury will not help you or other women designers in the long run; to the contrary, it only helps continue the sexist stereotypes of the past.[10] *Dress to complement your work, not to draw attention away from it.* Some students would find it especially easy to improve their jury attire if they only took the time to look at themselves in the mirror, preferably a full-length one.

Although dress may seem like a trivial issue that should not play any role in how your design work is

Figure 6-11 Your attire sends all sorts of messages to the audience.

evaluated, it sends signals to the jurors about how you perceive yourself. If you arrive at the jury wearing a wrinkled shirt full of ink stains, half of it neatly tucked in and the other half conspicuously dangling out the sides, and attempt to present work that appears to be finished, complete, and professional, you are sending out inconsistent messages. Some members of the jury may not take you seriously.[11]

So how should you dress before the jury? There simply is no one right answer. At some schools, juries are highly formal occasions where students take their one and only suit out of the mothballs, only to don it for a few hours and then return it to the closet where it will hibernate for another several months. At others, they are more informal events. My suggestion is that you not make too much of what you wear, but that you *simply dress in clothes that are neat, comfortable, and make you feel like you look your best—whatever that may be.*

Don't let nervous nonverbal behavior get the best of you. Fidgeting, rotating from foot to foot, jiggling keys in your pockets, scratching your head, covering up your mouth with your hands, nervously running your fingers through your hair—all these nervous habits distract the audience from what you have to say. What with some of the latest trendy hairstyles, I have recently seen many students with overgrown bangs routinely flick their head backwards during a jury presentation, simply to "clear the screen." Such routines lessen your credibility before the jury. The simplest way to avoid such patterns is to be aware of them and nip them in the bud. Practicing your presentation before a mirror or before another person will help prevent you from falling into this trap at the jury. Have a friend watch especially for this kind of nervous behavior during your actual jury presentation.

Don't speak only to your drawings and models. Although you may feel most comfortable facing your own work rather than those who are evaluating it, failing to establish eye contact with either the jury or the rest of the class weakens your presentation. Face your audience and maintain consistent eye contact. Staring longingly at your own work prevents you from being seen and heard by others.

Don't speak softly. This is a surefire way to bore not only the jurors, but the rest of the class as well. If the jurors right in front of you can't even hear you, how can you expect the students in the back of the room to understand what you are saying? In a trial run, practice speaking loudly enough to be heard. Have a friend stand in the back of the room and see if she can hear you. If not, speak up.

Don't speak too quickly. Most students have a tendency to speak too quickly, causing much of what they say to go in one ear and out the other. Slow down and take your time so that others can understand you.

Don't speak too casually. Too often students sound as if they are having a casual conversation with their studio-mates when they present their work before a jury. Their language and diction are sometimes extremely weak, punctuated by countless *you knows, I means, likes, and stuffs,* and so on. Unfortunately these may be the common expressions of the day, but when they are inserted into the jury presentation ad nauseam, they overwhelm whatever else you say. I once counted over 27 *you knows* during one minute of a student's jury presentation. Practicing with a tape recorder is one of the best remedies for this problem.

Don't use sexist language. You would be surprised just how many times I hear students consistently referring to the architect and the client as a male. Both men and women students are almost equally likely to make this error. To make matters worse, the typically all-male jury rarely calls attention to this pattern. Students often lapse into sexist stereotypes such as: "Here is where the secretary sits. She can easily see into the boss's office. The boss's office has a panoramic view of the entire open-plan office below him." Secretaries, teachers, librarians, nurses, and assistants are among the roles that design students most commonly stereotype (Figure 6-12). Such sweeping

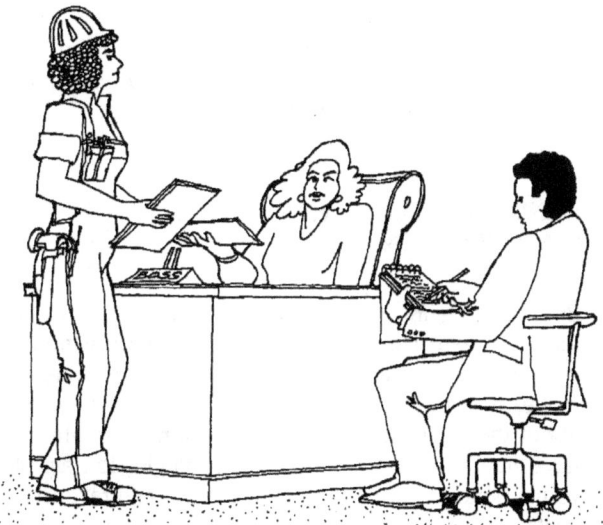

Figure 6-12 Avoid sexist stereotypes of secretaries, teachers, librarians, nurses, assistants, contractors, clients, and others.

generalizations only tend to irritate female jurors. Furthermore, they promote the notion among your classmates that not only the design but also the business world is still dominated by males. The way to avoid this is to use the more cumbersome *he or she,* or simply to speak in the plural whenever possible so that you simply refer to *them* or *they.* Another option is to alternatively refer to these roles as either a *he* or a *she,* as is the case throughout this book, suggesting that any role could be occupied by either a man or a woman.

Don't give the janitor's tour of the project. All too often, students use up valuable presentation time simply by taking the jurors through the project piece by piece. Not only can this prove to be incredibly boring, but if your drawings are clear enough, it is simply redundant. Catch yourself whenever you begin to do the following: "As you enter the building, you find..."; "On the right is..."; "On the left is..."; "Going up to the next floor is a...."

Don't ramble and try to fill up time. If you have nothing left to say, simply conclude your presentation. Don't speak aimlessly and in no direction at all. Remember that *in general, the shorter your presentation, the more effective you will be.*[12]

Don't keep talking after your time is up. This common practice can be quite irritating not only to the studio critic or moderator, who is trying to keep to a schedule, but also to jurors and other students who may have outside commitments immediately after the jury. Stick to your time limits.

Don't conclude by simply fading out. Too many students end their jury presentation just the way some would end a piece of popular music: They simply fade away. Some typically weak endings to a jury presentation include:

"Well, I guess that's it"; "I suppose that's all I have to say"; "I guess that about wraps it up." If you're only guessing, you are not sounding very confident about your project. Prepare an ending in advance and stick to it.

HANDLE QUESTIONS EFFECTIVELY: LEARN TO LISTEN

By preparing in advance and using some of the techniques already suggested, you may have surprisingly little trouble handling the jurors' questions. Nonetheless, no matter how much you prepare, you may still be anxious about the question-and-answer session, over which you have little control. Here are a few strategies to help place you in better command of this situation and respond in a professional manner.

Anticipate the jury's or client's questions and prepare some responses. While you are composing your presentation, ask yourself the following: *What are the five toughest questions someone could ask?* List them all and prepare your responses accordingly. Have a friend ask you these questions and critique your responses. Ask your friend to come up with some additional questions you may not have considered. Prepare some more answers and ask your friend to provide some helpful criticism.

Anticipate interruptions and prepare accordingly. All too often, jurors cut students off mid-sentence, and from then on, the jury seems to go straight downhill.[13] Those students who are least prepared, rambling or scrambling for words, are most likely to be interrupted. To prepare for this, plan ahead of time how you will respond if interrupted.

"You can always tell [the student] who really didn't do his homework, i.e. just kind of slapped something together.... Students who will verbally defend their project from any kind of criticism will defend it just by things they just made up just that minute. I think they should be taught that that's not the way to get the most out of a juror. The juror needs to be a good listener, and the student needs to be a good listener.

"... If somebody says something bad about [your project] and you instinctively feel it's right, you should press that juror for more information, not defend it to death." —William Callaway

"What helped me most in getting through design school was the encouragement of teachers and my own ability to adapt and be flexible. I don't believe that when you're in school you should be too rigid. I think I've always had [that] ability [and] I think that's always helped me very much. I'm still [very much] a student." —Joan Blutter

---

if possible, have your class ask your studio critic to inform the jurors that all students' presentations will be within a certain time limit and kindly ask jurors not to interrupt. This takes the burden off you. Or politely remind the jury: "I'd appreciate it if you could hold all questions until I have completed my brief presentation." "My presentation will be exactly five minutes. Afterwards, I will be happy to answer your questions." If you feel this type of statement distracts from the rest of your presentation, prepare a small sign to this effect that you can hold up before you begin to speak.

If all else fails and you are interrupted midstream, well within your time limit, then say: "Excuse me, but could you please wait until I have finished my presentation?" "Pardon me. In a few minutes I'll be pleased to answer your question, but right now I'd like to continue." "If I may...." Raise your voice slightly and continue, and don't let this brief episode throw you off.

Bring a tape recorder with you to the jury. Record your presentation, the jurors' comments, and those of the class. Play it back after the jury is over and you will be amazed at how much you can learn. When the tension of the moment is behind you, you can more easily retain and absorb their responses.

Listen carefully to the reactions of the audience, be it the jurors, your studio critic, or other members of the class. After someone has made a comment about your project, take a minute to simply rephrase what was just said in your own words, and check to make sure you understood them correctly. For example, "If I understand you correctly, you are suggesting that some of the spaces in my building are too dark. Is that correct?" Or "It sounds as if you believe this solution does not fit appropriately into the surrounding context. Is that the case?" "Let me see if I grasp your point. Here's how I interpret it...." "Are you saying that...?" If you truly do not understand or are ambiguous about something that has just been said, ask the juror to repeat a point. Don't worry about appearing stupid. To the contrary, asking for clarification lets jurors know that they have been heard (Figure 6-13).

Rather than simply continuing to extol the virtues of your project, something you should have already taken care of in your presentation, shift the discussion to a tone that is more constructive: "How would you suggest I remedy this problem?" "How would you suggest I allow more natural light into the building?" "What specifically could help this project tie in better with the surrounding buildings?" Instead of limiting the discussion to you and one particular juror, open the issue up to the other jurors and to the rest of the class. "Perhaps the rest of you have some ideas as to how this project can be improved. What might you all suggest?" As you ask this question, look to your left, right, and across the room to encourage more discussion rather than dialogue. Be open to the responses you receive. Note them down and consider them carefully after your presentation is over.

Figure 6-13 Listen carefully to the reactions of the audience. Check to make sure you have understood them correctly.

> "One of my students took graphic notes for himself, drawing overlays of his project during the reviews. While faculty offered advice, he sketched a response to this advice on tracing paper. The review was a working session for this student. He could ask, 'You mean, the entry could be something like this?' The faculty could return with, 'Yes, only try to open the space more to the vista you said was so important to you.' I found this student's technique to be most effective for using the final review as a learning experience, as well as an evaluative encounter."—Professor Robert Selby, University of Illinois at Urbana-Champaign

If someone asks you a question that you can't answer, don't be afraid to say, "I don't know." If the point raised is one that truly merits further exploration, you might add, "I don't know, but I will be sure to look into it." Or "I can't answer that right now, but I'll have an answer for you the next time we meet." It is far better to admit your deficiencies than to try to invent some wild idea at the last minute. By anticipating questions in advance, however, you minimize the chances that you will be stumped.

Don't be preoccupied with defending your work. The nature of the traditional academic jury encourages students to actively defend their designs. After all, it's really just a game of survival of the fittest—isn't it? But as so many practitioners have attested, this highly artificial system of attack and defense in school actually bears little resemblance to the interactions between designers and their clients. If it did, most designers would probably drive their clients straight out the door. The system currently in place—and the gladiator-like atmosphere that prevails—can be a major obstacle to a successful practice later in life.

How can you avoid getting caught up in this ironic twist? *The key is to view the question-and-answer session as an opportunity to better understand, rather than argue*

> "I think that students shouldn't be defensive at juries if faculty aren't on the attack. There isn't any need to be defensive. The main thing is to get something out of the jury."—Joseph Esherick
>
> "Listen carefully to first criticisms of your work. Note just what it is about your work that critics don't like—then cultivate it. That's the part of your work that's individual and worth keeping."—Jean Cocteau[14]

with, each other. See your interaction with the jury as an opportunity to understand and negotiate rather than simply to advocate your ideas at all costs.

LEARN HOW TO NEGOTIATE

What is negotiating? It is simply an effective way for people to deal with their differences. One of its major goals is to come up with something better than the results you could obtain without negotiating at all. "It is back-and-forth communication designed to reach an agreement when you and the other side have some interests that are shared and others that are opposed."[15]

Negotiating cannot be learned overnight; in fact it is a highly complex process. Negotiating skills may come more naturally to some people than to others, and for some it can even take years to master. Mastering these skills can help you both at the jury and in the office when you deal with clients and coworkers. This section represents only the tip of the iceberg. As is the case for time management, stress, and other topics addressed in this book, a wide variety of materials on this subject are available in any library or bookstore.[16] Next time you have a chance, skim through some of these sources and pick up whatever appears most useful to you.

One of the most effective ways to negotiate on a jury is to build up a working relationship with the jurors *ahead of time*, that is, before the jury itself. Ditto for clients and coworkers. The way you deal with someone you know, even if you don't know that person well, is quite different from how you respond to a total stranger.[17] It is more appropriate that the class as a whole, rather than you as an individual, meets the jurors in advance. This preventive approach can help you avoid many of the problems that commonly plague negotiators.

Separate the People from the Problem

Realize that your aim is not simply to deal with "the other side" in the abstract, but instead to deal with real human beings: the jurors and your classmates, or your clients and your coworkers. Your aim is to *establish a working relationship* so that you can be sensitive to other people's points of view, and vice versa. The purpose of the jury or

> "In professional practice, I believe it is important for young designers to understand that clients are human beings, and they've got to learn how to deal with clients. That is one of the most important aspects of my work. The only reason we can produce good architecture is because clients are willing to come along with us. The nurturing and handling of clients is the most important thing we do, and I spend a lot of time at it. It's the most time-consuming part of my work, and nobody tells you about it in school. Human relations, I think, are the most important factors that affect architectural practice."—Peter Eisenman

client presentation is not to score points and decide who wins or loses. For an interim jury or presentation to a client, the purpose should be to collectively arrive at a project that is greater than the sum of its parts—where your own ideas, coupled with those of others, work in concert to improve your design. *Picture yourself working side by side with the jury in order to attack the problem rather than each other.*

Realize that by understanding the roles of perceptions, emotions, and communication, you will help separate the people from the problem and become much more effective as a negotiator. Try to *avoid misunderstandings* whenever possible, but realize that misinterpretation is a common problem in almost any type of communication. One of the key points to remember is that no matter what you say or think, how others hear and perceive you can be entirely different (Figures 6-14 and 6-15).

Difficult though it may be, try to *place yourself in the juror's or client's shoes.* See if you can experience what she is going through as well, and if you can understand her viewpoint. *Remember that understanding someone else's viewpoint is not the same as agreeing with that person.* But it is often only through mutual understanding that you are able to reach a mutually agreeable solution.

Unfortunately, as this research has revealed, it is not uncommon for students to watch a juror explode in an emotional outburst.[18] Being on the receiving end of such an explosion can be extremely taxing. In these cases, one of the most effective negotiating techniques you can use is to simply *listen quietly without responding to any attacks. Then ask the juror to continue until the last word is spoken, leaving little steam leftover to vent later on.*

By contrast, if you believe you have been treated unfairly and feel that your own emotions are about to get the best of you, refrain from venting off your own steam. Instead of yelling and screaming or bursting into tears, simply *take a deep breath and exhale while counting to 10;* focus on exhaling as it will especially help calm you down. If you feel tears beginning to form, focus your eyes somewhere up high; this can slow down and sometimes stop the tearing process altogether. Then ask yourself: "Is there any merit of truth in what I just heard? From the other person's point of view, can I possibly see how they might say this to me?" If the answer is yes, then simply accept the criticism with no comment. Or say something like: "I think you do have a point here. I'll think that over carefully after the jury is over." However, if the answer to these questions is really no, then go ahead and simply state, slowly and calmly, something like the following: "I'm sorry, but I believe that on this particular point, my project is being viewed unfairly." Or: "Excuse me, but I believe that I will have to take issue with the point you just made. In fact, what I was trying to show was...." "It sounds as if you may be misinterpreting what I was trying to say. Let me more

STUDENT'S PERCEPTIONS

I have been up for three days straight slaving away on this project. This jury had better appreciate what I've been through.

I'm so nervous I don't know if I can even go through with this.

These 10 minutes in front of the jury are the most important minutes of the entire academic term.

JUROR'S PERCEPTIONS

This person looks like a wreck. His hair looks like it's been painted on and his clothes look like he's been living in them for days. It's a good thing his parents aren't here to see him!

He's had three entire months to work on this crazy project, but he looks scared stiff. What can he possibly be so nervous about?

Can I possibly last through another ten minutes? I am getting awfully uncomfortable in this dreadful chair, plus I am dying for a snack. I hope this guy talks fast.

Figure 6-14 The perceptions of students and jurors at the jury are often vastly different. Both should consider the other's vantage point.

DESIGNER'S PERCEPTIONS

This project is one of my most creative efforts to date. If I'm lucky, maybe it can win a design award or be published in one of the leading professional journals.

I'm giving this client the best possible price I can come up with for this project. She better not turn me down. Our office is slow these days and we really need the business.

CLIENT'S PERCEPTIONS

These ideas look too far out for me. And how come just about everything we discussed last time--our list of requirements and preferences--has been ignored?

This price is an absolute rip-off! No way will I pay anything near that. Why, I've always heard that designers are supposed to be one of the least expensive professions around! And besides, they hardly need my business. This office is such a mess, they must have work coming out their ears!

Figure 6-15 Designers and clients look upon design work from different perspectives.

clearly explain what I meant to say. . . ." In any case, keep in mind that standing up for your ideas and asserting yourself is not the same as defending your ideas at all costs. This distinction is key.

Focus on Interests Rather than Positions

An *interest* is what motivates you to take a particular position, that is, the motivating force behind why you believe or feel the way you do (Figure 6-16). The *position* you have usually been trained to assume at the jury is to both present and defend your design ideas. (Never mind the fact that you are rarely explicitly told just how to do this!) But your true interests are not to defend your ideas, but to learn more about designing and presenting your work and to do well in school, to earn a grade in the course that most closely reflects the results of your efforts, and to take one more step toward graduation. Among the jury's interests are to fulfill their teaching and evaluating duties and contribute their knowledge and expertise to an academic program. Education is an interest that both you and the jury share. By learning how you can improve upon your project, and what you have done well, you and the jury are working together to enable you to contribute to the field. Ultimately, the profession will be better off because of it!

In the world of practice, your interests include producing high-quality design work, establishing your professional reputation by gaining recognition from your peers, satisfying your clients and the users they represent, promoting and maintaining favorable business relationships, making money, and keeping work flowing into and out of the office. A client's primary interests are likely to concentrate on ensuring that the design project is completed in a timely and economical fashion, that her own needs and those of the people who use the space are satisfied, and reassuring herself that she has selected the right design firm. *Openly acknowledging these interests can help lead to more fruitful negotiations* between designers and their clients.

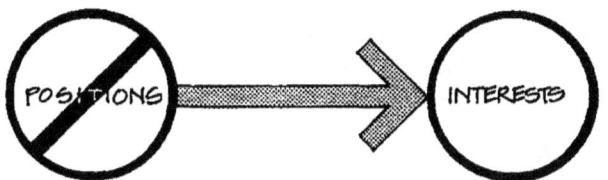

Figure 6-16 Both jurors and students must focus on interests, not positions. The same is true for designers and their clients as well.

One way to symbolically focus on interests rather than positions is simply to *avoid the attack-defense setup* in the first place where designers and jurors or clients are face to face, and where students stand and the jurors or clients sit. Instead, sitting together side by side can help reduce the inevitable feelings of conflict and lead to a more cooperative process.[19] Similar physical arrangements for professional presentations can also help promote better negotiations.

Produce Many Possibilities

You don't have to immediately respond to or act on any of the suggestions delivered at the jury. Instead, take the time to consider them at your leisure, once you have distanced yourself from the episode. With time on your side, you can produce design ideas that advance the interests you and the jurors share.

See the jury as an opportunity to come up with as many different options as possible, not as a fixed pie where the more you gain, the more jurors or other students lose. Negotiating is not a zero-sum game. Fixating on this simplistic view of juries can only lead to serious damage in the working world.

One way of generating many design possibilities at the jury or professional presentation is to rely on what expert negotiators call a circle chart.[20] This involves a four-step process shuttling back and forth between the specific and the general (Figure 6-17).

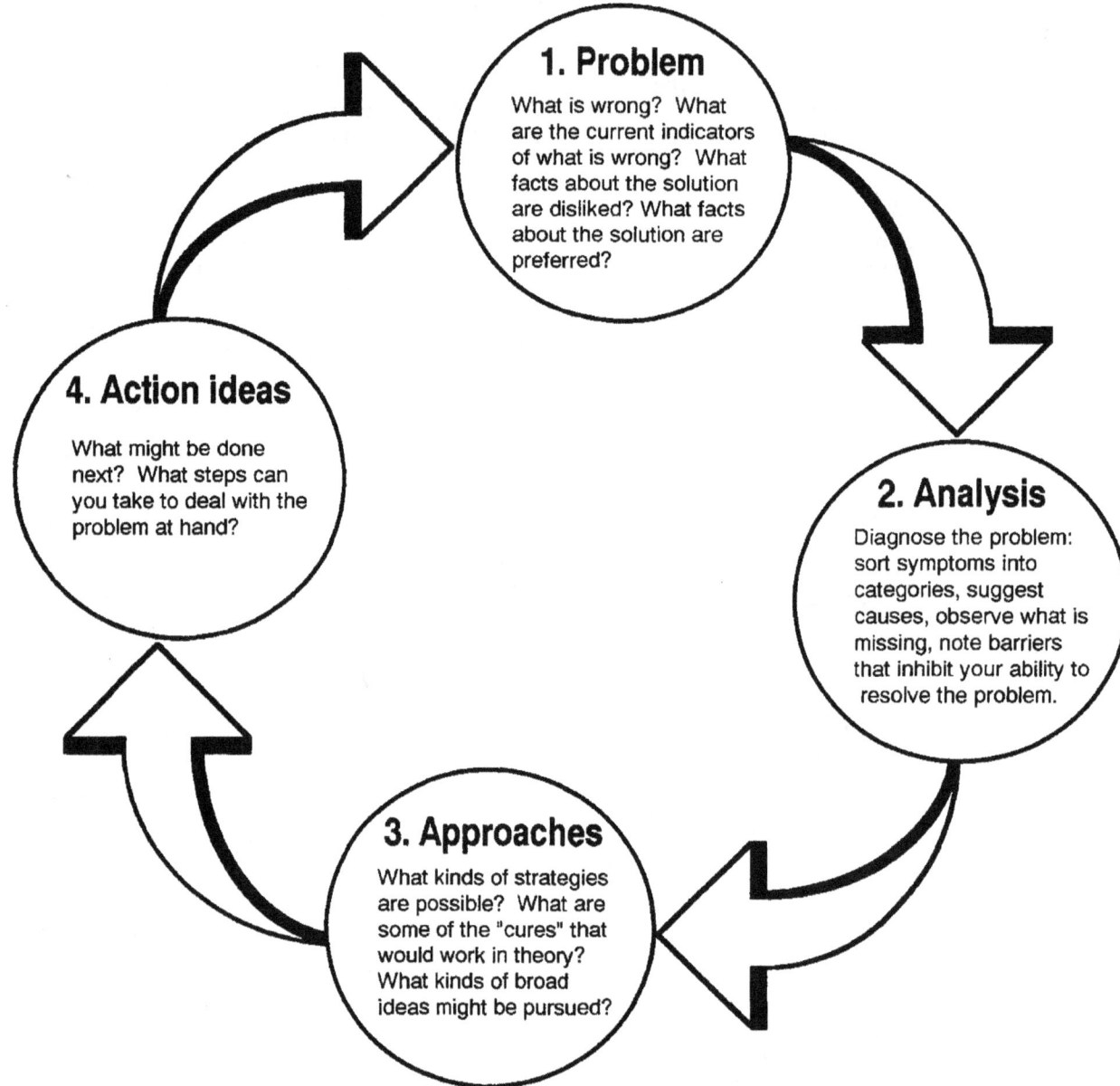

Figure 6-17 The circle chart developed by Roger Fisher and William Ury in their book, *Getting to Yes: Negotiating Agreement Without Giving In*, provides an easy way of using one good idea to generate others. It can provide a useful model for negotiating with jurors or clients.

Rely on Objective Standards Whenever Possible

You need criteria on which you can base your future work. Ask that the criteria the jury are using be spelled out in detail so that you can truly understand them.[21] Ideally these should be agreed on by all members of the jury as well as the class.

To understand these criteria at the jury, when a juror offers you an opinion, feel free to ask, "How did you arrive at that opinion?" "What standard did you use to determine that comment?" Your task is to understand the underlying reasoning behind that opinion. A prerequisite to this process is arriving at the jury with an open mind and being truly interested in the ideas that are offered to you and the rest of the class. Again, the same is true for professional interactions among designers, clients, public agencies, boards and trustees, and other audiences.

In sum, learning how to speak in public, how to listen, and how to negotiate are fundamental processes of both design education and practice.[22] Figure 6-18 provides a

LEARNING TO COMMUNICATE
SUMMARY CHECKLIST

PUBLIC SPEAKING

<u>Prepare in Advance</u>

___ Understand your audience and avoid jargon.
___ Plan to keep within your time limit.
___ Write and re-write a draft of your oral presentation.
___ Prepare a beginning, a middle, and an ending.
___ Write for the spoken, not the written word.
___ Plan out what you want to emphasize.
___ Be specific.
___ Experiment with different ways of delivery.
___ Watch and learn from experienced speakers.
___ Study how other visually-oriented professionals present their work.
___ Experiment with different ways of preparing notes.
___ Practice before a mirror, tape recorder, videocassette recorder, or another person and critique your performance.
___ Stage a "dress rehearsal".

<u>Zero in on a Few Key Points and Order Them Carefully</u>

___ Narrow down about 3-5 goals for your project.
___ Order goals from most to least important.
___ Identify specific ways that your design achieves your project goals.
___ Plan what you present and when and present your work sequentially.

<u>For a Dramatic Delivery...</u>

___ Emphasize key points.
___ Connect with your audience.
___ Highlight the strengths in your voice.
___ Listen carefully to yourself.
___ Coordinate your modes of communication.

<u>Avoid Strategic Errors - Don't...</u>

___ Begin with an apology.
___ Dress to distract from your work.
___ Let nervous, nonverbal behavior overpower your presentation.
___ Speak to your drawings and models.
___ Speak too softly or too quickly.
___ Let "ums", "you knows", and other annoying habits get in your way.
___ Use sexist language.
___ Give the janitor's tour.
___ Ramble.
___ Run overtime.
___ Conclude by fading out.

(continued)

Figure 6-18 Summary checklist of communication skills.

LISTENING

___ Anticipate the jury's or client's questions and prepare some responses.
___ Anticipate and prepare for interruptions.
___ Tape record your presentation and the jury's comments.
___ Listen carefully to the reactions of the audience.
___ Rephrase key comments from the jurors and ask for clarification.
___ Shift the discussion to a constructive tone.
___ Say "I don't know" if you need to.
___ Don't be defensive.

NEGOTIATING

Separate the People From the Problem

___ Establish a working relationship with the jurors.
___ Avoid misunderstandings and anticipate how others will interpret what you say.
___ Put yourself in the juror's or client's shoes.
___ Listen quietly to any attacks and encourage the juror to continue until finished.
___ To control your emotions, take a deep breath and exhale slowly.
___ If you disagree with the jurors' comments, calmly say so and explain why.

Focus on Interests Rather than Positions

___ Understand your own interests and that of the jurors or clients.
___ Avoid the attack-defense syndrome.
___ Sit together side-by-side if possible.

Produce Many Possibilities

___ Shuttle back and forth between the problem, analysis, approaches, and action ideas.

Use Objective Standards Whenever Possible

___ Ask jurors how they arrived at their opinions.

Figure 6-18 Continued.

summary checklist to help you with communication skills as you prepare for jury or client presentations. Excelling in all three areas can help improve the public's impressions of architects, landscape architects, planners, and interior designers. Rather than viewing them as temperamental, arrogant, artistic snobs who are solely interested in fulfilling their own agendas and defending their fragile egos, the public can view them in a more favorable light. Although speaking, listening, and negotiating are skills rarely taught in school, this may simply reflect the fact that many educators themselves are not well versed in these areas. Yet the experiences of the leading design practitioners interviewed for this book reveal that it is often exactly these strong communication skills, coupled with a strong expertise in design, that has made each of their firms a shining success.

> "What words of wisdom do I have for design students? Learn how to read and write and communicate." —Rodney F. Friedman

NOTES

1. Although the focus of this chapter is on oral communication skills, written skills are equally important. With few exceptions, such skills are also ignored in design education. But they are especially important to design professionals and to professional design juries that often require a short written statement to accompany graphic work.

   The College of Architecture and Planning at Ball State University has instituted an unusual program entitled Writing in the Design Curriculum to remedy this problem. It was initiated in 1985 and involves all second-, third-, and fourth-year students in studio classes. Its emphasis is on writing about design, about design processes, and about issues pertinent to the design profession. Writing consultants, instructors in the English Department's Writing Program, work together with design professors to design writing assignments, evaluate them, and assign grades.

According to Robert A. Fisher, dean, "When the program was first introduced, student reaction ranged from reluctant acceptance to low grade hostility. In this, our fifth year, students are not only accepting, but enthusiastic about the program." (Personal correspondence from Robert A. Fisher, August 23, 1990.) The program received an American Institute of Architects Education Honor Award. See Haynes, Jane C. (ed.), *Writing in the Design Curriculum 1989: Alternative Routes to the Imagination*, Muncie, IN: College of Architecture and Planning, Ball State University, 1989.

Another noteworthy model is at the University of Pennsylvania, which has instituted a Writing Across the University program. For further details about this program, consult Henry, Jim, "Writing Architecture," *Journal of Architectural Education, 43*:2 (Winter 1990), pp. 3-6.

The Conway School of Landscape Design in Conway, Massachusetts, is one of the few programs that emphasizes writing and speaking as part of its core curriculum. Students submit three to five pages of written work weekly, assessing progress toward their educational goals. In addition, every week they give presentations of their thoughts on design, which are evaluated by students and faculty. Students also make presentations to small and large community groups. See *Conway School of Landscape Design brochure*, Conway, Massachusetts, current version.

2. Student surveys revealed that they believe some of the chief goals of juries should be to teach communication skills. Out of 202 respondents to the question: "What do you think the goals of design project evaluations should be?" 79% responded "to learn to present my work professionally," 73% responded "to learn how to respond to criticism," 72% responded "to learn how to improve my communication skills, in general," and 72% responded "to learn how to improve my oral presentation skills."

3. This rather haphazard work schedule that is promoted by most design instructors is highly problematic. More on how instructors can improve the timing of assignments to help students better prepare for the jury is included in the Chapters 9 and 10.

4. More on how to overcome the jury jitters is described in Chapter 8.

5. In his biography of architect Charles Moore, David Littlejohn has stressed Moore's special ability to effectively listen to his clients as one of the keys to his success. He writes: "Moore can listen to clients—at least to those he likes—remarkably well, rather like a good psychiatrist.... In designing a house, he will try hard to discover not only such things as the clients' budget, space needs, daily round of activities, and conscious preferences, but also their *dreams*—the full array of their daydreams, memories, fantasies, and pretensions. Moore believes that the realm of the nonrational has been ignored by architects for too long, at severe psychic cost to the people who have to inhabit the places they design." See Littlejohn, David, *Architect: The Life & Work of Charles W. Moore*, New York: Holt, Rinehart and Winston, 1984, pp. 19-20.

6. Ironically, I have noticed that some of the students with the most carefully prepared oral presentations are those for whom English is not their native language. Perhaps because they fear lapsing into nervousness or forgetting the correct word or phrase, foreign students often tend to take more time preparing their oral presentations to the jury. As a result, they often sound more articulate than native English speakers.

7. A myriad of sources on public speaking is available. Here are just a few to help you get started: Bostrom, Robert N., *Communicating in Public: Speaking and Listening*, Santa Rosa, CA: Burgess, 1988; Gard, Grant G., *The Art of Confident Public Speaking*, Englewood Cliffs, NJ: Prentice-Hall, 1986; Gronbeck, B. *The Articulate Person: A Guide to Everyday Public Speaking*. Glenview, IL: Scott, Foresman and Company, 1983; Katula, Richard A., *Principles and Patterns of Public Speaking*, Belmont, CA: Wadsworth, 1987; Lucas, Stephen E., *The Art of Public Speaking*, 2d ed., New York: Random House, 1986; Mair, Alex, *How to Speak in Public*, Edmonton, Alberta, Canada: Hurtig Publishers, 1985; Sarnoff, Dorothy, *Speech Can Change Your Life: Tips on Speech, Conversation and Speechmaking*, Garden City, NY: Doubleday, 1970; Sarnoff, Dorothy, with Gaylen Moore, *Never Be Nervous Again: The World Renowned Speech Expert Reveals Her Time-Tested Method for Foolproof Control of Nervousness in Communicating Situations*, New York: Crown, 1987; Sprague, Jo, and Douglas Stuart, *The Speaker's Handbook*, 2d ed., San Diego, CA: Harcourt Brace Jovanovich, 1988; Vasile, Albert J., and Harold K. Mintz, *Speak with Confidence: A Practical Guide*, 3d ed., Boston: Little, Brown, 1983.

Various professional associations are specifically devoted to helping others speak more effectively. One of the best known is Toastmasters International (P.O. Box 10400, Santa Ana, CA 92711-0400), a nonprofit organization with over 6000 local Toastmaster clubs. Others include the International Association of Business Communicators (One Hallidie Plaza, Suite 600, San Francisco, CA 94102) and the National Speakers Association (3877 North 7th Street, Suite 350, Phoenix, AZ 85014). In addition, many private consulting firms offer seminars and training sessions in speech communication. One such firm is Dorothy Sarnoff Speech Dynamics (111 West 57th Street, New York, NY 10019).

8. In Chapter 10 I suggest that juries be held at least a few days after the projects are submitted. This allows the intervening period to be used to prepare the oral presentation, provided you keep some written record of your design as a reference.

9. Students in my team-taught studio courses have been subjected to the videotaping experience on numerous occasions prior to the actual jury. The class is taken to an on-campus simulated television studio a few days before the jury is scheduled, and all students are required to present their project before the class—and a video camera. We ask them to bring along as much of their project as they have completed,

be it a model, drawings, or for the truly desperate, simply a rough sketch on the blackboard showing what the final presentation boards will look like. Students are notified in advance of a time limit, usually anywhere from 3 to 10 minutes. Our television camera person is instructed to sound a 30-second warning and to cut off the presentation when time runs out. Often this occurs even when students are in mid-sentence.

After all the presentations are over, we then run through the video from start to finish, stopping it as needed to critique the students' presentation techniques. Every student in the class is asked to provide written feedback to every other student in the form of at least three positive points and three suggestions for improvement. They are also encouraged to enter freely into the discussion. All students are then asked to write a short statement noting their own impressions about their presentation and what they plan to do differently when the jury actually occurs.

In fact, most students dread this experience almost as much as the jury itself. Some have tried all sorts of excuses to escape from this particular day of class, usually pleading that they desperately need the time to continue preparing their work in studio. As a result, I have taken a rather draconian measure and made this one of the course requirements.

Despite their many protestations, once the experience is behind them students often cite this session as one of the most instructive parts of the studio, and they tend to remember it long after the course is over. Most importantly, the results of this before and after exercise, that is, the simulated jury and the jury itself, show dramatic improvements.

10. This point is especially important in light of the fact that women are still grossly underrepresented in the work force of environmental designers, especially as architects.

11. Personally, I have mixed feelings about the value of dress at the jury. While I believe it should not play a key role in how one's work is evaluated, because it really has little or nothing to do with the design project itself, I also know from experience that jurors often scrutinize a student's attire. While it may seem superficial to concentrate on style rather than substance, since design is a field that operates on both levels, it is logical to carry this argument to one's physical appearance as well.

12. Even members of the U.S. Congress are often limited to only two or three minutes when addressing the House floor. The ability to make a few key points in a short amount of time is one of the most effective public-speaking techniques you can learn.

13. Many of the interruptions all too common in the traditional jury system can be avoided by using some of the innovative jury formats suggested in Chapter 10. Applying assertiveness techniques can help you control interruptions effectively. Women are often in special need of such resources, especially as they concern responding to criticism. Many bookstores have a separate section for assertiveness guides. Browse through and select one that looks best for you. See, for example, Butler, Pamela, *Self-Assertion for Women*, new ed., San Francisco: Harper & Row, 1981; Hauck, Paul, *How to Stand Up for Yourself*, London: Sheldonn Press, 1979.

14. This passage was cited by Anthony Brandt in his introduction to Henderson, Bill (ed.), *Rotten Reviews II: A Literary Companion*, New York: Penguin Books, 1987, p. 17.

15. Fisher, Roger, and William Ury, *Getting to Yes: Negotiating Agreement Without Giving In*, New York: Penguin Books, 1981, p. xi.

16. Much of the following section is based on the national bestseller: Fisher, Roger, and William Ury, *Getting to Yes: Negotiating Agreement Without Giving In*, New York: Penguin Books, 1981. This book is an extremely valuable resource describing the method of principled negotiation developed at the Harvard Negotiation Project at Harvard Law School. Rather than being so soft as to make concessions too easily, or so hard as to be preoccupied with winning, principled negotiation allows you to reach agreements through a process that is fair: soft on the people, yet hard on the merits. See also Lewis, David V., *Power Negotiating Tactics and Techniques*, Englewood Cliffs, NJ: Prentice-Hall, 1981.

17. Some ideas for how your instructor can orchestrate this situation are offered in Chapter 10.

18. My hope is that by reading this book, both jurors and students will be better able to control their emotions at the jury. But books do not reach everyone, and ironically, those jurors who stand to benefit the most from reading this work are probably the least likely to read it.

19. More on this subject will be discussed in some of the upcoming chapters geared toward faculty and visiting critics. Research on personal space has demonstrated that sitting side by side is the preferred arrangement for cooperative work tasks. See Sommer, Robert, *Personal Space: The Behavioral Basis of Design*, Englewood Cliffs, NJ: Prentice-Hall, 1969.

20. Based on Fisher and Ury, op. cit., p 70.

21. Chapter 10 suggests that faculty ask jurors to spell out these criteria well in advance of the jury—ideally, shortly after the project is assigned—to help remove the mystery from the "mastery-mystery" phenomenon. This process is most effective when students are also involved in the discussions, so that the criteria are not one-sided. Involving both sides of the negotiating table in establishing joint criteria and standards helps yield more effective negotiations.

22. For an insightful account of how communication skills have been taught within a planning studio, consult Lusk, Paul and Min Kantrowitz, "Teaching Students to Become Effective Planners through Communication: A Planning Communications Studio," *Journal of Planning Education and Research*, *10*:1 (Fall 1990), pp. 55-59. The authors stress that planners must be skilled in receiving, processing, and delivering information in many different written, oral, and graphic forms. In addition, they must work well with groups in a variety of roles: as leaders, facilitators, consultants, team members, and mediators. (*Ibid.*, p. 56) The same can be said for interior designers, architects, and landscape architects.

CHAPTER 7
Dazzling Drawings:
Preparing Effective Graphic Presentations for the Jury

"Students should not enter work which is not really up to the level of which they're capable so that the juror when judging it doesn't have to feel that he or she never wants to judge again. That's how I feel all too often. Why waste my valuable time or even my interest? Why waste my interest in work less than that of which you're capable? And I resent it. I resent it in the professional world too with my trade sources who give me less than their best. Students all too often hurry to put a project together the night before it is due. The result is often sloppiness or a poor presentation. If you don't present well, how can you expect someone to judge you well?

". . . Slick or inventive presentations will immediately catch the jury's eye because we're all geared to look for excellence. After that, consistency is most important. When I add up my points that I give to various entries, I find that the most inventive submission doesn't always win because it was too lacking in other areas. What is most successful and most consistent along all the criteria will win. Consider the Miss America contest. The prettiest one doesn't always win. Instead, the person who wins is somebody who could sing a little bit and dance a little bit and look OK in a swimsuit and look OK in an evening gown and could answer a few questions. And when you add all the points together, she will come out even higher than the prettiest. So it's not just a beauty contest. Or an intelligence contest. It's all the parts put together. It's very hard to remember that you will win based on the little parts, not one big part. People always think it's the big picture. But it's not." —Larry N. Deutsch

"If you're going to prepare to enter competition, you better be damn good. The rather bratty designers say it is perfectly right to disregard the program and do what should be done: 'I, in my very limited and arrogant wisdom, know better than anybody.' Students better get over that feeling quickly. One of the principal things that all the young designers have learned from Frank Lloyd Wright is to confuse arrogance with genius. But it is not the same thing." —Lawrence B. Perkins

"One of the things that has given me strength as a student and as an adult professional is to focus on what I want to say that is important to me, my line of inquiry on an issue, my aesthetic values. Students should focus on what is important to them as opposed to trying to figure out what other people want. Ultimately, I believe that those people who contribute most to the culture have something of themselves to give; they are trying to pull something out of themselves and articulate their own point of view." —Martha Schwartz

CATCHING THE JURY'S EYE

Most of the designers interviewed for this book have received design awards themselves and many have won design competitions. Most have served on juries for professional design awards programs and professional or student design competitions where graphic work must stand on its own, without any verbal explanation. This insider's perspective offers an intriguing look at what is usually a hidden and secret process. Although the views they express are aimed at juries in professional design competitions, students will find them valuable for academic juries as well. How can you, as a submitter, catch the jury's eye?

Designers offer a wide range of opinions on this subject. Some firmly believe that there simply is no magic formula, and that the judging process is so subjective that it is virtually impossible to offer advice. Others, however, offer some valuable guidance to help increase your chances of victory:

> *"For practitioners submitting competition entries, one of the most important things is to please read the rules. I still serve as a consultant to HALO and their national competition, and when you're submitting an entry for lighting competition, know that you have to have a lighting plan. Know that you just can't send a pretty picture of a finished job. I've seen top notch work absolutely rejected because the rules were broken."—Joan Blutter*
>
> *"My advice to practitioners entering design competitions? Break the rules. Never obey the rules. Everybody who breaks the rules wins. We always do. Rules are made to be broken, especially in competitions.... Once the jury loves your design it doesn't matter what the rules were."—Peter Eisenman*

"What I find amazing is that jurors from varying points of view will agree pretty quickly on quality. How do you define quality? It's actually quite simple: a clarity of purpose and the realization of that purpose."—Laurence Booth

"I think that for a competition where you send in photographs, you should have someone other than yourself look at what you intend to photograph. If I'm working on a project and I spend a lot of time resolving a problem, I may think that aspect is the most fascinating element while other people may not understand what I'm talking about. So I wind up spending a couple thousand dollars photographing something that nobody else finds at all interesting or understands.

"... I believe a lot of awards are given that should actually go to the architectural or interior illustrators. It's the illustration itself that wins. The design is a work of art, an illusion, rather than a finished design in three dimensions. Most design competition juries award prizes far more on the basis of the illustration technique than on the design itself. If you don't have a good presentation technique, then I'm not sure it pays to even enter competitions."— The late Norman R. DeHaan

> *"Juries should be ... a critique of students' presentation capabilities, both verbal and graphic."—William Callaway*
>
> *"In professional awards programs, the submitter needs to find every way to help the jurors quickly get inside the complex. What was the purpose? What was the process? What was the meaning? What was the intellectual basis of the submission? Experienced jurors read quickly and you need to do anything you can to help them. I think one needs a mixture of very pointed, clear, and purposeful photography accompanied by brief statements of what is being shown."—Christopher Degenhardt*

> *"As a submitter, you should study how graphics can enhance your design. Without question one of the keys is to invest in a professional photographer, the best that you can afford. Many times you have photographs taken of a project before you even decide to enter competition. If you even have an inkling that you may want to submit this for a competition at a later date, try to think even before photographing: 'What would I enter this in? How will my project be best viewed?' For example, if you're entering a lighting competition, in many shots you would never want to shoot a large ceiling plane. You try to deaccentuate that. Instead, you need to show where the sources of light are coming from. And sometimes just by slightly changing the angle or the lens, you can have a photograph set up just as you would like it for your portfolio. Thinking about entering competitions should be an ongoing process. You can even think about it as you're first designing a project: 'How would this work in a competition? Would this be accepted? Can we do something different?' "—Jeffrey Werner*

"Your project stands a better chance of winning if the juror is grabbed by some idea of yours that seems particularly exciting or compelling. But then it's got to stand up to

> *"I think that plans, sections and models are the three critical elements of documentation, and to eliminate one or the other for an elevation is something that I don't agree with. If you make a model you have to make the elevation. If I were choosing how to describe or present architecture, I would rely, as a minimum, on those three elements. A plan and section are simultaneous and a model is both a facade and a three-dimensional representation. As a summary set of graphics, I would say that's the obligation.*
>
> *"... In the end, what is ultimately compelling to a jury is the three-dimensional manifestation of the design. An accurate and elaborate model is what ultimately convinces or doesn't convince a jury ... that's what is going to sell your scheme. You can eliminate a certain amount of speculation and you can actually visualize the design intention more easily."—Charles Gwathmey*
>
> *"The important thing in a competition is getting through the first cut, from 150 submissions down to 25. After the first cut, you've got a fair run at it because then people are going to ... spend the time to look at what you've done a little more carefully. To make the 150 cut you've got to have done something that grabs a juror's attention. ...*
>
> *"The thing that I always appreciate is [designers who use] words effectively. A lot of architects write atrociously and are very bad at explaining what their intentions are. The thing that really grabs me is just plain, simple exposition. It doesn't take fancy English and you don't have to be overly intellectual about it. Just be clear. The kind of design that grabs a juror's eye contains a clarity of exposition in terms of both graphics and language."—Steven Izenour*
>
> *"In a professional competition, you can't anticipate what the jury will decide. Never design for a particular jury. Instead of selecting work like their own, they will often be looking for originality—and for work very unlike their own. That's been our experience."—Ronette J. King*

close scrutiny. However, it's not going to get close scrutiny until it jumps forward."—Charles W. Moore

"The first element of judgment is the quality of the presentation. The quality of the presentation is the first demonstration of the design skills of the presenter, how well designed the presentation is, how beautiful it is, how suitable to the purpose. It is the first thing you judge because it is the first that comes to your eyes."
—Cesar Pelli

As you can see, there is no clear consensus about what constitutes "the most convincing" presentation to a jury. In fact, there simply is no such thing. Whether or not to break the rules is one bone of contention, with some designers arguing strongly in favor of maintaining the rules and a few others arguing against it. Those who comment on this issue feel strongly about it. Nonetheless, a number of designers stress the value of drawings that first "pop out" to the jury and later hold up to intense scrutiny, and the special power of models and photographs.

A SELECTIVE PROCESS

A wealth of information is available on preparing effective graphic presentations.[1] Any good environmental design library should offer plenty of sources to help you improve your graphic techniques and produce renderings that effectively communicate your ideas. Rather than repeat this detailed information, a subject for an entire book in itself, this chapter offers a few ideas to help organize your presentation so that it will make a favorable impression on the jury—whether it be in a classroom setting, a student design competition, a professional competition or awards program or any other type of presentation.[2]

Many program assignments and competition programs spell out the required number of drawings and the number and size of the boards. In school, usually these are presented in terms of fulfilling the minimum course requirements. For example, an architectural project may require a site plan, plans of two typical floors, a section, and an elevation. But which floors should you choose? Where should you cut the section? Which elevation should you show?

Due to space limitations and the logistics of mailing, many design competition entries are limited to a single board. What is the best use of such a limited amount of space? How can you put your best foot forward before a jury? Here are some simple rules of thumb that should help.

Often program requirements specify a minimum number of drawings. Check to see if more drawings are acceptable and if you have the time to do them. *If possible, try to show even more than the minimum that is required* (Figure 7-1). Students often skimp on sections, and yet in many cases, they are among the most effective communicators of your work. If a minimum of one section is required, see if you are permitted to show two or three. But be careful not to go overboard. I have seen some overly ambitious design presentations with 10 boards or more. Usually this is unnecessary and simply too much informa-

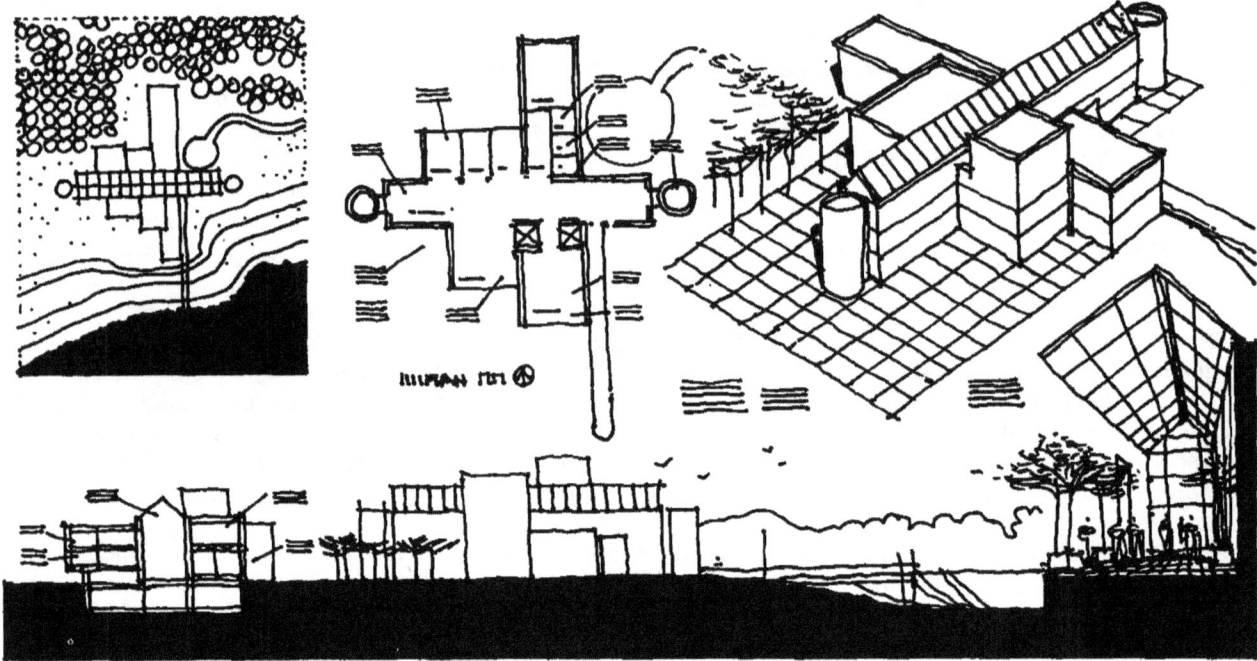

Figure 7-1 Most architectural projects require a site plan, floor plans, sections, and elevations. For each of these categories, carefully select exactly what you want to show, and if you have time, do more than the minimum that is required.

tion to digest. To make matters worse, it is often impossible to find a wall that will fit them all together.

Realize from the outset that whatever type of design project you are working on, be it an interior design, architecture, landscape architecture, or urban design project, the way you present your drawings is truly *an exercise in graphic design*. The knowledge and skills required for an effective graphic presentation may in fact be quite different from what it takes to design at a larger scale.

In fact, presenting your design work on a series of boards is somewhat like an experienced chef presenting an elegant meal on a plate. Each part of the meal—the appetizer, salad or soup, entrée and accompaniments, and dessert—requires its own preparation and presentation. Each arrives in a particular order and is tailor-made to look appealing in the proper dish. The dish itself is often specially selected to go with the food. Each item stands on its own, but each complements the other. The way each is presented is carefully studied and turned into an art form all its own, where through synergy, the whole is greater than the sum of its parts. Take a look at any good recipe book with high-quality photographs to see how this works.[3]

The drawings and models must speak for themselves. In a competition or awards jury, you are not allowed to explain or defend your work. If the jurors cannot understand what you are trying to show, your entry will be knocked out of the running. There is no second chance. But if you do have the opportunity to provide an oral presentation, as in a classroom jury, your talk should merely complement your boards. In any case the boards must still be easily understood. Keep this in mind whenever you prepare your boards. Assume you will not be present to help clarify points.

COMMUNICATE CLEARLY

Begin by considering exactly what it takes to most clearly communicate your design ideas. While you are mulling over what to show on your board, keep reviewing the following questions in your mind: What is the best possible use of this part of the board? What shows my project in its best light? What am I trying to emphasize through my design? For example, if your design features high-volume ceilings in major living spaces, be sure to highlight these spaces in your drawings. A section or perspective drawing of these spaces will communicate the added height that cannot be discerned from a plan. If the west facade of your building has something exceptionally special to offer and you can only show one elevation, then do not present the east facade. If the garden space you have designed in the front of the house is most impressive and you are only allowed one perspective landscaping sketch, then do not show the backyard space. Although it sounds like com-

Figure 7-2 Your boards should be strong, clear, and easy to read. Make sure that even the person seated farthest away from them in the room can see them.

mon sense, it is surprising how often these simple considerations are ignored. When a crucial drawing is missing and you must simply talk about it instead—if you have the opportunity to do so—your presentation loses power and the ability to convince the jury about the value of your ideas.

Arrange your boards and the drawings on each board to correspond to the order in which you wish to present your project. Plan out each drawing in a logical sequence so that viewers are not required to jump around in order to follow your presentation. Again, an analogy is in order. Compare the composition of your boards to the composition of a term paper. The processes are incredibly similar. In any written composition, we see a beginning, middle, and end. Each paragraph reflects a coherent set of ideas that are tied together from one sentence to the other. A major statement is made along with supporting points and evidence to buttress the argument. Generally speaking, paragraphs run from the general to the specific. Each paragraph is like a design drawing, and the paper as a whole is like a series of boards. Again, each ties into the other, and the whole is greater than the sum of its parts.

Your boards should be strong, clear, and easy to read (Figure 7-2). Before you draw a line, consider both the setting in which your work will be viewed and the person who will be the farthest away from it. Make sure that whatever you draw can be seen well even by that person who is at the greatest distance. This means that drawings and labels must be both large enough and dark enough to be seen.[4] If you are submitting a competition entry, try to envision the room where all the projects will be displayed and the typical distances between the jurors and your projects. If you are preparing for a classroom jury, have another student in the class help you with this. Display a set of drawings that you have presented before, perhaps for another class, and have a friend look at them from afar. Can they be seen easily? Does she have to squint to understand them? Think about projects in previous juries that elicited comments like, "You've got a really clear presentation." "Your presentation is easy to understand." Think about what made them this way. If possible, track down the student who presented her work and ask to study it carefully.

Design work published in professional magazines can provide some useful clues about how to present your work. The same is true for work shown in professional design exhibitions. These media are especially useful since they rely almost entirely on graphic communication, and the designer is not available to provide any further explanation. Your drawings should be just as clear and not need you to decipher them.

Every drawing should contain title, scale, and orientation. It is amazing how often these simple labels are omitted and how much confusion and frustration jurors experience as a result. Convention usually dictates that the north arrow faces up. However, this may be inappropriate for your particular project, for instance, if the front of the project faces east or west and you prefer that your plan be shown horizontally rather than vertically. If everyone in your class is working on the same project, you may all want to consult with your instructor and agree on a common convention that you will all use. In this manner, the jury will be on the same wavelength when they view each project and not have to spend needless moments reorienting themselves.

Scale is especially important. Drawings are often reduced for publication, portfolios, or other reasons, and without an accurate scale, the viewer is lost.[5]

If you have a tendency to be rushed and inadvertently omit title, scale, and orientation from your drawings, instead of waiting to add these at the end, consider drawing them on each of your boards when you first begin to prepare your final presentation. Some instructors refer to this as *starting by finishing*.

Be sure that your orientation throughout your drawings is consistent. Don't have north face up in one drawing and then have it down in another. Such contortions are unnecessarily confusing, making the jurors feel as if they need to be standing on their heads to figure out your work.

Ensure that all boards are finished to the same level of completeness. Try to picture an obviously *incomplete* set of boards, for example, lots of line work and lettering perhaps with some color on the first few, and only outlines, no notes, and no color on the last few. This type of uneven presentation immediately calls attention to that which is unfinished, thus detracting from whatever else you have done. Instead, consider the following sequence:

1. Outline all boards.
2. Freehand or hard line all boards.
3. Letter all boards.
4. Render or poche all boards.

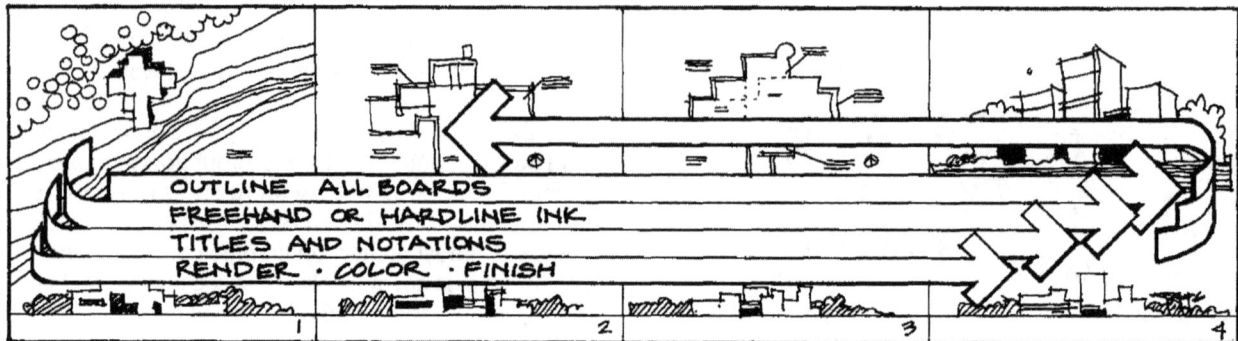

Figure 7-3 Flipping back and forth through all boards while you are preparing your final presentation allows you to present a project that looks complete.

The key is to keep flipping through all the boards at once and to produce them in a sequence that allows the last items on the list to be omitted if time runs out (Figure 7-3). For example, you may wish to color all your boards and save this task for last. If no time is left, however, and you never get to this stage, you still have a completed project. In this case, color is merely frosting on the cake, but it is not essential to communicating your design ideas; it is expendable.

THE VISUAL-VERBAL CONNECTION

Neatness counts. Since presentation means so much in design, even the slightest errors call out for attention. When jurors spot such mistakes, they naturally tend to look for more. Carelessness in presenting your final drawings can lead jurors to believe that you may also have been careless in conceiving your design. The entire process can domino and color the way in which they view the rest of your presentation. Using the computer is a tremendous aid in this regard as mistakes can be corrected easily and revised drawings printed out with minimal effort.

Spelling counts. Words are just as important as drawings on your boards. The number of spelling mistakes I have seen on final design presentations is appalling. And when misspelled words are enlarged to a size that is almost greater than life, the mistakes are called out as if they are advertised on a billboard. Even in this high-tech, computer era, with "spell check" and other electronic spelling devices, it is important to check a dictionary for any words that you include. Taking the time to do this will yield a more convincing presentation to the jury or to clients.

Labels and other identifying features, such as furniture, planting materials, and people are especially important. Do not forget them. In classroom juries, many students run through a litany of spaces that are simply not adequately identified on their drawings, with the expectation that jurors remember exactly what is where. It is virtually impossible for even the most experienced juror to memorize your project and its layout when such information is not provided. Showing people in your drawings whenever possible helps provide a sense of human scale as well as life and color.

Explanatory text should be well composed. Prepare a brief draft of any written material you want to include, such as concept or goal statement. Revise it several times before you produce the final draft. Have someone who knows nothing at all about your project review it with you and see if that person can understand it fully. Make it a point to develop your writing skills.[6]

PREPARE FOR LOGISTICAL DETAILS

Whenever possible, mount your boards so that they become stiff and you cannot see through them. For a classroom jury, find out what type of presentation surface is available and what types of supplies (pushpins, tape, etc.) you will need to bring with you. Gather these all ahead of time and be sure to have them with you when you arrive at the jury.

Practice your setup and takedown time before the jury. Figure out exactly what boards you want to show, and where, and practice with some mock-ups ahead of time. Better yet, if time permits, try it with the real boards themselves. One short rehearsal can save several precious moments during your actual presentation.[7]

In sum, preparing effective graphics is one of the most essential ingredients of a successful jury presentation. Paying attention to some finishing touches that are often overlooked can help the jury and clients view your work more favorably (Figure 7-4). By managing your time effectively, you can devote the time required to this important task.

PREPARING EFFECTIVE GRAPHIC PRESENTATIONS FOR THE JURY
SUMMARY CHECKLIST

A SELECTIVE PROCESS

___ Consult key graphics books.
___ If possible, try to show even more than the minimum that is required.
___ View your boards as an exercise in graphic design, such that the whole is greater than the sum of its parts.

COMMUNICATE CLEARLY

___ Keep asking yourself: What is the best possible use of this part of the board? What shows my project in its best light? What am I trying to emphasize through my design?
___ Arrange your boards and the drawings on each board to correspond to the order in which you wish to present your project.
___ Your boards should be strong, clear and easy to read. Consider the setting in which your work will be viewed and the person who will be the farthest away from it.
___ Study exemplary completed projects and analyze the graphic presentation style.
___ Every drawing must contain title, scale, and orientation. "Start by finishing" and include this information on each board before you begin your final design.
___ Be sure that your orientation throughout your drawings is consistent.
___ Ensure that all boards are finished to the same level of completenes by using the following sequence:
　　___ outline all boards
　　___ freehand or hard line all boards
　　___ letter all boards
　　___ render or poche all boards.
___ Flip through all the boards at once in the final production stage.

THE VISUAL-VERBAL CONNECTION

___ Ensure that your drawings are as neat as possible. Avoid anything that appears careless.
___ Check spelling on any words you write.
___ Be sure to include labels and other identifying features, such as furniture, planting materials, and people.
___ Carefully compose any explanatory text.

PREPARE FOR LOGISTICAL DETAILS

___ Mount your boards.
___ Practice your set-up and take-down time before the jury.

Figure 7-4 Summary checklist of graphic presentation skills.

NOTES

1. See, for example, Burden, Ernest, *Design Presentation: Techniques for Marketing and Project Proposals*, New York: McGraw-Hill, 1984; Ching, Frank, *Architectural Graphics*, 2d ed., New York: Van Nostrand Reinhold, 1985; Greenstreet, Robert, and James W. Shields, *Architectural Representation*, Englewood Cliffs, NJ: Prentice-Hall, 1988; Wahl, Michael Iver, *Design Presentations for Architects*, New York: Van Nostrand Reinhold, 1987.

2. Student surveys reveal that improving graphic skills should be one of the goals of design juries; 63% of 202 respondents expressed this opinion.

3. The photographs by Patricia Brabant in the cookbook series by culinary creator James McNair provide some excellent examples how composition can enhance the presentation of a design product: food. See, for example, *James McNair's Beef Cookbook*, San Francisco: Chronicle Books, 1989; James McNair, *Chicken*, San Francisco: Chronicle Books, 1987; *James McNair's Salmon Cookbook*, San Francisco: Chronicle Books, 1987; *James McNair's Squash Cookbook*, San Francisco: Chronicle Books, 1989.

4. I have seen many students prepare such timid-looking drawings in very light pencil that they can barely be seen from a few inches, much less several yards, away.

5. For example, an urban design plan drawn at the scale of $1'' = 100'$ on a $30'' \times 40''$ illustration board must be measured with a $1'' = 400'$ scale if reduced to 25% of its size in order to shrink to $7½'' \times 10''$, thus fitting easily on an $8½'' \times 11''$ sheet. If the original did not have a graphic scale, figuring the dimensions on the reduction becomes almost impossible. Similarly, an architectural plan drawn at a $¼''$ to $1'$ scale becomes a $⅛''$ to $1'$ drawing when reduced to half its size. In urban planning and landscape architecture drawings showing new cities, neighborhoods, large parks, and so on, it is also highly advisable to draw and label a line representing something like "20 minutes walking distance" in order for jurors and clients to immediately grasp how long it takes to walk from point A to point B. No matter how much the drawing is reduced, that line will always represent a 20-minute walk.

6. See note 1 of Chapter 6 about the writing curricula at Ball State University and the University of Pennsylvania.

7. Some faculty have told me that they have seen students intentionally take their time setting up their boards at the jury so that they have less time left for their presentation and for the jury's comments. What tends to happen instead, however, is that the individual session runs as long as it would otherwise, but that the delay in setup time throws off the rest of the students' presentation schedules. This is one of several reasons that juries often run overtime.

CHAPTER 8

Burnout on the Boards:

How to Handle Studio Stress

"My absolute inability to bring even the simplest design to paper is casting a shadow on many otherwise beautiful things and often makes me worry about my future profession. I am not capable of drawing a straight line. I could draw much better as a twelve-year-old. It seems to be almost a physical inability for me, because I immediately get a cramp in my hand and continually break the points of my pencils, so that I have to rest after five minutes. Even my handwriting is the same. It gets worse every day. In my darkest hour, I had never feared that things could be so hopeless." — Walter Gropius in a letter to his mother, 1907[1]

"The whole weekend I have been worried sick that I'm not going to get done. I had very little sleep and am coming down with a cold and a cough. I feel awful and hate architecture at this moment. I stayed up all night last night and feel miserable. I would do anything to get out of the jury right now. I wish I had an accident—just anything so that I wouldn't have to face the jury." —A design student

For many students, obtaining a design degree can seem like climbing Mount Everest. And each design jury appears as one of the steepest slopes along the way. While preparing for the jury, all that you perceive is that peak looming in the distance. The importance of other events diminishes greatly the closer you get. You become obsessed with scaling that overwhelming peak directly ahead. All the while, you contemplate turning back, or even worse, falling to your death!

The strong connection between juries and course grades is one important reason why they can sometimes be such nail-biting experiences.[2] As we noted earlier, speaking in public, one of the typical requirements of design juries, is in itself a source of great tension. The sheer excitement of completing a project also cranks up the adrenalin flow. But juries are not the only source of stress for design students. For many, the studio itself is a constant source of stress, where some days can be simply worse than others. An optimal level of stress is often needed to maintain interest and motivation in one's work. But when the level of stress becomes too high or out of control, you can't help but pay a price for it at jury time.[3]

In this chapter, we will take a look at what stress means and how it is manifested in both design studios and juries. More importantly, we will look at some ways you can use to help keep your stress level under control and ultimately avoid that all-too-dangerous phenomenon of burnout.

How do psychologists define stress? Stress occurs when demands placed on people exceed the resources they have available to deal with them.[4] Stressful events or situations can cause conditioned responses, as in the infamous Pavlov's dog.[5] These responses can be physiological, as in a rapid heartbeat or blood flow, or psychological, as in extreme fear. Such reactions are usually unpleasant and are often physiologically or emotionally disabling.[6] Anxiety, frustration, depression, and alienation are often spin-offs of stressful situations. When stress is prolonged over an extended period of time, it can result in burnout—complete mental and physical exhaustion that leaves one feeling helpless, depressed, and out of control. Most design students experience stress, while fewer burn out.

Numerous studies have documented that crowded living conditions, not unlike those found in most design studios, often result in high levels of stress. What appears to be a key factor influencing the level of stress one experiences under crowded conditions is *the level of control people feel they have over their environment. Students lack adequate control over their studio environment. This affects their work performance throughout the design process with spillover effects at the jury.* They may be interrupted at any time by another student who simply wants to take a break and chat, by their professor who may drop in unannounced even well after official class hours, or by other unplanned events. Some students who prefer to work with their radios and cassette players at full volume, and not under headsets, in effect take over the studio environment, forcing others to listen to music that they may not even enjoy. Such patterns distract and aggravate classmates, who may hesitate to speak up for fear of being socially ostracized. What we see in design studios, at their worst, is an exaggeration of the classic problems experienced by incompatible college roommates. These problems can be multiplied many times in especially large studios housing as many as 40 or 50 students working together around the clock.

In addition, some research has shown that people experience greater stress as a result of crowding when housed in a competitive, as opposed to a cooperative, environment.[7] Without a doubt, studios are highly competitive environments, despite the facade that they may be otherwise. More on competition and its role in the design studio will be discussed in Chapter 12.

Studios are also highly stressful environments in that they offer a minimal sense of privacy—the ability to control interaction with others. It is not unusual for students to complain about studio-mates with especially annoying habits at 4:00 A.M. Privacy is also a problem in many professional design offices as well. While some screen themselves off with various vertical barriers to try to achieve a sense of visual privacy, it is often impossible to screen out sounds, smells, and other types of intrusions. Many designers retreat into their own cocoon underneath their personal stereo headsets, surrounded by only those sounds they want to hear and trying desperately to ignore whatever else is around them.

But studio stress need not always be negative. In fact, preparing for a jury is not unlike preparing for a musical recital (Figure 8-1). In both instances, the preparation and practice may well be an even greater learning experience than the final presentation itself. The stress and strain while anticipating the performance may well activate the adrenalin, causing students to be even more productive than they would be otherwise. The key to handling stress effectively is to determine the level of stress that is optimal for you.

Being able to handle stress involves the ability to develop effective coping mechanisms. This can include developing *resources*—generalized attitudes and skills that work well in many situations, such as attitudes about your self-esteem, interpersonal communication skills, and so on. It can also include developing *styles*—generalized coping strategies, or habits that you use to handle stress. In some cases this may mean withdrawing rather than confronting the source of stress, denying the source of stress, blaming others, or being unable to solve problems in general. Finally, acquiring coping mechanisms involves

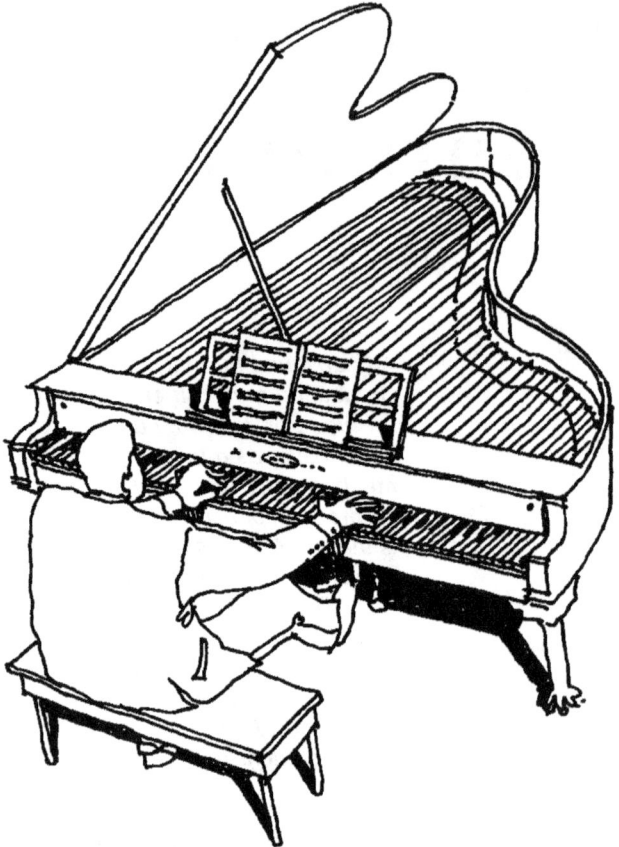

Figure 8-1 Preparing for a jury is much like preparing for a musical recital. The preparation and practice may be an even greater learning experience than the final presentation.

efforts—specific actions in particular situations that help reduce your sense of the problem and your level of stress, for example by appraising the problem, asking for help, beginning a new activity.[8] What follows is a combination of resources, styles, and efforts to help you effectively manage the stress of the studio subculture. As we have said before, no one technique will do the trick, so try whatever works best for you.

OVERCOME THE JURY JITTERS

One of the major reasons why some students become so terrified at juries is simply because they are doing all the wrong things: They've been up all night and are "running on empty," they haven't prepared their talk in advance, and they haven't stopped at all to think about the kinds of questions the jury may ask them. By changing some of these habits in ways we have discussed in earlier chapters, your level of tension should decrease. But if it doesn't, here are a few other techniques you can use to try to calm down.

Shortly before you present your work to the jury, use breathing as a relaxation technique. Here is an extremely effective way to bring down your tension level: Close your eyes and relax the muscles in your face. Begin to breathe deeply while you count down slowly from 10 to 1. Take your time exhaling. Feel your stomach going out as you inhale, and in as you exhale. Feel the air flowing through your nose.

Try the "Sarnoff Squeeze." Renowned speech consultant Dorothy Sarnoff has developed a technique that she claims is foolproof for controlling nervousness, especially shaking knees, dry mouth, and butterflies in the stomach.[9] She calls it the Sarnoff Squeeze. She learned it while acting in the Broadway musical "The King and I" with actor Yul Brynner. One night while waiting in the wings to go onstage, Sarnoff watched Brynner pushing a wall in a lunging position as if he were about to knock it down, grunting in the process. When she asked him why he was doing this, he explained that it helped him control his nervousness. She tried it and never suffered from stagefright again. She modified the technique so that it could be done inconspicuously.

The Sarnoff Squeeze is basically as follows: Sit in a straight-backed chair. With your rib cage high, incline forward slightly and put your hands together out in front of you with your fingertips pointing up and your elbows bent. Now push so that you feel an isometric force in the heels of your palms and under your arms. At the same time, say "sssssss," like a hiss. As you exhale, contract and tighten the muscles below the ribs. When you stop exhaling, relax the muscles and inhale gently. Believe it or not, contracting these muscles actually prevents your body from producing the fear-inducing chemicals noradrenaline or epinephrine. One of the greatest assets of the Sarnoff Squeeze is that it is unobtrusive. You can do it virtually anywhere and no one will notice. Next time you're "batter up" at the jury, try it.

Identify your stress points and then relax them (Figure 8-2). Nervous tics, furrowed brows, throbbing temples, or clenched jaws are telltale signs of tension in the *face*. Excessive pain and muscles knotting up afflict the *neck, shoulders,* and *back*. And the notorious butterflies seem to invade your *stomach* just as you realize you're one of the next to present. Plenty of techniques can help relax each area, but here are just a few. (1) Imagine yourself lying on a quiet beach, being warmed by the sun and pillowed by the sand. Hear the sound of the waves surrounding you. Relax. Now open your mouth and drop your lower jaw slightly. Keep this position for 10 seconds. (2) Make a face—that is, contort your face into an exaggerated mask, tightening your facial muscles. Hold your "funny face" for three seconds, then relax. Feel the tension melt away. (3) Tighten up your arm and shoulder muscles, then release them. Repeat this a few times to reduce the tension.

Take your mind off the stressor—even if only for a

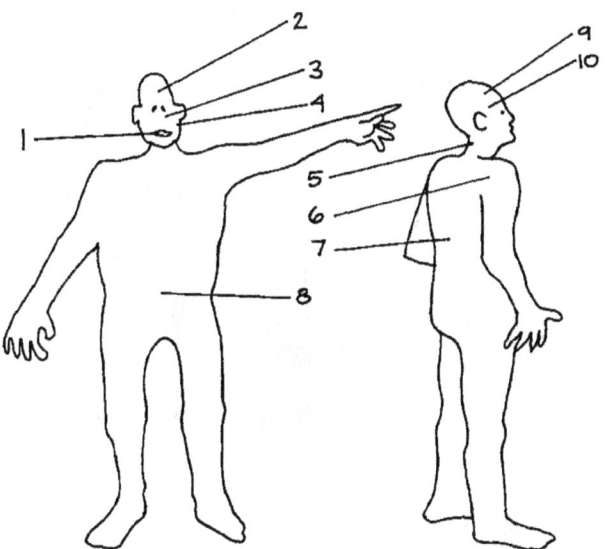

Figure 8-2 To help relieve stress before the jury, identify your stress points throughout your body and then relax them.

minute. Imagine the place where you feel most peaceful and relaxed: a beach, a swimming pool, a meadow, a forest, a bubble bath, or whatever most suits your fancy. Before the jury, find a strong visual image of this place and take it with you on jury day. The image can be a photograph you have taken, perhaps a drawing you have created, a postcard, even a photograph out of a magazine advertisement; it really doesn't matter. What is key is that the visual image be powerful to you. Have this image in your purse or pocket and glance at it whenever you feel the stress of the jury coming upon you.

Think positive thoughts and reduce negative chatter. Our thoughts are like tapes running throughout our heads. When we're tense, we often fixate on the negative reruns, for instance; "My last jury was a bomb, so this one will be too!" Or "I'm just not good at design, and I'll never get the hang of this!" "My parents are going to kill me!" Replace each of these negative thoughts with a constructive alter-

> *"Not being a stellar designer doesn't mean that you're a failure or that you're no good. Everybody in medicine doesn't have to end up being a surgeon. Indeed, a surgeon is very important, but there are many other forms of medical practice that are equally as important and respected. The same thing happens in architecture once you start practicing. There are many other elements of the practice that are equally as important and respected as design. But most schools are clearly centered on design. That, I know is a problem."—Cesar Pelli*

94 Burnout on the Boards: How to Handle Studio Stress

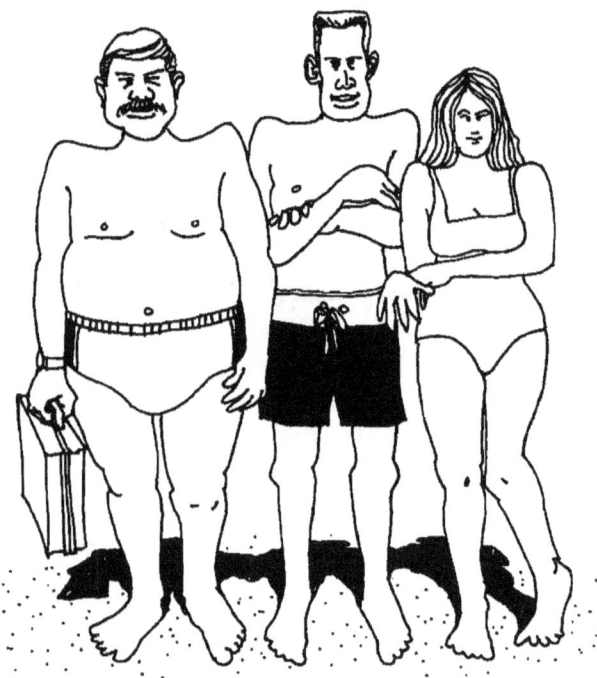

Figure 8-3 Change your image of the jury by imagining them all before you in their bathing suits.

native. For instance, "I know I've done well on previous juries, so I can do well on this one too," or "My presentation doesn't have to be perfect, it just has to be over!"

Remind yourself that design is not the most important thing in the world—even though your professors may not agree. Instead, tell yourself, "So what if I'm not tops at design. I'm sure I'll find other aspects of office life where I can be even better: selling our services to clients, organizing the staff to produce final drawings, or even administering the office." In fact, if your talents lie in promotion, production, or administration, you are likely to be in great demand.

Change your image of the jury by picturing them all before you in their bathing suits (Figure 8-3). Some speech consultants suggest you go even farther than that: Imagine them all sitting on the toilet! Or picture them in their casual weekend attire at the grocery store. In any case, take those jurors off the pedestal and picture them as normal human beings.

> "I usually imagine the jurors as my favorite relatives or close friends. Usually I see us in a living room, and then someone asks, 'Hey, can we see your project?' And I'll say, 'Sure!' This works great."—A design student

REDUCE STRESS BEFORE AND AFTER THE JURY

One of the biggest obstacles to performing well at the jury is sheer anxiety. Some of us are better worriers than others; some people make a career out of worrying. One way to get a handle on your worries is to write them all down. Think carefully about every single worry that is plaguing you, and write each one on a list. Make sure your catalog of worries is complete so that no stray ones are floating around to plague you later on.

As you can imagine, design students release all that pent-up stress and tension surrounding the studio and the jury in various ways, some healthy and some not. Diaries and interviews reveal that for many students, the biggest reward after the jury is sleep. Many go home to sleep for hours on end. After slaving away in design studio from a Wednesday morning until the jury on Friday at noon, one student went home and slept for 22 hours straight. Others tend to purchase their rewards in the form of a favorite compact disc or cassette tape, item of clothing, or other desirable item. Still others indulge in excessive alcohol consumption, drug abuse, wild parties, joyrides, and the like.

Whether or not your desk crit or jury went as planned, you can deal with stress and unreleased tension in several ways. Select whatever techniques work best for you.[10] Here are some tips.

Maintain a regular exercise program. Exercise and intense physical activity have long been effective relievers of stress, and they can provide a healthy escape from the sedentary activity of the drafting table. Find some friends to go walking or running together with outside of studio. Swim laps at the nearby pool. Engage in a sport and stick with it. Walking just 20 minutes a day can accomplish wonders.

Set aside a notebook and spontaneously write down your feelings in a form of free association. Don't even think about what exactly to say or how to say it, but just spit it out. Keep writing until you have nothing more to say to the jurors who angered you. Four-letter words are perfectly acceptable in this context. Don't show what you have written to anyone else, but keep it "for your eyes only." If it makes you feel better at some point, stage a private ceremony where you dramatically destroy whatever you have written. Stomp on it, shred it, crumple it up, scatter it over a garbage dump, or watch it burn away in your fireplace. These symbolic acts can help you release your negative

> "I coached the freshman water polo team and got myself through school. I had a lot of fun."—Joseph Esherick

emotions and get them out of your system—without harm to yourself or anyone else.

Go to a natural setting with few people around where you can become as angry as you like without anyone watching. If you live near the ocean, for example, stand in front of the sea, open up your hands and stretch them out in front of you toward the crashing waves. Let the waves absorb your anger and suck it away from you. If you live in a flat area, an open plain or prairie can serve the same function.

If one of your housemates has a pet, spend some time with it to help you relax. Pets offer unconditional love and companionship, and they certainly won't think less of you after a bad jury. Spend some time stroking a cat or petting a dog, and you will find that it can be quite therapeutic.

If they live nearby, spend some time with some small children that you enjoy. Play games with them and share their toys. Just keeping up with a three-year-old is sure to take your mind off the studio and jury experience and give you a fresh perspective on life.

Do you have access to a punching bag at a nearby gym? If so, beat your heart out and think whatever you like about the juror or critic who treated you unkindly.

Remember a time when you felt elated and enthusiastic about life: when you learned of your admission to college, the first time you traveled abroad, your first visit to a national park. Focus on that experience and try to capture the same feelings again today.

Buy some relaxation audio- or videotapes. Listen to ocean waves, a forest rain, or a desert thunderstorm and take your mind off your troubles.

Take a slow, gentle bath while listening to your favorite relaxing music. Plan to stay there for at least a half hour. To prevent any unnecessary anxiety while in the tub, disconnect your phone or turn on an answering machine.

BROADEN YOUR HORIZONS

The amount of hours spent in studio are more like those in the working world than they are like those of other courses. For many students, studio requires the time commitment of a half-time job, if not greater. At most schools, studio class hours range from about 9 to 20 hours per week. Add in the additional hours most students spend in studio outside of class, along with their obligations for other required courses, and there is little free time left. The long hours chained to the drafting table are a major source of stress—but they don't have to be. That preoccupation with the design project often precludes students from engaging in other activities. By organizing your time well, you can engage in activities that can not only reduce stress but also broaden your educational experience.

Attend a concert, performance, or lecture on a topic that has nothing to do with design. Not only will you find this relaxing, but you may also learn something in the process. Check out your university newspaper for a list of campus events.[11] Carve out the time in your schedule to attend whatever interests you.

Experience and learn from the other fine arts. If you feel so inclined, try out painting, sculpting, or playing a

> "For students, a key point to success in school is exposure. Don't be caught in the academic world of your studio. At a good design program there are a lot of guest lecturers brought in who show slides of their work. I think that . . . is where you really can see it all come together and experience the totality of design beyond academia."—Jeffrey Werner

> "I've been on several scholarship juries and I always disturb other architects because I make a habit of asking the applicants whether they cook, or what's the last piece of symphonic music they've listened to—or what are the last four books they've read. I ask these questions because I think that design students are often very narrow minded in their design approach. I tend to feel very uncomfortable with students like that. . . . If they're really interested in the visual aspects of the world, then they should also be interested in painting and sculpture and landscape. They should seek as broad a cultural base as possible.
>
> ". . . A lot of the schools tend to become terribly design oriented, to the exclusion of almost everything else. Students' experiences become much too limited. . . . You find students being asked to design concert halls who have never been to a concert except some rock concert in a field somewhere. . . . It's just unbelievable."—The late Norman R. DeHaan
>
> "I learned a lot when I was in school from fine arts classes in painting, drawing, and print-making. I was always good at these classes. I also developed a real interest in theater design. Fine artists think a different language from architects and designers as do video and film people, musicians, and dancers. They're entirely different worlds. Listening to them and their languages, their jargon, so to speak, and trying to comprehend the print-making medium brought in a different perspective that really enriched my approach to design. I may have added a little poetry to the fine arts and tried to apply it to my design work. I do find that I tend to bring these different languages together. And I encourage our design staff to do that too—to get out there and get involved in other mediums."—Ronette J. King

> "A design education should be very broad. I believe that reading, listening, and generally being gregarious are among the most important components of a design education. You can't sit around reading novels and not know how to draw. It's not going to get you anywhere. You have to do both, but you shouldn't do one at the expense of the other. I rely enormously on reading, and largely on fiction." —Joseph Esherick
>
> "The architectural curriculum [while a student at Cornell University from 1948 to 1954] was very rigid and assumed that everything should be learned in a uniform sequence. It was also assumed that we would not become seriously concerned with electives. One of my friends scandalized the faculty by abandoning his design thesis because he had become preoccupied with reading Melville. One might think that an educational institution would rejoice in having cultivated a strong interest in literature, but in a professional curriculum departures from routine are seen as a problem. Cornell offered some marvelous distractions at the time. Vladimir Nabokov was lecturing on the European novel, Clinton Rossitor on politics, and David Daiches on poetry. Unfortunately, the architecture programs seemed cut off from all this. We had to cut required classes to get to the lectures and there was little hope of taking these courses for credit. Sadly, this isolation is still true of many professional programs." —John F. Hartray, Jr.

musical instrument. Not only will these relax you, but you may find some interesting connections between these other art forms and your own work.

Read widely outside your field. Reading can be relaxing and help you take your mind off the problems at hand. It can benefit you in several ways and help make you a much more educated person, not simply one who has been technically trained in a narrow specialty. A number of designers interviewed for this book admitted that reading outside the design professions was not only relaxing, but a fundamental component of their education, both while in school and ever since they graduated.

REDEFINE THE STUDIO SUBCULTURE: THE ROLE OF SLEEP AND FOOD

To Sleep, Perchance to Dream

Statistics indicate that most Americans sleep between 6 and 9 hours per day, with an average of 7 to 8 hours. But individuals' needs are different. How much sleep do you require? To test yourself, select a conventional sleep schedule of 11:00 P.M. to 7:00 A.M. and maintain it for about a week. Then switch to a 1:00 A.M. to 5:00 A.M. schedule, cutting down your sleep to 4 hours. If you still feel alert and well rested and can perform well even on the new schedule, your sleep requirement is only 4 hours. If this doesn't work for you, try another variation and test yourself again. Become aware of your own sleep barriers, your minimum sleep requirements, and use them to your advantage in your studio work. In general, you need enough sleep to be alert the next day.[12]

Studies of partial sleep restriction done for a few consecutive nights closely parallel the sleep patterns of design students the week before the jury. The research indicates that the following day, individuals typically show a drop in performance only when they are engaged in boring, routine tasks. On routine vigilance tests, however, individuals tend to become less motivated. What's interesting to note is that once studies are completed, however, people prefer to return to their usual amount of sleep, explaining that it simply made them feel better.[13]

Design students routinely stay up all night before the jury; some practitioners do the same before a competition deadline. The all-nighter syndrome has become one of the classic rituals of design education. For some, it may even be a symbol of machismo. But before your next all-nighter, consider the following: What are the effects of going without sleep? And what can you do about them?

Scientists have documented a strong relationship between one's body temperature cycle and fluctuations in performance and alertness. As body temperature decreases at the low point of the biological day, performance and alertness also decrease. People who stay awake for 24 hours at a time show peak performance near the middle of the day and their worst performance from 3:00 A.M. to 5:00 A.M. Performance may also show a "post-lunch dip" around 2:00 P.M. Nonetheless, even when people have been up all night, their performance starts to improve around 6:00 A.M.[14]

One of the nation's leading sleep researchers conducted a study of young student volunteers who were forced to stay awake for 48 hours at a time. The volunteers were tested regularly. Despite their increased sense of fatigue throughout the duration of the study, their performance on complex intellectual tests was not affected. *But what did deteriorate with time were attentiveness, the ability to follow simple routine, vigilance, and mood.* Students became increasingly depressed. The volunteers were tested repeatedly and results showed that they became progressively worse on almost all tasks except for those that were most complex and engaging. Willingness, motivation, and performance on low-level, boring tasks seem to suffer the most, causing errors of omission rather than commission.[15]

Another classic study of sleep deprivation for 51 hours obtained similar results, showing that during the first night, sleepiness tended to come between 4:00 and

6:00 A.M. During the second night, the subjects' moods worsened, tempers flared, and they struggled to stay awake. Again the pressure to sleep was most persistent during the early morning hours. The following day they became much more serious and grim, losing interest in whatever they were doing. They could do whatever they were told, but did so apathetically. Basically they became "'flattened' people doing a dull job in a dulled way."[16] Studies of even greater sleep deprivation reveal that after three days, momentary confusion, loss of train of thought, bursts of irritation, a spacy feeling, and general apathy are common symptoms. Even though when engaged in some short-term intensive effort, some people are able to "come out of it," they are likely to be confused, unable to concentrate or pay attention.[17]

The effects of sleep deprivation from the classic studio all-nighters are similar. Students' confusion and inability to concentrate on their design work sometimes results in accidental knife injuries and other calamities. Because low-level, boring tasks are among the first to go, it is no surprise that so many students appear at the jury with beautiful drawings that lack title, scale, orientation, and other identifying labels. And their proclivity toward bursts of irritation may simply exacerbate the psychological impact of a negative jury. So what can be done about all this?

Make the all-nighter syndrome a thing of the past (Figure 8-4). Don't let peer pressure convince you that it is the "macho" thing to do. Plan your time accordingly by using some of the techniques suggested in Chapter 4 so that you do not have to stay up all night. Faculty too can play an important role by making the studio inaccessible to students during the late night hours before a jury.[18]

There is no magic formula about how much sleep you should get. *Simply try your best to sleep as much as you normally do.* Your performance at the jury and your ability to retain and respond to criticism will be markedly improved.

Figure 8-4 Staying up all night can have harmful psychological and physiological effects. By learning how to budget your time properly, the all-nighter syndrome can become a thing of the past.

Some People Eat to Live...

Eating properly is a basic component of a healthy life-style. Few design students eat well around jury time. When your body is under stress, it uses higher-than-normal amounts of nutrients. When you release the hormone adrenalin, your body's metabolism speeds up and you need more B vitamins to help metabolize food for energy. You also need more vitamin C to help produce the adrenalin. The increased production of adrenalin causes you to release magnesium from your body—which may result in classic symptoms of stress such as muscle twitches and spasms, forgetfulness, depression, and a tendency to be startled easily. *Junk foods are almost always lacking in these nutrients, resulting in "empty calories."*[19]

Eating on the run, skipping meals, munching on unhealthy snacks, and drinking high doses of caffeine merely exacerbate the heavy toll stress is already taking on your body. If you are without food for several hours, your hormones change temporarily, and when you finally do eat, your blood sugar will first climb too high and then drop too low, often resulting in your soon feeling sleepy, anxious, and unable to concentrate. Alcohol can also make things worse by robbing the body of magnesium and vitamin B value.[20] So what kinds of foods can help you perform your best under the stress of studio?

Many dietitians argue that a nutritious, well-balanced diet is best: a combination of proteins (meat, fowl, fish, cheese), starches (breads, cereals, crackers, rice, pasta), fruits, vegetables (starchy, dark green, or deep yellow), and milk (milk or yogurt) every day (Figure 8-5). Don't reach for that Milky Way. Have an orange, strawberry, or kiwi instead. Proteins provide energy for athletes; they can do the same for designers too. Too many starches and carbohydrates can make you sleepy, so don't overdo them.

Not everyone agrees with these recommendations from the American Dietetic Association, however. Natural hygienists are highly critical of what they call "antiquated myths" about "the basic four food groups".[21] They provide convincing scientific evidence that dairy products are disease-producing, causing excess mucus that clogs and irritates the body's respiratory system and leading to such illnesses as hay fever, asthma, bronchitis, sinusitis, colds, runny noses, and other ailments.[22] Such maladies are common afflictions among design students. They also point to mounting evidence about the harm done by animal products. What is most important for a healthy diet, according to natural hygienists, *is to drink lots of water and eat high-water-content food (fruits and vegetables), to combine food properly by not eating proteins and starches at the same time, and to eat fruit correctly by having it alone on an empty stomach, preferably before noon.*[23]

Eat foods high in vitamins B and C and magnesium, especially dark green vegetables (spinach and broccoli), nuts, legumes, seafood, and whole grains.

Figure 8-5 Eating a well-balanced diet can be a tremendous energy booster before the jury. It is far preferable to the typical student diet of junk food from vending machines.

Eat at regular intervals and don't skip meals. Bring in healthy snacks from home like fruit, carrots, celery or nuts to have on hand at your studio desk. This way you will avoid the temptations from nearby vending machines.

Avoid caffeine and alcohol. Even though you think they may be helping you, they can actually make you feel worse. If you are struggling to stay awake, go home and sleep. Don't rely on coffee and coca-cola to keep you up. Bring in fruit juices from home to drink instead.

Encourage your school administrators to provide some small-scale, high-quality food service near the studio if at all possible. At some colleges and universities, cafes and small restaurants offering healthy foods are located directly in the environmental design building. Wurster Hall at the University of California, Berkeley, and Gund Hall at Harvard University are two such examples. Such spots provide a welcome alternative to the vending-machine junk food typically provided in most studio buildings. Even a small, portable kiosk selling sandwiches, salads, a variety of fruits, and healthy drinks will suffice. Such informal gathering spots are a much-needed retreat for students, faculty, and visitors to socialize and relax. If resources are scarce, students can take the initiative by helping to organize such facilities themselves.

In sum, reducing stress, exercising, and monitoring your sleeping and eating habits work in tandem with time management, communicating effectively, and other self-management skills (Figure 8-6). By developing these abilities, you should be able to survive the studio experience more successfully. Ideally, aim for a healthy life-style that allows you to place your studio work in perspective.

LEARNING THE ART OF STRESS REDUCTION
SUMMARY CHECKLIST

OVERCOME THE JURY JITTERS

___ Shortly before you present your work to the jury, use breathing as a relaxation technique.
___ Try the "Sarnoff Squeeze".
___ Identify your stress points and then relax them.
___ Take your mind off the stressor--even if only for a minute.
___ Think positive thoughts and reduce negative chatter.
___ Remind yourself that design is not the most important thing in the world.
___ Change your image of the jury by picturing them in their bathing suits.

REDUCE STRESS BEFORE AND AFTER THE JURY

___ Maintain a regular exercise program.
___ Set aside a notebook and spontaneously write down your feelings; free-associate.
___ Go to a natural setting where you can become as angry as you like without anyone watching.
___ Spend some time with a pet to help you relax.
___ Spend some time with small children that you enjoy.
___ Punch a punching bag.
___ Remember a time when you felt elated and enthusiastic about life, and take yourself there.
___ Buy some relaxation audio- or video tapes.
___ Take a slow, gentle bath while listening to your favorite relaxing music.

BROADEN YOUR HORIZONS

___ Attend a concert, performance, or lecture on a topic that has nothing to do with design.
___ Experience and learn from the other fine arts.
___ Read widely outside your field.

REDEFINE THE STUDIO SUBCULTURE: THE ROLE OF SLEEP AND FOOD

___ Make the all-nighter syndrome a thing of the past.
___ Sleep as much as you normally do--especially the night before the jury.
___ Eat a nutritious, well-balanced diet with lots of fruits and vegetables.
___ Eat foods high in vitamins B and C and magnesium: especially dark green vegetables, nuts, legumes, seafood, and whole grains.
___ Eat at regular intervals and don't skip meals.
___ Avoid caffeine and alcohol.
___ Encourage your school administrators to provide small-scale but high quality food service nearby the studio, if possible.

Figure 8-6 Summary checklist of stress reduction skills.

NOTES

1. Letter from Walter Gropius to his mother dated October 21, 1907, cited in Winifried Nerdinger, *Walter Gropius: The Architect Walter Gropius Drawings, Prints and Photographs from Busch-Reisinger Museum, Harvard University Art Museums, Cambridge/Mass. and from Bauhaus-Archiv Berlin. With Complete Project Catalog*, Cambridge, MA: Busch-Reisinger Museum, 1985, p. 29. Gropius had such trouble with drafting that he left the university in Munich, Germany, after only one semester. He continued his studies in Berlin a year later, but had such difficulties with the lectures that he again interrupted his study after four semesters, before he actually began his design training. He gained his primary design training through the office of Peter Behrens. It appears that Gropius never did learn to draw, and he considered the translation of a design concept into a drawing to be a support activity. Through conversations with coworkers, scholars have reconstructed that throughout his career as a designer, Gropius verbally outlined his ideas in detail to the specific designer, and then only in the rarest cases did he draw even a thumbnail sketch. After the designer drew up preliminary plans, Gropius further explained his ideas and indicated directions for further work. Designs were formed step by step through discussion. (Ibid., p. 31.)

2. The survey of 103 American Institute of Architecture Students administered in Phase 3 addressed this issue. In response to the question, "At your school, how often are jury grades the same as course grades?" students were evenly split: 33% responded "always," 33% "some of the time," and 34% "never." In answer to the question, "At your school, how often do faculty who serve as jurors contribute to the students' jury grades?" 43% said "always," 26% "sometimes," and 31% "never." In answer to the same question regarding visiting critics, 18% said "always," 32% "sometimes," and 50% "never." In response to the item, "At your school, how often does the instructor take the comments of guests into account on an informal basis in helping determine students' jury grades?" 38% said "always," 30% "sometimes," and 32% "never." Most agreed that the grading system varies from one instructor to another. These results indicate that at most schools, juries are tied into the grading process, thus making them a source of greater tension than they would be otherwise.

3. Furthermore, intense levels of stress often lead to procrastination, thus exacerbating many of the time management problems described in Chapter 4.

4. Lazarus, Richard S., "The Stress and Coping Paradigm," in C. Eisdorfer and D. Cohen (eds.), *Models for Clinical Psychopathology*, New York: Spectrum, 1981, pp. 177-214, cited in Kaplan, Howard B. (ed.), *Psychosocial Stress: Trends in Theory and Research*, New York: Harcourt Brace Jovanovich, 1983.

5. Kelly, Desmond, *Anxiety and Emotions: Physiological Basis and Treatment*, Springfield, IL: Thomas, 1980.

6. Levi, Lennart, *Preventing Work Stress*, Reading, MA: Addison-Wesley, 1981.

7. Epstein, Yakov M., "Crowding Stress and Human Behavior," in Gary Evans (ed.), *Environmental Stress*, New York: Cambridge University Press, 1982, pp. 133-148; Freedman, Jonathan, *Crowding and Behavior*, San Francisco: Freeman, 1975.

8. Kaplan, op. cit., pp. 162-163.

9. Sarnoff, Dorothy, with Gaylen Moore, *Never Be Nervous Again: The World-Renowned Speech Expert Reveals Her Time-Tested Method for Foolproof Control of Nervousness in Communicating Situations*, New York: Crown, 1987. See especially pp. 66-76. The next few paragraphs are paraphrased from the passages on pp. 67-69.

10. Literally hundreds of books are available on stress. Investing in a few good books on the subject is well worthwhile. Some of the following ideas are derived from Davis, Steven Andrew, *How to Stay Healthy in an Unhealthy World*, New York: Morrow, 1983; Gillespie, Peggy Roggenbuck, and Lynn Bechtel, *Less Stress in 30 Days: An Integrated Program for Relaxation*, New York: Signet, New American Library, 1986; Kaplan, Howard B. (ed.), *Psychosocial Stress: Trends in Theory and Research*, New York: Harcourt Brace Jovanovich, 1983; Lerner, Helene, with Roberta Elins, *Stress Breakers*, Minneapolis, MN: CompCare Publishers, 1985; Levi, Lennart, *Preventing Work Stress*, Reading, MA: Addison-Wesley, 1981; Mechanic, David, *Students Under Stress*, Glencoe, IL: Free Press, 1962; Nucho, Aina O., *Stress Management: The Quest for Zest*, Springfield, IL: Thomas, 1988.

11. I am often amazed at how few design students regularly attend campus events outside their major. While some may attend departmental guest lectures regularly, it is rare to see design students at concerts, plays, museum exhibits, and lectures on campus. More often than not, their excuse is that they are simply buried in studio and can't afford the time. Your college tuition helps support a variety of entertaining, informative events and it is wise to take advantage of them.

12. A fascinating discussion of biological clocks and how they control sleep, alertness, mood, and performance can be found in Coleman, Richard M., *Wide Awake at 3:00 A.M.: By Choice or by Chance?* San Francisco: Freeman, 1986. See especially p. 96. For those readers especially curious about sleep deprivation, the *Guinness Book of World Records* cites Maureen Weston of Peterborough, England, as the world-record holder for sleeplessness. She was able to stay up for 449 hours (18 days, 17 hours) during a rocking chair marathon in 1977. See *Ibid.*, p. 92. Even design students don't come close to this.

13. Ibid., p. 98

14. Ibid., p. 17

15. Goleman, Daniel, "Staying Up: The Rebellion Against Sleep's Gentle Tyranny," *Psychology Today* (March 1982), pp. 24, 27-28, 30-32, 35.

16. Webb, Wilse B., *Sleep: The Gentle Tyrant*, Englewood Cliffs, NJ: Prentice-Hall, 1975, p. 122.

17. Ibid., p. 124.

18. In Chapter 9 I suggest that faculty make a conscious effort to leave students alone during the final week before the project is due, and simply be available to help those students who need them. This will avoid the unnecessary "change orders"

from well-meaning instructors who offer criticism after it is too late.

19. In a highly controversial legal case, a poor diet of junk food was blamed as a major cause of diminished mental capacity. In the infamous "Twinkie defense" of Dan White, former member of the San Francisco Board of Supervisors and murderer of the city's mayor, George Moscone, and fellow supervisor Harvey Milk, the lawyer for White's defense was able to convince the jury that during the months preceding the fall 1978 assassinations, his client suffered from "diminished mental capacity" from an overabundance of junk food, especially Hostess Twinkies. As a result, White, who might otherwise have faced a conviction of premeditated murder and been sentenced to life in prison or the death penalty, was convicted of voluntary manslaughter and imprisoned for only a few years. He was since released and committed suicide.

20. See, for example, Davis, op. cit. pp. 49-50; Storm, Jackie, "Stressed Out? Good Food Can Help," *Women's Sport & Fitness*, 9 (September 1987), pp. 54-55.

21. Diamond, Harvey and Marilyn Diamond, *Fit for Life II: Living Health: The Complete Health Program!*, New York: Warner Books, Inc., 1987, p. 17.

22. Ibid., p. 243.

23. Ibid., pp. 28-44.

PART 4

WHAT FACULTY AND VISITING CRITICS CAN DO

"Men give away nothing so liberally as their advice."
—François de la Rochefoucauld

"Be slow of tongue and quick of eye." —Miguel de Cervantes

"Think like a man of action and act like a man of thought." —Henri Bergson

CHAPTER 9

Delivering Constructive Criticism

"Securing competent men for juries is no easy task.

"... Wise architectural criticism seldom suggests a solution, it suggests only a road, or perhaps several roads, by which a solution may be reached. ... The great critic never teaches architecture, he only suggests a method by which the problems of architecture may be attacked." — F. H. Bosworth, Jr. and Roy Childs Jones's thoughts on design criticism in the 1930s[1]

"Criticism will always be more useful when it informs the future than when it scores the past." — Wayne Attoe in Architecture and Critical Imagination[2]

"... There has been great talk recently of a number of jurors who have forgotten the insecurities and sensitivity of those just beginning to equip themselves for the architectural profession: a humiliating and personally degrading bootcamp of a jury can be much like Drano in the eyelids for a student (Figure 9-1).

"... What good can such personal attacks do when meant to injure rather than educate? To give a student a swift kick rather than a general direction can only provide frustration that will kill that spark to explore. ... What you [the juror] say in those forgotten five minutes will be remembered by the student for years to come." — David Schlensker, editor of an architecture student newsletter[3]

A CRITIQUE OF CRITICISM

Before we begin our analysis of criticism in the jury, let us take a minute to look at the broader implications of what it means to be a critic, be it on the jury or at the studio desk. Unfortunately in the design fields, the words *criticism* and *critic* have pejorative connotations and are often equated with expressions of disapproval. More importantly, however, these words imply the passing of judgment. The design professions are not alone in this regard. Art critics, food critics, and film critics are often cited for their pithy judgmental remarks such as "For the best clam chowder in Boston, you must dine at ..."; "Absolutely sensational—one of the year's ten best films!" "A summer sleeper."

Some scholars have defined criticism as "a form of studied discourse about works of art. It is a use of language designed to facilitate and enrich the understanding of art." In this light, four procedures of criticism have been outlined: description, interpretation, evaluation, and theory, evaluation being neither necessary nor sufficient for criticism.[4] Many distinctions among types of criticism have been drawn: exploratory versus argumentative, applied versus theoretical, "connoisseurship," and others. Andy Grundberg, a photography critic for the *New York Times*, sharply rejects the latter. According to Grundberg, "connoisseurs," be it of wine, photography, or design, make proclamations of "good" or "bad" based on their own particular tastes. The supporting reasons for these proclamations are rarely given, and without the benefit of explicit criteria, they are merely idiosyncratic, don't lend themselves readily to discussion, and are not informative.[5] Unfortunately, designers often play the role of connoisseur while serving on juries. Relying primarily on criticism based strictly on their own personal taste can create chaos and confusion for students.

Criticism at design juries can be viewed from a sociological perspective, such as that sketched by Herbert Gans in his classic book, *Popular Culture and High Culture*. *Mass* or *popular culture* refers to that which is imbibed by the masses. *High culture* refers to the art, music, literature, and other symbols preferred by the well-educated, "cultured" elite, as well as their styles of thought and feeling. *Taste cultures* consist of values and their cultural forms—music, art, design, literature, drama, comedy, poetry, criticism,

Figure 9-1 Here is how one design student pictured his response to jurors' destructive criticism, complete with tar and feathers. (Source: Clayton Haldeman.)

> "The one thing I learned... which has carried me all along to this day, 20 years later, and to my own teaching... and I always tell people who teach: do not ever assume the skills of a student. Do not ever assume it. If you do, you will do terrible things to that person. The truth is that no teacher ever really knows the capacity of skills and the direction of skills of a student." —Ronette J. King
>
> "I think that a student has to be fairly strong to withstand some of these juries and come out of them with self-confidence.
>
> "...A juror shouldn't serve unless they're prepared to spend some preparation time. There's a certain amount of danger in shooting from the hip. If you're not familiar with the project you ought to have enough time to clearly read the problem statement, visit the site, and understand what's going on. Ninety percent of success as a juror may just be showing up, but I think the jurist needs to be more than 90% successful. I think the [rest] is showing up prepared." —Christopher Degenhardt
>
> "[When I was in school, I was in a class with a] classic middle-guard football player, and he was BIG. The guy could draw up a storm, but his hands—and his fingers—were that big around. And I remember one of the instructors telling him, 'Those are the hands of a butcher, those are not the hands of a designer.' I don't think people realize how devastating an off-hand comment like that can be.... Teachers don't realize how much power they have over students. I think they have to be careful of what they say and do to people.
>
> "... The whole thing is about when you were four years old and you hold it up and say, 'Mommy, Mommy, look what I did!' That's why it's so personally devastating and hard because it's your heart on the paper that you're holding up. And [negative criticism at a jury] is as if the mother of the four year old kid had turned around and said, 'That's a terrible picture!'" —William Callaway
>
> "I think that one of the worst things that happens with juries is to get some outside critic who comes in and who doesn't bother to take the time to learn anything about the project and starts to shoot from the hip.... It's amazing how many times you're asked to go and serve on a jury and the faculty don't tell you what the project is even about. You just walk in and you're supposed to start this spout of wisdom.
>
> "... What the faculty ought to do is to not say this is wrong or this is right, so much as this would be a way to advance the process." —Joseph Esherick
>
> "I know people who were devastated by this experience and really never recovered... people who did not survive well in this climate of criticism... I think that today people should be seriously reexamining that whole educational process to determine whether or not there is an alternative way of positively reinforcing the learning experience rather than using the criticism mode exclusively." —Donald J. Hackl
>
> "Faculty should be responsible for seeing that the jury comments are organized and to the point, and not simply a vehicle for a jury member to show how smart he is. If there is any value to it at all, it is to help the student to see how he might have thought more clearly in general or in some detail. And not just for the faculty to be a loose, unled rabble." —Lawrence B. Perkins
>
> "When I am in the Standard Jury System, the only options open to me to encourage dialogue/dissent/discussion are to: (1) encourage students to talk—often I try not to talk until a student voices something; (2) realize my position of power and not say things that are insulting or derogatory; and (3) realize that as a faculty member I am talking about the students themselves. All of us have heard and said the following: 'We are not talking about you, we are talking about your work.' This is a strange statement, because while true, it is also false. The students certainly don't believe it. When they hang up their work, they feel they are hanging up part of themselves. I think if we acknowledged the intimate connection between students and their work, we actually might talk about it quite differently." —Professor Thomas Dutton, Miami University.

news—and the media in which they are expressed—books, magazines, newspapers, records, films and television programs, paintings and sculpture, and architecture, as well as in ordinary consumer goods like furnishings, clothes, appliances, and automobiles.[6]

Extrapolating from Gans's work, *one of the hidden agendas of criticism at design juries is to acculturate students from popular, or mass, culture into high culture.* This is accomplished through the transmission of the taste culture of the environmental design professions. An unspoken mission of jurors is to ensure that these taste values are not only transmitted but imbibed by students. That is why, for example, if an architecture student's final design clearly resembles a tract house built by a developer, jurors are likely to pounce. They may even question why that student is even bothering to study architecture if her design looks just like that of the mass building industry.

In his book, *Architectural and Critical Imagination*, Wayne Attoe suggests that criticism is broadly concerned with evaluating, interpreting, and describing. Rarely is criticism concerned with just one of these.[7] Attoe also draws distinctions among three types of criticism. *Normative criticism* is based on norms—doctrines, systems, types, measures, or standards. Judging whether or not an architectural design fulfills building codes is one example. *Interpretive criticism* is impressionistic, evocative, or advocative; the critic tries to make us see the environment in a particular way. Interpreting a place based on how it makes you feel is one example. *Descriptive criticism* is biographical or contextual, describing physical phenomena, events in the life of the designer, or the historical context that influenced design decisions. Describing the historical events that influenced the professional development of Frank Lloyd Wright would be an example of descriptive criticism.[8] As Attoe concludes, "criticism is first and foremost about the critic, not about the object criticized."[9] How true! Consider the following:

> "*The reviewer knows of no psychiatrist who agrees with Szasz and is sorry to consider his book a total waste of time.*"—Review of Thomas S. Szasz's 1962 seminal book, The Myth of Mental Illness[10]
>
> "*There is plenty of hot air in this particular balloon, but I don't see it going anywhere.*"—John Russell's New York Times *book review of Tom Wolfe's* The Painted Word[11]
>
> "*... a copyeditor's despair, a propounder of endless riddles.*"—Atlantic Monthly's *review of the 1962* Webster's Third New International Dictionary of the English Language[12]
>
> "*The New York audience, the night I went, gave the play a standing ovation. A cynical friend maintains that Broadway audiences always do this to justify to themselves the mountainous cost of the evening out....*"—*Drama critic Robert Cushman's reaction in* Observer *to Peter Shaffer's 1981 smash hit* Amadeus[13]
>
> "[*The public should*] *weep over the lifelessness of its melody and harmony, so derivitive, so stale, so inexpressive.*"—*Music critic Lawrence Gilman's reaction to the 1924 premier performance of George Gershwin's classic,* Rhapsody in Blue[14]

This brief critique of criticism provides a useful framework from which to view criticism at juries. My experience as a participant-observer and accounts from students, faculty, and practitioners have confirmed that design critics have a strong tendency to overemphasize the negative. In a typical 15-minute review of a student's work, jurors' comments tend to run about 12 minutes on its weaknesses and only about 3 minutes, if even that, on its strengths. *This disproportionately negative slant tips the scale in such a way that often students can't even recall if the jurors said anything at all good about their work*. Recipients of criticism naturally tend to focus on negative aspects that others point out and often overlook any positive remarks that were made. A pianist may give a marvelous performance of a classical concerto, but if she lands on the wrong note at the very end of the piece, she will undoubt-

Figure 9-2 Most people have a tendency to dwell on negative criticism and ignore whatever positive is said about their work. A pianist who gives a flawless performance of a classical concerto until her grand finale on the wrong note is likely to be obsessed with her mistake, no matter how great the applause. Design students are the same way. One devastating remark from the jury, and whatever favorable has been said tends to be erased.

edly be plagued by her mistake long after the concert is over (Figure 9-2).

A faculty member once suggested delivering all the positive criticism first, and then following it with negative remarks. The reason for this, apparently, is that once the negative comments are made, in the recipient's mind, they tend to overshadow and obscure all subsequent remarks. This notion is worthy of further study.

Others have suggested focusing on what the student identified as being most important in the project, that is, the project's goals and what she was trying to accomplish. The jurors' role is then to comment on the extent to which these goals were achieved.

My own personal strategy as a juror, whenever possible, is generally to *begin with specific, positive points, insert the negative points in the middle, and close with some more general positive points at the end*. This allows my critique to provide a balance of the positive and negative, and to end on an upbeat note. The student is not left just standing there hanging his head in despair.

In order to make my comments in this order, I rarely am the first juror to speak. Speaking spontaneously does not allow me to offer my thoughts in this order. Instead, I generally need a few minutes to write down and organize my reactions. I write them in two columns: positive and negative (Figure 9-3).

What is needed is an appropriate balance between negative and positive criticism. Although it may not come naturally, if you try hard enough in your role as juror, you

POSITIVE

Specific

+ Clear distinction between what is new and what is existing
+ Strong set of plans, including not only floor plans but also lighting, landscaping, and site design
+ Clear, clean drafting
+ Title, scale and orientation are clearly indicated
+ Good before and after images
+ Much natural light
+ Attractive swimming pool area

General

+ Overall this design truly enhances and improves upon what is currently on the site. It has the potential to change the image of this place and turn it into a major tourist destination.

NEGATIVE

Specific

- From the rear view, the exterior of the pool addition does not tie in well with the rest of the project.
- The arrangement whereby two private guest rooms overlook an interior pool is odd. These rooms may be dark and noisy. The view is good and it would be better if a more public space overlooked the pool, thus offering a special benefit to more visitors.
- The corner window of one of the children's rooms looks right into the parents' bedroom.
- Due to the way the building is oriented, a good part of the pool area will be in the shade for most of the day. Sunbathers will likely be unhappy with this.

Figure 9-3 Before offering criticism, think about the positive and negative points you would like to make. Think of both general and specific criticisms in each area.

can always find at least some aspect of a project to praise. Maybe the design concept has even greater potential than the student recognizes. Maybe the labels are exceptionally clear. Perhaps the sheer amount of work displayed is commendable.

Results from this research indicate that from the students' point of view, the key issue is not whether or not criticism is positive or negative, but rather *how the criticism is delivered*. What's wrong with how criticism is delivered at juries? It is often:

- Too personal
- Too vague
- Too destructive

STOP, LOOK, AND LISTEN

Before one begins to deliver design criticism, it is essential to absorb what students are both showing and saying. Getting a good grasp of the project and understanding it as fully as possible are prerequisites to being able to deliver criticism that is both intelligent and useful to students. Yet this is not always easy to do.

Serving as a juror can often be a taxing experience, and jurors must arrive prepared to help educate students. In fact, my own performance as a juror is greatly affected by the amount of sleep I have had the night before. Not surprisingly, this sounds quite like the same situation that design students face. Getting a good night's sleep before a jury can help you be more alert and attentive as a juror.

To be an effective juror, you must take the time to study the project in front of you as carefully as you can. This means looking at and interpreting all drawings and models; these can often include several separate components that must be absorbed simultaneously. At the same time, you must not only hear but carefully listen to the student's oral presentation; often this presentation calls attention to particular highlights in the drawings and models. And while all this is going on, you must be thinking about how you will respond: What will you say, and how will you say it? Even the most talented designers and the most articulate spokespersons can find it quite a challenge to juggle all these tasks at once.

Being a good listener is an acquired skill. *It is paramount that jurors first listen, then evaluate.* Review the techniques suggested in Chapter 6; they apply just as well to jurors as they do to students. As psychologist Carl Rogers has stated,

> "Real communication occurs, and this evaluative tendency is avoided, when we listen with understanding. What does this mean? It means to see the expressed ideas and attitude from the other person's point of view, to sense how it feels to him, to achieve his frame of reference in regard to the thing he is talking about."[5]

One way that counselors and psychologists suggest to improve your listening skills is to practice the technique of *active listening*. This simply involves briefly restating what another has just stated in your own words, and then giving the other person the opportunity to verify whether or not your interpretation is in fact correct. My own suggestion is that jurors engage in this practice immediately after the student has finished her presentation. For instance, as a juror you might say, "So, as I understand it, your major concept in this design project is. . . . Could you please tell be briefly, am I interpreting you correctly or not?" After the student's response, ask for a few minutes of silence before you begin your comments. This will allow for some time to concentrate on the design work you have just seen and to prepare some thoughtful remarks. It will also allow the more verbally oriented to jot some of their comments down in writing. This will make for a more coherent, organized, and concise response.[16]

Active listening also means that each person hears out the other's point of view. In other words, *do not interrupt the student's presentation*. Unfortunately, too few design critics heed this advice. Perched at the edge of their seats, jurors often leap prematurely into the criticism mode even before students have finished presenting their work. This not only throws the students off guard, making it more difficult for them to remember the criticism you may offer, but it also can disrupt the train of thought of the other critics on the jury. After hearing you speak, other jurors may think that now it must be their turn. They may start speaking before they have had enough time to organize their thoughts. This abrupt shift in focus from the project presentation to critical response can have a catalytic effect that in turn can render a critique session much less valuable to the students.

Jurors, too, need to be sensitive to each other. The do-not-interrupt rule applies here as well. At many schools, this pattern of interrupting tends to reflect various subconscious "pecking orders." Deans and department chairs are more likely to interrupt faculty, senior faculty are more likely to interrupt junior faculty, some "stellar" visiting critics interrupt faculty, and more likely than not, men interrupt women. Studies of speech patterns have shown that women, more than men, often believe that cutting someone off in mid-sentence is rude. They are less likely to do the interrupting, and when interrupted, they often fall silent.[17] In order to welcome women into the design professions — as students, educators, and jurors — male jurors ought to pay particular attention to this trend and hear out their female counterparts. The dynamics that occur within the jury are extremely important. Jurors must realize that their jury style is sending messages to both students and other jurors about what and who they think is important. To avoid the dominance of any one juror, some design faculty develop a pattern so that jurors rotate their order of speaking.

FOCUS ON THE PROJECT, NOT THE PERSON

Let us next examine how criticism can be *much too personal*. Although students are often advised not to take criticism at the design jury personally, when the criticism is directed at themselves rather than at their project — for example, being told they are better off selling dresses, repeating freshman design, or getting out of the profession altogether — how can they help but see it as a personal attack? *Before you say a word, stop to think how you would feel if you were in the student's shoes. Apply the Golden Rule: Do unto others as you would have them do unto you.*

Whether it is positive or negative, criticism *aimed at the person rather than at the project* can be equally irritating. If a juror says to a student, "You're really a talented designer!" what does this really mean? Specifically what was it about the student's design work that prompted that comment? Without that information, the compliment, although well tended, does little to inform or educate. It is simply a pat on the back. "This is an excellent project because it communicates very clearly" is more meaningful. Similarly, if a juror remarks, "You'll never make it as an interior designer!" what does this mean? Why won't the student do well in the field? Without having seen the student's entire array of work over several years of schooling, how can a juror fairly condemn the student to future failure? The message that comes across from this statement simply boils down to, "You're no good."

Marriage and family counselors often suggest directing criticism toward specific behaviors rather than at one's personality as an important step in helping couples get along more harmoniously. For example, rather than telling your spouse, "You really are a stupid fool, aren't you?" you are likely to get a more favorable reaction by saying, "You knew we were planning to be away on vacation that week. I wish you hadn't asked your mother to come and visit us at exactly that time! Can you please call her and ask her to visit at a later date?"

At the jury, shifting the focus from the person to the project can have the same effect (Figure 9-4). *Simply taking the word "you" out of your comments will go a*

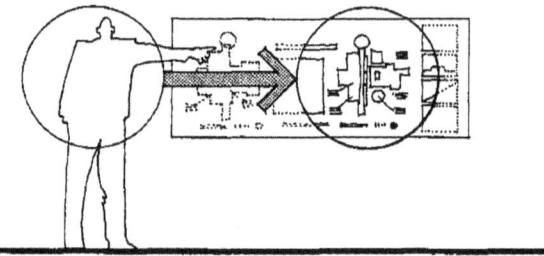

Figure 9-4 Shifting the focus from the person to the project will help relieve a great deal of pressure that students experience at the jury.

PERSONAL ATTACK

You don't seem to have any idea what you're doing here.

I don't think you have really thought this project through enough.

You really haven't solved the problem.

You haven't spent enough time on this yet.

CRITICISM OF THE PROJECT

The project does not look finished yet. I can't understand what exactly is a section and what is a plan. Please provide adequate labeling to help explain each individual drawing.

The concept is an appropriate one, however it is not yet well enough elaborated in your design scheme. Next time try to illustrate specifically how your concept is carried out throughout your design. Be sure to highlight this in your drawings and in your oral presentation.

I see floor three but not floor two, which will be substantially different. We need to understand how each floor will be in order to better understand how the entire building will work.

In order for this project to satisfy building codes, it needs more stairways, fire exits, spaces for mechanical systems, and a service area for the restaurant.

Figure 9-5 Critique the design project, not the person who created it. Your words will have an altogether different impact.

long way. For the untrained, this requires a constant effort, so the trick is to think carefully before you speak. Figure 9-5 contains selected excerpts from actual jurors' comments and shows how to improve them.

You can also add a qualifier to what you are saying in order to help the students place your comments in perspective. For instance, "Keep in mind that what I am saying now is directed to this specific project in this stage of your professional development. I'm sure your future projects will be much improved."

BE SPECIFIC

Another serious problem with the way criticism is delivered at juries is that it is often *much too vague.* Jurors often tend to speak in superlatives, using words like *marvelous, awful, dramatic,* or *horrible.* Again, the student's reaction is often, "So what?" Such abstract words really don't do much to inform the student. Other jurors simply fail to give a reason or rationale behind their reactions. Just as students are advised against telling the jury that they chose a particular design just because "I liked it," jurors are cautioned against responding in the same superficial way. While preparing your response to a project, try to always keep in mind that ultimately *how you react is not nearly as important as why you react the way you do.* Figure 9-6 shows some examples.

Separate out which comments apply directly to the project at hand and which can be generalized to other projects. *Instruct students to listen for insights from the jury that can apply to their future work,* whether it be a school, a railroad station, or a zoo.

If you are truly uncertain about your reaction to a project, it is far better to acknowledge this openly rather than to begin rattling off some vague comments in the hopes of sounding intelligent. Chances are that no matter how hard you try, students will still be confused by what you have to say. *Don't hesitate to say, "I don't know."* Or, "Right now I have mixed reactions to some of your design decisions. It's difficult for me to resolve them in just a few minutes when you have spent so much time on this project. I need more time to think about what I have seen."

In some cases, *statements of opinion are less instructive than raising questions.* Instead of saying, "I really don't like this project," try saying, "I wonder in what other ways some of your project goals could be achieved. What do you think?" Address your question not only to the student presenting, but also to the rest of the class. Encourage a group discussion on the subject. Asking questions allows students to become more involved in the jury process. As a juror, you come across as less judgemental and more helpful.

VAGUE

This project has a wonderful feeling about it.

I really like it. I don't know why, but I do.

This is really ugly.

Something about it just rubs me the wrong way.

SPECIFIC

The relationships between solids and voids here, i.e., the massing of the buildings and the innovative use of open spaces between them, can create a very exciting space for pedestrians. This project would satisfy William Whyte's criteria in his well known book and film, The Social Life of Small Urban Spaces.

The building is much too massive for the site. It overwhelms its surroundings and dwarfs some of the historic structures nearby. The fenestration pattern needs further study as well. Right now the proportion of windows to building solids looks inappropriate--the windows are too small, like little holes in the walls.

Figure 9-6 Be as specific as possible in delivering criticism. Vague statements do not mean much to students.

OFFER SOME GUIDANCE

Criticism needs to be constructive rather than destructive. What exactly distinguishes one from the other? Destructive criticism offers few suggestions about how to remedy an unsatisfactory situation. Students cannot really learn much from it, except that they must have "done something wrong." By contrast, constructive criticism points out the negatives, but is phrased in such a way that students can take further action to improve. Some loose direction or guidance is given (Figure 9-7).

Psychologists and learning theorists have clearly demonstrated the educational value of positive as opposed to negative reinforcement.[18] The same principles that apply to teaching animals and small children apply to design students. Before lashing out at what students have done wrong, consider what they have done right. Aim for praise, not punishment.

Certain key phrases can help shift the emphasis to constructive criticism: "The project would be greatly improved if..."; "It would be better if..."; "In case you get a chance to work some more on this project for your portfolio..."; "If class lasted another two weeks..."; "What would help is..."; "My suggestion is..."; "If you had a chance to start this project all over again..."; and so on. One technique is simply to try to shift your grammar to the subjunctive conditional tense—*if, then* types of statements. Another is simply to imply the future in your comments, even if this particular project really has no future (i.e., it is officially "over"): "Next time..."; "In any future work on this project..."; and so on. Yet another technique is simply to avoid the word *not* in your critiques.

As a faculty member or visiting critic, you may find it especially taxing to try to come up with kindhearted comments when you are presented with work that is obviously incomplete and a last-minute, rush job. This is particularly the case when you know that a student is capable of producing work of much higher quality. Under these circumstances, you may be tempted to express your anger directly at the student during the jury (Figure 9-8). While the feeling may well be justified, *chastising the student in public can sometimes make matters even worse.* As psychologist Carol Tavris has demonstrated through her ground-breaking research, taking anger out on others can often do more harm than good.[19] In fact, Tavris's research has debunked the myth of the so-called ventilationist theory that is still widespread among clinical psychologists, psychiatrists, and the general public—that is, that expressing your anger is healthy for you. To the contrary, Tavris points to countless studies that prove just the opposite: Getting anger out of your system can lead to unhappy side effects, both for yourself and others.

My suggestion is that *projects that are unfinished can be discussed in great depth during interim juries, but they*

> "My puppy is going through obedience training. I have learned through my dog trainer that animals learn more quickly with positive reinforcement. The more negative you are, the less quickly they will learn. What's true for animals is also true for people.... Students are especially sensitive about their own self confidence, whether or not they're capable of doing design, and whether or not they really know what they are doing. That's why it's important to be constructive without being overly negative."—Ronette J. King

DESTRUCTIVE	CONSTRUCTIVE
That's about the worst project I've ever seen.	This project needs to be reworked so that the scale of the furniture relates more closely to the scale of the room. Right now the furniture completely overpowers the space. If you had more time to work on this project, the next thing to do would be to either scale down the furniture or scale up the space.
This class needs to throw out everything they've done so far and start from scratch.	
Come and stand next to the window and let me look through your ear. I see light!	
	The landscape that has been proposed is too monotonous. It is basically a large, green lawn with only a few trees added on for good measure. The emphasis shown is purely two-dimensional--and overly horizontal. What is needed is more volume and depth to create some greater interest and excitement in all three dimensions.

Figure 9-7 Phrase your criticism so that it is constructive rather than destructive.

Figure 9-8 Publicly chastising students for poor or incomplete design work does little to enhance their self-esteem. Such condescending behavior can easily help spawn inferiority complexes. Chronically poor students must be counseled—but in private.

be excluded altogether from final juries. In this way you are not comparing apples with oranges, so to speak, that is, criticizing some projects that are completely finished alongside others that are only 60% or 70% complete. Eliminating discussions of unfinished work altogether from final juries will provide a strong incentive for students to complete their work on time. More on this is presented in Chapter 10.[20]

Students with chronically incomplete or lamentable design work need to be counseled—but in private. *If you have students in your studio whose design work consistently looks truly hopeless, meet with them alone in your office, close the door, and tell them candidly—but tactfully—what you think.* In this case, comments like the following are entirely appropriate: "Design seems to be very difficult for you, as it is for many others. I'm afraid that you may become increasingly frustrated with the field the longer you stay in it. I know this is hard to take, but I really think you might be better off pursuing a different field of study altogether. You may want to think this over for awhile and decide for yourself what is best for you." Although the student still may become flustered or upset, the impact of such advice is entirely different when delivered in private, and not broadcast in front of peers. Some of the more sensitive instructors I know always keep a box of tissues tucked away in their desk drawer to have on hand for such occasions. At times like this, they are much appreciated.

You may have noticed one inherent difficulty in trying to improve the way in which criticism is delivered. In order to be careful not to fall into the usual patterns, language must be used with extreme care. It is often a challenge to try to sound articulate while thinking quickly on your feet. Unless we are able to slow ourselves down, it is nearly impossible to censor every word that comes out of our mouths. Careful, thoughtful criticism is usually more easily delivered in written rather than oral form. Might it be unrealistic to think that, as jurors, we can effectively deliver criticism in such a spontaneous setting, while we ourselves are "on the hot seat"? We will talk more about this in Chapter 10 when we discuss some alternatives to design juries.

WRITE IT DOWN

Interviews with students reveal that when it is offered to them in a coherent manner, most design students relish written criticism about their work. Unfortunately, written criticism is a rare component at most design juries.[21] But *writing down critical comments can help jurors to be more precise and informative than they would be otherwise.*

The School of Architecture at the University of Illinois at Urbana-Champaign strongly suggests that its faculty provide written juror comments to students. The course instructor generally collects these written comments from the jurors, reproduces them after the jury, and then distributes them to the students. After an interim jury, many students choose to pin up the jurors' comments in front of their studio desks so that they have a constant reminder of the criticism they received, and try to act upon the jurors' comments during their subsequent work on the project.

But doesn't this simply add one more task to the already overloaded juror? This is true. However, the payoff is extremely great. *Student surveys, interviews, and diaries confirm that all too often, what students hear at the jury goes in one ear and out the other.* Yet written criticism can have a much more long-lasting effect. A simple analogy is that between a telephone conversation and a letter. While a phone conversation is much more spontaneous and free-flowing, it is virtually impossible to remember exactly what the caller told you once you both hang up the phone. You are both attempting to listen to each other and respond at the same time. But a letter, on the other hand, allows you the opportunity to read the message over as many times as you like, without your own reactions getting in the way.

Written criticism has the disadvantage, however, of being unable to express tone and voice inflection, and once delivered, it cannot be questioned easily, unless students seek out the jurors individually. In contrast to the temporary nature of oral criticism, what is written tends to acquire an aura of truth or permanence. As one design student put it, "In this sense, it is a double-edged sword. Where it can help tremendously, it can also be lethal." *If you choose to provide written criticism, be careful exactly what you write and how you write it.* Picture how you would feel if you were on the receiving end.

At Urbana-Champaign, written criticism is delivered in a variety of formats. Some instructors simply scribble quick notes, either in written or graphic form. Others take the time to write or draw carefully enough so that the students can read and understand it. Students report that while "chicken-scratch" is virtually useless, the legible responses can be invaluable.

Some design instructors provide jurors with special forms purposely created for that jury. These may be quite general or highly specific, depending on the instructors' preferences. Students tend to prefer those forms that are not simply open-ended, but that contain some more specific information about certain aspects of their project, for instance, the degree to which the students met their intended goals. In developing these forms, instructors should be cautioned not to ask for too much. I have seen some forms that have asked for detailed ratings on a scale of 1 to 10 for some 15 items or more. In the traditional jury format, this makes the jurors' job much too difficult. Asking only about a few key items, such as site planning, fit into context, and so on, is usually sufficient. Or even more generally, simply ask for strengths, weaknesses, and suggestions for improvement, not unlike the postoccupancy evaluation (POE) questions discussed earlier. Some examplary jury evaluation forms are provided in Appendix C, Figures C-2 and C-3.[22] Tailor-make these to suit the needs of the particular project at hand. You may wish to use different forms for interim and final juries.

One way around the logistical difficulties of having jurors deliver written criticism is to ask students to assume this task.[23] Ask them to bring a tape recorder to the jury and to transcribe the comments afterwards. Or ask them to have two friends write down the juror's comments. Chapter 10 describes some of these ideas in greater detail.

CONSIDER YOUR OVERALL VERBAL AND NONVERBAL COMMUNICATION STYLE

In addition to thinking carefully about exactly what you say, and trying to deliver more well balanced, specific, constructive, and less personal criticism, jurors would do well to begin thinking about their overall communication style and how they come across to students. Both your verbal and nonverbal communication influence your ability to be an effective design critic.

Just as students need to improve their public-speaking abilities, so do certain members of the jury. Again, the techniques suggested to students in Chapter 6 apply to jurors as well. Some jurors may speak too quickly or softly or have a tendency to mumble. No wonder other students in the room start getting fidgety—they can't even hear what the juror is saying. It is important to *address comments not only to the student who is presenting but to the rest of the class as well.* This means establishing close eye contact with all parties in the room—presenters, jurors, the studio critic, and the rest of the class.

Maintaining eye contact with the students presenting their work helps them understand that you are paying attention to what they are saying. Occasionally nodding your head, smiling, and giving other nonverbal signs of acceptance can also help boost the student's self-confidence during a presentation. Naturally, you shouldn't overdo this lest you, yourself, become a visible distraction. It is equally important to spend time establishing eye contact with the project—looking it over carefully and trying to clearly understand it. This may mean having to get up out of your chair to take a closer look. When students see you carefully examining their drawings and models, they realize that you are indeed interested in their work.

Nonverbal communication — anything that transcends spoken or written words — is just as important as verbal communication[24] (Figure 9-9). Data from the observations of 130 student jury presentations revealed that most faculty showed signs of nervous, nonverbal behavior such as avoiding eye contact, covering up the mouth or chin, twiddling fingers, tapping feet, and scratching. Such signs of tension are transmitted to students, who are already in the same shape or worse.

Facial expressions, bodily motions, voice quality, and physiological responses all convey messages between jurors and students, between jurors and the rest of the class, and among jurors themselves. Smiles, frowns, grimaces, raised eyebrows, twisted lips; posture, body movements, gestures; the tone, pitch, level, intensity, and inflection of your voice, as well as the spacing of words, emphases, pauses, and silences; quickened breathing and other physiological responses send signals to students about what you are really thinking and feeling about their work. Nonverbal behavior punctuates verbal messages much like periods, question marks, exclamation points, and underlines punctuate the written word.[25]

Nonverbal behavior, or body language, can modify interpersonal communication in at least four different ways: confirming or repeating what is being said, denying or confusing, strengthening or emphasizing, or regulating or controlling.[26] For instance, leaning forward while someone is speaking tends to confirm what you are saying. If you express anger toward a student whose work is incomplete or inferior, yet say that with a smile, you are denying or confusing what you are saying. Stalking out of a room or speaking loudly and with carefully phrased pauses can strengthen or amplify your message. Gesturing with your hands and clearing your throat send a signal to other jurors that you are ready to speak, thus regulating or controlling the conversation.

Figure 9-9 Jurors must pay careful attention to the nonverbal messages they are sending to students and other jurors.

Jurors with minor physical disabilities such as nervous movements, tics, or hearing loss need to be sensitive to how these can affect students. One professor described a colleague with a hearing aid who kept the battery in his shirt pocket. Quite often, the battery would make a sharp whistling noise, something that devastated students in the middle of their jury presentations. Not knowing what the sound was, the students thought that the old professor was signaling his disapproval to other jurors. In this case, simply notifying the class about the situation would have rectified the problem.

It is important that jurors be aware of how they are behaving nonverbally so that they realize the subtle, subconscious messages they may be sending to students and others on the jury. Ultimately, *jurors need to try to maintain consistency between their verbal and nonverbal behavior.* For example, if you tell a student, "It looks as if you have an interesting project here," while at the same time your eyes are wandering nervously about, you are scratching your head, frantically tapping your foot, and displaying an unfriendly scowl on your face, you are sending inconsistent messages. While your verbal behavior may imply a positive connotation, your nonverbal behavior implies just the opposite. Maintaining consistency between what you say and how you — and your body — say it helps reduce the tension and confusion that students experience "on the hot seat."

Nonverbal behavior is highly complex and difficult to interpret. It differs greatly from one person to another, and people on the receiving end often interpret it differently as well. Nonetheless, the key to sending and receiving nonverbal communication effectively within the context of design juries is to be sensitive to the fact that not only the student, but you, too, are "on the hot seat," and that your every move is being scrutinized.

HELPFUL DESK CRITIQUES

What about design criticism in its more private form — at the desk? In general, the same principles apply. As in the design jury, faculty engaged in desk critiques should try to avoid the attack-defense, win-lose syndrome that does little to educate. Put more simply, *"Honey will get you farther than vinegar."*[27]

The timing of desk critiques is key. As we have noted earlier, criticism — no matter from whom — provided at the last minute is simply too late. Past a certain stage, substantive criticism about the design is of little use, as it can cause serious domino effects that cannot be resolved by the deadline. *Once students are in the production stage of their drawings and models, professors are best off simply remaining "on call" for those who need technical assistance. At these times, it may even be a good idea for the professor to legitimately "disappear."*

While the desk crit is a more private form of criticism than is the design jury, it is more public than it appears at first glance. In the bullpen-like arrangement of most design studios, acoustic privacy is near impossible (Figure 9-10). So while instructors may think their words are only being heard by the student at hand, in fact her *neighbors are within easy earshot and can often pick up every word.* Faculty need to keep this in mind whenever they hold a desk crit. Nonetheless, desk crits provide opportunities to discuss specific aspects of a project in greater detail and to monitor students' progress on a regular basis.

Design critics have different ways of operating, and no one technique is perfect. Some prefer to whip out a pencil and draw their criticism, saying little if anything to the student. Criticism is performed strictly in the visual mode, and many students find this highly informative. Others prefer to engage in a dialogue with the student, exchanging ideas in a "reflection-in-action" mode, to use Donald Schön's term.[28] Some faculty offer specific suggestions, while others simply raise questions for the student to ponder over. What is most important to remember, however, is that the project is the student's, not yours, and that designing the project for them will not help them learn much in the long run.

Among the possible outcomes of desk crits in the design studio, as Schön has eloquently described, are students as "counterlearners," who are only concerned with giving their instructor what they are looking for, or students as "overlearners," who mechanically misinterpret the messages from their instructor and apply them inappropriately to other situations.[29]

As is the case in design juries, *both faculty and students tend to overlook the importance of nonverbal behavior at desk crits.* It is quite common in many design studios to observe professors hovering over their students' desks while the students remain seated. This is often simply because no stool is available. Some professors prefer to critique work while standing. To some students, however, being sandwiched in between their studio desk below and their towering professor overhead is quite intimidating (Figure 9-11). This is especially the case with shorter students and taller professors, and with students and faculty of the opposite sex. Students in these situations experience an invasion of personal space, making them feel so uncomfortable that it interferes with their ability to digest the criticism. The discrepancies in height also reinforce the traditional image of the design instructor as the "studio master," with the student slave at his side. *My suggestion is that desk crits generally take place while both parties — the critic and the student — are seated on stools or chairs of equal height.*

A common problem with desk crits is that students often forget what they are told. As a design instructor, this can get extremely frustrating, as day after day, you see the same mistakes being made over and over again. An effective remedy that some faculty have tried is to *require all students to have a tape recorder at their studio desks.* These days, most seem to have them already. Ask them to record each desk crit they receive. They can then play it over again to themselves at their leisure, under their headsets if they like, and the messages are sure to get across.

Professor Stefani Ledewitz at Carnegie Mellon University has developed an unusual approach to desk crits. Believing that the individual crit is an inefficient use of studio time, prompting students to become overly dependent on the instructor for guidance, she initiated a simple system of *"shared crits." Students who sign up for desk crits are asked to attend not only their own crit, but also the crits just before and after theirs. This creates a rotating group of three students sharing the crits.* The instructor can refer to points made in a previous crit rather than

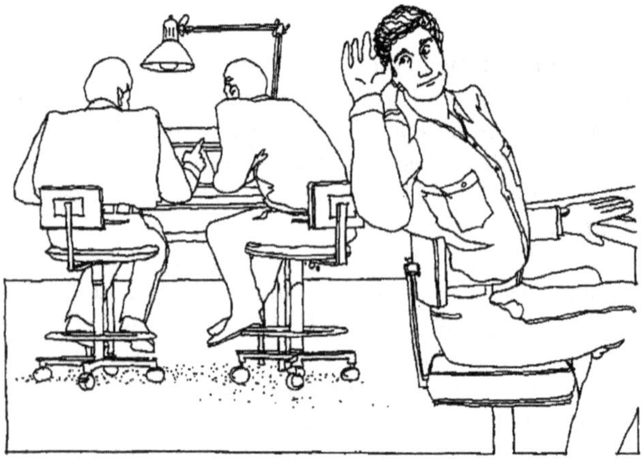

Figure 9-10 Keep in mind that even at a desk crit, what you say can be easily heard by others nearby. Design studios are perfect breeding grounds for eavesdroppers.

Figure 9-11 Be sensitive to students' personal space needs when conducting a desk crit. Towering over students who are seated at their desks can make them feel invaded and intimidated, thus interfering with their ability to listen to your comments.

repeat them for each student. Also, students become more familiar with each other's work and can learn from both similarities and differences between other projects and their own. Most importantly, students are encouraged to engage in a critical dialogue with each other about their projects. This enables them to practice critical skills and to be helpful to each other. An incidental advantage of this system is that the student who is "next" during any crit serves as the timekeeper and is generally much better than the instructor at keeping the crits on schedule.

Expanding on Professor Ledewitz's experiences, one can easily see that *the desk crit need not be completely private nor individual.* In fact, students can learn a great deal from the work of others, especially under circumstances that are more relaxed than the jury. Professors who continually make the rounds in desk crits often feel extremely rushed knowing that the next student in line is anxiously awaiting their arrival. As a result, students and faculty often cannot get into any great depth on any particular issue. *By contrast, conducting small-group pinups can prove to be a much more effective teaching/learning technique than the old-fashioned private tutorial.*

If you have a class where students are working on different types of projects, group those with similar types of projects together; one group may deal with housing, another with offices, and so on. If the class is all working on the same project, group students together by the particular types of problems they are having, or by the concepts they are developing, or by the goals they believe to be most important. Encourage all students in the group to assist each other not only while the work is pinned up, but throughout the design process. Dividing a studio class up into small groups can make the desk crit process much more efficient time-wise. If three groups of five are established, you may end up spending an hour with each of them, having ample time for discussion and exchange of ideas. This is far preferable to trying to quickly circulate around all 15 students within the same three-hour period.

In attempting to create more effective desk critiques, *design instructors can draw upon the world of medicine.* Every time a doctor sees a patient, she pulls up his chart to review what transpired during his last visit. She then enters notes onto the chart reporting what the problem was and how it was addressed (i.e., what medicine was prescribed, what type of shot was administered, and so on). Each time an entry is recorded, she also notes the date that the visit occurred. Professors can use a similar system with design students. Simply record and date the problems the student was having and the advice that you or others offered during a desk crit. The next time you meet with the student, check to see what specific progress has been made on those particular issues. These charts need not be private documents. In fact, they may even work better when they are not. The chart can be posted at the student's desk for others to view. Students can be encouraged to provide assistance to their classmates with specific problem areas as they arise, and add their own notes to others' charts as well as their own. Suggest that students with problems in similar areas gather periodically on their own in small groups to discuss how each is approaching these issues. Such activities help foster a cooperative, collaborative effort in studio.

WORKSHOPS AND ORIENTATION SESSIONS FOR DESIGN CRITICS

Learning how to become a good critic is no easy task. To believe that educators and visiting critics can acquire these skills overnight is naive at best. Simply taking some of these points into account is a step in the right direction. To go even further, however, *short workshops and orientation sessions with faculty and visiting critics, perhaps at the beginning of each school year, would help.* One of the short-term goals of such sessions is to *identify inappropriate jury behavior,* thus preventing some of the atrocities from occurring. One of the long-term goals is to *improve the way in which jurors serve as role models to students.* Repeated exposure to role models who deliver competent, capable, and tactful criticism will inevitably rub off on students, many of whom will be future jurors themselves. The feared studio master can become a valued source, mentor, and simply a more experienced colleague.[30]

My suggestion is that such sessions be required of anyone who serves on a design jury—be it a faculty member, visiting critic, or student. The course need only last a few hours or so, but those few hours are likely to be long remembered. Ideally the facilitator should have strong skills in psychology, counseling, interpersonal relations, human resource development, or a similar field. Role-playing is an especially effective technique that can be used to help communicate what it feels like to be on both the sending and the receiving end of design criticism. *Place instructors in the roles of students for even five minutes, and they may be forever changed!* Sessions could be videotaped and played back to see both how you as a critic come across to others and how others respond to you. If visiting critics find it impossible to attend, they could be sent brief, summary handouts from the workshop as required readings prior to their participating on the jury.

These sessions could be conducted through professional associations of design educators as an ongoing component of their annual conference programs. "How to Become an Effective Design Critic" could become a regular item on conference or meeting agendas of the Interior Design Educators Council (IDEC), the Council of Educators in Landscape Architecture (CELA), the Association of Collegiate Schools of Architecture (ACSA), the Association of Collegiate Schools of Planning (ACSP), and similar organizations of design educators. Participants could be trained to help arrange similar workshops on their own campus. Closer to home, these workshops could be run through university counseling centers; they often emphasize interpersonal communication skills and delivering criticism to others. Or they could be administered through campus offices for instructional development, much like the mini-courses offered for teaching assistants. It is indeed ironic that many teaching assistants at the university, and all teachers of primary and secondary education, must go through compulsory training in learning how to teach, while university professors are allowed to "waive the course." While they may indeed be experts in the design fields, they still need to be educated about how to educate.

If we assume, as so many participants in this research have pointed out, that one function of the academic jury is to simulate future interactions between professional designers and clients, or among designers themselves, then improving the interpersonal communication skills between faculty and students can have great benefits for the design professions in the long run. Practitioners who are effective communicators and good listeners are likely to attract good clients who may want to hire them again and again.

IS CONSTRUCTIVE CRITICISM ENOUGH?

One of the chief ways in which criticism can be delivered more effectively in both juries and desk crit sessions is to actively try to encourage greater dialogue between students and jurors. Receiving criticism strictly from a professor or a visiting critic is not enough. By nature, these relationships are hierarchical, with students perceiving the critics as authority figures. When criticism only comes from these authorities, students are less likely to feel free to discuss and debate their own points of view. Instead, student interviews and diaries reveal that most feel they are better off simply keeping their mouths shut. *The tension provoked by their subservient role and the structural inequality interferes with their ability to retain and truly learn from the criticism.* As Professor Thomas Dutton of Miami University of Oxford, Ohio, aptly points out,

> The main problem with this [jury] system is that it is not dialogical. And it never will be because of its structured asymmetrical relations of power. I just take it as a fact of life that there is little or no dialogue if there is not a rough equality of power among the participants. And if there is no dialogue there is no learning. We have all heard the despicable comments made by faculty before— "next time try drawing with your hands instead of your feet," or "I haven't seen anything this bad since . . ." or "Your building doesn't turn the corner very well, does it?" All of these comments are facilitated by power imbalance. No faculty member would say such things to a colleague, who, more or less, is on an equal footing. Check out the following quote.[31]

> "True dialogue takes place only among equals. There is no dialogue across the boundary between masters and servants, for the master will listen only as long as his power remains intact and the servant will limit his communication to utterances for which he cannot be punished. In fact, to recommend dialogue in a situation of inequality of power is a deceptive ideology of the powerful, who wish to persuade the powerless that harmony and mutual understanding are possible in society without any change in the status quo of power."[32]

Redefining the nature of the power relationships between critics and students is indeed a tall order, and it goes well beyond delivering constructive criticism at design juries. This leads us to some key questions: How can students become empowered? Can the jury system, as we now know it, be so radically transformed? Or does this require a different type of system altogether? *Can we simply administer medication to numb the pain—or is major surgery required?* We will address these questions in the final chapters.

NOTES

1. Bosworth, F. H., Jr., and Roy Childs Jones, *A Study of Architectural Schools*, New York: Scribner, 1932, pp. 56, 184.

2. Attoe, Wayne, *Architecture and Critical Imagination*, New York: Wiley, 1978, p. xii.

3. Schlensker, David, "An Open Letter to the Faculty: Sledgehammers and Broken Glass," *Rickernotes*, University of Illinois at Urbana-Champaign, School of Architecture Student Newsletter (April 14, 1989), p. 3.

4. Weitz, Morris, *Hamlet and the Philosophy of Literary Criticism*, Chicago: University of Chicago Press, 1964, p. vii, as cited in Barrett, Terry, "A Consideration of Criticism," *Journal of Aesthetic Education*, 23:4 (Winter 1989), pp. 23-35, quote from p. 24.

5. Grundberg, Andy, "Toward a Critical Pluralism," *Afterimage* (October 1980), reprinted in Thomas Barrow et al. (ed.), *Reading into Photography: Selected Essays, 1959-82*, Albuquerque: University of New Mexico Press, 1982, pp. 247-253, cited in Barrett, op. cit., pp. 26-27.

6. Gans, Herbert J., *Popular Culture and High Culture: An Analysis and Evaluation of Taste*, New York: Basic Books, 1974.

7. Attoe, op. cit., p. 8.

8. Ibid., pp. 9-10.

9. Ibid., p. 8.

10. This passage was cited in Henderson, Bill (ed.), *Rotten Reviews II: A Literary Companion*, New York: Penguin Books, 1987, p. 72. This unusually entertaining, enlightening book provides countless examples of the extremely subjective nature of criticism.

11. Ibid., p. 76.
12. Ibid., p. 42.
13. Ibid., p. 68.
14. This excerpt from Gilman's criticism was drawn from Baldridge, Charlene "Gershwin," *Performing Arts, San Diego Edition*, 2:8 (August 1989), p. 13.
15. Rogers, Carl R., *On Becoming a Person: A Therapist's View of Psychotherapy*, Boston: Houghton Mifflin, 1961, pp. 331-332.
16. The moments of silence can be used most effectively with some of the alternative jury techniques described in Chapter 10 that do not require each student in the class to present a project to the jury. These techniques remove the intense time pressure all too common in most juries, thus allowing jurors to be more thoughtful and reflective in their comments.
17. Butler, Pamela E., *Self Assertion for Women*, new ed., New York: Harper Collins, 1981.
18. Skinner, B. F., *The Behavior of Organisms*, New York: Appleton-Century Crofts, 1961; Watson, J. B., *Behaviorism*, New York: Norton, 1930.
19. Tavris, Carol, *Anger: The Misunderstood Emotion*, New York: Simon & Schuster, 1982.
20. One issue that some instructors might raise is that they often do not know whether or not a project is completely finished until the students' final jury presentation. In Chapter 11, I suggest that the due date for the project and the presentation date be different, thus allowing the instructor enough time to preview the work and to weed out whatever is incomplete.
21. The survey administered in Phase 3 asked students the question: "At your school, how often do students receive written feedback from *other instructors* who served as jurors?" Most (84%) answered "never." When asked how often students received written feedback from *visiting critics* who served as jurors, 89% answered "never." And when asked how often students receive written feedback from *classmates*, 86% replied "never." These answers reflect the combined responses 1 and 2 on a 5-point scale where 1 was "never" and 5 was "always."
22. For another excellent example of criteria that can be used to evaluate design work, consult the "Working List from a Member Firm" cited in Franklin, James A., "Keys to Design Excellence," in Vonier, Thomas (ed.), *In Search of Design Excellence*, Washington, DC: The American Institute of Architects Press, 1989, p. C-3.
23. The *Design Studio Handbook* at my own university specifies that "Since guest reviewers may or may not submit written comments concerning each project, students are encouraged to team-up with a partner and take thorough notes for one another of all comments made during a partner's presentation." Consult: *Design Studio Handbook*, Champaign, IL: School of Architecture, University of Illinois at Urbana-Champaign, 1990, p. 7. This handbook, updated periodically, is a useful reference to students and faculty alike. Along with a brief section on evaluation and grading for architectural design studios, it also includes summary outlines of design studio courses, descriptive summaries of design seminar courses, a directory of design faculty, and other information. It is especially useful for entering students and faculty who may be unfamiliar with the jury process.
24. Knapp, M. L., *Nonverbal Communication in Human Interaction*, 2d ed., New York: Holt, Rinehart & Winston, 1978.
25. Egan, Gerard, *The Skilled Helper: Model, Skills, and Methods for Effective Helping*, 2d ed., Monterey, CA: Brooks/Cole, 1982, p. 64.
26. Ibid., pp. 64-65.
27. For a fascinating account of how this principle works in training musicians, see Hoff, Helen, "Honey Will Get You Farther Than Vinegar," *Music Education Journal*, 71:2 (October 1984), pp. 24-28.
28. Schön, Donald A., *The Reflective Practitioner*, New York: Basic Books, 1983; and Schön, Donald A., *Educating the Reflective Practitioner: Toward a New Design for Teaching and Learning in the Professions*, San Francisco: Jossey-Bass, 1987.
29. Schön, *Educating the Reflective Practitioner*, p. 155.
30. This distinction was drawn by Lusk, Paul, and Min Kantrowitz, "Teaching Students to Become Effective Planners through Communication: A Planning Communication Studio," *Journal of Planning Education and Research*, 10:1 (Fall 1990), pp. 55-59, quote from p. 58.
31. Personal correspondence from Thomas Dutton, May 11, 1990.
32. Baum, Gregory, *Truth Beyond Relativism: Karl Mannheim's Sociology of Knowledge*, Milwaukee, WI: Marquette University Press, 1977, pp. 43-44, cited in personal correspondence from Thomas Dutton, May 11, 1990.

CHAPTER 10
Alternatives to Traditional Design Juries

Although it will go a long way toward helping create a more favorable atmosphere in which to learn, improving the way in which criticism is delivered will not solve all the problems that students experience in design juries. Some of these, admittedly, are endemic to the jury system. Hence, they will persist.

It is indeed ironic that throughout the term, design instructors encourage their students to be creative, go out on a limb, take a risk—and then when it's all over most of those same instructors rely on the same technique they've been using for years.[1] This pattern directly conflicts with findings from many educational research studies demonstrating that *instructors who provide a variety of flexible options for interacting with students create climates where students learn more.*[2] Using the same technique over and over again can be as boring as eating a hamburger every night for dinner. Students—and faculty—need variety. Just as faculty express their creativity in their own design work, so, too, can they use the jury process as a creative outlet.

A few daring faculty have been willing to experiment with innovative ways of presenting and evaluating student design work. This chapter presents some of these alternatives, ranging along a continuum of minor to major modifications of the traditional system. At the end of the chapter is a summary of the common traits shared by many of these approaches.

A MATTER OF SEMANTICS

In considering these alternatives, it is natural to pose the question, should we continue to use the word *jury* or should we begin to call it something else? The issue here is simply one of semantics. In an effort to reduce the legalistic, adversarial analogy, some faculty prefer to call them *reviews*, *critiques*, or *presentations*.

One word of caution, however: It is quite easy to simply come up with a new name, but still maintain the traditional jury format. I have seen this happen on many occasions. In fact, over the years, many faculty have approached me saying, "We don't have juries at our schools. We have reviews. So we don't have any of the problems you are describing." But when I probe more deeply, I often find that the process is virtually identical to that of the traditional jury. In these cases, changing the name is meaningless and may simply mislead students. *What is most important is not what they are called, but how their deficiencies are remedied.* A name is simply a name, and nothing more.

In each instance, faculty must consider exactly what they are trying to accomplish: *What are your goals for this session? Is the jury's primary goal to evaluate? Is it simply to present finished work? Is it to obtain feedback to improve subsequent work on a project? Is it to discuss the design process as a whole in the context of a specific project? Is it to communicate graphically? Is it to communicate orally? Is it to learn how to negotiate with clients? Is it to emulate a design office in some other way? Or is it something else?* Depending on your answers, you may choose to call the session a different name.

My own preference is to eventually rid ourselves of the term *jury* because of the many negative connotations it has come to have over the years. Change is slow to occur, however, and I realize that this will not happen overnight. Juries imply judgment, yet, as you will see, that is not what all of these alternative models intend to do.

Furthermore, I have come to believe that the term *jury* in the design professions has actually been misused. If we think back to our earlier legalistic analogy, what is a courtroom jury really like? In fact, the jury plays only one of several important roles. Along with the jury is a judge,

Figure 10-1 The term *jury* has been misused in design education. Faculty and visiting critics are actually the jurors, prosecuting attorney, judge, and in the worst cases, executioner—all rolled into one.

prosecuting, and defense attorney. The latter two are each given time to present their clients' case, along with all the necessary supporting evidence. In simple terms, the role of the prosecuting attorney is to attack, while the role of the defense attorney is to defend. The role of the judge is to announce the sentencing. The role of the jurors is to listen and decide the case, but not respond publicly until all the evidence is heard. In fact, they never speak publicly until the case is officially over.

In the traditional design jury, there simply is no defense attorney, and the "victim" is frequently reduced to stuttering incoherently, an experience painfully reminiscent of that classic scene in the film *Billy Budd*. The faculty and visiting critics, whom we typically refer to as the jury, are actually the jurors, the prosecuting attorney, and the judge, all rolled into one. And when they really do "rip the project to shreds," as many students have indicated, they even assume the role of executioner (Figure 10-1).

Throughout most of this chapter, I have continued to use the term *jury* simply for convenience's sake.[3] As many of the following examples came from other faculty who also use the term *jury*, I have chosen to stick to their own words. Nonetheless, various models could more adequately be described as presentations, critiques, reviews, workshops, working sessions, or otherwise. *Whether or not the term jury remains, the current system should be changed and changed quickly.*

SOME PREREQUISITES

Before describing some alternative models in detail, let us review some of the important parameters to consider when designing a critique session.[4] Although the list in Figure 10-2 is not all-inclusive, it provides an overview of the variables that can affect how your critique session will proceed. For each of these parameters, consider the implications for how students will think, feel, and act—all of which will ultimately influence how much they will learn.

One of the chief parameters that affects the jury process is the influence of jurors' comments on the students' grades. This parameter seems to vary from school to school. In fact, *several educators strongly suggest that jurors have nothing at all to do with the grading process.* Jurors are only viewing the students' final product, while the course instructor is intimately familiar with the students' progress throughout the term. As such, the instructor is more qualified to make an accurate assessment of the students' work. Relieving jurors of the responsibilities of grading helps make the jury a less stressful experience for them as well as for the students.

Some instructors may wonder, How can I evaluate students' design work without any outside assessment from jurors? By using the sample jury evaluation forms in Appendix C, Figures C-1 to C-3, or your own variations, you can assess design work along a consistent set of criteria that can be easily explained to students. Relying on the medical model of the desk critique with the aid of a chart to monitor students' progress throughout the term, as described in Chapter 9, can also provide a reliable measure of the quality of students' designs.

Most of the approaches suggested on the next several pages have already been tried out at various educational institutions. Our concentration here is on what has worked especially well for students, faculty, and visiting critics. Why not try some of these alternatives for yourself?

SPELL IT OUT

Each school needs an established, mutually agreed upon written statement that describes the purposes of design juries. This will allow students, faculty, and visiting critics to use juries more effectively. Questions like these need to be addressed:

> What are the overall goals of juries?
> What specific objectives are we trying to achieve through the use of juries?
> How will we know if these objectives have been met?

These kinds of issues should be discussed on an ongoing basis, perhaps starting at the beginning of each school year. One possible setting in which this can easily occur is during a departmental faculty meeting. Some visiting critics and students ought to be invited to participate in the discussion. New faculty should also be encouraged to add their viewpoints, as they are likely to have some fresh, new ideas.

Whatever policy statement is agreed upon, it should be distributed and made widely available to students,

PARAMETERS THAT AFFECT DESIGN CRITIQUE SESSIONS

TIME

Amount of notice and preparation time given to jurors
Time between completion of the work and the critique
Time allocated for each student's presentation
Time allocated for each critic's reaction
Total duration of the critique

PRESENTATION FORMAT

Traditional drawings, usually on either 20" x 30" or 30" x 40" boards
Models
Number of drawings and models

Technique used to produce drawings and models:
- drawn by hand
- drawn using computer aided drafting techniques
- produced using video-imaging techniques, such as photo-montage or other ways of simulating environmental changes

Nature of the medium used
- black and white
- color

Generation of work
- first generation (actual drawings and models)
- second generation (reproductions in slides, photographs, or other media)

Primary mode of communication
- graphic
- oral
- written

PROCEDURES

Presence or absence of students (i.e. open vs. closed session)

Number of and composition of critics
Number of students' work displayed at once

Order in which critics comment
Order in which students are evaluated

Opportunity for students to respond to the critics

Pre-crit orientation for critics
Pre-crit review of student work
Pre-crit instruction to critics to decide division of labor and establish ground rules

Relationship between the critics' evaluations and the students' grades

ABILITIES TO BE EVALUATED

Conceptualization of the problem
Problem-solving ability
Response to the requirements and constraints of the assignment
Drawing skills
Model-building skills
Oral presentation skills

Figure 10-2 Parameters that affect design critique sessions. Keep them in mind in planning any student presentations.

faculty, and visiting critics. This policy statement should be reiterated at the start of each jury session.

MASTER THE MYSTERY

Invite jurors to meet with students when the project is first assigned and, together, to establish the criteria that will eventually be used to critique the project. What constitutes a "successful" design solution to this problem? What are the most important issues that must be addressed? List the major points from this discussion on the blackboard, have someone copy them down, and xerox them off for each student to have as a reference throughout the duration of the project.

If the jurors are unable to make it to this early session, meet with them, call them up, or ask them to respond to some of these questions in written form. Then share this information with the class. Enlarge these criteria into poster size and display them in studio to serve as a reference throughout the duration of the project, as well as at the jury itself.

Some instructors use these sessions as "briefings" at which students explain how they perceive project's salient

CHARACTERISTICS OF THE WORK TO BE EVALUATED

Aesthetics
Function
Economic considerations (economy of construction, of urban land, etc.)
Environmental considerations (impact on the quality of land, air, and water)
Contextual relationships
Ability to satisfy user needs
Social considerations (impact on social pride in the neighborhood, city, etc.)

ROLES OF PARTICIPANTS

Students as creators of the design solution
Students as critics

Course instructor as coach of creators
Course instructor as critic
Course instructor as advocate

Critics as generalists
Critics as specialists:
- graphic communication
- oral presentation
- materals selection and technical execution
- structures specialists
- user-needs specialists
- building type specialists
- quasi-clients
- users
- historic preservation specialists

Figure 10-2 Continued.

characteristics and focus, such as the program site, historic precedent, and some conceptual directions beginning to emerge. At such sessions, students become teachers and vice-versa.[5]

Notifying the jurors well in advance of the jury is essential. All too often a seemingly casual encounter between two design instructors in the hallway, where one simply asks the other, "Do you have a minute?" turns out to be an invitation to serve on the jury. The professor arriving on the scene could be taken totally off guard. Immediately placed on the spot, the natural tendency is to begin shooting from the hip and engage in "grandstanding." As a result, much precious critique time is often wasted. Jurors need to be invited well ahead of time — at least a week or two — so that they not only have the proper time to prepare, but also to be in the proper frame of mind.

Alternatively, have the jury, together with the instructor, write the program for a studio class project. This involves jury members in the process from the very beginning. Rather than working with someone else's assignment, the project is partly their own. As such, they are likely to have a vested interest in it and be more explicit in articulating their ideas.

BE PREPARED

Being prepared requires minimal faculty effort but yields great benefits. Give all jurors a copy of the project assignment and design program well in advance of the jury — say a week ahead of time.[6] Provide them with a brief description of the educational goals for the course, the amount of time that students have spent on this particular project, and the students' skill level. For instance, if you are teaching a graduate course, how many of your students have a prior degree in design? How many were trained in different disciplines? What kinds of disciplines are these? How many students are returning after spending time in the working world or at home raising children? Such background information is sometimes useful for the jury to know.

At this time, be sure to spell out the jurors' roles. Do you want them to grade students' work? Do you want them to emphasize certain issues? Do you want them to focus on particular problems that have been plaguing the class? Are the students presenting their final work, or will they have more time to complete it once the jury is over? *Are you trying any new or innovative techniques (such as any of the ones suggested here) that are unfamiliar to the jurors? If so, carefully explain the technique and what you expect — and do not expect — from them. Repeat the process with students as part of a jury orientation session.* This last step is extremely important if you want to ensure the success of some of these new techniques. Otherwise old habits are likely to be repeated.

Ask the jurors to phone you if they are unclear about any aspect of the program or their role in the jury or if they have any additional questions. Or ask them to arrive about 15 minutes before the jury begins to meet with them privately. In any case, clarify these issues ahead of time. Advance preparation helps save valuable time at the jury.

KEEP THE ORIGINAL CAST OF CHARACTERS

Try to ensure that the jurors who serve on both the interim and final juries are the same. This allows jurors to monitor students' progress over time. How did students respond to prior jury criticism? What other new ideas may have arisen in the meantime? Do not invite one group to evaluate the projects midstream and an entirely different cast of characters to evaluate the final work.[7] Students find it much less confusing to hear feedback from the same group of people twice rather than from an entirely new set of people who are unfamiliar with their project.

CHANGE THE CALENDAR

Schedule the final jury one or two weeks before the time it would normally be. The project must be complete enough to be easily understood and evaluated, but not necessarily in the final presentation stage. Students are more likely to take the jurors' remarks seriously if they know that they can eventually act upon them. Following the jury, discuss as a class the most important issues that have been raised, what you agree or disagree with, and where to go from here. Comments delivered at the jury can thus be incorporated into the students' final design, and part of the students' grade will depend on the extent to which they responded to the criticism they received. Jurors do not participate in grading student work. Instead, part of the instructor's grade includes how well students' final designs responded to the jury's comments.

DROP THE FINAL JURY

Consider eliminating the final jury altogether since most students do not find it very instructive. Instead, improve the procedure for conducting interim juries using some of the techniques suggested below. In this case, the instructor can determine the final grades without the usual input from jurors, basing the grades on the degree to which students improved throughout the term and the degree to which they have met their potential.

CURFEW

One of the simplest ways to improve the jury process is to establish an early deadline. Require that all projects be submitted well in advance of the jury session. Most faculty who have tried this technique have found that a minimum of two to three days prior to the jury is best; midnight the night before will not do.

Students and faculty who have tried this technique find an amazing improvement in the jury. Faculty note that students' performance at the jury is markedly improved, and students report that they are much better able to retain and learn from the jury's comments. It is one of the smallest gestures that faculty can make, but it offers one of the highest payoffs.

If you are going to try to implement a curfew, it is essential that you strictly enforce the deadline; otherwise your intentions can easily go out the window.[8] Before you know it, everyone in studio will ask for "just 10 more minutes" to complete their project. The key is to tell students exactly what you will do well ahead of time, when the project is first assigned, and then stick to it. If the work is incomplete, take it as is, but do not allow the student to present the work at the jury. Instead, have that student make up the assignment after the jury is over, evaluate it privately, and drop the grade accordingly.[9] By so doing, *students will begin to view the jury as a privilege, not a right.* Continuing to accept late work merely perpetuates the notion that deadlines are not important, but they are. Students must be penalized for lateness, no matter how good their work is. Just as many instructors of English drop the grade if a student's paper arrives a few days late, design instructors should do the same.

PREPARE A SCHEDULE

Another simple technique is to prepare a printed schedule for the jurors and the class listing the order of student presentations. Assign students to particular time slots, and stick to them. Preparing such a schedule ahead of time can ensure equal time for students presenting and discourage the common tendency to offer the first student 45 minutes of criticism and the last student only 5 minutes. Assign someone to serve as timekeeper if you do not take on this task yourself.

SPOTLIGHT A FEW

Select only a small sample of two or three projects to be discussed in great detail by the faculty critic, the jurors, and the rest of the class. The aim is to try to bring up as many relevant issues as possible for only a few projects, thus avoiding the "saturation point" reached when a long series of solutions to the same problem fails to generate a lively discussion. This arrangement has the twin benefits of making both the students' and the jurors' tasks much more interesting. Faculty who have tried this technique report students and jurors welcome the change. Stefani Ledewitz at Carnegie Mellon University explains:

> *At the outset I asked all the students and other reviewers (both faculty and invited community representatives, etc.) to look at all the submissions and select three most "commendable." Then I tallied the results and the three most commended were discussed by everyone together. Instead of having the students present, I asked anyone who had selected the scheme to talk about why he or she had picked it, and the discussion went on from there to talk about all sorts of issues about the project. After reviewing those schemes, we broke into three small groups to review the other twelve schemes (four apiece).*

I liked it, and the students and a couple of reviewers also mentioned to me that they liked it. It gave everyone a chance to get into the project together and hear the full range of perspectives, but not require that everyone sit through 15 reviews. I like to start all juries with well-documented projects to insure that everyone understands the projects as quickly as possible, and the selection process naturally identified three well-developed and well-presented schemes.

I thought the most successful aspect of it was that the discussion was actually carried on more by the students than the invited reviewers. In fact, students mentioned that they had looked at the work very differently because they, too, were expected to judge it. They said they looked much more closely at it than they would have at a typical review. They also felt much more comfortable not standing up in front of the group, but sitting beside their reviewers, and thought it was easier to have a discussion about the project. (I think it affects the behavior of both student and critic.) The reviewers told me they found it very interesting, and more fun because there was a lot more discussion than usual. It was just an experiment, but it seemed to have worked surprisingly well.[10]

Based on Professor Ledewitz's experience, Appendix C, Figure C-4, shows an example of a general form that can be used to help narrow down the selection process.

STAGE AN OPENING NIGHT

A more dramatic variation on the current jury system is to redefine the basic structure of the event. Rather than seeing it as a series of individual vignettes, with every student's turn in the spotlight, think of it as the entire studio's work that is on display. In this sense, the jury becomes more like the opening night for a new museum exhibit or a concert performance. The orchestra as a whole (i.e., the class) performs, but no solo performances are given. The role of both jurors and class is to respond to the exhibit (Figure 10-3).

Before this event takes place, find a room—or set of adjacent rooms—that is large enough to display all the work at once. It may require holding the jury in a different campus building or even somewhere off campus. Encourage students to help make the space look attractive and well lit. Assign each project a number. Place a few comfortable chairs in front of each exhibit, along with a folder coded with the project number.

Each student should be required to prepare a brief, a one-paragraph or one-page written statement explaining their project's goals and how and where they have achieved them. The text should tie in to the drawings as much as possible, preferably with specific references. For instance:

The interior is enhanced through the use of a wide variety of textures and colors (see Perspective Draw-

Figure 10-3 Holding an exhibit of student work, along with a folder for comments beside each project, can provide a welcome alternative to the traditional design jury. At any instance, students, faculty, and visitors are all actively involved in the review process, making it a more lively experience.

ing of Entry Lounge). The sense of verticality is achieved through high-volume ceilings in strategic locations, such as the entry lounge and health spa (see Perspective Drawing of Entry Lounge and Section A-A).

This statement should be prominently displayed alongside each exhibit. Extra handouts should also be available at each exhibit site so that people can refer to it easily while sitting down and studying the project themselves, without having to strain their eyes and wander back and forth from the statement to the drawings and model.

First ask everyone to take a brief stroll around the room in order to take a look at every single project. This is essential so that everyone is operating within the same frame of reference, having viewed the entire range of work and not zooming into great detail in any one of them. Then ask them to write their comments, being certain to include the project number, and place them in the folder in front of each exhibit.[11]

Writing down feedback for every single project is time consuming and may not be realistic, depending on the size of the class. In this case, divide the students and jurors into smaller groups and have them review only a select number of projects. Try to ensure that at least two jurors and two students review each project, thereby providing the student with at least four different sources of feedback.

Be sure to schedule at least a half hour for some general discussion at the end of this session. Try to focus the discussion on the following types of issues:

What is the range of work we have seen here today?
How would you assess the overall quality of the projects?
To what extent did students achieve their goals?
How do you think the users would respond to various design solutions?

To what extent do these projects fit into the adjacent context?

Encourage the jurors and students to cite specific examples when answering these questions and to always state the reasoning behind their opinions, referring to the projects by number rather than name.

The chief advantage of this technique is that it causes the drawings and models to speak for themselves. In this sense, it more closely approximates the process of submitting work to a professional design competition, for publication, or responding to a request for proposal. In these cases, the screening process typically occurs without the designer being present.

THIS TIME IT'S FOR REAL

Before you assign the next hypothetical project or the most conveniently available design competition program, stop to think if the following arrangement may satisfy the educational goals of your course: Assign a project with a "quasi-client." The relationship simulates what would occur in a professional setting, but students are not being paid for their work. In some cases, quasi-clients may be able to reimburse the class as a whole for incidental expenses, but no salaries for professional services are paid.

In order to avoid potential competition with practitioners, instructors must clearly indicate to quasi-clients that the primary purpose of the project is to educate students and that *it is not a substitute for professional work*. The instructor must clearly inform the quasi-client of the educational goals of the course. Together, instructor and quasi-client can structure the project in such a way that it meets those educational goals. Nonprofit bodies, such as religious institutions, schools, and other organizations with limited funding, are often the best-suited quasi-clients for academic design projects. Such organizations are often faced with small-scale projects that would not normally require the services of a design professional and that most practitioners would not be interested in taking on themselves.

Select the quasi-client carefully. She should be personable and excited by the prospect of working with students. She should be willing to commit several hours to meet with students not only at the jury, but throughout the design process, especially at the beginning. She must be willing to provide some basic information that can be passed on to students, as well as, perhaps, to offer a tour of the existing facilities, arrange for special meetings with staff members, and so on. Develop a mechanism for fielding student questions. For instance, they can be assembled on a weekly basis and one student is assigned to call in the queries. Either the quasi-client or someone on her staff should be assigned to respond promptly.

Figure 10-4 Bringing clients and users into the studio throughout the design process to review in-progress and completed student work can help the jury better emulate the professional work environment. As a result, students' transition from school into practice is easier. Students find working with clients and users an exciting alternative to hypothetical "paper projects."

Invite the quasi-client as well as various types of users (executive, middle management, and clerical staff, for example) to serve on the jury (Figure 10-4). This lay group can be used either alone or in tandem with other design faculty and visiting critics. Ideally, this group should have contact with students at the very outset of the project and perhaps at some point midstream, if at all possible. This provides the opportunity for more informal dialogues among users, quasi-clients, and designers that can *help students to learn how to negotiate with clients—rather than simply to present and defend their work*—when they enter the world of practice.[12]

Faculty members who have routinely tried this technique make a convincing case for its widespread adoption. In fact, many have found it one of the most effective motivators for students to produce high-quality work. My own students have produced designs for single-family homes, schools, urban plazas, bicycle path systems, shopping malls, and other settings.[13] In some cases, the quasi-clients have been so impressed with the students' work that, with the assistance of a licensed practitioner, they eventually constructed solutions based in part on the students' ideas. What better compliment to pay to a design student![14]

Not only are students accountable to someone who is truly interested in their work, but also they are offered an important viewpoint that is usually unavailable to them. Quasi-client jurors are often unusually appreciative of the students' work. With a direct interest in the problem at hand, they welcome the opportunity to view a variety of solutions spanning the entire range of the class. Students often raise issues that they, themselves, had not considered. Compared to the typical jury composed of design faculty and practitioners, at times quasi-clients are more articulate in their assessments of various design schemes. Having had direct, hands-on experience with similar types of spaces and how people have reacted to them, the criteria they use to assess student work are usually quite clear. The issues they raise are usually dramatically different from those brought out in a traditional jury composed of design faculty and visitors.

The use of quasi-clients and users helps transport design education out from under what some have called paper projects to a situation that more closely approximates the working world. As educator Anthony Ward has written,

> *I have become convinced that paper projects in studio play a large part in the adoption, by students, of an elitist attitude towards the wider community. In my own work I have thus attempted to confine myself and my students to real-world problems with real clients, real sites, real budgets and most importantly, real human contact.*[15]

Ward argues that isolating the studio from the wider social environment merely insulates students from the realities of design practice, creating a self-indulgent illusion that tells them that the only criticism that really matters is what comes from within the profession. Perhaps it is simply a reflection of the actual value system within the profession, but if so, then that, too, is misguided. Paper projects tend to encourage a highly unrealistic view of what design practice is all about. A student's fantasy and imagination are all that matter. Satisfy that urge to create, and you will be fulfilled. In fact, design practice tends to be messy, chaotic, and unpredictable. Clients' needs change midstream, budgets are drastically cut, and rules and regulations challenge the designer's creativity. By contrast, working with a quasi-client not only brings students down to earth, preparing them for what is to come, but also helps build confidence in their design abilities.[16]

If one of your goals is to educate future professionals to respond to the needs of their clients and users, then it is hard to find a better way to conduct and evaluate student design work. In so doing, you can help improve the image of the design professions to the public.

POSTDESIGN EVALUATION

Anthony Antoniades of the University of Texas at Arlington has invented an unusual "Post-Design Evaluation".[17] Before the academic term begins, the instructor works with a well-known designer to select a building project for the students. The project selected has already been designed in the architect's office, but has not been published. The designer provides the instructor with the program as it came into the office. Disguising the specific location and site, but selecting comparable geographic and site constraints, the instructor assigns the same design program to the class. He also provides relevant information, such as design principles pertaining to the project, along with some historical and contemporary precedents for the specific building type. Students are encouraged to conduct additional research on their own.

The review process involves individual desk crits, group pinups, a final presentation to interested faculty, and *a summary brochure*. The final presentation serves as an exhibition of drawings and models, and feedback is randomly given. The session ends with the instructor disclosing the real project as built, or if a competition, the assembly of entries along with the winners. Students are asked to contrast their solution with that which has actually been built.

The brochure is in the format of a magazine article, along with necessary visual documentation. It is sent directly to the architect, who is asked to provide written comments on each of the student projects. When the designer's feedback arrives, usually during the subsequent term, the class is reconvened. Students are shown slides of their projects, which the instructor had taken during the semester break, along with the architect's written comments which they may keep for their files. Sometimes the class accepts the architect's comments, while on other occasions they may not. In any case, the feedback seems to elicit a lively discussion about design issues.

One of the greatest strengths of this technique is that it relieves the stress of most design juries. It gives students the opportunity to work on a simulation of a real, rather than a purely hypothetical, project. It allows them to receive feedback from an experienced practitioner in a nonthreatening fashion, via written correspondence rather than personal reproach. As Professor Antoniades states, it also provides an "opportunity to extend the bonds of the studio beyond the semester," by meeting after the course has officially ended, a rare occurrence.[18] Among the disadvantages are that it is difficult to organize and is time consuming for both the instructor and practitioner. The designers in question must complete the evaluation and provide useful, informative feedback to students whom they will probably never meet face to face.

JURY DUTY

Some instructors require their students to attend several juries per term for other classes. For example, sophomores are required to attend senior juries, senior students are required to attend graduate juries, and so on. Their assignment is to observe and criticize the work presented, note the jury's comments, and reflect upon how what they learned can apply to their own work—either to current, previous, or future projects. Because they and their classmates are off the "hot seat," they are in a good position to be able to carefully critique the work. Students bring in their written assignments to class to discuss their "jury duty" with other class members.

GIMME SHELTER

Robert Levy of Syracuse University assigned a project whereby students built enclosures and shelters within their studio.[19] On jury day, each juror received a clipboard with several copies of an evaluation sheet, one for each team. Each reviewer was required to visit each group, but was free to go alone or with other jurors and to spend as much time as they liked. The teams stood in their shelters and waited for the reviewers to arrive. The instructor collected the evaluation sheets from the jurors, wrote up a summary of the results, and distributed it to the class. Another variation of this model is to monitor the public's reaction with a postoccupancy evaluation (POE), suggestion boxes, and personal observation.[20]

How did students react? Professor Levy explains, "The students had a good time, the atmosphere was relaxed, communication [was] established on an informal level. . . ."

DO UNTO OTHERS . . .

Art Stamps at the Institute of Environmental Quality in San Francisco has tried an unusual method of evaluation in a design course intended to teach students how to design for other people's feelings.[21] Students drew perspective sketches of various places in their designs and then were asked to guess how other people would respond to these sketches. Other people were asked to write down their responses to the same sketches. Students' grades were based on how well they anticipated others' responses. They repeated the entire process three times so that they could improve their designs as well as their knowledge of how others would respond. Professor Stamps reports:

> *People's reactions have proved to be most interesting. After some initial confusion, the students adapted to the fact that there were not going to be any juries in the traditional sense of the term. After the class, the students were extremely appreciative; in fact, they had a tendency to follow me around no matter what course I taught.*
>
> *My own reaction was elation: I tried a direct, no-safety-net empirical experiment based on three different lines of thought (representing architecture through perspective drawings; representing people's feelings through measurements of pleasure, arousal and dominance; and learning through cycles of objective feedback), and it all worked the first time! What more could anyone ask?*

IF AT FIRST YOU DON'T SUCCEED . . .

Howard Ray Lawrence at Pennsylvania State University asked students to submit their design work "as many times as is necessary to achieve excellence."[22] The students in the class were the judges of excellence. At first, most students were willing to pass all their classmates' work, applauding after each project was presented. The instructor openly expressed his concern that students were being overly generous in their assessments, and he placed a limit on the number of acceptable "best" projects. Once the limits were in effect the class became more serious. How did students react? They learned what constitutes high-quality work and appreciated the opportunity to view excellent work among their peers. And, as Professor Lawrence explains, "They finally conducted the studio themselves. . . ."

SHOW ME YOURS . . .

Juan C. Bertotto of the Savannah College of Art and Design requires that each student prepare a one-page written statement describing the project's concept, resolution, and merit prior to the jury.[23] The instructor also randomly assigns each student to study and evaluate a classmate's completed project. Peer reviewers are instructed to assume the role of an impartial design critic. At the jury, each student reads the written statement and further explains her project. Then, the assigned peer reviewer offers an evaluation of that project. This peer review allows the jurors to rapidly get a grasp on the project and someone else's assessments of its merits and flaws.

What has been the reaction to this approach? According to Professor Bertotto: "Generally, students balk at having to compose essays." However, they seem not to when the assignment is presented in stages, that is, when a rough copy of the statement is presented once the project's parti has been approved, and this copy is later refined for presentation to the jury.

> *The system of peer review has been positively received by most students. Those students who have an exaggerated concept of the value of their own work—seldom the best students—are the ones who have the greatest problem accommodating to the system.*
>
> *The jurors have been pleased. . . . The intervening peer review gives the jurors further time to study the project and view it under the light of the peer's more intimate assessment.*

The instructor moderating the jury needs to keep a close eye on the time in order for the system to work. Nonetheless, jurors often proceed more rapidly once the peer review has highlighted some of the important issues. In any case, students appear to accept criticism from peers more readily than from faculty, especially ones that they do not like or respect. Variations on this theme are certainly possible, perhaps in combination with some of the other approaches already discussed.

ROUND-ROBIN

Thomas Dutton and his colleagues at Miami University in Oxford, Ohio, have tried a number of variations on design juries.[24] The round-robin format has involved four critics who talk with students individually about their work. All students hang up their work in one room, and jurors rotate from student to student. Four reviews occur simultaneously. When their work is not being reviewed, students participate in a review nearby. Professor Dutton reports: "The advantage of this system is that it allows for dialogue—a back and forth conversation. Students feel freer to disagree with critics and/or demand some justification for opinions expressed by them. The disadvantage of this system is that no common discussion takes place..."

Peter Prangnell at the University of Toronto has used a similar system that involves students at all levels of a five-year program.[25] He adopted the format from his experiences as a visitor at the Massachusetts Institute of Technology and the University of Oregon during the 1970s. The final review is conducted two weeks before the end of the project so that suggestions can be incorporated into the final design. A sign-up sheet is prepared listing faculty teamed with visiting critics. (See Appendix C, Figure C-5, for an example of how to orchestrate a round-robin jury.) Through a ballot system students sign up for available time slots; whoever draws #1 has free choice. Faculty chair the sessions, and their aim is to lead discussions that span disparate projects. Students are encouraged to discuss each other's work, so first-year students talk about fifth-year work and vice-versa. The faculty member who chairs the review session provides written minutes of the proceedings, summarizing the discussion and reccommendations given to each student in her session. A copy of each student's minutes is given to the student's professors (studios were team-taught) and is taken into account in assessing a grade for the project. Professor Prangnell reports:

> Students appeared to support it! Certainly it did not produce the hysteria and trauma so evident in the "final" performance [of the traditional jury]; certainly it did not permit grand-standing on the part of critics. My guess is that faculty and critics found it hard—they had to find connections between projects and orchestrate discussions rather as seminar leaders do.

Cynthia Weese, one of the designers interviewed for this book, participated as a visiting critic in one of Professor Prangnell's reviews while he was visiting at Washington University. She found the format refreshing and exciting:

"It's a marvelous way to do it. It's hard work for the jurors, but the students get so much out of it. Jurors are talking only to students; there is little opportunity for posturing."

ROUND-ROBIN—STANDARD

The standard round-robin system is basically similar to the previous one; however, after about two or three hours the entire class reconvenes to discuss three to five schemes. Both critics and students select the schemes that will be discussed, usually based on the array of issues they raise, not because they are considered "the best." Professor Dutton comments: "This review system is rather nice because it allows students to receive personal feedback, and there is a time for discussion of issues not related to student performance."

STUDENT REVIEW

For the student review system, Professor Dutton arbitrarily divides students and their work into four groups. Each group moves together to discuss the merits of each design scheme in every other student group. The instructor sometimes offers questions for each group to consider, such as "Which scheme is the strongest in concept?" "Which has the best organization?" "Which is the most provocative?" Because students often disagree among their answers, they learn that there really is no one "right" way of solving a design problem. In addition, each group must write down five good points and five not-so-good points about each project. This offers each student written comments about his work. When every group has studied all the projects, the entire class, along with the instructor, discusses the projects. Professor Dutton concludes, "I have found that students are very insightful and often make excellent commentary when given the chance...."

Robert Selby at the University of Illinois at Urbana-Champaign uses a similar format that he sometimes calls the "County Fair."[26] A standard critique form is placed on each desk. Students are asked to visit each desk and write helpful advice in each category. They are also asked to place a dot on a grade scale. Professor Selby notes that "students (like faculty) sometimes find that grading is hard, [while] advising is easier."

JURORS ON TRIAL

Edward R. Ostrander and Ronald Beckman at Cornell University have been experimenting with several variations on the jury theme.[27] For "Jurors on Trial," faculty invite a jury of design professionals to view student design work. The instructors grade all projects before the review. No oral presentation by the students is necessary. In front of the students, jurors respond to questions such as: How well can you understand the designers' intentions? What aspects of the project communicate most and least clearly?

Students then ask themselves: How well did the jurors understand the projects—in general as well as in detail? Based on their answers, they assign grades to the jurors. In this case, the jury becomes a learning experience about how well student design work communicates to others. Its greatest strength is that it allows students to step into the shoes, to some extent, of those who will eventually be viewing their work, offering them a vantage point that is rarely available.

PROFESSOR AS ADVOCATE

Here is another innovative technique from the two professors at Cornell: In this case the studio instructor, rather than the students, presents all the work done by the class. Each student briefs the instructor before the presentation to the jury or board of experts. In presenting the work of her class, the professor assumes the role of senior partner in a firm. In this instance, students are forced to communicate their ideas clearly and explicitly, because someone else, rather than themselves, must explain it to the audience. This model closely reflects what actually occurs in most design offices when only the senior partners appear before clients to present the work of their staff. Many of the designers who do the detailed, day-to-day work on the projects remain behind the scenes.

CLOSED SEMINAR/VIDEO REVIEW

Professors Ostrander and Beckman have experimented with a variation of the video model. This involves videotaping each student presenting her finished work to the rest of the class, with no outside jurors present. In effect, the presentation is done in the format of a closed seminar. The instructor's role is to encourage the class to ask questions and make comments, but the instructor himself withholds any critical remarks. During the next few days, the instructor reviews the video presentation individually with each student. At that time, the student is well rested, and the instructor may have already previewed the work and be prepared with notes to make constructive criticism.

YOU OUGHT TO BE IN PICTURES

Videotaping can be used in several ways, and this relatively simple technique offers an enormous payoff (Figure 10-5). Not only can the video prove extremely useful in

Figure 10-5 Using a videotape to help students practice their jury presentations is an excellent way of improving students' skills in communication. By reviewing their performance along with the instructor and other students, students are more likely to accept criticism from others and, even more important, to develop the ability to critique themselves.

helping students prepare for the jury in advance and improve their public-speaking skills, but also it can provide an irreplaceable source of feedback after the jury is over. Students can watch their performance, evaluate how well both they and their project are coming across, and replay the jurors' comments as many times as they like until it truly sinks in.

If a video camera is not available, a tape recorder is the next best substitute. As an instructor, you can either record the entire session yourself and make it available to students to play back on their own, or you can simply require every student or teams of students to bring in their own machines.

The use of any kind of recording equipment as an evaluation technique is most valuable if you tie it into some kind of short assignment.[28] Otherwise it might just end up as a form of cheap entertainment. You can also make this assignment in teams of two or three students so that each is required to evaluate not only her own work, but those of classmates as well. I suggest that you not only require students to watch the videotape or play back the tape, but to take notes of their own based on this replay and to write down some specifics. For instance,

> What are the greatest strengths of your oral and graphic presentation?
> What are your greatest weaknesses?
> What did the jurors say to you?
> Do you agree or disagree with their comments, and why?
> List three things that you will do differently the next time you prepare and present your work.

Questions like these encourage the students to become involved in active listening, that is, restating in their own words what was said to them, much like faculty are encouraged to do. You, too, can go over the individual tapes with the students and address some of these same issues in writing. This technique can also assist future designers in understanding how they come across to clients, public agencies, regulatory commissions, and other audiences.

THE BUDDY SYSTEM

Assign each student to two "buddies," fellow class members, who can write down the feedback that is received on their partner's project. This should prevent the comments from going in one ear and out the other. The buddies can also assist the student in hanging up drawings, placing the models properly, and preparing immediately before and after the jury.

THE BROCHURE OR PORTFOLIO PRESENTATION

A few faculty have experimented with a novel technique that involves students submitting their work in a brochure or as part of their portfolio, much as they would do to a prospective employer[29] (Figure 10-6). Upon completing their design work, students are responsible for preparing a small brochure that encapsulates their work, presenting all drawings in reduced format. If models are required, they must also prepare slides of their models and submit these along with the brochure. A short written statement summarizing their goals for the project should also be included.

The brochure can be reviewed in a variety of ways: by the studio critic in the privacy of her office, by the jury behind closed doors, or by students in a more public setting. Critics and jurors can add written feedback before returning the brochure, perhaps along with an individual meeting with the student.

One disadvantage of this technique is that the detailed information available in large-scale drawings is reduced to such a scale that it may be lost or hard to read. Nonetheless, professional design publications and booklets describing the winning entries of design competitions are also published at a small scale and readers have become accustomed to understanding the drawings at this scale. A striking advantage of this technique is that the projects instantly become easy to transport, thus allowing instructors to review them at their leisure, be it in their office or even at home.

Students have reacted to this technique with enthusiasm. Not only does it represent an interesting departure from the norm, but also it helps them prepare their work in

Figure 10-6 Asking students to prepare a final design presentation as a portable brochure, much like that seen in professional publications, allows the work to be reviewed by many people either in public or in private. Students' work is already in the form they will eventually need for their portfolios when they begin job hunting. Students have reacted enthusiastically to this technique.

the format in which they will eventually have to prepare it for their portfolio. Usually this task is done on their own time, after class is over, and often near graduation time as they are frantically seeking a job. Having the documentation of their project already in their portfolio puts them one step ahead of their competition.

MEET ME AFTER CLASS

Some design instructors never ask jurors to grade students' projects or to have any input in the grading process whatsoever. Instead, they compile the grades themselves based on the students' progress throughout the academic term. Some schedule individual student conferences to discuss progress on their design work at various intervals.

DEAR JOHN...

Some faculty prefer to write each student a personal letter at the close of each project. The letter assesses the student's performance and notes her specific assets and liabilities in a wide range of areas. At the end of the letter is a grade for the project. The instructor encourages students to compare their letters with those sent to other students. Students are asked to keep these letters and show them again to their instructor should they request a letter of recommendation at a later date. In addition, the instructor delivers a written summary evaluating the class's performance on the design project to the entire class.

SELF-EVALUATION

Based on the concept-test model of studio instruction described by Stefani Ledewitz,[30] M. Joe Numbers at the University of Idaho has developed an insightful set of questions that can best be used at interim juries and desk crits.[31] Some are asked of the individual student, while others are presented in the form of a class group discussion:

1. What do you like/dislike about your design?
2. What issues have/have not been addressed at this point? What are the major issues that are influencing this design problem? Which of these issues have high versus low priorities? What are the consequences of changing the priorities of these issues?
3. What are the formal issues of this problem?
4. What areas of this design are/are not resolved at this point?
5. What is the basic concept (parti) of this design?
6. What are your design intentions for this project? For this client? And how does your design incorporate, express, and fulfill these design intentions?
7. What is the original precedent or prototype for this design? Is this precedent appropriate?
8. What would happen to the proposed design if the scope, program, site, client,... were to be radically altered?
9. Should this preliminary solution be developed further or completely discarded? If it should be developed further, then what additional knowledge/information is needed to further develop this design solution? How will this additional knowledge help in evaluating and testing this design concept?

Using these questions reflects a critique process that shifts the focus from the instructor to the students, forcing them to explain the rationale behind their designs. According to Professor Numbers:

The act of phrasing [students'] response in the manner of "I don't like this aspect..." seemed to take them out of a purely defensive mode of response and put them on a more objective footing. Comments from their peers also took on the form of helpful suggestions rather than criticisms....

Assigning a number priority to the issues (e.g., highest to lowest), enables the students to better concentrate their time and efforts towards resolving these issues. As you know, we often focus on relatively minor details in the early design stages to the detriment and neglect of the truly important issues. This discussion was very enlightening in this regard....

...this line of questioning further reduces the adversarial, finger-pointing stance which arises when the instructor abrogates the responsibility for finding fault or deficit with the student's work....

The students respond with a visible amount of relief and enthusiasm when they are given the opportunity to take charge of the process and incidentally their "destinies" in this manner.

I have found that critiques conducted with this approach will generate a more satisfying level of discussion, more student participation in the discussions, and a greater degree of enthusiasm as the students realize they are able to control the design process.

In addition, the finished designs appear to be more fully resolved and better informed when this approach is taken. This approach has also proven the value of interim critiques as an effective learning/teaching tool.

COMMON THEMES

Increased Student Participation

In sum, what many of these alternative techniques try to do, especially those that represent the most radical departures from the status quo, is to shift the emphasis from an individual public defense to a more democratic debate and discourse. *Including the students as key players* is essential. Experiences with these techniques have clearly demonstrated that a student who actively participates in the jury process is much more likely to learn something than one who simply appears on cue for 10 minutes and later disappears into the audience. As participants rather than as spectators, students are much more able to absorb new information and place it in their own mental contexts. According to cognitive-learning theorists, hooking new ideas into life as you already know it leads to more meaningful learning. It also helps students reframe or recast the design problem, a fundamental aspect of reflective learning.[32]

Focus on the Design Process as Well as the Design Product

Emphasizing more general discussion and debate, not focusing on any individual project but on the class' work as a whole, is another important benefit of many of these new techniques. *This shifts the discussion from the final design product to the ongoing design process.* How students approach a problem and arrive at a solution—the series of decisions that must be made, the trade-offs and turnabouts in developing design ideas—are issues that can be raised and discussed in depth. In the traditional jury system, with the clock anxiously ticking away and the constant pressure to move on to the next project, jurors typically don't have enough time to discuss these points in detail.

Clarifying Criteria and Demystifying Design

Some of these innovations attempt to spell out criteria used to evaluate design work, thus helping to demystify the design process. As a result, they *help make the evaluation process somewhat less subjective*. While design can never be a truly objective process, with crystal-clear rights and wrongs and formulaic solutions, some of these techniques help establish group-derived general criteria that can be applied to specific projects.[33] Involving jurors, instructors, as well as students in the development of the evaluative criteria helps reduce the individual subjectivity of the jury. Jurors no longer appear as mysterious masters to the students, and students no longer suffer from mysteria mania. In short, juries become somewhat more predictable events.

A Higher Level of Learning

By focusing on the process and not the product, *learning will be increased to a higher level.* In fact, the problem with the one-by-one approach is that discussion generally fixates at a relatively low level, focusing only on individual problems. Furthermore, many of these problems are the same from project to project; when the jury continues to call them out, they begin to sound repetitive. Each project is viewed in relative isolation, apart from the context of the rest of the class. Time rarely permits an overall comparison of information across the board to analyze, evaluate, and synthesize all the projects as a whole.

Learning theorist Benjamin Bloom, who has had a tremendous impact on the field of education, argued that levels of learning can be classified into several types: *knowledge, comprehension, application, analysis, synthesis, and evaluation.* This list reflects a range from lower to higher levels of learning.[34] One can argue that at its best, the traditional jury system may provide opportunities for all these levels of learning to occur, but only for each student's individual project. *By engaging in a more broad-based discussion across the board, jurors and students can begin to analyze, synthesize, and evaluate the entire class's response to a design project.*

Not All Students Need Be Present

Many of these alternatives overturn the myth that each student must present her work before the jury. In fact, *it is not essential that all students present their work before the jury. The jury can be a much more educational and enriching experience when not everyone presents his or her work.* Students need to understand this too, especially those raised during the "me" generation, who may have come to expect individual attention and their chance to be on stage. But it is this very attitude, often shared by faculty alike, that not only drags the traditional jury down but also, for many, turns it into a big yawn. The new generation of students can be easily rid of this expectation if the faculty simply introduce these innovations in the beginning levels of design studios.

Less Tension and No Public Humiliation

Another feature that many of these techniques share is the ability to reduce the levels of stress and tension that students experience. *Stress can be a positive pedagogical tool, provided it is used in moderation.* In the case of design juries, an optimal level of stress is high enough to motivate students to put their best foot forward, but not so high that it interferes with their ability to function.[35]

The traditional jury system has allowed stress to get out of hand. Moreover, public humiliation at an extremely poor jury performance can be so nerve-wracking that it has a negative impact on students' self-image. Numerous educational studies have discovered a strong reciprocal relationship between self-concept and school achievement.[36] Research supports the notion that an instructional atmosphere that is distant, cold, and rejecting (not unlike design juries at their worst) is far less likely to enhance students' self-concept, motivation, and learning.[37]

Problems in student design work need to be called out and corrected, but the key is how and in what context this is done. Perhaps our colleagues in other disciplines, where criticism is delivered in private and on paper, have something to teach us. They probably have good reasons for not placing students on display in front of the class and offering them a public point-by-point account of what they have done wrong. Ironically, the old juries of the Ecole des Beaux Arts, conducted behind closed doors, may not have been such a poor model after all. Granted, these juries had many faults—chief among them that students were totally excluded from the review and grading process, literally left in the dark about how others viewed their work. But subsequent attempts to improve upon the old model may have simply gone overboard in the opposite direction.

Less Time

Many of these alternatives *can end up taking much less time than traditional juries.* Examine the traditional jury from a pure cost-benefit analysis. This research has demonstrated that the costs to faculty are high, while the benefits to students are few. Take a jury of six hours' duration. Say four faculty members are present—the course instructor and three guest critics. Six hours times four instructors equals 24 person-hours spent at the jury. Where else on a university campus is so much faculty time spent evaluating student work for just one assignment?[38] And if students are not getting much out of them, is all this time worth it? I don't believe so.

Marathon jury sessions have been known to last well over two or three hours, and sometimes even seven or eight hours or more. To expect students and jurors alike to maintain their attention span for so many hours is absurd. *During what other circumstances is anyone expected to sit still for so long?* The average movie only lasts about two hours, a long one is over two and a half, and even *Gone with the Wind* is only four hours long. To ask people to sit through a double feature that is not nearly as entertaining is simply too much.

Different Physical Environments and Presentation Media

Finally, some of these models *imply different kinds of rooms and furniture arrangements, as well as different presentation media, than what we generally see at traditional juries.* It is indeed ironic that environmental designers—of all people—are often sitting and standing in the most inappropriate spaces when reviewing student work. The seating arrangements are often hard and uncomfortable, and our bodies soon tell us it is time to get up and move around. Studio desk stools are often the only furniture available to students, and a few hours on those are usually enough to make you want to take a 10-mile hike as soon as possible.

More comfortable seating is needed, and visual access must be improved. Students, jurors, and the studio critic need to be able to see and study the work presented without squinting and having to rearrange their bodies in all sorts of awkward contortions. All three groups need to be able to see and hear each other as clearly as possible.

For some of these models, a conference room with one large table and chairs is more appropriate than the traditional studio environment. In fact, this arrangement comes closer to simulating what usually occurs when a designer and a client meet. If given enough time, students can photograph their boards and models prior to the jury so that they can be shown in slide form, large enough so that even someone in the back of the room can see them well. For students who produce their work using computer-aided drafting systems, computers can be hooked up into equipment that enlarges documents onto a large screen for easy viewing.

For small-group discussions of selected projects, having several large tables much like those found in campus libraries, along with a few chairs, is appropriate. Or, a few exhibit boards can be spaced evenly throughout a room, along with small groups of seating in front of each.

Experiment and Evaluate

Some colleagues have found it helpful to offer students a range of options for when and how they want their work to be evaluated. As a group, through the democratic process, students select the methods they believe to be most helpful for their particular stage of the design process.

These innovative techniques call for a pluralistic approach, so that the benefits of some techniques can compensate for the deficiencies of others. Systematically experimenting with various presentation and feedback methods, such as those presented here, and continuing to assess students' reactions to them can help us fine-tune the jury process. Experimentation and evaluation must go hand in hand. With both major surgery and a few cosmetic touches to help them reach their fullest potential, juries—or better yet, "presentations," "critiques," "reviews," "workshops," and "working sessions"—can and should continue to play an important role in design education.

NOTES

1. This statement was based on Professor Edward R. Ostrander's presentation at a workshop on "The Design Jury: Human Developer or Human Detractor?" at the 21st annual Environmental Design Research Association Conference (EDRA 21), Urbana, Illinois, April 1990.

2. Flanders, Ned, "Some Relationships Among Teacher Influence, Pupil Attitudes, and Achievement," in Amidon, Edmund J., and John B. Hough (eds.), *Interaction Analysis: Theory, Research and Application*, Reading, MA: Addison Wesley, 1967.

3. At my university, faculty have drawn a distinction between *reviews*, which refer to open sessions when students are present, and *juries*, which refer to closed sessions to select prizes, awards, and submissions for national competitions.

4. I am indebted to Professors Edward R. Ostrander and Ronald Beckman of Cornell University for the following list, which they originally prepared as a handout at a recent Environmental Design Research Association Conference. This list reflects some minor adaptations of and additions to the original version. For a summary of the conference workshop presentation, consult Beckman, Ronald, Edward R. Ostrander, Kathryn H. Anthony, and Matthew Gilbertson, "The Design Jury: Human Developer or Human Detractor," in Selby, Robert I., Kathryn H. Anthony, Jaepil Choi, and Brian Orland (eds.), *Coming of Age: Proceedings of the Twenty-First Annual Conference of the Environmental Design Research Association*, (EDRA) Oklahoma City: EDRA; 1990, p. 77.

5. Professors Robert Selby and James Anderson at the University of Illinois at Urbana-Champaign have routinely relied on this technique. They have also invited review faculty back to consult with students individually to discuss and evaluate their projects in progress. They have used outside consultants as well: a librarian for a library project, a police chief for a new police station, and so on.

6. At my own campus instructors are encouraged to give every juror a copy of the design program at least one week before the actual jury date. This procedure has worked quite well.

7. The University of Illinois at Urbana-Champaign has developed a computer software program that ensures that faculty members are assigned to both the interim and final juries of the same class. Faculty members plug in their teaching schedules and times they are available, and those who teach their own studios plug in the number of hours of jury time they need and the number of jurors they are allocated. (This formula varies depending on the level of the class. Generally, graduate studios merit greater jury time and more jurors than do undergraduates. Master's thesis students are offered the most evaluation time.) For further information about this computerized program, write to the Chair, Design Committee,

School of Architecture, University of Illinois at Urbana-Champaign, 608 East Lorado Taft Drive, Champaign, IL 61820.

8. Logistically, this means that all projects must be collected and stored in a locked room to prevent access to them overnight. Your office or a department storeroom will do. Alternatively, you may want to have all students turn in their studio keys and simply leave the work in studio. However, the more desperate students may find their way into the studio in the middle of the night. All submissions should be logged in detail in a record book, so that the next day, a brand new board doesn't magically appear before you. After the projects are collected, encourage students to leave the studio, go home, relax, and get a good night's sleep before the jury. Consider instituting a policy stating that students who continue to work on their projects after the curfew are disqualified from the jury.

9. Ironically, such students may end up producing better projects since they will have benefited from the jury's comments. However, in fairness to those who finished on time, they should not be graded on the same scale as everyone else.

10. Personal correspondence from Stefani Ledewitz, October 29, 1990.

11. The Conway School of Design routinely uses written feedback as part of their students' project presentations, along with oral feedback. Cards are passed out to the audience, and those who wish can provide written comments. According to Ruth Parnall, a faculty member, "It takes a while to learn to be a critic here, since the focus of comment is expected to be not so much on the details of the design as whether the design decisions are well supported.... Given free range of comment, the critics are expected to offer it in an educational way—no terrorism, no artistic tantrums.... So each event is supposed to be an intelligent discussion among reasonable people." (Personal correspondence from Ruth Parnall, October 30, 1990.)

12. By using this approach, faculty and students will find an audience especially receptive to the results of environment-behavior research, discussed in Chapter 5. Having a long-term interest in the final outcome of the project, quasi-clients are usually anxious to learn how users have responded to previous design solutions. More on the importance of the team approach to design is discussed in Chapter 12.

13. For more specific information about some of these projects, consult Anthony, Kathryn H., "Environment-Behavior Research Applied to Design: The Case of Rosemead High School," *Journal of Architectural and Planning Research*, 4:2 (1987), pp. 91-107; Anthony, Kathryn H., "Applying Environment-Behavior Research to Design: From the "Real World" to the Studio Round Trip," in Quinn, Patrick, and Thomas Regan (eds.), *The Discipline of Architecture: Inquiry Through Design. Proceedings of the 73rd Annual Meeting of the Association of Collegiate Schools of Architecture (ACSA), 1985*, Washington, DC: ACSA, 1986, pp. 312-321; Anthony, Kathryn H., and Craig Sutton, "Los Angeles Civic Center's West Mall: A Multi-Media Presentation of an Environment-Behavior Research and Design Study," in Brian Orland (ed.), *Prospect, Retrospect, Continuity. Proceedings of the Annual Conference of the Council of Educators in Landscape Architecture, Urbana, Illinois, September 19-21, 1985*, Urbana: Department of Landscape Architecture, University of Illinois at Urbana-Champaign, 1985, pp. 63-66; Anthony, Kathryn H., Byron Ely, Norman Murdoch, Larry Derr, and E. Terry Irvine, "A Follow-up of Some Applied Environment-Behavior Research Projects Conducted in the Los Angeles Area," in Lawrence, Denise, Reiko Habe, Art Hacker, and Drury Sherrod (eds.), *People's Needs/Planet Management: Paths to Coexistence. Proceedings of the Nineteenth Annual Conference of the Environmental Design Research Association (EDRA), Pomona, California, May 11-15, 1988*, Washington, DC: EDRA, 1988, p. 317.

14. Several other colleagues at the University of Illinois at Urbana-Champaign have routinely used this technique, including James R. Anderson and Robert Selby, as well as Edward R. Ostrander and Ronald Beckman at Cornell and Anthony Ward at the University of Auckland in New Zealand. For more on Professor Ward's particular approach, consult Ward, Anthony, "Ideology, Culture and the Design Studio," in *Design Studies*, 11:1 (January 1990), pp. 10-16; Ward, Anthony, "Biculturalism and Community Design in New Zealand: The Whakatane Project," in Hardie, Graeme, Robin Moore, and Henry Sanoff (eds.), Changing Paradigms: EDRA 20, 1989. Proceedings of the Annual Conference. Oklahoma City, OK: Environmental Design Research Association, 1989, p. 198.

15. Ward, Anthony, "Ideology, Culture and the Design Studio," op. cit., p. 13.

16. Ibid.

17. This is not to be confused with the term *postoccupancy evaluation*, described in Chapter 5, which refers to assessing the performance of a building or space after it has been occupied. More on Professor Antoniades's teaching techniques and the results of his students' work can be found in Antoniades, Anthony C., *The Poetics of Architecture*, New York: Van Nostrand Reinhold, 1990.

18. Personal correspondence from Anthony Antoniades, June 25, 1990.

19. Personal correspondence from Robert Levy, September 8, 1990.

20. Edward R. Ostrander and Ronald Beckman at Cornell University have suggested this as a technique.

21. Personal correspondence from Art Stamps, III, April 8, 1990.

22. Personal correspondence from Howard Ray Lawrence, June 4, 1990.

23. Personal correspondence from Juan C. Bertotto, May 10, 1990.

24. Personal correspondence from Thomas A. Dutton, May 11, 1990.

25. Personal correspondence from Peter Prangnell, August 21, 1990, and September 7, 1990. As former chairman of the Department of Architecture at the University of Toronto, he was able to experiment with both the curriculum and the review process.

26. Personal correspondence from Robert I. Selby, April 30, 1990.

27. This technique and others were described in detail in their presentation at a workshop on "The Design Jury: Human Developer or Human Detractor?" at the 21st annual Environmental Design Research Association Conference (EDRA 21), Urbana, Illinois, April 1990.

28. This practice has proven successful in helping train doctors how to interact with patients. See Cassata, D. M., R. M. Conroe, and P. W. Clements, "A Program for Enhancing Medical Interviewing Using Video Tape Feedback in the Family Practice Residency," *Journal of Family Practice, 4* (1977), pp. 673-677.

29. I learned of this technique from the second set of architecture student surveys at California State Polytechnic University, Pomona.

30. Ledewitz, Stefani, "Models of Design in Studio Teaching," *Journal of Architectural Education, 38*:2 (Winter 1985), pp. 2-8.

31. Personal correspondence from M. Joe Numbers, May 10, 1990.

32. Schön, Donald A., *The Reflective Practitioner*, New York: Basic Books, 1983; Schön, Donald A., *Educating the Reflective Practitioner: Toward a New Design for Teaching and Learning in the Professions*, San Francisco: Jossey-Bass, 1987.

33. Many designers are quick to point out that, as Bryan Lawson argues, "... it seems unreasonable for designers to expect to find a process which will protect them from the painful and difficult business of exercising subjective judgement...". See Lawson, Bryan, *How Designers Think: The Design Process Demystified*, Boston: Butterworth Architecture, 1988, p. 62. Yet many well known designers interviewed for this book admit that in school, design is evaluated in far too subjective a manner, thus making the design process unnecessarily mysterious to students.

34. Bloom, Benjamin, *Taxonomy of Educational Objectives: Handbook I: Cognitive Domain*, New York: McKay, 1956.

35. This notion is somewhat akin to the theory of environmental press used to explain optimal environments for elderly. See Lawton, M. Powell, *Planning and Managing Housing for the Elderly*, New York: Wiley, 1975.

36. See, for example, Jersild, Arthur T., "Characteristics of Teachers Who are 'Liked Best' and 'Disliked Most,'" *Journal of Experimental Education, 9* (1952), pp. 139-151; Purkey, William W., *Self Concept and School Achievement*, Englewood Cliffs, NJ: Prentice-Hall, 1970, pp. 1-17, 43-65. Scores of additional studies have addressed this same topic.

37. Hamachek, Don E., "Towards More Effective Teaching," in Hamachek, Don E. (ed.), *Human Dynamics in Psychology and Education*, 2d ed., Boston: Allyn & Bacon, 1972, pp. 231-246.

38. At the University of Illinois at Urbana-Champaign School of Architecture, for instance, all full-time design faculty members are required to participate in 30 hours of jury duty per semester. Other institutions require similar time commitments, with some expecting even more.

PART 5

JURIES IN PRACTICE

"One cool judgement is worth a thousand hasty councils."
— Woodrow Wilson

"The measure of a man is the way he bears up under misfortune." — Plutarch

CHAPTER 11

How Do Practitioners View Professional Design Juries?

A Critique of Awards Programs and Design Competitions

"This whole competition system is wrong—and I'm sick of it. It is too much to ask a man to spend months of study and work, and thousands of dollars all on a chance and then to have to work by political methods to hold what you may have won fairly by merit. After the Washington University [competition] is over I am through with it once and for all. The strain is too great. I can't understand why [Charles] McKim and other men of equal standing submit to it." —Architect Cass Gilbert in a letter to his wife, Julia, 1899[1]

"I think we have design competitions because architects are egotists. Architects place very low value on their own ability, on their own time, and on the value of their services. They will undertake competitions with the hope that they will achieve individual recognition as a result of submitting the winning solution. The artistic ego overwhelms the philosophical, economic, and moral prudence of engaging in these activities. It's tragic but true." —Donald J. Hackl

"Designing a building isn't a competitive sport. Everyone should contribute to the outcome and everyone should win. Architecture is frozen politics." —John F. Hartray, Jr.

ACADEMIC AND PROFESSIONAL DESIGN JURIES

As we have seen, juries in educational settings are plagued by a host of problems. Are the problems of design juries unique to academia? Or do some of the same issues surface in professional design juries? To begin this analysis, let us compare academic and professional juries along a few critical dimensions: the purpose of each, the review process, the criteria used to evaluate the design work and the nature of design criticism and how it is delivered (Figure 11-1).

Purpose

As we described in Chapter 3, the purpose of academic design juries is not crystal clear. However, in a general sense, they are conducted largely to evaluate student design work. In the case of registration exams, which fall midway along the continuum of academic to professional design juries, it is to evaluate applicants' competence to enter the profession. The purpose of awards and competitions juries is to select winners.

A distinction must be drawn between the two major ways in which juries are used in the design professions: in design competitions and in design awards programs. Design competitions involve projects that are not yet built and that in some cases may never be built. By contrast, design awards programs focus attention on projects that have already been completed. Both design awards programs and design competitions are often intended to draw public attention to the design fields. They can also focus attention on the development of an especially important product, building, or site.

Awards for both completed projects and competition

> "Regarding professional design competitions, the sad thing today is that most designers are too busy to even enter, and that is a shame. Through entering a competition, you do receive great rewards in addition to awards. And what I believe is good about it is the whole process itself and the exposure that it can offer." —Joan Blutter
>
> "It is very easy to win design competitions. I know how easy it is because I've been a juror in competitions where there have been only 30 or 40 entries, when the world assumes there have been 3000. And out of 30 or 40 you're never going to have total excellence. So your chances are really very good as your sampling is smaller. If 30 or 40 people enter and you're really good, you're going to win because there are usually three or four awards. It's a secret that people don't know; so few enter." —Larry N. Deutsch
>
> "I think that competitions in practice should be used more often. In Japan, design competitions can help reduce some of the political pressure inevitable in public projects." —Minoru Takeyama
>
> "I think a competition is the place to take risks. I think that you can break the rules within the constraints. In other words, you could have a totally different interpretation of the problem, which is different from not answering the problem." —Charles Gwathmey
>
> "I think the basic weakness of the people who enter competitions is the inability to look out of the clients' eyes to see what looks good for them. Call this prostitution or salesmanship or just good service, depending on your point of view. It's some of each maybe." —Lawrence B. Perkins
>
> "As an office we've done 30 or 40 competitions in 20 years. We placed in half of them, received an honorable mention, we won one, which hasn't been built. When you look at the dollar value of (competitions), we could have done a lot better if we'd gone to Las Vegas with that money. On one level you have to say it's a pretty inefficient way to work. On every level it seems that we're almost dumb to enter competitions because we all lose our shirts." —Steven Izenour
>
> "After a design competition, we try to hear the tapes back from the jury so that we can hear their quotes. This is very important, because you are hearing people who don't know your name or the identity of the firm. They are responding to your work as pure design.... When the entrant isn't around, the jury is far more honest. And it's fascinating how quickly the jury can get to the bottom line." —Ronette J. King

A COMPARISON OF ACADEMIC AND PROFESSIONAL JURIES

	Academic	Professional		
		Registration Examinations	Awards	Competitions
Purpose	Evaluate student work. Occasionally select winners for competitions and awards.	Evaluate examinations to demonstrate applicants' entry level competence.	Select winners for completed projects.	Select winners for projects not yet built.
Review process	Open deliberations except for competitions and awards.	Closed deliberations.	Closed deliberations.	Closed deliberations.
Evaluation criteria	Rarely made explicit.	Extremely explicit with formal grading criteria given to all jurors. Strong emphasis on jurors' consistency and fairness.	Tends to be slightly more explicit but still generally vague. Post-facto criteria.	Tends to be more explicit. Often spelled out in competition program, but still often intentionally vague.
How criticism is delivered	Oral, on-the-spot.	Written notification by mail.	Formal announcement. Public ceremony. Publication in the press and professional journals.	Formal announcement. Public ceremony. Publication in the press and booklets. Jury report.

Figure 11-1 A comparison between academic and professional design juries, with juries for professional registration exams falling somewhere in the middle. Certain aspects of juries in the professional world have much to offer those in academia.

entries are used to help establish the reputation and enhance the credentials of design firms. As some of the profession's most effective marketing tools, awards are usually highlighted in firm brochures and in presentations to potential clients. In academia, placing in a competition or receiving an award for a completed project is usually one of the bases for faculty promotion, tenure, and salary increases. Both vehicles serve as important indicators of how peers review design work.

The Review Process

While most academic design juries are now "open" and the public is invited to view the judging process, a few are clearly the opposite. Juries for student design competitions are typically closed. In this case, juries usually involve a select group of jurors meeting in a closed session, with the results publicly announced after they adjourn. This format most closely resembles that of the professional design jury.

State registration examinations are judged by a jury in closed sessions. Professional design awards, for example, by a local chapter of the American Institute of Architects, American Society of Landscape Architects, or American Society of Interior Designers, are also judged in closed sessions. The same is true of juries for professional design competitions. The transformation of the jury process from closed to open that occurred in design education has not occurred in design practice. One might speculate that the process has remained closed in order to protect the professional integrity of the firms entering, in order to protect the confidentiality of the jurors' comments, or simply because the purpose is altogether different.

The Evaluative Criteria

In academia, the criteria behind what constitutes a successful design project are rarely, if ever, made explicit before, during, or even after the jury. This is especially true when the professor has written an assignment of his own, as opposed to using a published competition program. Because postjury class meetings are relatively rare, few students and instructors have the opportunity to discuss the evaluative criteria used by the jury even post facto.[2]

In the case of professional licensing examinations, the criteria for judging are made most explicit, moreso than in any type of jury. Figure 11-2 shows the grading criteria used for the 1990 Architect Registration examination (ARE). This grading process is outlined in detail in the *Juror's Manual*, which states: *"We cannot overstress the importance that every grader accept and apply the established grading criteria whether or not they personally agree with the criteria."*[3] The authors of the *Juror's Manual* acknowledge that the ability to serve as a juror for the ARE is quite different from that required to teach or practice architecture. Nonetheless, this format provides a model that can be readily adapted into design education.

In professional design competitions and awards programs, the call for entries and competition program often, but not always, include a statement about the criteria used to evaluate the submissions. Often these criteria are intentionally written in vague language in order to encourage a wide variety of interpretations among the solutions. Many designers welcome the vague nature of the program, arguing that creative breakthroughs often occur in spite of, or at variance with, the program. Rightly or wrongly, competition winners frequently break some of the rules. Some contend that creatively reinterpreting the competition program is possibly the most important creative act of the design process, an act central to concept development.

Lawrence Witzling and Jeffrey Ollswang's book, *The Planning and Administration of Design Competitions*, provides another useful model for academic design juries.[4] The authors suggest that every design competition problem statement clearly defines the project's goals, objectives, design features and attributes, requirements, recommendations and options, and evaluative criteria. Evaluative criteria are defined as "those principles or standards which the jury agrees to use in making its decisions."[5] The authors recommend:

> *The problem statement should contain explicit evaluative criteria which the jurors are obligated to apply in their selection process. These criteria must relate directly to the objectives as well as the required and recommended design features or attributes. When possible the evaluative criteria should be ordered according to priority.*[6]

They suggest that the announced objectives of the competition form the basis of the evaluative criteria, and that any criteria must be reviewed and approved by the jurors in writing. They note, however, that competition jurors should also be given full authority to apply additional criteria of their own as needed. While the book offers some thoughtful suggestions for establishing and maintaining a basis for jurors' decisions, what is not clear is the degree to which these guidelines have been implemented routinely in practice.

The Nature of Design Criticism and How It Is Delivered

After the jury for the professional competition or design awards program is over, some of the jurors' comments explaining the criteria for selecting the winning entries may be published in booklets or trade journals. The *Handbook of Architectural Design Competitions*, published by the American Institute of Architects, calls upon jurors to write a report explaining the rationale for their final selection. According to the handbook, this report has three functions: (1) as written evidence to competitors, the sponsor, and the public that the evaluation and selection proceedings were conducted fairly; (2) as an educational document describing the criteria for evaluating architec-

GRADING CRITERIA USED FOR THE 1990
ARCHITECT REGISTRATION EXAMINATION (A.R.E.)[1]

PROGRAM REQUIREMENTS

Development of All Programed Spaces
Conformance to Square Footage Requirements
Compliance with Required Spatial Relationships

DESIGN LOGIC

Circulation
Spatial Relationships/Proportions/Adjacencies
Compatibility to Existing Context

CODE COMPLIANCE

Fire Separations
Means of Egress
Accessibility Requirements for Physically Challenged Individuals

TECHNICAL ASPECTS

Material Selection and Wall, Floor and Roof Assemblies
Structural Systems and their Integration
Mechanical Systems and their Integration

COMPLETENESS AND CLARITY

---

[1] Source: Adapted from handout given to jurors at the June 1990 grading session of the National Council of Architectural Registration Boards (NCARB) Architect Registration Examination

Figure 11-2 The grading criteria used for the 1990 Architect Registration Exam. If criteria are so explicit for the exam, why can't they also be explicit for the academic jury?

---

tural design; and (3) as a historic document listing the winners and explaining why certain designs were chosen.[7] The handbook states: "A jury report should be accurate, comprehensive, and succinct. Each juror should have ample opportunity to offer comments and suggestions, but the report as a whole should speak with one voice."[8] This documentation process provides yet another useful model for design education.

Jurors' comments about the winning entries for professional design awards may also be announced at a public awards ceremony. Award ceremonies are often gala public events, and the winning entries usually receive formal recognition in various trade publications, exhibits, and local newspapers (Figure 11-3). In these instances, the focus is usually on positive criticism, although this is not always the case.

During my debut as a juror for a professional architectural awards program, the awards program advisor pulled us aside and strongly urged us to focus on the positive in the upcoming public ceremony. (During our jury deliberations earlier that day, by contrast, we were encouraged to say whatever came to mind.) At this gala event, a formal sit-down dinner and slide presentation, our role was to present the awards to the winning designers and discuss

Figure 11-3 Design awards ceremonies are often high-visibility gala events intended to promote a favorable image of the design professions to the public. They are the counterparts of the Academy Awards in the movie industry.

how we arrived at our decisions. I naively asked the advisor to explain his request. To my amazement, he informed us of previous incidents when jurors presenting the awards made scathing remarks about the deficiencies of even the winning projects. This occurred despite the fact that *not only the designers, but also their families, friends, and clients, were often sitting in the same room.* Once again, I felt as if I had arrived from another planet.

Since that time, as a member of the audience for professional design awards juries I have witnessed several such embarrassing scenes, causing me to believe that this kind of behavior at juries may be somewhat common. I have watched winning designers anxiously dash up to the podium to receive their awards against a backdrop of enthusiastic audience applause, and then stand quietly at attention to listen to the jurors' remarks about their work. Their faces, beaming at first, literally dropped. The sparkle in their eyes vanished. The wind was instantly knocked out of their sails. And one can't help but wonder how the clients, who have already paid out large sums of money for their project, must feel when hearing about all their designers' mistakes. Such tactless comments can easily take a toll on the award-winning designers and their guests, putting a palpable damper on this exciting event.

In sum, some — but not all — of the serious shortcomings of educational juries are remedied by professional design juries. The private nature of the review process spares those who do not fare well public humiliation and embarrassment. The evaluative criteria are generally made somewhat more explicit, especially in the professional registration exam. The documentation of jury deliberations in a jury report helps provide entrants with at least some clue to the jury's decisions. Only the results and the winning entries are discussed publicly, and emphasis is generally much more positive. Educational juries can easily benefit from some of the strengths of professional juries, thus helping reduce their sense of mystery to students.

In professional design jury presentations, the overall emphasis is much more on the positive. Even so, just as in school, some jurors at awards ceremonies still make a habit of humiliating the winning designers in public. *By so doing, they contribute to the public image of design as a self-effacing profession. If the image of the design professions to the public is to improve, this unintentional self-destructive behavior must be stopped.*

Despite some similarities with juries in academia, professional design juries raise a host of problems not found in educational settings. With the marked increase in the use of design competitions in the United States and elsewhere during the past decade, it is an opportune moment to step back and take a look at how well design juries work in practice. We will first examine design awards programs and then design competitions.

THE PROS AND CONS OF DESIGN AWARDS PROGRAMS

Each of the major professional design organizations has its own design awards programs — often at local, regional, state, and national levels. The American Society of Interior Designers (ASID), American Society of Landscape Architects (ASLA), American Institute of Architects (AIA), American Planning Association (APA), and Environmental Design Research Association (EDRA) each has separate awards programs. Design awards programs are not restricted to these professional organizations, however. In various localities, different types of awards programs can be found. One such example is San Diego, California's, unusual Orchids and Onions Program, which we will discuss later. Design magazines such as *Progressive Architecture* and some federal agencies like the National Endowment for the Arts also sponsor their own awards programs.

How do designers evaluate design awards programs? As can be expected, their responses vary greatly. The next few pages reflect their thoughts and sentiments.

On the positive side, a tremendous value of design awards programs is to help recognize outstanding talent in the field. After all, everyone needs a pat on the back once in awhile. Because the pay scale of designers compared to that of many other professions is relatively low, and because public recognition of designers in the United States is not what most designers believe it ought to be, awards programs provide one of the few ways to reward design professionals for a job well done.

I think professional juries certainly serve a good purpose. It's a wonderful outlet for people to be able to

> *submit quality work and to have it reviewed by their peers. Although there's great diversity in design and people come from different philosophical backgrounds, I think bringing together a group of varied jurors is a very good method to review work of an area or region, or nationally. It's very encouraging to the individuals when there is some kind of recognition by their peer group. — E. Fay Jones*

For jurors, the process is an enlightening experience. Jurors can often learn much from each other and about the region in which the projects are being judged. This type of education is often best obtained through the jury experience.

Because only completed projects are generally eligible for design awards, clients have already paid for design services. Whether or not they win any design awards, firms are still paid for the work they have produced. This is not always the case in design competitions.

Decisions about design awards juries are highly subjective. What one juror favors may not be the preferred choice of another. What one year's jury selects may be entirely different from what next year's jury chooses. This aspect of design awards juries is both encouraging and discouraging. On the one hand, designers must realize that if their work does not win an award, it may be due to the composition of the jury and the individual preferences and predispositions of the jurors, rather than to their projects' deficiencies. Hence it is often worth resubmitting the same project for yet another awards program at a later date, where a fresh jury may view one's work in an altogether different light.

What is somewhat disheartening, however, is that with subjectivity comes unpredictability. Entering an awards program is often a gamble at best. Kay Kaiser, architecture critic of the *San Diego Union*, eloquently described some of the problems with the design awards program sponsored by the San Diego chapter of the American Institute of Architects (AIA):

> *Many San Diego architects see the list of well-known jurors from other cities and know that their work doesn't stand a chance of winning. From reading the architectural press, local architects know that one juror likes only white buildings and that another rejects everything that isn't symmetrical and redolent of ancient Rome. If another juror is quoted as saying that nothing worthwhile has been built west of New Hampshire since 1936, that statement alone will keep many local architects out of the game.*
> *...Under these conditions, architects figure they have a better chance of winning if they bet on the horse with the nice eyes at Del Mar [Race Track].*[9]

Along these lines, architect Frank Welch has cleverly argued: "Architects look lovingly on cherished work like parents view their newborn — with perspectives askew. We professionals have set up awards programs — official baby-judging contests differing in meaning and attitude from year to year and from jury to jury."[10]

Serving on a jury can be an extremely taxing experience when literally hundreds of projects have been entered. The same problem is true for design competitions as well. Projects are shown in rapid succession and jurors often have only a few seconds to try to absorb and retain what they see. A casual review of submitted work often does not do justice to design firms that spend hundreds and thousands of hours, not to mention dollars, preparing their submissions. Just as in academia, jurors are often under severe time pressures, constantly looking at the clock.

> *I've been on a lot of professional juries where you're looking at from 50 to 150 presentations, and you're supposed to go through them in a few hours. You eventually get to the point where you put them up and if not one person on the jury raises their hand about something positive, you put it aside and then you go on.... Jurors with ready wits can easily determine who's going to win by taking the lead in conversation. Someone else is then embarrassed to disagree. — The late Norman R. DeHaan*

A few designers believed that awards juries served no useful purpose except to "hand out candy." They stressed that such juries merely serve as "rewards" rather than "awards" and that they really do not advance the profession in a significant way. Others speculated that professionals in other fields, such as doctors and lawyers, may mock the design professions for what appears to them as merely a backslapping process.

Among the more noteworthy drawbacks of awards juries is the fact that as out-of-town jurors, they are often unfamiliar with the local urban context. Many jurors are often incapable of adequately judging the extent to which a new project fits into its surroundings. In fact, instead of recognizing those more modest projects that "fit in," design awards juries often pay more attention to work that "stands out."[11] It is also possible for a jury to give an award to a project that local citizens utterly despise. Public reaction to a new project and how it fits into its local context is usually overlooked altogether.

Others have cited the oddity of giving awards to projects before we know how the public or the people for whom they were built react to them. While projects usually must be completed to be eligible, they need not have been occupied for a specified length of time, and generally no information whatsoever is collected about people's responses. As a well-known scholar cleverly observed, "Giving out awards to buildings before they have been fully occupied is like giving an award to an airplane before you find out if it can fly, or to a boat before you found out it doesn't sink."

In the eyes of the public, some notorious design award winners have turned out to be bitter losers. One of the more illustrious examples is the mammoth 2764-unit

Pruitt-Igoe housing project in St. Louis, Missouri, designed by Hellmuth, Yamasaki and Leinweber and built in 1955, hailed as an example of outstanding design and the recipient of an award from the American Institute of Architects soon after it was built. In 1972, after a turbulent history of vandalism, muggings, and murders, and a myriad of social problems, the city demolished its three central blocks by dynamite.[12]

Another famous award-winning example is the Art and Architecture Building at Yale University, designed by acclaimed architect Paul Rudolph and built in the early 1960s. Apparently an oppressive and inflexible building for its occupants, it became the target of angry arsonists who in 1969 set it afire and destroyed the three upper floors.[13] As psychologist Robert Sommer has written,

> It is difficult to understand how a building that made so many people so uncomfortable that some even tried to burn it down could merit a citation for good design. . . . Professional disinterest in popular tastes is a dangerous trend for a democracy . . . to the extent that it [the system of architectural awards] encourages professional disinterest in popular response to buildings and favors monumental structures, it provides support for hard architecture.[14]

Design awards are often the result of changing climates of architectural opinion and the world of fashion. Some critics might opt for a breezy neo-classicism while others no doubt would prefer the chill of deconstructivism. In fact, little scientific research has been conducted to test the validity of design awards. One can't help but wonder, Are awards being given to the right projects? Are awards valid indicators not only of the opinions of design professionals, but also of the public? One of the few studies to test some of these ideas yielded provocative results.[15] Jacqueline Vischer and Clare Cooper Marcus were hired as consultants to evaluate a national housing design awards program run by the Canadian Housing Design Counsil (CHDC). They used four sets of criteria to evaluate several housing projects, some of which had received awards and some of which had come very close. The evaluation criteria included designers' criteria for submitting their work, expressed in their short written texts accompanying their submission; the design awards jury's criteria as expressed during two working sessions; on-site observation and evaluation of a set of user needs criteria developed from postoccupancy evaluations of about 100 multifamily housing schemes;[16] and resident surveys.

Findings indicate that all four sets of criteria overlapped to a certain extent, especially concerning the overall appearance of the project and some aspects of livability. However, the criteria of the jury and those of the residents differed so sharply that their rank ordering of the housing schemes was reversed.[17] This study raises some critical issues about the ways in which design projects are evaluated. Whose values are most important? Can aesthetics be achieved without livability — and can the reverse be true?

In sum, design awards have their pluses and minuses — and some of these minuses are serious shortcomings. However, compared to design competitions, they are far less controversial.

THE PROS AND CONS OF DESIGN COMPETITIONS

What Are Design Competitions?

Some of the world's best-known and best-loved spaces and places are the results of professional design competitions. The old Paris Opera in France, the Sydney Opera House in Australia, and the Town Hall in Stockholm, Sweden, are just a few international examples. In the United States, the White House, the Washington Monument, the Capitol, the Lincoln Memorial, and most recently the Vietnam Veteran's Memorial, all in Washington, D.C.; the Chicago Tribune Administration Building in Chicago; Union Station and the Gateway Arch in St. Louis; the Public Library of the City of New York; and Boston's City Hall were all designed by competition winners (Figure 11-4). Competitions have a long history. In fact, the first recorded competition was for an Athenian War Memorial on the Acropolis in 488 B.C.[18]

A wide variety of design competitions exist in the United States today, and it is important to distinguish among the different types available. *Project* or *implementation competitions* are intended to lead to the construction or installation of a project. By contrast, *idea* or *concept competitions* are aimed at generating ideas, such as improving specific building types, revitalizing urban neighborhoods, or using materials in an unusually creative way. Competition sponsors include professional groups such as local chapters of the American Institute of Architects, public interest groups, potential clients, or some combination thereof. Typically professional and public interest groups sponsor concept competitions often as a consciousness raising or public relations device, while clients can also sponsor them as a way of generating ideas to help offer future solutions to real problems. A professional advisor, for example, a designer, a member of the sponsor's staff, or a volunteer chapter official, manages the competition. The time the professional advisor and staff spend to develop the program can range from only 12 hours or so to over 1,000 hours over a few months. Part of this time involves publicity. Sponsors use direct mailings, professional newsletters and journals, newspapers, and other media to advertise competitions. Client and mixed sponsored competitions appear to attract the greatest interest.[19]

Concerning eligibility requirements, they can be open, limited, or invited. In an *open competition*, any licensed design professional is eligible to enter, and entries are

Figure 11-4 Some of our most beloved national landmarks are the results of national design competitions.

anonymous. In the United States and Germany, open competitions are most prevalent, attracting anywhere from 10 to 700 entries. Cash prizes are awarded along with special recognition for honorable mentions and other noteworthy projects. In a *limited competition*, only a portion of the design profession is eligible—for instance, only those residing in a particular geographic area. In an *invited competition*, a small number of firms may be commissioned (i.e., paid) to prepare conceptual designs under the guidance of a project program and a professional advisor or competition coordinator. Such firms are selected based on their fame and expertise. Student competitions may be open to all schools or restricted to a small group of schools. Prizes include cash awards, scholarships, traveling fellowships, and other awards.[20] Competitions can be conducted at a local, regional, state, national, or an international level.

From start—the competition announcement, followed by a question-and-answer period—to finish—when the jury selects the winners—the competition process can take almost a year. Concept competitions end when the results are publicized and disseminated, while implementation competitions conclude with contract negotiations. Post-competition publicity efforts can involve public exhibits of award-winning entries, reports on local television stations, or press coverage in local newspapers, in many cases. However, some competitions result in little or no public exposure.

Most open competitions are conducted in a *single stage*, with the required presentations limited to drawings, brief concept statements, and perhaps photographs of models. The form and scope of the entries are usually specified. In the case of more complex projects, competitions may be conducted in *two stages*. Based on the results from the first stage, a limited number of designers is invited to further develop their work for the second stage. Winners from the first stage generally receive prize money to help defray some of their expenses involved in preparing the second-stage entries. Two-stage competitions combine the advantages of the open and invited competition, where the first stage is open but the second stage is restricted only to finalists. Although competition juries are usually composed of a panel of expert design professionals, in some cases, especially the more complex two-stage competitions, the jury also includes non-designers as well.[21]

Recent years have also witnessed the proliferation of so-called *quasi- or design-develop competitions* that involve packages of developer groups, such as builders, architects, planners, financiers, and others who submit a combined proposal. In these cases, the evaluation criteria are broadened to include not only design, but also social benefits, financial costs, and other considerations.[22] These are almost always invited competitions. Jurors for design-develop competitions often include cost-estimators, developers, or construction managers.

In the United States and Europe, competitions have been used increasingly in the past decade, especially to help select the designers of major projects. While in the 1960s the American Institute of Architects approved an average of about 10 competitions per year,[23] by the late 1980s the yearly average was about 10 times that amount. One recent estimate is that the number of design competitions in the United States increased between 1975 and 1985 by 1000%. Today, between 1500 and 2000 architectural firms and individual architects regularly enter design competitions.[24] In some European countries, design competitions are used even more widely than they are in the United States. In 1980, for instance, over 500 design competitions were held in West Germany, and competitions for any public-sector building costing over a set fee level were held in France.

Design Competitions: A Pandora's Box

When we begin to take a serious look at design competitions, we are inevitably opening up a Pandora's box. Again, the following reflects the designers' viewpoints.

On a positive note, it is sometimes only through the use of design competitions that young, previously unrecognized talent is discovered. The example of a design competition that designers most often cite as a shining success is that of the Vietnam Veterans Memorial in Washington, D.C., where then Yale student Maya Ying Lin's sensitive, simple solution rose to the surface. Were it not for that design competition, her stunning project would never have been built. Competitions can often yield unparalleled examples of design excellence.

For young designers, entering design competitions can be a relatively quick route to fame and fortune—if they win. The prestige and publicity accompanying the receipt of a competition award help to quickly establish a designer or design firm as one of the leaders in the field. Given the intense level of competition for many of these awards, winning is certainly a major accomplishment that deserves recognition.

As is the case for awards juries, many designers find that serving on design competition juries is an education in itself. The exposure to a wide cross section of ideas and design talent is often something that jurors find exhilarating.

A distinction can be drawn for spaces and places where design competitions are either highly appropriate or, by contrast, entirely inappropriate. *The general consen-*

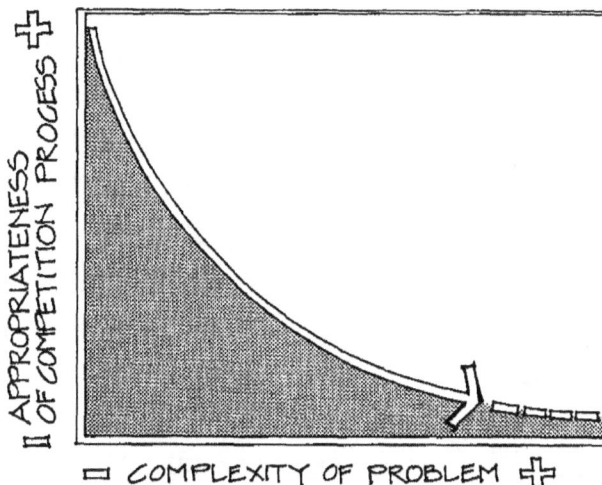

Figure 11-5 Design competitions may be more appropriate in some cases than others. The more complex the project, and the more diverse the users, the less appropriate competitions may be. Competitions are often most appropriate for symbolic buildings and landmarks.

sus is that the simpler the project, or the more symbolic or artistic its goal, the more appropriate is the use of competitions. Conversely, the more complex the project, the less appropriate competitions usually are (Figure 11-5).

> *Competitions are a good means of uncovering talent and of designing symbolic or monumental projects. The Vietnam Memorial Competition was a good illustration of both these goals. Poetry is best produced by individuals working alone. A building committee is not likely to arrive at the concept for The Vietnam Memorial or the Washington Monument.*
>
> *Competitions are not appropriate for the design of more complex buildings, or where there are planning questions which require the formation of a consensus. This is one of the most important functions of the design process, and it can't be done without a dialogue.*
> —John F. Hartray, Jr.

On the downside, design competitions raise many serious ethical issues. The analogy between the design professions and the legal and medical professions is quite common. As architect Rodney F. Friedman points out (Figure 11-6):

> *Can you imagine a surgeon entering a competition to remove somebody's appendix—for free? Hell, no! Or an electrical engineer or an attorney working for free? We are a self-destructive profession. I don't do anything for free. Right now the ethics in this profession are just all right down the drain.*

To add fuel to the fire, designers do so willingly! The concern that designers are being taken advantage of through the use of design competitions is extremely widespread, causing many practitioners to be angry and bitter. And

Figure 11-6 Competitions in the design professions have become routine, but in other professions competitions are rare. Imagine a competition among surgeons to see who has performed an operation most successfully—with no charge!

justifiably so: In open design competitions in the United States, the vast majority of designers are not paid for their work. Hundreds of firms spend countless hours of staff time and significant amounts of money to prepare and submit their competition entries. And with the exception of the lucky winners, everyone else loses. Even for the winners, the monetary rewards rarely come close to covering the real costs involved.[26] In almost any other profession, this practice would be viewed as a colossal waste of both time and money. In invited or limited competitions, designers are often partially reimbursed for their expenses, but rarely is a major portion of their costs covered. Again, design competitions are often a losing financial operation and many designers find them exploitative.

Often the project that is the subject of the competition is not even built after all, despite earlier intentions of doing so. Financial constraints, the election of a new mayor, a corporate merger, and other obstacles often get in the way. In many cases, it is entirely possible to win even an implementation competition yet never see the project built, thus making the whole process merely a hypothetical exercise much like in design school. In these instances, designers are simply being used as a free means of gathering ideas.

To make matters even more complex, upon submission of a competition entry, ownership is generally transferred to the competition sponsor. This raises yet another ethical dilemma, as in this case designers are not only working for free but also literally giving their work away for others to use, if they so choose. Designers' rights to their own work are thus severely restricted. Again, a counterpart in another profession is not to be found.

> "I have very mixed feelings about professional design competitions. I think that unpaid competitions are really an exploitation of the profession. God knows we're not the best paid profession. We are eager to enter these competitions, but I really think that in a way they are degrading and demeaning. The paucity of money is an insult. The amount of work they require is an insult. And the fact that someone is going to be using our work in order to raise money when the project is not yet a reality—it's ridiculous! I could kick myself sometimes. Some competitions pay each team $5,000 or $7,000 for their entries, and the teams will have ¼ scale models and drawings. There's usually a huge amount of work for which they are not paid, however. This work is often done by students who are not paid. That's no way to run competitions. We're being used."—Martha Schwartz
>
> "More and more design competitions are becoming exploitative. They demean the profession. They demean the participants. And they demean the people who advocate them—all because of this fundamental failure to understand what architecture really is."—Donald J. Hackl

One of the most compelling drawbacks of the widespread use of competitions is that they basically go against the grain of what design practice is supposed to be all about. Most competitions prohibit communication with the client or users who will ultimately be affected by what is built. Only the professional adviser is privy to this information, and communication between the professional adviser and design competitors is limited to brief, written questions and answers. Thus the rich dialogue among designer, client, and user—the ability to discuss ideas back and forth and to listen to each other—is altogether absent. Many designers stress that this dialogue is indeed fundamental to the design process, and as a result, refuse to even enter competitions.

> I don't like design competitions because I need much closer contact with a client in order to do good work. Design competitions do not allow you to deal directly with clients' problems. They foster the notion that architects are completely independent types of people. The whole idea behind design competitions is to produce something that is actually unrelated to any expression of clients' needs. —Joseph Esherick
>
> Why am I, in general, against juried design competitions? Because of the way we work with clients. I believe it is impossible for an architect to produce an excellent solution without the ability to interface on a very intimate level with his or her client. A successful building must be more than aesthetically pleasing; it must also be both functionally and economically sound.

In the case of design competitions, the client does not have the opportunity to interface with his or her architect at the level of intimacy that is fundamental to creating a great work of architecture. —Donald J. Hackl

In addition to satisfying the clients' and the users' needs, competition winners must also satisfy the public. *At bottom, competitions are a very public enterprise: Public bodies often sponsor major design competitions and pay for them with public money, and the result is a public building or space.* But how does the public react? One of the few studies to assess reactions to the winning entries of design competitions reports favorable reactions by special interests, the general public, and the media; however, the responses were from "individuals intimately involved with their respective competitions, who may have viewed other impressions in an unduly favorable light."[27] The opinions of the person on the street, who had no prior involvement with the competition process, were not asked.

By contrast, some fascinating research by Jack Nasar and Junmo Kang raises some disturbing questions about professional design competitions. The researchers conducted a *postjury evaluation* of the recent Ohio State University Design Competition for a Center for the Visual Arts. Using the criteria stated by the jury for their selection of the winner, the researchers assessed public responses to the entries. Results showed that the public ranked the winning entry, designed by Eisenman/Robertson and Trott & Bean, as third or fourth out of five. Instead, they consistently rated the entry by Arthur Erickson and Feinkopf, Macloce and Shappa as their first choice.

Public evaluations of the five competition entries were consistent and profoundly different from the "expert" jury's choice. The difference was not simply one in the degree of preference but one in direction. The jury's first choice was among the least liked by the public.[28]

Along these same lines, Andrew Seidel conducted a survey of design competition entrants, jurors, and sponsors and found that respondents' experiences with competitions were mixed. Although respondents pointed out that competitions encourage quality design, promote new ideas, and generate public recognition, two-thirds of those surveyed did not believe that in the competition in which they participated the best design won. Two-thirds recognized that opportunities for eventual users of the project to participate were limited, and over four-fifths believe that the general public has little involvement. Over half believed that every entrant does not receive fair consideration and that jurors are biased towards well-known designers. Most believed that competitions cost architects more money and took more time and effort than regular means of obtaining a commission.[29]

Does the increasing popularity of professional design competitions signal an increasing elitism in the design professions—where fashions and trends preferred by the experts are placed on a pedestal high above the public's reach?

On the other side of the coin, professional competitions basically turn over the decision-making process to a group of strangers, the jurors, who in fact may have no long-term commitment to the project or to its geographic locale. Thus clients are often giving away the most important decision they can make: the selection of the designer.

Clients who hold competitions aren't really very smart. The process doesn't give them good architecture because they're cutting themselves out of the process at the very point when the architect is formulating the most important things about your building. You've suddenly isolated yourself from any exchange. And that's just idiotic. —Steven Izenour

The common practice of hiring students and recent graduates to help prepare competition entries is also one that many designers view as unethical. Working into the wee hours of the morning much like in design school, their contributions often go unrecognized. When the deadline is reached, they are often fired from the job. As one student put it, "We are used like a piece of toilet paper. Once we serve our purpose, we are thrown away." Furthermore, the use of students as a contemporary form of slave labor to help prepare competition submissions can unintentionally misrepresent the true capabilities of a firm. This raises a disturbing question: would some firms participate in competition if it were not for the cheap labor that students provide?

The medium through which competition entries are submitted also has an effect on how they are judged, and this, too, can often serve to misrepresent a firm. Talented artists are often hired with the express purpose of completing competition entries, but in many cases, they may not be contracted to actually do the work. Furthermore, poor delineation of an otherwise strong design concept will generally be enough to toss the entry out of the final round of judging. Because of shipping and handling limitations, drawings often must be done at such a small scale ($1/16$ inch = 1 foot or even smaller) that important details crucial to understanding the design concept must often be omitted.[30]

SOME ALTERNATIVE MODELS

The overwhelming problems inherent in professional design juries, especially in design competitions, lead one to believe that the current model has simply become outdated. Perhaps it is time to consider some refreshing, new ways to evaluate design work. These models can retain the basic concept of the design jury, that crucial element of peer review. The importance of aesthetics and design innovation as one of the chief criteria for evaluating design work can be maintained. Thus a revised evaluation system need not fly in the face of current practices. But additional criteria can be added to achieve a more well balanced evaluation. Future changes to professional design juries ought to reflect a field where aesthetics is but one of several categories that deserve recognition.

Orchids and Onions

Along these lines, San Diego's innovative Orchid and Onion Awards, a community awareness program, incorporates public response as a key ingredient. It is one of the few awards programs of its type in the country. Members of the general public are asked to nominate from San Diego's planned and built environment both *"orchids," that is, successes, well-design solutions that contribute to the community, and "onions," that is, disappointments and missed opportunities.* As its official ballot indicates, an Orchid's "contribution to the community brings a sweet, refreshing fragrance," while "no matter how you slice it, [an Onion] brings tears to your eyes."[31] Nominations are solicited in the following categories: architecture, city and regional planning, environmental solutions, historic preservation, interior design, landscape architecture, graphic design and signage, and fine arts. A jury of design professionals and members of the public then selects the final award winners from the nominations received. The announcements are made at a large public ceremony. San Diego's successful program could well serve as a model nationwide.

The Rudy Bruner Award for Excellence in the Urban Environment

Another innovative awards program is the Rudy Bruner Award for Excellence in the Urban Environment. Created in 1985, the program is an outgrowth of the organizers' dissatisfaction with traditional design awards programs. In their book, *Urban Excellence*, which describes the award program in detail, Philip Langdon, Robert Shibley, and Polly Welch argue that by having jurors look only at slides, photographs, plans, and written materials, the process "all too often ends up going astray; the panelists who pass the final judgment may not understand the projects thoroughly enough, and the lessons of the award competitions may be ambiguous or even misleading." According to the authors, among the greatest shortcomings of traditional awards programs are that they:

- Do little or no on-site inspection
- Report only the good news about the winning projects instead of presenting a balanced story; the projects' shortcomings, which may hold lessons for others, tend to go unacknowledged

- Do not make explicit some of the significant assumptions about what constitutes quality
- Focus on the artifact—the project, the object, the place—and neglect to examine processes and values that were important aspects of the award winner
- Celebrate only one type of actor or professional—such as the architect, developer, or builder—rather than tell about the full range of professional, political, social, financial, and other actors that bring successful construction into being[32]

The projects that receive awards as part of this innovative program integrate aesthetic concerns as well as social, political, and economic issues. The award is not just for an applicant, but rather it is for a place and all the people who helped make that place great.[33]

Members of the Environmental Design Research Association (EDRA) assist in defining the award's approach, in creating and writing the announcements and application package, and in the selection process. Only built projects are eligible. A selection committee, each of whom represents a different specialty within the urban development field, meets twice. The first meeting is to determine which of the nominated sites merits a closer look. Next, two professional consultants who serve as evaluators visit those sites, in many cases, interviewing passersby, photographing the buildings and spaces from all sides, and collecting other relevant information that goes above and beyond what the applicants provide. The second meeting of the selection committee is to review the evaluators' findings and to select the winning entry. One entry receives an award, and the others are presented certificates commending them for their valuable qualities.

Incorporating Public Opinion: Prejury Evaluations

Psychologist Robert Sommer suggests two simple ways of creating a design awards system more responsive to user needs:

> 1. *No building shall be nominated for an award until it has been open and in use for at least twelve months.*
> 2. *Some effort shall be made to systematically obtain and include the opinions of the building's occupants in the decision process.*[34]

Based on the results of their research, Jacqueline Vischer and Clare Cooper Marcus suggest that three evaluative approaches be addressed by design awards juries: appearance, construction quality, and livability.

> *First, does the development look interesting and attractive? Is it aesthetically and functionally appropriate to its context? Second, does the building work? Is it well-built? Third, is the development enjoyed and appreciated by the people who are living there? Does it fulfill their day-to-day social and psychological needs?*[35]

They stress that while these approaches overlap somewhat, applying one at the expense of the other is insufficient. These approaches reflect the age-old twin concerns of form versus function. In fact, the Canadian Housing Design Counsil incorporated some of the findings from their research into subsequent design awards programs. More in-depth jury site visits have been employed, and the jury is required to interview managers and residents in each project to assure that projects selected for awards are also liked by their inhabitants. All jury members are required to visit each project on the short list.[36]

Jack Nasar and Junmo Kang, based on their research, suggest that competition sponsors commission *prejury evaluations (PJEs)* to identify how the public will respond to a variety of proposed design solutions. They could then select a jury who will take the results of this evaluation into account during their own deliberations. The researchers stress that this does not imply locking the jury into the results from the PJE, but rather simply ensuring that public reaction is considered seriously along with other design and technical issues.[37] Although the costs of such a PJE would be relatively minor, the benefits to the public and community at large could be great.

A Pluralistic Approach

In rethinking their awards programs, the design professions could benefit from examining the awards programs routinely used in the music, television, drama, and film industries. Consider the well-known Grammy, Emmy, Tony, and Academy awards programs, or for those who despise the glitz and the glitter, those somewhat less ostentatious programs like the Cannes Film Festival. Awards are given for not just one but a variety of categories. The Academy Awards, for example, recognize not only best picture, best actor, or best actress. They also present awards in the director, cinematography, screenplay, editing, musical accompaniment, costumes, and other categories. Making a film is a complex, sensitive process that involves the talents and skills of a diverse group of professionals. Each contributes in a unique way to the betterment of the whole. The awards programs reflect this division of labor by giving out a variety of awards. On occasion, new award categories are added to reflect the changing nature of the industry.

Depending on your point of view, the best film of the year may be the one that rakes in the most awards across all categories, rather than that which is officially awarded "Best Picture." Like other art forms, in film the whole is often greater than the sum of its parts. The categories awarded are not contradictory but rather complementary. This Gestalt view applies to architecture, landscape architecture, and interior design.

In the world of film, too, discrepancies sometimes occur between the critics and the public. A smash box office hit may not receive one Academy Award (although in reverse, once a film receives an award, it usually becomes a hit at the box office). But the truly stellar films—for instance *The Last Emperor* (1987), *Rain Man* (1988), and *Driving Miss Daisy* (1989)—usually do well in both arenas. *The values of the profession as reflected by the critics need not contradict those of the public; at their best, they can complement each other. The same is true in design.*

One could thus conceive of an awards program that recognized design innovation and the advancement of the profession from a purely aesthetic standpoint (form), or *Best Design Innovator;* livability and the responses of the public (function), or *Most User Friendly;* and construction (yet another aspect of function), or *Most Well Built.* But in addition, we might include awards for the *Best Concept Statement;* the *Best Graphic Presentation;* the *State of the Art* of a particular type of product, building, or site; *Most Harmonious Fit into the Local Context; Best Contributor to the City Fabric; Most Cost Effective;* and so on. Rewarding these diverse aspects of design submissions will better reflect the complex nature of contemporary and future design practice.

How should we assess some of these new categories? Since so few precedents exist, experimentation is a simple first step. For the Most User Friendly category, for instance, the vast literature of environment and behavior provides guidelines for a variety of building and site types, from housing and office to hospital design and from parks and playgrounds to urban plazas. Experts in the environment-behavior field who are familiar with this informative literature need to be incorporated as jurors for this award category. Short surveys and interviews with users and passersby at the specific projects being reviewed can supplement the information derived from postoccupancy evaluations and design guidelines. Similarly, structural engineers can serve as experts to judge project construction.

Looks Can Be Deceiving

The use of a diverse team of experts to assess various criteria necessitates that a good deal of the judging be done locally, thus allowing jurors to actually visit the project submissions rather than simply to speculate about them from photographs and drawings. Judging three-dimensional work based on two-dimensional submissions can be deceptive. In many instances, design awards jurors may actually be judging the photography, not the design.

By actually visiting the projects that are being considered, jurors can experience how a place looks from a 360-degree perspective. *Human beings tend to look more pleasant from the front than from the back or the side; some of us look more pleasing from a distance than we may from up close. Spaces and places operate under the same set of rules. In addition, visiting the sites allows jurors not only to see, but to hear, smell, and touch spaces in a way that drawings do not permit.* Some of the most successful spaces in the world are so because they are a joyful experience throughout all five senses — sight, sound, touch, smell, and taste. These sensations can not possibly come across through a camera lens. Based on the decisions and reports of local jurors, more well informed decisions can be made later at the national level.

Many of these concepts can be applied to both awards programs and design competitions. In the case of competitions, although jurors do not have the benefit of visiting a finished product, several of these criteria can be evaluated even before the project is constructed. A jury will arrive at a more well informed set of decisions through in-depth site visits, familiarity with the local context, and some knowledge of public sentiment about the project and its surroundings. Public opinion about various proposed solutions should be carefully monitored and incorporated into the jury's final decision. But it is also likely that both the public and the jurors may favor certain aspects from several proposed solutions. In this case, how can only one solution be chosen?

The Finnish Formula

To help solve this dilemma, and to help address some of the disturbing ethical issues raised by design competitions, we might look to some successful European examples. In Finland, for instance, the results of building competitions are generally used to select the architectural firm for a project, and it is usually, but not always, built exactly as submitted. The winner of a building competition usually is awarded the project, which is then developed further in cooperation with the competition promoter. In town plan competitions, certain elements of the winning entry combined with successful elements from other entries receiving second or third place are usually used as *the basis for further work on the project*, with the winning team doing the work. In some large-scale urban design projects, the team designing the first-place entry is chosen to design the master plan and some of its buildings, while the teams who placed near the top are selected to design other buildings covered in the plan (Figure 11-7). And the winner often acts as a consultant who supervises the project when it is developed further.

In Finland, the ratio of open to closed competitions is usually about one to three in favor of closed competitions. Firms who enter closed competitions are always paid standard architects' fees set by the Finnish Association of Architects (SAFA). Here too, however, competitors often tend to exceed the estimated amount of work upon which the fee is based. Usually the competition is based on a preliminary design scheme for which the prize is 10% of the total cost required to complete the design. In open competitions, firms compete for prizes along with other competitors.

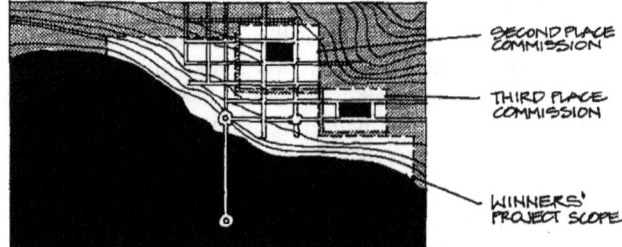

Figure 11-7 Many American designers feel "ripped off" by design competitions. Competitions in Finland and other countries appear to avoid many of the problems found in the United States. In Finland, the firm that places first in a design competition is often awarded the master plan and selected buildings in a new development, while those that place near the top are awarded commissions for other buildings in the project site. Payment for design work seems to be the norm rather than the exception.

Design firms are encouraged to contact the client or sponsor only when an organized visit to the competition site is specified in the competition program. This is not the custom in open competitions, however.

And what about the jury selection? The promoters of competitions, usually town and local authorities who sponsor about 90% of these competitions, select the jurors. In addition, SAFA selects two architects as members of the jury. The judging panel must be approved by SAFA's competitions committee. The promoter also selects its representatives and appoints them to the judging panel. The majority of jurors must be professional members, usually architects. However, the fact that many nonarchitects also serve as jurors helps to provide a well-balanced means of assessing the submissions.[38]

The results of major Finnish design competitions are published in a special monthly journal entitled *Architectural Competitions in Finland*, where a summary article provides detailed explanations of the rationale behind the jury's decisions.[39] These articles address the competition as a whole and the extent to which the entries met a variety of criteria. In contrast to most published accounts of American design competitions, these articles do more than simply highlight the winning entries along with some stray comments from the jurors. Instead, they provide a systematic analysis of how well the program needs are met by the submissions as a whole. In many cases a section is included stating, "Further work should strive to pay attention to the following..." and a list of important issues is spelled out.[40]

The Finnish approach is in fact a very logical one. Instead of simply choosing the "best" or "winning" project and building it as is, the process involves *selecting the best aspects of all the submissions and incorporating them into a new solution* after the competition is over when the project is actually realized.

When Are Competitions Appropriate?

The appropriateness of open versus invited design competitions must be reexamined. The distinctions among various project types that John F. Hartray, Jr. points out are quite useful. Following his logic, open competitions might indeed be appropriate for monumental, highly symbolic projects, whose use is relatively simple. Or, as Donald J. Hackl suggests, open design competitions ought best to be used for projects for which there is no precedent—as a type of exploration or innovation. But when a complex project with a diverse group of users is involved, then a limited competition, based on one of the models suggested above or a variation thereof, or no competition at all is preferable.

Nonetheless, no matter what alternatives are chosen to evaluate professional design work in the future, jurors of any proposed or new projects are faced by the same dilemma: "Time makes the final judgement."[41]

NOTES

1. Gilbert, Cass, personal correspondence to his wife, Julia, dated September 20, 1899. From the Collections of the Manuscript Division, Library of Congress, Box 6, 1899, File 1. Architect Cass Gilbert wrote regularly to his wife, Julia. While he was angry about the Washington University Competition, which he lost, he continued to enter competitions throughout his life.

2. These postjury sessions can be quite instructive, however, and provide a useful teaching/learning technique for students.

3. For the Architect Registration Exam, the selection of jurors who have graded in the past is based on their previous performance, while the selection of new jurors is based on education and experience. A trainer familiar with the examination criteria conducts the training at each grading session, providing continuity from one session to the next. Before the grading begins, the trainer reviews the exam and the grading criteria and explains the application of the criteria for several sample solutions. The trainer also explains the scores used in that process. Jurors are asked to grade some of the training samples and to indicate the scores they give to each sample through a show of hands, and they are required to adjust their scores to the standards of the majority. "Any juror who presumes the right to set individual standards is being unfair to the candidates whose solution will be scored by that juror... we do not expect jurors to give 1's to solutions that other jurors have scored 4. This degree of divergence in scoring cannot be tolerated." *June 1990 Juror's Manual*, Washington, DC: National Council of Architectural Registration Boards, 1990, pp. 1, 3.

4. Ollswang, Jeffrey, and Lawrence Witzling, *The Planning and Administration of Design Competitions*, Milwaukee: Midwest Institute for Design Research, 1986.

5. Ibid., p. 95.

6. Ibid., p. 93.

7. *Handbook of Architectural Design Competitions*, Washington, DC: American Institute of Architects, 1988, p. 17.

8. Ibid., p. 18.

9. Kaiser, Kay, "Design Awards Need to Go Back to the Drawing Board," *San Diego Union* (Sunday, July 8, 1990), Section F, p. 2. Kaiser's controversial article created such a stir that it prompted a tart rejoinder by the design awards chairman in the local American Institute of Architects chapter newsletter. See Stout, Russ, "Chapter Design Awards Controversy Continues," *San Diego Architect* (September 1990), pp. 5-7.

10. Welch, Frank, "On Juries and Jurying: Standing in Judgment of Architecture," *The Bulletin: San Diego Chapter, American Institute of Architects* (April 1985), pp. 6-7.

11. Lethbridge, Francis D., "The Honors Awards Program in Retrospect," *American Institute of Architects Journal* (May 1973), p. 22.

12. Wolfe, Tom, *From Bauhaus to Our House*, New York: Farrar, Straus & Giroux, 1981, pp. 80-82. The situation at Pruit-Igoe was so complex that it is unfair to pin the blame solely on the architects. Many articles have been published chronicling the tragedy of this housing complex and the unusual set of circumstances that led to its demise.

13. Zimring, Craig M., and Janet E. Reizenstein, "A Primer on Postoccupancy Evaluation: Uses and Techniques of an Increasingly Valued Tool," *AIA Journal* (November 1981), pp. 52-58, citation from p. 58.

14. Sommer, Robert, *Tight Spaces: Hard Architecture and How to Humanize It*, Englewood Cliffs, NJ: Prentice-Hall, 1974, pp. 130-131.

15. Vischer, Jacqueline C., and Clare Cooper Marcus, "Evaluating Evaluation: Analysis of a Housing Design Awards Program," *Places*, 3:1 (Winter 1986), pp. 66-85.

16. Cooper Marcus, Clare, and Wendy Sarkissian, with Sheena Wilson and Donald Perlgut, *Housing as if People Mattered: Site Design Guidelines for Medium-Density Family Housing*, Berkeley: University of California Press, 1986.

17. Vischer and Cooper Marcus, op. cit., p. 80.

18. Seidel, Andrew D., "Design Competitions Receive Mixed Reviews," in Alexander, Ernest R., and Lawrence P. Witzling (eds.), *Journal of Architectural and Planning Research*, 7:2 (Summer 1990), pp. 172-180.

19. McGaughan, A. Stanley, "Architectural Design Competitions," in Wilkes, Joseph A., and Robert T. Packard (eds.), *Encyclopedia of Architecture: Design, Engineering & Construction*, 1, New York: Wiley 1988, pp. 694-705. For an excellent discussion of design competitions, consult Alexander and Witzling, op. cit. See especially Alexander, Ernest R., Dennis J. Casper, and Lawrence P. Witzling, "Competitions for Planning and Urban Design: Lessons of Experience," in Ibid., p. 142-159; and Alexander, Ernest R. and Lawrence P. Witzling, "Planning and Urban Design Competitions: Introduction and Overview," in Ibid., pp. 91-104. Much of this section is based on these key sources.

20. McGaughan, op. cit., pp. 694-695; Alexander and Witzling, op. cit.; Alexander, Casper, and Witzling, op. cit. Alexander, Casper, and Witzling's analysis of 16 concept competitions revealed that AIA and public-interest group sponsored competitions offered an average of $1,500 in prize money, while the mixed and client-sponsored competitions awarded an average of nearly $35,000. This huge discrepancy helps explain why the latter attracts so many more entries.

21. McGaughan, op. cit., pp. 695-696.

22. Ibid., p. 696; Alexander and Witzling, op. cit.

23. Spreiregen, P. D., *Design Competitions*, New York: McGraw-Hill, 1979, p. 287.

24. Gutman, Robert, *Architectural Practice: A Critical View*, New York: Princeton Architectural Press, 1988, pp. 70-71.

25. Wynne, G. G., et al., *Winning Designs: The Competitions Renaissance*, New Jersey: Transaction, 1981, cited in Nasar, Jack L., and Junmo Kang, "A Post-Jury Evaluation: The Ohio State University Design Competition for a Center for the Visual Arts," *Environment and Behavior*, 21:4 (July 1989), pp. 464-484, cited on p. 466.

26. Lewis, Roger K., *Architect? A Candid Guide to the Profession*, Cambridge, MA: MIT Press, 1985, p. 208.

27. Alexander, Ernest R., Lawrence P. Witzling, and Dennis J. Casper, "Planning and Urban Design Competitions: Organization, Implementation and Impacts," *Journal of Architectural and Planning Research*, 4:1 (1987), pp. 31-46, citation from p. 43.

28. Nasar, and Kang, op. cit., p. 478.

29. Seidel, op. cit.

30. McGaughan, op. cit., p. 704. One design professional recounted a frustrating story of a competition with unrealistic size requirements. The final illustration boards were so large that the person accompanying them had great difficulty squeezing them through the door of an airplane!

31. *Play Your Card! 1989 Orchid & Onion Awards. Community Awareness Program Official Ballot.*

32. Langdon, Philip, with Robert G. Shibley and Polly Welch, *Urban Excellence*, New York: Van Nostrand Reinhold, 1990, pp. 2-3.

33. Ibid., p. 4.

34. Sommer, op. cit., p. 136.

35. Vischer and Cooper Marcus, op. cit., p. 80.

36. Ibid., p. 81.

37. Nasar and Kang, op. cit., p. 482.

38. Much of the above information was derived from personal communication from Antti Pirhonen, architect, competition secretary, SAFA, Finnish Association of Architects, August 16, 1990, as well as personal correspondence from Matti Nurmela, another Finnish architect who serves on the editorial board of the *Finnish Architectural Review*, July 30, 1990.

39. *Architectural Competitions in Finland*, merged with *Finnish Architectural Review.*

40. "Open Design Competition for Maanika Municipal Offices," *Architectural Competitions in Finland* (7-89), p. 23.

41. Kaiser, Kay, "Prized Projects. Jury Bends Rules a Bit in Local Competition," *San Diego Union* (Sunday, July 2, 1989), Section F, pp. 1-2, quote by juror Romaldo Giurgola, Fellow and Gold Medalist of the American Institute of Architects, p. 2.

PART 6

EPILOGUE

*"Merely ignoring a problem will not make it go away....
Nor will merely recognizing it."* —Cullen Hightower

"A gem can not be polished without friction, nor man perfected without trials." —Chinese proverb

CHAPTER 12

Should Juries Be Jettisoned?

A Retrospective Critique of Criticism in Design Education and Practice

"The traditional model of the design school has been the old fashioned meat chopper, clamped to the edge of the table (campus), and into whose hopper were funnelled a carefully selected variety of (mostly male) individuals. With an incestuous faculty turning the crank, these individuals were all thoroughly indoctrinated in fixed craft skills, middle-class values and normative attitudes, and reduced to a common specification by the single curriculum die of the professional stereotype; and were eventually extruded in homogenized format for immediate consumption in existing professional offices." —Philip Thiel in "Architecture and the Beginning Student"[1]

"It is not for nothing that our beloved discipline has the highest dropout rate of any subject studied at a university." —Martin Pawley in "My Lovely Student Life"[2]

"It is no coincidence that some of the greatest architects of our century—Sullivan, Wright, Corb, Mies—either did not attend or did not finish a professional architecture program. As with our best writers, those architects, who for lack of a professional degree would now face considerable difficulty practicing at all, wanted to change not just architecture, but the world. Each, in his own way, felt estranged from the system of values and the built environment as he found it. And each had strong, idiosyncratic beliefs that might not have stood up before the collective critique of his superiors, but that sustained and enriched his architecture.

"... Louis Kahn and Alvar Aalto are two acknowledged masters in this century who were formally educated in design, although we now gauge their genius by the degree to which they rebelled against that training.

"... Some have made it through the mill of design education to become great architects, but one wonders about those who did not or those who despaired of even trying." —Thomas Fisher, Executive Editor, Progressive Architecture[3]

"... there remains ample evidence that many members of the profession lack a sufficient sense of professional self-worth. The nature of architectural criticism as taught and practiced in schools of architecture is regarded by some as contributing to this destructive pattern." —James R. Franklin, Robert G. Shibley, and Thomas Vonier in In Search of Design Excellence[4]

SHOULD JURIES BE JETTISONED?

Should juries be jettisoned? This is the key question raised by this research. Needless to say, the answer is not simple. After thoroughly examining the reactions of students, faculty, and practitioners, it is tempting to draw the conclusion that we are better off without them. To a certain extent, this is true. Who could argue that being "thrown into a bullring," "crucified," "put before a firing squad," or "thrown to the sharks" is a beneficial learning experience? Is it not time to put an end to this medieval inquisition?

Consider the following analogy: Your old car has been giving you trouble. Most of the time, it still runs and gets you where you want to go, but all too often it breaks down, leaving you stranded and upset. Should you continue to spend hundreds of dollars on a poor investment? Should you pay for a major overhaul—or abandon it altogether?

Design education is faced with the same choice. Should juries be scrapped? In their present form—as seen in architectural programs at most universities throughout the English-speaking world—yes! It is time to upset the apple cart. This research has clearly demonstrated that the jury system—especially in architecture—is in dire need of either: 1) a major overhaul or 2) abandonment. I am advocating structural change in the jury system through achieving a greater balance of power among students, faculty, and practitioners. The rigid hierarchy among these three groups must begin to loosen up.

What I am arguing for, in essence, is a reformist approach. While some of the reformist measures in of themselves are quite modest, when taken together, they should have profound consequences for design education and, in turn, practice. By implementing some of the reforms spelled out in this book, as well as others yet to come, juries—in their future incarnations—can and should continue to play an important role in design education. The system has been so severely tarnished by misuses and abuses that a few minor touch-ups are not enough to solve its many problems. The weakest aspects of juries must be abandoned, hopefully never to reappear, while the strongest features can be retained.

Aspects that should be maintained include debate and discussion about design from many different viewpoints, even those of the students, leading to even greater dialogue than the current system offers; and the opportunity to deliver, receive, and learn from constructive criticism of your own work and that of others. The ability not only to produce high-quality design work but also to criticize it are hallmarks of a good design professional. This much-needed dialogue is essential to the future growth of the environmental design professions.

Aspects that must be eliminated include the psychologically destructive and sometimes unethical behavior stemming from antagonism, fear, boredom, insensitivity, and competition—all of which promote unhealthy attitudes toward design practice.

PROMOTING DEBATE AND DIALOGUE ABOUT DESIGN

What can be done in academia to promote even greater discussion and debate about design, in addition to or in lieu of juries? To begin, students need a more well rounded, holistic education. This point came across over and over again in the interviews with leading design practitioners, many of whom strongly believe that design schools have become too much like trade schools. By expecting students to leap immediately into design and place a high priority on the case-study method, educators have overlooked some other crucial aspects. Several designers argued strongly that the studio has become too dominant a part of students' education and that it is time for its role to be redefined. A number of them suggested that the studio need not be the only way to learn about design.

Equal Rights for Nonstudio Courses: The Medical and Legal Models

Courses other than design studio can provide welcome opportunities for extended discussions and debates, not focused on any one project per se but rather on broader issues that affect the profession at large. Courses in environment and behavior, culture and the environment, history, theory, research methods, preservation, and other special topics can all provide enlightening sources of information and insight for design students. Such courses tend to emphasize developing writing skills and fine-tuning the thought process, and they can be incredibly valuable for designers. Students must draw upon a richer base of information and experience than studio typically provides. They need the freedom and time to discover the library, to participate in campus events, and to lead a more well rounded life-style. They need to be educated in the broad sense, not merely trained. Even Frank Lloyd Wright recognized the need to educate rather than simply train his design students at Taliesin by requiring them to read classic works by Socrates, Jefferson, Thoreau, Emerson, and Lao-Tzu.

Lecture and seminar courses often require students to read widely and broaden their horizons—perfect breeding grounds for stimulating intellectual discussions—but in most current design programs nonstudio courses have been given low priority. As architectural educator Diane Ghirardo has written, "Whatever the other curricular requirements, including coursework outside architecture, it is always made clear by the design faculty that the only class that really counts is the studio."[5]

A comparison between design studio courses and

others in the architectural curriculum reveals some telling trends. The amount of credits assigned to nonstudio courses, compared to studios, is abysmally low. To make matters even worse, they are often offered at inconvenient hours, in leftover spaces, and with little faculty support. Resources in the form of teaching assistantships, space, and equipment are almost always poured directly into the design studios.

Even the jury itself is evidence of the strong support given to studio. Most faculty are expected to devote several hours to "jury duty" each term in order to assist design instructors, but those who teach other courses have no such support. On this note, one architecture faculty member who taught non-studio courses raised an interesting point: "I refused to serve on design juries unless design critics would assist me in grading my final examinations. This was thought by design critics to be a joke . . . but I was deadly serious."

Whether intentional or not, at many design programs, a caste system has been created among faculty; the designers who teach studios are the "haves," while the rest of the faculty are the "have-nots." *An end to this imbalance is long overdue.*

In this regard, *design educators ought to draw upon the lessons learned from medical and legal education*, where reading, attending lectures, doing lab work, and review are part of the learning requirements for each topic. In both law school and medical school, the case method is supplemented by a heavy dose of readings and discussion. Both place a strong emphasis on research and its implications for the profession, and both expect its faculty to be aware of current research in the field. Both stress a close connection with the client. And both begin at the graduate level, thus allowing undergraduates to obtain a liberal arts education prior to their specialization. Design educators have much to learn from the educational curricula of other professions, and they need to begin exchanging information. In sum, a better balance of courses is necessary. Too much theory can leave the graduate unemployable, but too much applied experience reduces her potential for long-range development.

Academic curricula, course scheduling, administrative priorities, accreditation criteria, and the "hidden curriculum" conveyed to students need to be carefully reexamined and restructured. The star system, so prominent in the design professions, has permeated design education as well. With the design studio as the shining star of the curriculum, other important aspects of students' education have long been shortchanged (Figure 12-1). A heated debate was raised a number of years ago about design studios and their role in architectural education. The findings of this research suggest that it is time to rekindle that discussion.[6]

Various options must be considered, including reducing the number of hours devoted to studios. Studios can

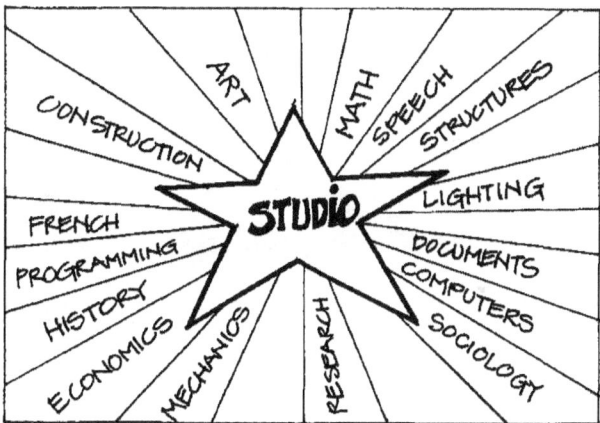

Figure 12-1 The studio has long been the star of design education. Although studios are certainly important, other courses in the curriculum have been shortchanged as a result.

still remain open during nonclass hours for students, but class meeting times with faculty can be reduced. Consequently, students will no longer be overwhelmed by the sheer numbers of hours they must commit to studio. And design professors will be free to teach other courses as well, thus diversifying their own experiences and contributing in more diverse ways to their programs.

Yet education need not be a zero-sum game. Without a doubt, studios must continue to play an important role in design education, but they must now share that role with other courses as well. *By implementing more effective teaching and learning techniques such as those described throughout this book, such as reforming design juries, replacing the labor-intensive desk crits with more shared reviews, and using time more productively, the hours spent in studio can be used more efficiently.* The costs to students and faculty will be low, and the benefits will be high.

But granting equal rights to nonstudio courses is not the only way to stimulate discussion and debate about design. Encourage students, visiting practitioners, and faculty to participate in a variety of teaching/learning formats, such as *panel discussions, colloquia, exhibits, debates, role-playing exercises, workshops, and small-group discussions.* With the exception of the debate, these formats create less adversarial roles than what is typically seen in design juries, thus promoting a more favorable model of designer-client interaction. Several designers stressed the need for this in their interviews. Many of these formats can be used to encourage discussion across the disciplines of architecture, landscape architecture, urban planning, and interior design. By inviting participants from each of these departments, the multidisciplinary field of environmental design—which has become fragmented to a fault—can become more united. Most campuses have centers for instructional resources that are replete with detailed descrip-

Figure 12-2 Holding panel discussions about design-related issues can be an effective way of stimulating interaction among students, faculty, and practitioners.

tions of such innovative teaching/learning techniques, along with ways to ensure their success. Many of these approaches are specifically designed to increase student participation and involvement with the subject matter; design educators must take advantage of them. The following sections offer but a few suggestions.

Panel Discussions and Colloquia

Invite a panel discussion of students, faculty, and visiting practitioners to discuss design ideas (Figure 12-2). Examine a design-related controversy in your local area and invite members from different sides of the fence to express their views. Address socially relevant issues such as homelessness, the burgeoning elderly population, and the AIDS epidemic, and invite nondesigners who are intimately involved with these issues as members of the panel. Encourage the audience to consider carefully issues raised by the panel. Have the moderator set aside a few minutes to solicit written questions from each member of the audience and sift through the most interesting ones for discussion.

Exhibits

Most design programs have an assigned space for exhibits. Take advantage of these exhibits to help stimulate discussion. Rather than simply hanging up the work, select a mixture of faculty, students, and practitioners to react to them. The group need not even include whoever's work is being shown; in fact the discussion can be more revealing when the artist is not present.

Display recently completed design work, either by students, faculty, or practitioners. They can even be works that have been published in magazines. Display several copies of each design, and then stage an event at which students and faculty react to the work. Place tracing paper over each and have students annotate the drawings with their reactions (Figure 12-3). Identify positive points (+) as well as negative points (−) and the reasons why these are so. Ask students to incorporate the results of environment-

Figure 12-3 Placing tracing paper over completed drawings displayed at an exhibit can be an effective way of critiquing each other's work.

behavior research into their notations and to cite specific research findings wherever relevant. Discuss the reactions as a group.

Debates

Invite people with distinctly opposing viewpoints to discuss pressing design or environmental issues, or even current political issues that impact the design professions. The purpose is not to reach agreement but simply to articulate and develop different perspectives on a problem. Include students as part of this debate. Have them sign up in teams to join the side that they favor. Include student representatives to argue as part of the debate panel and have student team members provide them with input as needed. Clearly define the pros and cons of the issue and vigorously argue both sides. Set aside some time to allow the audience to add its opinions on large pinup boards. Discuss the different viewpoints that arise. Or seek out controversial articles or books and assign students to argue for or against the author.

Role-Playing Exercises

Simulate a real-world design project to include the full spectrum of actors. For instance, assign students to the roles of developer, the city planning commission, city council persons, members of the public, and others. Have them react to various student design proposals for the same problem. Compare their reactions and have students reassess their solutions in light of these different perspectives.

Workshops and Small-Group Discussions

Invite representatives of various user groups such as physically challenged individuals, single-parent families, and the elderly to set up and lead workshops with design

Professional Ethics and Design Education   161

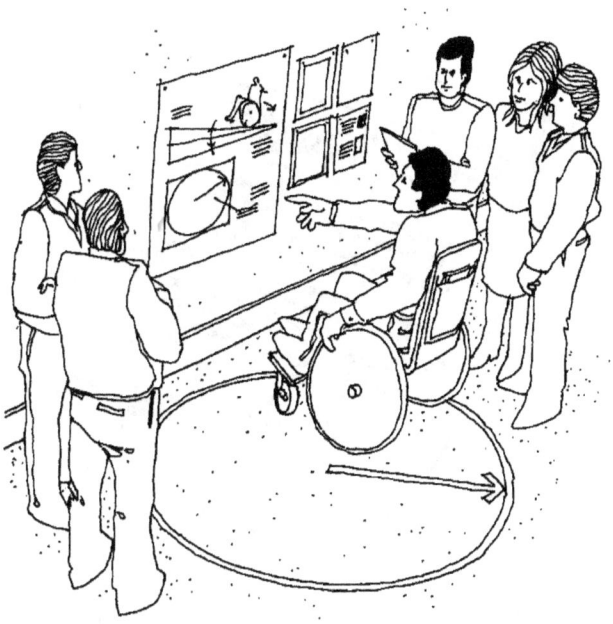

Figure 12-4 Bring in representatives of different user groups to help set up and lead workshops with design students.

students, faculty, and practitioners (Figure 12-4). Focus on a specific design-related issue and divide the audience into small groups to tackle particular aspects of the problem. *Assign to each group a leader, a specific task, time limit, and end product.* Have the workshop leaders circulate among each group to clarify points and answer questions. Ask group leaders to display and briefly present the work of each group. At the end, have workshop leaders, together with the audience, reflect upon all that has been accomplished.

Critical Questioning

Invited lecturers can be asked to prepare *discussion questions* for the audience either before or after their presentations. Students must be actively encouraged to ask critical questions of invited guests, not simply to applaud and walk out the door. Enough time needs to be allowed for such question-and-answer sessions to occur.

Team Work

More team projects are needed to promote informal discussions among students in a nonthreatening environment. In fact, encouraging team work in school is essential to the future of the design professions. Several studies have increasingly demonstrated that more often than not, team work is a key to successful design practice, but that sadly, the academy does not reflect this. Some landmark research conducted by sociologist Judith Blau, involving interviews with over 400 Manhattan architects over a five-year period, revealed that repeat clients like to see many different people in the firm sharing the work and responsibility for their projects. Team practice is consistently found to be conducive to multiple commissions. Similarly, Dana Cuff's fascinating case studies and field work in architectural offices provide a sharp distinction between design problems in the office and in the university. She argues convincingly that the isolation of the academic design studio results in practitioners who are untrained in the social art of working with clients and consultants, in negotiating contracts, working with regulatory agencies, and so on. Her research has confirmed that team work with independence — key individuals working together to make key decisions for the larger group of contributors — is a fundamental ingredient of built projects that professionals, the public, and their creators agree have high design quality.[7]

In sum, the point is to educate well-rounded individuals, not just to train highly skilled professionals. In this cost-cutting era, many of these techniques cost far less than what programs spend to invite well-known practitioners.

PROFESSIONAL ETHICS AND DESIGN EDUCATION

At their very worst, juries are examples of professional misconduct. In another context, offensive behavior often exhibited in juries could possibly result in professional sanctions such as censure, professional ostracism and boycott, suspension or expulsion from professional society membership and withdrawal of professional privileges, malpractice suits, or suspension or revocation of license to practice.[8] Educators are protected from punishments such as these. Under the protective cloak of academic freedom, jurors have felt free to say whatever they wanted. *But they have taken academic liberty to mean academic license.* The result has been a relatively widespread misuse of the system and a literal free-for-all, often at the students' expense.

Two documents speak directly to this issue and have grave implications for design juries.

> ... *As teachers, professors encourage the free pursuit of learning in their students. They hold before them the best scholarly and ethical standards of their discipline. Professors demonstrate respect for students as individuals and adhere to their proper roles as intellectual guides and counselors. Professors make every reasonable effort to foster honest academic conduct and to assure that their evaluations of students reflect each student's true merit. They respect the confidential nature of the relationship between professor and student. They avoid any exploitation, harassment, or discriminatory treatment of students. ...* — Statement on Professional Ethics from the American Association of University Professors[9]

... In fulfillment of the obligation to the student, the educator—(1) Shall not unreasonably restrain the student from independent action in the pursuit of learning. (2) Shall not deny the student access to varying points of view. (3) Shall not deliberately suppress or distort subject matter relevant to the student's progress. (4) Shall make reasonable effort to protect the student from conditions harmful to learning or to health and safety. (5) Shall not intentionally expose the student to embarrassment or disparagement....
—*Code of Ethics of the Education Profession*[10]

In the most abusive design juries, students are treated with utter disrespect, and the confidential relationship between professor and student is violated. These conditions are harmful both to learning and to students' psychological health, and students are indeed exposed to embarrassment and disparagement. And when professors and students compete in the same design competitions, students are often exploited.[11] *It is time for design education to begin addressing these serious ethical issues to prevent further abuse of the jury system. Professional codes of ethics are needed for all fields of design education.* These codes should be distributed to all faculty and visiting jurors, and jury behavior may be monitored through informal peer pressure. Faculty need to be made accountable for their words.

A few enterprising faculty once explained an unusually effective technique they used to help make their colleagues more accountable for their jury behavior. These faculty had watched countless students become devastated and depressed at the final jury of their educational career, only days away from graduation. They were concerned that as a result of this final jury experience, students would leave the university with a bitter taste in their mouths. So they did something bold and brash: *They invited the students' parents to attend the final jury presentations.* Only those students with completed projects were allowed to present, and unfinished work was not discussed. The jury discussion took on an altogether different flavor, and the atmosphere was one of celebration rather than degradation.

One colleague noted that at his school, applicants for faculty positions are asked to participate in juries as part of their job interviews. Other professors carefully observe how the applicants behave on the jury. If they come across as too insensitive or harsh to students, they simply are not hired. For those faculty who are already firmly in place, gentle peer pressure from colleagues and administrators needs to be applied. Those who behave inappropriately at juries need to be counseled and advised by their peers. If problems persist, they can be addressed by department heads and other campus administrators. A variety of mechanisms already in place on most campuses can be used to monitor faculty behavior. If the problem becomes chronic, and the faculty member in question is not yet tenured, such behavior could even constitute grounds for firing.

Figure 12-5 Just as design faculty need a code of ethics that identifies appropriate and inappropriate behavior, design students need their own "Bill of Rights" to prevent further abuse of the jury system.

Design students, too, have the right to demand the following, their own "Bill of Rights" (Figure 12-5):

With their professors as role models, students have the right to learn the best scholarly and ethical standards of their discipline. They have the right to expect that professors demonstrate respect for them as individuals, adhering to their proper roles as intellectual guides and counselors. They have the right to demand that professors make every reasonable effort to foster honest academic conduct and to assure that evaluations of student design work reflect each student's true merit. They have the right to expect that the confidential nature of the relationship between professor and student will be respected. They have the right to be free of any exploitation, harassment, or discriminatory treatment based on their sex, race, age, clothing, or otherwise.

Students have the right to (1) independent action in the pursuit of learning; (2) access to varying points of view; (3) expect that their design ideas shall not be deliberately suppressed or distorted; (4) be protected from conditions harmful to learning or to mental health and safety; (5) be free of intentional exposure to embarrassment or disparagement.

Students have the right to demand that their design education accurately reflect the realities of the world of professional practice, with a responsibility not only to their future employers and to the design professions, but also, and equally important, to clients, to users, and to the public at large. They have the right to demand that their design work be evaluated with these diverse responsibilities in mind.

COMPETITION AND ITS EFFECTS ON DESIGN EDUCATION AND PRACTICE

The competitive spirit, so endemic to design education and practice, underlies both the jury process and the entire design studio experience. Without it, the rationale behind the jury system crumbles. A final critique of the jury system must, then, critically examine what is at the very core of the process: the nature of competition itself.

Alfie Kohn's award-winning book, *No Contest: The Case Against Competition*, makes an extremely compelling case against the use of competition in virtually every walk of life. In shaping his argument, Kohn draws upon the results of hundreds of studies from diverse fields such as education, social psychology, sociology, psychoanalysis, leisure studies, evolutionary biology, and cultural anthropology, as well as philosophy and literature.[12] He rejects the use of competition even if kept in its "proper perspective" or used with "parenthetical qualifications," arguing that most writers fear losing all credibility if they take this extreme position. According to Kohn, *the problem is not only with the way we compete or the extent of our competitiveness; it is with the fundamental nature of competition itself.*[13] Much of my conclusion has been inspired by Kohn's provocative book, which has profound implications for design education and practice.

As noted in Chapter 2, despite the comaraderie, fellowship, and social bonding that occur in academic design studios, design students are often fiercely competitive. The cooperative appearance of the studio is for many only a transparent facade. Students within the same studios routinely compete with each other for grades, favorable comments from the jurors, competition prizes, and awards. While one can easily argue that students in law, medicine, and other professions are also highly competitive, they are not sitting next to each other side by side working individually on the same project, day after day. As some have argued, "the practice of solitary rivalry begins in the studios."[14] The public nature of the studio and the jury process exacerbates the competitive atmosphere. Contrast this with the cooperative model in place in many professional design offices, where team projects are the norm.[15] *This mismatch between the academic and professional design studio is a fundamental flaw in design education. After years of working competitively in studio, it may take even more years—if ever—to learn how to work cooperatively.*

The competitive, dependent atmosphere of the design studio places undue pressure on students. As a result of their preoccupation with winning and their reluctance to share their ideas with their competitors, they often fail to be receptive to the criticism they receive. In fact, a recent study conducted by the American Institute of Architects reveals that one of the most important "trade secrets" of firms that have achieved design excellence is the ability to critique their own work. Constructive board criticisms help them to continually refine and improve their design at many stages of the design process.[16]

Kohn argues convincingly that the case for competition does not hold up well under close scrutiny. The cases in its favor are built on four myths:[17]

1. Competition is inevitable, part of human nature.
2. Competition motivates us to do our best (i.e., we would cease being productive if we did not compete).
3. Competitions provide the best, if not the only, way to have a good time.
4. Competition builds character and is good for self-confidence.

These myths form the basic rationale behind the jury system in design education and practice. *Kohn debunks each of these myths with convincing evidence, concluding that even the phrase "healthy competition" is a contradiction in terms.*[18] *Countless studies clearly demonstrate that people prefer cooperation over competition, provided they have experienced both in some fashion.* In fact, it is not unusual for some people to say they prefer to compete, but to change their opinion when they experience firsthand what it is like to work or play in an environment without winners and losers.[19]

In answer to the key question, Do we perform better when we are trying to beat others than when we are working with them or alone? the evidence is overwhelmingly clear: almost never.[20] In fact, several studies have demonstrated that competition and achievement are negatively linked.[21] This is true in artistic endeavors as well; as some have argued, "Competitions are for horses, not artists."[22] In the win-lose framework, those whose temperaments are best suited for competition succeed, but the competitive nature is not equivalent to artistic ability.[23] The same can be said for the design studio, both in education and practice. In fact, a recent study of publicly sponsored developer/architect competitions revealed that almost half of those surveyed did not believe that design and development solutions are more creative than those achieved without competitions.[24] Among the proven consequences of competition are the loss of community and sociability, heightening of selfishness, anxiety, hostility, and obsessional thinking.[25] Competition discourages generosity and encourages distrust. People lose their ability to empathize with others and therefore are less inclined to help.[26] More often than not, competition can lead to unreliable and impoverished communication, suspicious attitudes, and oversensitivity to differences and threats.[27] *All these symptoms are well displayed in the design studio, albeit sometimes in subtle ways.*

Design competitions are a zero-sum game. In both student and professional design competitions, most competitors lose most of the time. By definition, not everyone can win and very few do. Most competitions result in just one winner, perhaps a few in second or third place or honorable mention. *Everyone else loses.* True, open competitions provide a unique opportunity for budding young stars to be discovered—*if their designs receive an award.* But what about the other 99% of the entrants who also expend tremendous amounts of time, energy, and money, only to retreat into oblivion? Repeating this process over and over again, as designers often do, does little for one's self-esteem: "To lose—particularly in a public event—can be psychologically detrimental even for the healthiest among us. At best, some exceptional individuals might emerge without *damage* to their self-esteem, but it is difficult to see how losing can *enhance* it.... Competition drags us down, devastates us psychologically, poisons our relationships, interferes with our performance."[28] The process of internalizing failure and seeing yourself as a loser can be debilitating. Furthermore, repeated exposure to design competitions encourages even greater hero worshipping of those lucky few who "beat the odds." As the handful of winners in a field of losers, the stars of the profession shine even more brightly, and those at the top of the hierarchy seem even further beyond reach.

Kohn's dramatic conclusion aptly describes the design studio environment, especially in academia:

> *Strip away all the assumptions about what competition is supposed to do, all the claims in its behalf that we accept and repeat reflexively. What you have left is the essence of the concept: mutually exclusive goal attainment (MEGA). One person succeeds only if another does not. From this uncluttered perspective, it seems clear right away that something is drastically wrong with such an arrangement. How can we do our best when we are spending our energies trying to make others lose—and fearing that they will make us lose? Can this sort of struggle really be the best way to have a good time? What happens to our self-esteem when it becomes dependent on how much better we do than the next person? Most striking of all is the impact of this arrangement on human relationship[s]: a structural incentive to see other people lose cannot help but drive a wedge between us and invite hostility.*[29]

Competition in education will not disappear. Grades are a stubborn reality of academia. And competition in the design professions will not vanish, either. Like it or not, it is a fundamental reality of the marketplace and it will continue to be. *But in both design education and practice, competition has been used to excess. The disturbing trends that Bosworth and Jones noted in the 1930s are still true today, over half a century later.*[30] *In fact, design faculty and students probably speak about "competition" more than any of their counterparts on campus. The design professions are drenched in competition—but they may also be drowning in it. It has invaded the professions like a virus, worming its way through the system and slowly devouring it.* In every instance where competition is the norm, we must stop to consider another alternative.

Can't design education become somewhat more like a ski lesson or a music lesson, where the goal is not to outdo all your competitors but to improve upon your own abilities? Tomorrow's performance should be better than today's. Students' subsequent designs should be better than their previous ones.

Whenever possible, cooperative rather than competitive efforts should be encouraged to better emulate the professional office environment. Fewer design competitions ought to be required in school, thus reducing the "architectural football" syndrome where schools compete against each other. Design education need no longer be dominated by a series of contests with judges and prizes. When faced with the option of assigning a competition to their class, faculty must seriously ask themselves, Is this competition really serving the students' best interests? Or, at this stage in their development, does another assignment better meet their educational goals? Some competitions can best serve as optional, extracurricular activities.

In some instances, the reward system ought to be altered. Why not reward those teams of students who work best together? Ironically, by awarding prizes to individual students for their winning designs, we may be reinforcing a pattern of secrecy and competition.[31] The subtle distinction between *reward* (something tangible or intangible that is given in return for a good job, good service, or attainment of a goal) and *award* (a judgment or final decision, something tangible that is conferred or bestowed on the basis of merit) is crucial. Rewards can be shared by many, while awards go only to a chosen few.

Juries in practice, in both professional design competitions and design awards programs, are also in need of reform. *The current practice of exploiting designers and expecting them to deliver thousands of hours of work free of charge should not continue. It has left damaging scars on the profession and inevitably will continue to do so.*[32] Many designers are outraged at this practice and rightfully so. The public spanking of one designer by another that is sometimes displayed at design awards ceremony leaves its marks, too. Negative criticism of built work is sorely needed, but gala events with family, friends, and clients are not the place for it. Airing the profession's dirty laundry in front of the rest of the world smacks of cruelty.

The composition of the professional design jury, the nature of the awards, and the jury process itself must be altered to reflect more accurately the diverse public that often sponsors them. Some of the innovative jury models from abroad as well as the United States, especially San Diego's Orchids and Onions Program (perhaps with an emphasis on Orchids rather than Onions) and the Rudy Bruner Award for Excellence in the Urban Environment, serve as highly useful prototypes. As sociologist Herbert Gans has argued, desirable taste cultures must respond to and express the demands of their users. Ideally, he argues, the demands of both users and creators should establish a symbiotic, egalitarian relationship wherever possible so that neither dominates the other.[33] Cultural pluralism should be the goal.

SEX, STARS, AND STUDIOS

The competitive model of design education is very much a male model. The highly competitive nature of the design studio, the unusually public nature of juries, and the vulnerability of the public defense make many females uncomfortable. Researchers in women's studies have gathered strong evidence that women require greater effort to manage their emotions than do men. Through their socialization and upbringing, many women have worked to become experts at showing deference and trying to appear "nice." Some have referred to the requirement to induce or suppress feeling in order to sustain the outward countenance as "emotional labor." Coordinating mind and feeling, the private and the public face, and disguising hurt and anger are often painful processes.[34] As a result, for women the need to "defend" one's work—and oneself—before a typically all-male jury can take a heavy emotional toll. The glorification of the studio all-nighter as a badge of courage is also a phenomenon to which many women can not relate. The personal costs of design education, especially for women, may simply be overwhelming.

The athletic and military analogies that many design instructors routinely use in design studios can be a sore spot for women students, none of whom were star football or basketball players in their schools; they may also offend some gay students as well. Instead, the "chosen few" women may have earned the distinction of valedictorian or homecoming queen, where competition was not for physical ability but for good grades and popularity. Many women are simply not involved in sports at all, except for individual exercise programs where the purpose is to develop and improve one's own physical abilities. As a result, the debut in the design studio and in the jury is a rude awakening— and in some cases, a turn-off—for many women.

As many designers pointed out in their interviews, for better or for worse, design is an "old person's profession." A strong paternal thread runs throughout the fabric of architectural education and practice. Maternal threads are simply not part of the design fabric. The paternal model creates an atmosphere of "Father knows best" that permeates the design studio.[35] Students' rigid dependence upon their instructors and jurors for criticism often leads them to overlook a most valuable source of criticism: their own. Yet it is just this ability that can aid tremendously in the professional world.

The absence of women as authority figures in architectural education and practice inevitably leads to repercussions on the jury as well. The star system in the design professions has long been a galaxy full of men. *The problem lies not with the stars themselves, but with the system that worships them.* With few women as stars, authority figures, and role models, students' work shown at design juries continues to be inspired primarily by that of male role models.[36] The galaxy has not included designers of color either. The predominance of the white male stars leaves minority students with no role models of their own.

The charismatic leaders who have catapulted to the top of the star system in the design professions, especially in architecture, are almost exclusively male. While architecture has plenty of heroes, it has few heroines. Denise Scott Brown, a stellar designer and planner in her own right, has delivered a shocking account of her own mistreatment by publishers, clients, and others in and around the design professions. The turmoil she underwent poses a dramatic contrast to the worldwide acclaim accorded her star designer husband, Robert Venturi. Scott Brown raises the provocative question, Is there room at the top for women in the architectural star system? Her own experiences seem to demonstrate, unfortunately, that at least for now the answer is no.[37] The notion of charisma in architecture has historically been and continues to be sex-linked to a machismo male model. However, as Scott Brown aptly points out, "The star system, which sees the firm as a pyramid with a Designer on top, has little to do with today's complex relations in architecture and construction."[38]

Scott Brown partially attributes today's star system in the profession to contemporary American architectural education with its deep roots in the turn-of-the-century French Ecole des Beaux Arts. Note the stinging connection to design juries in her description of the Ecole and the star system:

> *It was a rip-roaring place and loads of fun, but its organization was strongly authoritarian, especially in its system for judging student work. The authoritarian personalities and the we-happy-few culture engendered by the Beaux-Arts stayed on in Modern architecture long after the Beaux-Arts architectural philosophy had been abandoned; the architecture club still excludes women.*[39]

This research has documented that compared to men, women are significantly more dissatisfied with juries, studios, and their design education in general. To add to this, about two-thirds of the women architecture faculty who responded to a 1990 survey stated that they thought sexism was inherent in architectural education in general.[40] Women are still underrepresented in architectural programs as both students and faculty, as well as in the profession, and it should be no surprise.[41] Many schools are now under pressure to hire more women faculty and to increase their female student enrollment. Yet with the antiquated, traditional jury system in place, and the bizarre subculture of the design studio, it is no wonder that relatively few women seem to be attracted to the field. My hope is that by reforming the design jury and reexamining the ways in which studios are conducted, and by creating a situation that is more democratic and less hierarchical, we will create a learning environment that is more welcoming to women. In so doing, we can also create an atmosphere in which students of color—still grossly underrepresented at all levels of the design professions—also feel at home.

But sexism is only part of a larger problem that continues to plague design education: the "superiority complex" promoted by the star system. Although many sensitive architects form the exceptions that prove the rule, too many others routinely belittle the role of the landscape architect, the interior designer, and the urban planner whose work is complementary to their own; rather than recognizing the valuable contributions of their counterparts, many architects view them as mere obstacles that get in their way. To these individuals, the architect is the unacknowledged legislator of the design world; all others must remain subservient. This divisive attitude is clearly communicated in academia and is often carried on into the world of practice. Rivalries between these academic departments are quite common, even when they are housed under the same roof. Just as architects tend to look down on their counterparts, students and faculty in smaller departments sometimes have mixed feelings of admiration, fear, and resentment toward the mammoth architecture programs which, by sheer virtue of their size, have greater visibility, power, and control within the university. This phenomenon on the part of architects is not simply "Father knows best," but rather "I know best." As architectural educator Diane Ghirardo has written,

> *Regularly disparaged are clients (they do not understand architecture); the public (corrupted by consumerism); urban planners (number-crunchers with no taste); construction workers (no pride in their craft); everyone who produces buildings in the absence of those three letters—AIA; and finally, almost everyone who does wear AIA after their names. Only in the rarest of studios is the client perceived as anything but an obstruction to be firmly removed; and certainly not as a collaborator; at best the client is a vague abstraction to whom all manner of emotions and poor thinking can safely be attributed. Even less frequent is an emphasis on teamwork or collaboration among architects....* [42]

Ghirardo calls to mind the image of Sylvester Stallone in the smash film *Rambo* (1985), whose rugged individualism strikes a resonant chord with that of the design student and his heroes. Rambo's refusal to yield to authority, his hatred of bureaucracy and technocracy, and his ferociously authoritarian egomania embody the values that many design instructors convey to students. The Rambo-run-rampant nature of the studio has created an illusion that satisfying one's creative urges is all that matters. The Howard Roark figure in Ayn Rand's classic, *The Fountainhead*, perpetuates this myth.[43] To many designers—in school and in practice alike—he has become the controversial symbol of their profession; in fact, a number of designers interviewed for this book called for the immediate abandonment of such Rambo-like figures as Roark and Frank Lloyd Wright as cultish heroes in the field.[44] But on this note, let us conclude with where this symbolic illusion all began: The Ecole des Beaux Arts.

THE ECOLE DES BEAUX ARTS MODEL IN RETROSPECT: THE DESIGNER AS ARTIST

In retrospect, the fiercely competitive educational environment and the original jury system created by the Ecole des Beaux Arts have remained relatively unchanged a century later. The predominant role model conveyed by this system has been that of an artist driven by individual creativity. While in the meantime, functional, structural, social and psychological, and other issues have been tossed in for good measure in architecture, landscape architecture, and interior design curricula, the design studio—with *the image of the designer as an individual artist first and foremost—has reigned supreme*. The "stars" that students and practicing designers worship are promoted in the same light.

But not everyone has accepted the star system with welcome arms. Even several "stars" interviewed for this book, as well as other well-known designers, have been highly critical of the degree to which students are wrapped up in the star system. Again, Denise Scott Brown makes a convincing case:

> *...Schools can and should reduce the importance of the star system by broadening the student's view of the profession to show value in its other aspects. Heaven knows, skills other than design are important to the survival of architecture firms. The schools should also combat the student's sense of inadequacy about design, rather than, as now, augmenting it through wrongly authoritarian and judgmental educational techniques. With these changes, architects would feel less need for gurus, and those they would need would be different— more responsible and humane than gurus are asked to be today.*[45]

In his penetrating analysis, *Architectural Practice: A Critical View*, sociologist Robert Gutman explains how this artistic image promoted in school translates into problems in practice.

> *...Architecture attracts students who assume that practice permits an unusual degree of individualized, creative self-expression. These egotistic attitudes are encouraged in schools of architecture. The tempera-*

ment of architects reinforced by educational experiences yields an employee population who probably are more prone than other professional workers to insist on autonomy... older architects and principals [tend] to adopt a dictatorial manner. In turn, younger architects are inclined to demand greater autonomy than they are capable of exercising...

... The ideals of the profession tend to equate excellence in practice with design excellence, frequently ignoring the quality of professional service or the performance of the building....

... One might assume that firms celebrated for the design quality of their work would be good situations for architects with artistic talent, who would work happily and effectively in these settings. But it often turns out that such firms are dreadful employers for people who wish to exercise these skills, because the principals make all the interesting and important design decisions, while the majority of the staff is relegated to drawing up plans and details. Sometimes gifted designers do better in a firm with a strong commercial orientation, where their skills are more exceptional and therefore more highly valued.... Firms that do small projects... are frequently more stimulating environments for talented designers.... These offices may reproduce the atmosphere of old-fashioned ateliers, in which the principals serve as critics of schemes developed by young designers. However, because these offices are managed haphazardly, they often have a short life. If an atelier-type firm does survive and grow, it is usually as a result of having installed bureaucratic management techniques. However... this is exactly the setting some of the best design architects abhor, and they then quit....[46]

Along these lines, architectural educator Martin Pawley has been equally critical of the gap between architectural education and the real world in Great Britain and Western Europe:

Their education, in so far as it prepares them for any career at all, prepares them for a prima donna role as "form-givers" to a society eager for their help and advice. The career of "form-giver" does not exist; neither does the society eager for their help and advice.... The war of nerves is thus the pitting of obsolete training against an obstinate reality.[47]

The widening gulf between education and practice has been the source of several rumblings during recent years. The tectonic plates have been shifting and may soon be ready to explode. In the United Kingdom, Peter Buchanan writes:

In Britain, and in most other countries too, architectural education is based upon an increasingly irrelevant role model, that of the architect as an elite professional independent of and superior to the building industry and each architect, if not actually a principal in his own firm, at least a job runner and designer aspiring to genius.

... As a result, the architectural studio often resembles a kindergarten of uninhibited free expression—except that the finger-painted smudged pencil finish overlies hours of painstaking drafting and the wackiest schemes tend to be the most self-consciously trendy, if not downright derivative.

The emphasis on unshackled and uncritical creativity has led much student design far from the fundamental disciplines of architecture and into the realms of bad art. The celebrated creativity may flatter the ego it issues from and those who feel they have liberated it, but it has nothing to do with humble service to a client.[48]

While the Beaux Arts model may well have been appropriate during the nineteenth century when the Ecole began, it has been long outmoded.[49] Its influence on design education around the world has been widespread and long-lasting. *But the increasingly complex nature of the professional world—reliance on design teams and joint development efforts, and larger and more complex design projects—has left the designer trained as a solo artist, engrossed in competitive, individual pursuits, out in the cold.*[50]

The field of architecture especially has undergone significant transformations, placing an inordinate stress and strain on architects. Gutman describes in detail several conditions that have led to these transformations. He points to the artistic identity as a partial explanation of why the profession is currently faced with extremely serious challenges. Unlike other professions, such as law and medicine, architects have been reluctant to establish other subsidiary professionals like paralegals or pharmacists to help provide an adequate division of labor and regulate the supply and demand in the profession. Nor have architecture schools taken measures to limit the number of students who enroll in their programs, as law and medical schools have done.[51] As a result, *competition among design firms has never been greater.* He argues:

... The combination of diversity and fragmentation [in the architectural profession] are major factors that help to explain why architecture is populated by a higher proportion of alienated and disappointed men and women than any other major profession, why so many firms are badly managed, and why when offices are managed efficiently, they achieve work of dubious architectural quality. Of all the challenges facing the profession, the problems of motivating architects and sustaining office morale and performance may be the most difficult to address.[52]

The foregoing analysis of the jury system begins to address this challenge. The verdict on juries is now in: It is time for a shakeup in design education and practice. By encouraging a less authoritarian structure in the schools, a cooperative over a competitive atmosphere, and by evaluating students with a balance of both praise and constructive criticism, educators and visiting design critics can help create a healthier atmosphere in which students can learn and grow. By acquiring some of the all-important skills of research, time management, stress management, and communication, students can become better equipped not only to master design juries, but also to make that all-important leap from education to practice. And by restructuring professional design juries to become more responsive to the designers who compete, the clients who pay, and the public that lives and works in the spaces created, the environmental design professions can help enhance their image to society at large.

This book has sought to expose the jury system for what it is and to unravel some of its hidden agendas. It has sought to demystify the process and to offer a fresh angle of vision. Just as Dorothy and her friends traveled the dangerous yellow brick road, so do students journey on the hazardous trail of the university. Just as the Scarecrow, the Tin Man, and the Lion sought a brain, a heart, and courage, aspiring designers seek knowledge, compassion, and confidence. Just as Oz ruled over the Emerald City, so have expert jurors ruled over the world of design. Just as "I am Oz, the Great and Terrible" terrified Dorothy and her friends, so do the words of jurors continue to terrify students. But as L. Frank Baum wrote in his classic children's story, it was all an illusion:

> *The Lion thought it might as well to frighten the Wizard, so he gave a large, loud roar, which was so fierce and dreadful that Toto jumped away from him in alarm and tipped over the screen that stood in a corner. As it fell with a crash they looked that way, and the next moment all of them were filled with wonder. For they saw, standing in just the spot the screen had hidden, a little, old man, with a bald head and a wrinkled face, who seemed to be as much surprised as they were. The Tin Woodman, raising his axe, rushed toward the little man and cried out, "Who are you?"*
>
> *"I am Oz, the Great and Terrible," said the little man, in a trembling voice, "but don't strike me—please don't!—and I'll do anything you want me to."*
>
> *Our friends looked at him in surprise and dismay.*
> *"I thought Oz was a great Head," said Dorothy.*
> *"And I thought Oz was a lovely Lady," said the Scarecrow.*
> *"And I thought Oz was a terrible Beast," said the Tin Woodman.*
> *"And I thought Oz was a Ball of Fire," exclaimed the Lion.*
> *"No, you are all wrong," said the little man meekly. "I have been making believe."*
> *"Making believe!" cried Dorothy. "Are you not a Great Wizard?"*
> *"Hush, my dear," he said. "Don't speak so loud, or you will be overheard—and I should be ruined. I'm supposed to be a Great Wizard."*
> *"And aren't you?" she asked.*
> *"Not a bit of it, my dear; I'm just a common man."*[53]

And just as Dorothy and her friends realized that they only had to look inside themselves to find the answers to their own problems, so must we in design follow their example.

So we come to the end of our inquiry into the design jury system. But the end of this exploration is only the beginning of a refreshing, new era: the renaissance of design education and practice. Where will this new era take us? Only time will tell. Juries continue to be on trial; the final verdict is in your hands.

NOTES

1. Thiel, Philip, "Architecture and the Beginning Student," *Journal of Architectural Education*, 27:1 (February 1974), pp. 13-20, 34, quote from p. 17.

2. University Grants Committee, "Enquiry into Students' Progress," *RIBA Journal* (April 1968), as cited in Pawley, Martin, "My Lovely Student Life," in Gowan, James (ed.), *A Continuing Experiment: Learning and Teaching at the Architectural Association*, London: Architectural Press, 1975, pp. 17-25, quote from p. 17.

3. Fisher, Thomas, "Editorial: The Way to a Design Education," *Progressive Architecture*, 71:3 (March 1990), p. 9.

4. Franklin, James R., Robert G. Shibley, and Thomas Vonier, "A Summary of Lessons and Issues from the 1989 Initiative," in Vonier, Thomas (ed.), *In Search of Design Excellence*, Washington, DC: The American Institute of Architects Press, 1989, pp. x-xiv, quote from p. xiii.

5. Ghirardo, Diane, "Authenticity or Rambo Redux?" *Architectural Review*, 185:1109 (July 1989), pp. 47-49, quote from p. 48.

6. Rapoport, Amos, "Architectural Education: There Is an Urgent Need to Reduce or Eliminate the Dominance of the Studio," *Architectural Record*, 172:11 (October 1984), pp. 100, 103; Beckley, Robert M., "The Studio Is Where a Professional Architect Learns to Make Judgments," *Architectural Record*, 172:11 (October 1984), pp. 101, 105.

7. Blau, Judith, *Architects and Firms: A Sociological Perspective on Architectural Practice*, Cambridge, MA: MIT Press, 1984, pp. 109-111; Cuff, Dana, "The Social Art of Design at the Office and the Academy," *Journal of Architectural and Planning Research*, 6:3 (Autumn 1989), pp. 186-203; Cuff, Dana, "The Origins of Excellent Buildings," in Vonier, op. cit., pp. 77-89.

Along these lines, Robert Nisbett has aptly written "Despite the American creed of individualism, which locates motivation and achievement in the recesses of the individual mind and character, human accomplishment in almost any form is the product of association, usually in small and informal structures whose essence is a high degree of autonomy. . . . This isn't to diminish the superlative powers which lie in certain individuals, but simply to call attention to the context in which these individuals thrive." Nisbet, Robert, *Twilight of Authority*. New York: Oxford University Press, 1975, 269.

8. Rich, Martin, *Professional Ethics in Education*, Springfield, IL: Thomas, 1984, p. 135.

9. "Statement on Professional Ethics," *Academe* (July–August 1987), p. 49. The complete statement is available from the American Association of University Professors in Washington, DC. The most recent version was adopted by the Council as Association policy and endorsed at the 73rd Annual Meeting in June 1987.

10. "Code of Ethics of the Education Profession," adopted by the 1975 National Education Association (NEA) Representative Assembly," in Rich, op. cit., p. 147.

11. It is not uncommon for design professors to assign a competition to a class, have them work on it for several weeks, hold the jury as usual and hear the juror's comments, and then, after the students' work is completed and the top entries are sent on for national judging, to enter the competition themselves. This practice occurs so often that it has rarely been questioned.

12. Kohn, Alfie, *No Contest: The Case Against Competition*, Boston: Houghton Mifflin, 1986, p. 8.

13. Ibid., p. 9.

14. Ghirardo, op. cit., p. 49.

15. A study of design excellence conducted by the American Institute of Architects revealed that while some of the most successful firms are primarily driven by competition even within the office, others strive to avoid internal competition. One firm distinctly switched strategies in order to create a more cooperative, collaborative work environment, and their staff reports a marked improvement in their work. See Franklin et al., op. cit., p. 101; Cuff, op. cit.

16. The study cites: "The critique process, or the process by which architects criticize and develop their designs, appears to play a central part in producing excellent work. It is mentioned consistently by architects and firms whose work is recognized as distinguished." Franklin et al., op. cit., p. xi.

17. Kohn, op. cit., p. 8.

18. Ibid., p. 9.

19. Ibid., p. 32; See also Kohn, Alfie, "It's Hard to Get Left Out of a Pair," *Psychology Today* (October 1987), pp. 53-57.

20. Kohn, *No Contest*, pp. 46–47.

21. Ibid., p. 53.

22. See Amabile, Teresa M., "Children's Artistic Creativity: Detrimental Effects of Competition in a Field Setting," *Personality and Social Psychology Bulletin*, 8 (1982), pp. 573-578, cited in Kohn, op. cit., p. 54. Along these lines, music critic Will Crutchfield has written, "The emotional stamina to tough it out through round after round, as the competition winds on and the stakes rise, does not necessarily go along with the emotional sensitivity to make five minutes worth of truly remarkable Chopin." See Crutchfield, Will, "The Ills of Piano Competitions," *New York Times* (May 16, 1985), p. C25, cited in Kohn, op. cit., p. 54. Bela Bartok once said, "Competitions are for horses, not artists," in Battaglia, Carl, "Piano Competitions: Talent Hunt or Sport," *Saturday Review* (August 25, 1962), pp. 31-33, 39, quote cited on p. 31, cited in Kohn, op. cit., p. 209.

23. Kohn, op. cit., p. 54.

24. American Institute of Architects and The National Endowment for the Arts, *A Study of Publicly Sponsored Developer/Architect Competitions*, Washington, DC: American Institute of Architects Press, 1988; See also Seidel, Andrew, "Design Competitions Receive Mixed Renews," *Journal of Architectural and Planning Research*, 7:2 (Summer 1990), pp. 172-180.

25. Kohn, op. cit., p. 78.

26. Ibid., pp. 140, 142.

27. Deutsch, Morton, *The Resolution of Conflict: Constructive and Destructive Processes*, New Haven, CT: Yale University Press, 1973, p. 353.

28. Kohn, op. cit., pp. 109, 114.

29. Ibid., p. 9.

30. Bosworth, F. H., Jr., and Roy Childs Jones, *A Study of Architectural Schools*, New York: Scribner, 1932.

31. At my own university, on a few occasions I have witnessed certain talented design students walk away with high-paying cash awards for seductive-looking projects, all the while knowing that their arrogant behavior was despised by their studio-mates.

32. Some practitioners argue that the notion of placing minimal value on the work of design professionals originates in the academic design studio. Students are given relatively little course credit for what amounts to many long hours of class time. The system tends to reinforce the idea that design work is not worth much at all.

33. Gans, Herbert J., *Popular Culture and High Culture: An Analysis and Evaluation of Taste*, New York: Basic Books, 1974, p. 122.

34. See Hochschild, Arlie Russell, *The Managed Heart: Commercialization of Human Feeling*, Berkeley: University of California Press, 1983. The book won numerous awards and was one of the New York Times Books of the Year, 1983. In a nutshell, Hochschild describes from a feminist and humanist perspective the process of estrangement from personal feelings and its role as an occupational hazard for women.

35. This "Father knows best" attitude is clearly illustrated in the passages between Quist and Petra, the studio critic and the design student, described by Donald Schön in his well-known work, *The Reflective Practitioner: How Professionals Think in Action*, New York: Basic Books, 1983.

36. For a discussion of how the role models in architectural history have been dominated by men, see Kingsley, Karen, "Gender Issues in Teaching Architectural History," *Journal of Architectural Education*, 41:2 (Winter 1988), pp. 21-25.

37. Brown, Denise Scott, "Room at the Top? Sexism and the Star System in Architecture," in Berkeley, Ellen Perry, and Matilda

McQuaid (eds.), *Architecture: A Place for Women*, Washington, DC: Smithsonian Institution Press, 1989, pp. 237-246.

38. Ibid., p. 240.

39. Ibid., pp. 241-242.

40. This survey of 210 women architecture faculty, was the first of its kind. When asked if they believed sexism to be inherent in the curriculum of their school's own program, about half the women agreed.

    The total number of women faculty in architecture departments of Association of Collegiate Schools of Architecture (ACSA) member schools was 651 while the male architecture faculty numbered 3492. 81% of the women architecture faculty were in either nontenure track or nontenured positions, 18% were tenured, and only 5% were full professors. Contrast this with 62% of the males either in nontenure track or nontenured positions, 38% with tenure, and 23% as full professors. The ratio of tenured males to tenured females is over 2:1. The study showed that compared to men, women are over-represented at the lower-status and under-represented at the higher-status levels of architectural faculty. See Groat, Linda N., and Sherry Ahrentzen, *Status of Faculty Women in Architecture Schools: Survey Results and Recommendations. Developed and Completed by the ACSA Task Force on the Status of Women in Architecture Schools*, Washington, DC: ACSA Press, 1990.

41. The situation in landscape architecture and interior design is not quite the same. At some schools, interior design programs are almost the opposite, dominated by women students and faculty. Landscape architecture and urban planning appear to attract a higher percentage of women students and faculty than does architecture.

42. Ghirardo, op. cit., p. 49.

43. Rand, Ayn, *The Fountainhead*. Indianapolis, IN: Bobbs Merrill, 1943. A more contemporary critique of the role of the architect is also provided in the play *Benefactors*. See Frayn, Michael, *Benefactors*, London: Methuen, 1984.

44. Tom Wolfe's *From Bauhaus to Our House* offers a scathing critique of the superiority complex of the architectural profession. His book triggered a strong backlash among designers, many of whom failed to see the humor in his writing. See Wolfe, Tom, *From Bauhaus to Our House*, New York: Farrar, Straus & Giroux, 1981.

45. Scott Brown, op. cit., p. 243.

46. Gutman, Robert, *Architectural Practice: A Critical View*, New York: Princeton Architectural Press, 1988, pp. 108-110.

47. Pawley, Martin, "Demilitarisation of the University," in Gowan, James, *A Continuing Experiment: Learning and Teaching at the Architectural Association*, London: Architectural Press, 1975, pp. 115-125, quote from p. 121.

48. Buchanan, Peter, "What Is Wrong with Architectural Education? Almost Everything," *Architectural Review*, 185:1109 (July 1989), pp. 24-26, quotes from pp. 24-25.

49. A number of educators have sharply criticized the "charrette" system that originated in the Ecole des Beaux Arts on the grounds that it promotes an image of the design process that is both unrealistic and superficial.

50. Economist Robert Reich has made a similar argument. He uses the term *collective entrepreneurialism* to describe what he believes to be the wave of the future. "Individual skills are integrated into a group whose collective capacity to innovate becomes something more than the simple sum of its parts.... Innovation is inherently collective and incremental." See Reich, Robert B., *Tales of a New America: The Anxious Liberal's Guide to the Future*, New York: Vintage Books, 1987, p. 124.

51. Gutman, op. cit., p. 98.

52. Ibid., p. 110.

53. Baum, L. Frank, *The Wizard of Oz*, New York: Schocken Books, 1983, (originally published 1900) pp. 96-97.

CHAPTER 13
Leading Practitioners' Reflections on Design Juries

This final chapter features selected excerpts from the interviews with designers. Each entry opens with a brief description about the designer and his or her firm, along with some representative examples of their work. Their comments address how they experienced juries while they were in school, what they think of juries in education today, and how they view juries in practice. More specific information on the methodological approach can be found in Appendix A. Note the following abbreviations that are used in the photo captions: Fellow of the American Institute of Architects (FAIA), Fellow of the American Society of Landscape Architects (FASLA), and Fellow of the American Society of Interior Designers (FASID). Also note that in some cases, the order of paragraphs has been changed to clarify the flow of the text.

It should come as a pleasant surprise and perhaps as an inspiration to students that many of these stellar practitioners were not shining stars in school. In fact, several were "late bloomers." Many offer refreshing, valuable advice to both students and faculty based on their unique vantage points. Notice the remarkable similarities between the views of many practitioners and the experiences of today's design students; throughout the interview process, I found this astonishing. Some of these designers are satisfied with the status quo and aptly point out the inherent strengths of juries. Others clearly call for sweeping changes to the jury system and to the design studio in both design education and practice. They argue forcefully and convincingly that such changes are long overdue, thus providing substantive support for the case made throughout this book.

CAROL ROSS BARNEY

Carol Ross Barney (Figure 13-1) received her Bachelor of Architecture degree from the University of Illinois at Urbana-Champaign in 1971, where she also continued her graduate studies in the early 1980s. She is currently president of the Chicago firm Ross Barney & Jankowski, Inc., founded in 1981. Among her many achievements, Ms. Ross Barney chaired the jury for "Many More," an exhibition of women in American architecture, and she recently served as the Chair of the AIA Women in Architecture Committee. She has received Distinguished Service Awards from the Chicago Chapter as well as the Illinois Council of the AIA. She has also served on Honor Award juries for the Wisconsin Society of Architects and the Washington, D.C. Chapter AIA.

The firm's recent projects include the U.S. Post Office for Glendale Heights, Illinois, recipient of the 1989 Distinguished Building Award from the Chicago Chapter of the AIA, and the Automated Guideway Transit System at O'Hare International Airport in Chicago.

How did I do in school? That's an interesting question. I was uneven. I started out kind of slowly, seeing that it was a really big place with a tremendous amount of distractions, but I finished up fairly strong. But in my very first studio class I got a D. The professor gave everybody in the class D's and F's and C's and he gave one A and one B. After that I never got below a B on studio course as a final grade.

Figure 13-1 Carol Ross Barney.

I had a pretty good experience in school after I realized that I wasn't supposed to be creative. Instead I was supposed to learn what they were teaching me and give it back to them. Then studio experiences became much easier once I figured that out. It took me a while to realize that what you had to do was figure out what the design professor had to offer and then just take that from the class. After that I did a lot better. Before that I tried to express myself, but after that I tried to learn what they had to teach.

You probably shouldn't teach design to 17- and 18-year-olds. You really have to be older to understand what it's all about. When I look back on my education I think I missed a lot because I was too young. What helped me the most was finally becoming mature enough to absorb what was being taught, or even to absorb what you see. One of the most important things in design is being able to look at a design and to reuse that experience—the texture, the color, the shape and form of it. There's just too much happening to you when you're 17 or 18 years old to do this effectively.

One of the things the faculty did to us in school was to make us rename every space in our design, like a bathroom or a bedroom, and get us to think about this seriously. It had to be called something other than what we were familiar with. It's harder to do when you're 18. When you're 18 you always want to tie it back to something that you know and feel comfortable with.

You get out of architecture school and you start designing buildings and you discover that the real reason you design something is because "you like it." But that wasn't a valid reason for argument in design school. If the jurors asked, "Why did you do this?" you couldn't say, "Because I like it." You had to have a rationale for your design decisions.

When I was in school it was in vogue to be very tough on students in juries. I remember that on one jury when I was in school, there was a student who was on a swimming scholarship, which was extremely unusual. I don't think anybody in architecture school ever did anything athletic. And he spent no time working on his projects. And so at the jury one of the jurors got up and said, "Son, you'd better decide if you're going to swim or be an architect," which was absolutely devastating, especially in front of the rest of the class.

In retrospect I think juries are good. Daily I'm in a position where I have to explain myself and review work for the client. How well you do that really makes a difference in the type of work you'll build. If you can impress your ideas upon the client, you can get a much better product. Clients can walk all over you more easily than your professors because they're paying the bills.

The thing about going to school that was just great was that you get all these different ideas. Sometimes students inadvertently have ideas. They don't even know they're having them and they are great ideas. It was refreshing.

My advice to students is to figure out what their critic is trying to teach. You may not agree with it, but at least you'll have a rational reason to disagree with it. You'll get more out of your education and do better. It shoulds like selling out but it really isn't. When you're in school you have to regard that time as a total absorbing experience. That's hard to do in a profession where you're supposed to be priding yourself on your creativity.

I think the most important thing to realize about design education is the problem-solving process.

There's no reason on the earth why a woman can't be an architect. There's this traditional relationship with construction that scares a lot of women off. I think that the successful architect is so much more universal than math or construction that it really precludes some sort of gender-based advantage. But I am worried about the fact that there aren't more women going into architecture school today. About 25-30% women is the average on most campuses and it's not improving. It's been that way for seven or eight years. Something outside the profession or the mere entry to the profession is discouraging women from choosing this as a career.

My firm is now almost ten years old and I have at long last discovered why people call this an old man's profession. It has nothing to do with being a man. But it does have to do with being old.

I think that professional design competitions are questionable. Maybe they are most appropriate only for the most important civic projects. Designers who are truly successful are good at selling their ideas. This can be an acquired skill.

JOAN BLUTTER

I don't think I did as well in school as I have done in the field because I sincerely believe that design is an evolving process. Design [ability] can come to you [immediately] or it can be an agonizingly long process. Students should not be discouraged when ideas don't come as quickly as they would like. Eventually design sensibilities will evolve, but all the things that you've learned of course are in your brain so that eventually all the things you think you're missing in your abilities come [second nature]. There are no quick shortcuts to [good design ability], even though some people are quicker [at developing them] than others.

My advice to students and jurors is not to be arrogant. The faculty should not be arrogant either. They should not expect perfection from students. What I'm just saying is not necessarily just for designers. It's for the world in general. It applies to all things in life.

My words of wisdom to students and young practitioners would be: Do not be afraid of your own thoughts. And never stop seeing. Try, if you can, to always keep your vision.

[In professional competitions] jurors should read the rules and judge the portfolio and judge the job based on what the competition is about and not necessarily from their own personal judgment on the project as a whole.

Another great mistake a lot of professional juries make is to be swayed by the look of the presentation rather than the substance of the design. [It is also] very important for the designers to watch their spelling. We don't judge

Figure 13-2 Joan Blutter, FASID.

designs for correct spelling but, to most jurors, it's difficult to say that it doesn't matter because spelling errors show carelessness on the part of the designer.

Sometimes it's very difficult to stay within rules of a competition because you have to give the designer who is presenting the license to be creative, and this may mean breaking the rules.

One factor that can sway a jury is having immaculately clean, caring entries. You've got to show the juries that you cared about the project. If two entries are equal in aesthetic and character, the one who has taken the trouble to care is going to win. It doesn't have to be an elaborate presentation.

LAURENCE BOOTH

It [the jury system in academia] is very inefficient. And it's very undisciplined. It has no rigor. . . . If they taught medicine this way, we'd all be dying.

When I was in architecture school, I had one experience in which a teacher criticized my design saying, "You've been drawing these strange buildings. Why don't you get into the program and learn how to do [things right]. We're trying to teach you something and you're just not trying to

---

Joan Blutter (Figure 13-2), president of the Chicago firm Blutter/Shiff Design Associates, has over 25 years of experience designing residential and commercial interiors. She has routinely advised industry on product, marketing, and design concepts. Her work has been published widely in trade magazines and national consumer publications, and she has been a repeated guest on talk shows throughout the Midwest. She has served as national secretary and regional vice-president of the American Society of Interior Designers (ASID), chairman of the ASID National Industry Foundation, and president of the ASID Illinois Chapter. She also has served as ASID National Competitions chairman and as a consultant to HALO on its national lighting design competition. Throughout her career she has received various awards, including the 1979 Designer of the Year Award from ASID.

learn." And I said, "Well, I came from California and I'm interested in the kind of direction [I've explored]." They didn't have a wider range. Architecture has got to be something more than just backing up toilets, which it was [when I was in school]. Each generation has its own fetish. For a while it was Post-Modernism and now it's Deconstructivism, where buildings look like they were put through the Cuisinart.

As a student, I thought the jury system was educational. The good side of the jury system is you do see judgmental processes in action. So you see a juror looking at a project and trying to grapple with it. But ultimately the process could be done by a silent jury.

I never thought that verbal presentation was terribly important because designers don't make architectural judgments verbally. They make them intuitively. There was never any question about if a project was good or bad. All you had to do was look at it.

Some jurors were very good at conveying their criticisms to students. It's hard to do. Some jurors were very effective at giving comments that helped students and other jurors weren't. And the outcome was very arbitrary. I used to think if they taught medicine this way we'd all be dying. Can you imagine teaching heart surgery by saying, "Well, bring the patient in and start at it. Well, that one died.

Figure 13-3 Laurence Booth, FAIA.

I don't know what you did wrong. Try it again. I know intuitively you're going to figure this out." That's the way they're teaching architecture, isn't it?!

If I were in education I'd work on [improving the studio system]. It's not an effective way of teaching because it's so haphazard. How do you know that students understand anything as they go from one level to another? I don't think it's a question of drawing ability because architecture just isn't an artistic profession. It's management and it's an organization process. There's a lot more to the architecture profession than just design. You can be a very good designer in school and not succeed at all in real life because you have not mastered the other skills that you need to integrate with your design abilities.

A jury sometimes degenerates into a situation where the jurors themselves are competing. And if you have a juror with a strong, dominating personality, the juries can get to be tedious, becoming a vehicle for a lot of grandstanding.

Juries are too long and tedious. They should be 10-minutes maximum, but there's no way to keep the time limit under control. It's unfair to students who come last. Depending on your sequence jurors can be tired. So to me it's a very, very sloppy process.

To just get through design school you have to have certain skills just to organize your materials and your time. Whatever you can do to increase those organizational skills I would reinforce because school is a matter of time. Watch people working in an office. Look at someone's desk, you can tell right away if they're effective or not. Now sometimes they're not just tidy but there's something about the way they organize their belongings. The ones that are

---

Laurence Booth (Figure 13-3) completed his Bachelor of Architecture at the Massachusetts Institute of Technology in 1960 after earning his Bachelor of Arts degree from Stanford University in 1958. He also studied at Harvard University. He is currently design principal at the firm Booth/Hansen & Associates, Ltd., in Chicago. On numerous occasions Mr. Booth has served on American Institute of Architects (AIA) awards juries, as well as on juries for the Rome Prize of the American Academy in Rome. For several years he served on the board of directors of the Chicago Chapter of the AIA. Mr. Booth has also served as president of the Chicago Architecture Club and on the board of directors of the Society of Architectural Historians. Booth/Hansen & Associates has earned 20 Distinguished Building Awards and several Interior Awards from the Chicago Chapter of the AIA; Record Home awards from Architectural Record; Progressive Architecture awards; and the Gold Medal Excellence and several Excellence in Masonry Design awards from the Masonry Council of Metropolitan Chicago. Recent projects include the Terra Museum of American Art, North Pier Terminal Building and the Omni-Morton Hotel in Chicago; the Shoreacres Golf Club at Lake Bluff, Illinois; and the Kinkead Pavilion at Krannert Art Museum on the campus of the University of Illinois at Urbana-Champaign.

more organized are more effective, obviously, and I don't think it's just a prejudice I have.

I'd say that educators should forget about juries and just have students pin up freehand drawings and pictures and then let them be graded and posted in a display room. Actually, what's wrong with juries too is that they occur and then everything's gone. They ought to display the projects for two weeks or so, along with the grades. To me, that would be pretty educational.

What's a good alternative to the typical design jury in school? In a class of 30 students, you could select, say six projects to discuss in the jury. You need to convey to students that even though we didn't talk about your project, you're still going to learn something important. It's awkward when you see poor projects and you still have to find something to say about them — it's just very taxing. So why bother? You either qualify for the jury or you don't. Next time maybe you will. That would be a way to focus energy, then, and have a good three hours on a few projects that are selected. The discussion can center on not so much what you as an individual did but, instead, what is the problem all about? What were the ranges of solutions to the problem? How can you think about the problem? And how can you best understand how to approach this problem and others?

One of the problems with architecture is that it's bogged down with individualism. You're put on the spot: "It's my project." That's a real heavy load and it gets in your way. In fact, design is really a team sport.

Design is a team activity. Succeeding in practice is a matter of developing skills to work and develop as a team. It's like basketball. It's constantly moving well. Learning design is not like teaching basketball by teaching people to shoot free throws. Someone who can only shoot baskets well will not necessarily help the team. It takes much more than that.

WILLIAM CALLAWAY

In undergraduate school I did pretty badly. I had just over a 2 point average as I recall. I was still really a youth of the '50s. I was having a good time. It drove me crazy because I was always having trouble with grades. I wasn't really that serious of a student, actually. I grew to really like the profession and I really love it now, but I didn't do very well in undergraduate school.

In graduate school, I wasn't at the top of the class, but I was much more serious about what I was doing. I don't necessarily think that my grades directly relate to how much I learned. Anyway, (I was) not a star student.

I was really terrified of coming off the farm and going to Berkeley. The whole design [experience] was just incredible. Professors were talking in strange languages and I didn't have a clue what the hell was going on.

William Callaway (Figure 13-4) received his Bachelor of Landscape Architecture from the University of California, Berkeley, in 1966 and his Master of Landscape Architecture from Harvard University in 1971. Mr. Callaway joined the SWA Group in 1967 and is currently president and design principal in SWA's Sausalito, California, office. He has received Honor Awards from the American Institute of Architects (AIA), the American Society of Landscape Architects (ASLA), and the California Council of Landscape Architects (CCLA). To date, the SWA Group has coveted about 200 design awards at the national, state, and regional levels from the AIA, ASLA, CCLA, National Association of Home Builders, U.S. Department of Housing and Urban Development, Landscape Architecture *and* Progressive Architecture *magazines, and elsewhere. SWA's services cover landscape architecture, urban design, land planning, environmental management, and photography/audiovisual. Noteworthy projects include the luxury resort landscaping for the Hyatt Regency Scottsdale at Gainey Ranch; Citicorp Plaza and the Seventh Street Market in Los Angeles; Sidney Walton Park in San Francisco; the Concord Pavilion in Concord, California; the Phoenix Tower roof garden in Houston, Texas; the Boca Raton Beach Club in Boca Raton, Florida; the Newport Center and Fashion Island in Newport Beach, California; the Village of Woodbridge in Irvine, California; and the Orange County Performing Arts Center in Costa Mesa, California.*

Throughout undergraduate design school I found that the faculty was not very encouraging, with one exception. This professor appeared to be the only human, really warm person in the whole school. And she helped a lot because she made it feel like you weren't going to lose a little finger. She was a warm person, and she was willing to talk. She didn't have a presentation of herself or her material that was intimidating. She genuinely cared about her students. I think teachers sometimes tend to be proving something to themselves....

I believe that professors need to spend some time setting up the jury well and instructing the jurors. Most of the time they just try to get people to come in at the last minute (with) very little background on the projects and virtually no background on the students.

Most of the time [juries in school were unfair or] chaotic. Many jurors are feathering their own nests rather than helping a student.

Sometimes faculty set up juries for all the wrong reasons. So I think that the more they can focus on their mission to teach students, then the more they can tailor juries to what that student needs. The instructor is the only one that knows who their students are, what they need,

Figure 13-4 William Callaway. (Photo: Dixi Carillo)

and how they need to be taught, and whether they need encouragement or not. A jury is the moment of truth.

I think that the best juror is the best listener.

It's hard to conceive a project being done by a team at the conceptual stage. Other people can improve and enrich a design, but I think it still is responding to a major idea. You know the old cliché of design by committee. If everybody gets their way you end up with something mediocre because you've compromised it. If you just tried to choose a color by a team [you'll] very likely end up with beige. But I'm not demeaning that process because I think that teamwork is invaluable for bringing you up to that point. I think even once you're at that point, then you can go back into the team and ask for input and ideas.

If you don't have a passion about what you're doing, then you probably should be in another profession, because it can get real discouraging along the way. Money can't be a primary goal, so you've got to get something else out of it, like peace of mind or satisfaction. Students need to realize how many roles a [landscape architect can play]. It's unrealistic to think that [one person] could perform all the roles of a landscape architect. Not everybody can be a brilliant designer.

Even though you may not have a blazing talent in [large-scale] design projects, you may be very good at small-scale design which is less complicated. I don't think you should give up one way or another.

Both left-brain and right-brain people are needed in an office. You need some left-brain people to keep the place from being chaotic: people that are neat and tidy and think linearly, and that pull things together. A successful practice requires people with diverse skills. Therefore, students should not think, "if I can't design brilliantly, then I'm no good and I should get out of the field altogether."

Jurors shouldn't be afraid to say what they think but I think that their comments should be well considered. I think that's true of a jury. In a jury you have to listen to what a person is saying and read between the lines about how skilled this person is. It's good if the instructor hands out some background on the student, particularly in graduate school because so many times you have people who are English majors that can't draw very well. They're much different from the student who has had four years of undergraduate [design] school and then worked in an office for two years.

Most professional design competitions are done for the wrong reasons. Either the clients or sponsors don't know what they want or they don't have any money. So they hold a competition primarily as a means to generate some ideas that they can publish and then apply for funding. What's good about competitions is that for younger professionals, it frees them from all constraints. But [considering] the low success rate of competition entries, I don't think it's worth the effort. The only reason we enter competitions is for internal morale.

Professional competitions are also a way of testing the talent of your younger people. In addition, it takes so much energy to enter a competition that it requires the stamina of young people.

CHRISTOPHER DEGENHARDT

In terms of providing some intellectual basis for design and looking at problems comprehensively, I'll say with all due humility, that I think I was a good student. I would say synthesis was probably my greatest strength as a student.

I think it's very easy to be on a jury and only identify what's bad. Most critics tend to put emphasis on being critical, whereas a true "critique" embraces the idea of saying both what's bad and what's good.

I think that the faculty ought to take some time to brief the jurors so that the jury fully understands the level at which they're critiqueing, what the expectations of the program are, what the professor expected the students to learn. Students should view the jury as part of their education and not just as part of their grade.

One of the things I realized after the end of my formal education is the tremendous value of *looking* at other projects. You really ought to be looking all the time at different products, doing many comparisons, recording ideas, seeing what works and what doesn't, and how problems were solved. All these things become part of your vocabulary. It occurs to me that this process is very

Christopher Degenhardt (Figure 13-5) received a Bachelor of Science degree from Wye College at the University of London in 1963 and a Diploma of Landscape Architecture Design from the University of Newcastle upon Tyne, England in 1964. In 1967 he completed his Master of Landscape Architecture at the State University of New York at Syracuse. He has also been a member of the Design Review Board for the University of California, Berkeley. Based at the San Francisco headquarters of EDAW, he has been involved with the management of EDAW's major projects in the United States and around the world. His special expertise is in large-scale development of landscape architecture and planning projects.

Selected EDAW projects under Mr. Degenhardt's supervision include a Comparative Land Use Study of 12 countries in Europe; the planning of major resort and visitor destinations including Northstar-at-Tahoe near Lake Tahoe, California, Dragon Valley in Korea, and Sun River in Oregon; and waterfront revitalization projects in Washington, D.C., San Francisco, and St. Paul. He has also supervised major park and recreation and natural resource management plans such as Minneapolis Parkway and the 23,000-acre San Francisco Bay National Wildlife Refuge and the Nisqually Wildlife Refuge in Washington. Recently he directed land use planning for the Mission Bay Specific Plan in San Francisco.

Figure 13-5 Christopher Degenhardt, FASLA.

similar to learning the English language. You've got all the words stored in your brain, and you need to select the right one for the right situation. You need to acquire that vocabulary. And you need to do it by continually observing and experiencing. The key is to be able to take pieces of that vocabulary, and synthesize and adapt and change them for specific needs.

... However, I think one has to be careful not to overdo that. I have a friend who's a composer and song writer, and I was talking to him one day about how he went about [composing]. I said, "You must listen to an awful lot of music," and he said, "Yes and no. When I'm not writing, I do, but when I'm writing and composing, I don't listen to any at all." "You can't get input and output at the same time."

Professional design competitions can be very frustrating. Typically, if one gets to the final stages, it's through the process of elimination. An easy consensus is very rare. When you try to pick the winner out of the last half dozen of a hundred or so, it's very difficult. A jury tends to want consensus and yet since they don't always agree, they argue and argue until they can get a clear majority. Such juries are frustrating; but on the other hand they've always been broadening, and as a juror I always learn something.

Over the years our firm has won many awards, but all our submittals don't win. And I'm sometimes surprised by what wins and what doesn't. I think that's a bit like how you get a project sometimes.

There certainly is occasion for a design competition. At the same time, I would have to say I find it a decidedly overused practice. There tends to be a certain lack of realism because you're operating without a client, and I feel that a client is an essential component of nearly every design problem. I also believe there are several wrong reasons for having competitions. One is that I think they can be used as a cheap way of getting a lot of ideas. The profession should resist that. If design becomes so selfish and so arrogant that it does not and will not respond to a client's needs, then we're not serving the client properly and we're not tailoring our design to our clients' needs. Instead, we're tailoring design through our own preconceptions. Put yourself in the client's shoes. [The client] needs to recognize that in selecting [this type of] designer he is selecting a preconception of style. If that's what he's going to do, he may as well go shopping because he's not going to get a tailor-made suit. He won't be able to select the style, the cloth, the stitching, and the buttons. Instead, he's going to go shopping until he finds something he likes.

THE LATE NORMAN R. DEHAAN

They had a rigid educational theory in the architectural school of IIT (Illinois Institute of Technology) in the mid '40s. The theory was that if you had talent it would blossom after you graduated. The first important thing [for the student to learn was] how to put a building together and to understand the technical requirements. If you weren't an inherently good architect you'd at least make a good draftsman. As there were only eight in my freshman class, we were not keen on the odds.

In the first two years of school you simply were given assignments and you had to produce excellence in those assignments—drawing all the brick courses and sections from steel. There was nothing creative. It was all technical ability. The only creative areas—two: one was the freehand class of Mr. Kreible, a marvelous old character, when we complained one time because we had such ugly models and he said that anyone could draw a beautiful woman, it took an artist to make a work of art out of an unattractive person. And the voids. You always had to draw the voids before you got into the topic. The other creative area was in the axiometric projections required by Walter Pederhans.

I think that juries in design education today are fine. It seems to me, though, that what a jury says in front of students and in public is entirely different from what a jury may say in private.

I think the student should be told beforehand if their projects don't meet certain technical criteria, then their work can be set aside. It would be more profitable for the students to be given a more detailed analysis of the jury's criteria and reasons for selecting the top projects rather than hear sarcastic remarks about every single one of the rejections.

I don't think a student's written or verbal presentation should be preachy. It's amazing how many students preach. Maybe it's their only chance to get on a soap box. And if you're looking at a competition where there's going to be a few hundred entries, preaching and wordiness tend to turn the jury off. I think you should explain why and what

Figure 13-6 The late Norman R. DeHaan, FAIA, FASID. (Photo: Bruce Powell)

Norman R. DeHaan (Figure 13-6) studied under Mies Van der Rohe at Illinois Institute of Technology (I.I.T.). He was president of Norman DeHaan Associates, DeHaan Inc., and vice-president of Interior Distributors Incorporated in Chicago. He has held such positions as national president and chairman of the board of the American Institute of Interior Designers, founding national president of the American Society of Interior Designers (ASID), president of the ASID Education Foundation, and chairman of the American Institute of Architects (AIA) Interior Architecture Committee. Mr. DeHaan served on numerous juries and panels for the ASID, AIA, National Endowment for the Arts, National Institute for Architectural Education, the Chicago Architecture Foundation, and the Smithsonian Institution, and authored numerous design publications. He was a past president of the Chicago Chapter of the AIA and a governing member of the Art Institute of Chicago, and vice-president/president-elect of the International Federation of Interior Architects/Interior Designers, a 29-nation organization headquartered in Amsterdam.

Mr. DeHaan's firm specializes in interior design and architectural remodeling and commercial design advisory services. Its emphasis is on the interior design of condominiums, offices, hospitality/food service facilities, institutions, and retail stores. Selected projects include the Member's Dining Room at the Art Institute of Chicago; Lake Point Tower Club; dining facilities at Michael Reese Medical Center, Northwestern Memorial Hospital, and the Museum of Science and Industry in Chicago; the O'Hare Hilton in Chicago; the Hillcrest Country Club in Long Grove; the Ravisloe Country Club in Homewood, Illinois; and the Westwood Country Club in St. Louis, Missouri. Mr. DeHaan died in 1990.

you've done concerning the design aspects and place less on the moral aspects. It's terribly easy to sound like you're criticizing everybody else's standards but you're own, and that's very slippery ground to be on. Unless you really know how to write you have to be very careful what you say.

I've never been on a jury where specific ground rules were laid out and followed. It seems to me that if the jury can have a few minutes to establish certain criteria for successful projects, then at least the student wouldn't be thrown into complete despair.

It would be refreshingly nice if a jury explained to the students each of their own personal criteria and design interests and they were therefore going to concentrate on those projects which fell within their area of expertise. I don't think they do that often enough on juries. I think it's very difficult for a student who is unaware of the fact this happens on juries.

Design faculties—and those who administer professional competitions—tend to select jurors that like to work together. Therefore you often get a very slanted jury. If the faculty is involved in selecting a jury they should explain why they have selected individual members, whether they have diverse or similar opinions, or whether they all follow a certain school or "ism." It is only fair to the student.

The other thing I think students and designers should understand is that many juries tend to judge on a visual basis, rarely in three dimensions. What you see on the covers of design magazines are often not interesting places to visit because they photograph beautifully in two dimensions, but when you're actually there, it is less sensational. Sometimes it's the work you can't photograph that's really the most sensational.

I think that a sense of humor is essential. Ms. Cornelia Congor, who was the grande dame of design and decorating here in Chicago, was asked at one of the ASID student conferences, what she felt was the most important trait for a designer to have, and she said, "A sense of humor, my dear, a sense of humor." She said, "There's enough ill will in the world and if you don't have a sense of humor, take up dentistry."

It seems to me that if faculty are asking students to design something specific then there ought to be some required reading that goes along with the assignment. Once they get out in the real world they've got to start doing some research.

I think design students themselves should get involved in something outside of their career, not just because that's how you meet clients, because that isn't always so. But I think that if you're in a creative position then you owe it to society to give something back to society and do something more.

I believe that if you've hung out your shingle and you're married and your wife is working and you have no work in the office, then you tend to enter design competitions. If you have work in the office and are busy, you tend not to enter competitions. Maybe that's not fair but I think it's quite true.

If clients want to have an open competition, at some point they should say that they seek a conceptual [design] and compensate the designers for their work.

Concerning practitioners serving as jurors, if they do not agree with the program, they should not serve on the jury. It never happens that way, however, instead they simply change the rules. I think that practice is not only unethical but very unfair to the entrants.

It would be unique if the rules of a design competition stipulated that NO award will be given to anyone who doesn't comply with the published criteria. If a design is so outstanding, but had no business in the competition, they should give recognition on the side, but it shouldn't be a part of the competition. You do come across this phenomenon frequently. They just have this great idea for a dish pan but the competition is for a tea kettle. But if it's the most gorgeous dish pan they've ever seen, some jury will give the award to the dish pan.

Design firms often spend over a million dollars on one of their competition presentations, so to have a couple of jurors make little sarcastic remarks doesn't do the profession any good. It's claimed that one of the reasons architects are so bitchy is that they're treated so badly in their juries as students.

LARRY N. DEUTSCH

When I was a student I did very well in the subjects in which I was most interested, and did not do very well in those in which I was not interested. In my major, ¾ of my courses were A's and B's, but ¼ of them were C's and in some cases D's because I didn't think they were well taught. Other students and professors didn't see me as a star student. I think they perceived me as a unique student, but not as a star. A star to me means somebody who's really superbly talented and capable in the design or art field and I don't think I was at that time.

I was unique in that I always looked beyond what was obvious to try to see how my thoughts or actions were relating to other concepts in the larger scheme of things. I have a social consciousness that is not always relating just to my art, but I practice some of it through my art and through my design.

My most devastating experience as a student was during one summer at the University of Arizona summer school in Guadalajara, Mexico. I discovered that it is easier to enjoy Guadalajara, Mexico, but not to learn or study as much when you're out of a controlled environment. There was too little structure and not enough responsibility on my part at that age. It was my sophomore year of college. I was 19 and the professors there didn't care whether you did well or not. I received an Incomplete grade because I

> *Larry N. Deutsch (Figure 13-7) graduated from the University of Arizona in 1963 with a Bachelor of Fine Arts degree. He is president of the Chicago firm Larry N. Deutsch Interiors, Ltd. In 1977 he received second place in the National Barcalounger Competition for the best design of a multipurpose room. In 1986 he was honored by the Merchandise Mart in Chicago for outstanding Achievement in Design.*
>
> *Mr. Deutsch has been a board member, vice-president, and Education Committee chairman of the Illinois Chapter of the American Society of Interior Designers (ASID). In 1984 he was chairman of the ASID National Conference in Chicago and in 1986 he was business chairman of the National Conference in Los Angeles. He is an ex-officio member of the National ASID Industry Foundation Steering Committee. He has also served as president of the River North Association, a civic group representing Chicago's art and antique shopping district. His firm's work has been featured in such publications as* Architectural Digest, House and Garden, House Beautiful, Better Homes and Gardens, *and* The Designer. *The firm specializes in residential and commercial design. Notable projects include a duplex in Chicago's Water Tower Place, homes from Boca Raton to Beverly Hills, a luxurious Manhattan apartment, and a major brokerage firm in Chicago.*

Figure 13-7 Larry N. Deutsch.

had a very nice professor who gave me a year to make up the grade. I finally made it up and I think got a D.

I dreamed continuously that I had not graduated and would not graduate. It's a dream that many people have, even after they've graduated from college. But it related directly to this incident because I knew that I had really failed both myself and my professor who had given me an extra chance.

In retrospect what helped me get through design school was the thought that I would eventually get out of school. I have never been a school person. I wanted to quit high school in my senior year but my counselor allowed me to go to school from 8:00 in the morning until noon and then work full-time from 12:30 P.M. for the rest of the day during my entire senior year. When I went to the university I didn't have much more interest in school than I had in my senior year. I only looked forward to the end of the four years which was a requirement to get a degree. And during that maturation process I discovered that I would never want to be intensely steeped in schooling, like many people who enjoy it, because I enjoyed the real world much more. There are two kinds of people—the real-world people, as I am, and the scholarly people who live in a world of books and education and research, of which I'm not a part.

When I'm invited in for a jury, I don't just look at a student's project and say "Terrible" or "Good." I write what I feel might be valuable to the student based on what I perceive that student does or does not know. I don't think it does any good to say, "I liked this because it was bright and clever and brittle in its approach to design." What does that mean? Rather, I write, "Your color was murky" or "Your line drawings were uneven. Your pencil should have been sharpened." I'm very specific because I think that it's only when you tell someone exactly what is expected of them that they have the opportunity if they're interested to use that information.

I think it's more important to see whether the project submitted works or doesn't work. It really doesn't matter if parts work but the whole doesn't. No professional or businessman will pay you for a project that had great potential but was a failure, so you have to learn that. And I think that's not often taught in school.

I think that if jurors are more honest in what they see, whether it's brutal or not, that is far better than being evasive and too kind.

As a student, I had a lot of motivation and my professors recognized it, and that's why I think that motivation is perhaps more important than talent. It's nice if you can be Picasso and have great motivation to paint all day and all night and also have exquisite genius talent, but that's really for very few. Talent will not carry you sometimes as much as motivation, in my belief.

While I was experimenting with black shapes on a white sheet of paper, I remember asking my professor in two-dimensional design, "How will I know when it is good two-dimensional design?" And he responded, "You'll know it when you see it. I can't teach it other than to tell you to continue to experiment with these shapes and you will recognize it when it is approached." And I thought to myself, "Well, if that isn't the biggest crock." And I went back to doing dozens and hundreds of these sort of things, and all of a sudden some started to look right, even to an unpracticed eye. Some didn't look right. Some seemed unbalanced but not purposely unbalanced. Some seemed to have energy from their imbalance, but it was different from just an imbalance. And some seemed perfectly balanced and floated properly. And as weeks and months went by, I kept saying to my professor, "This is the weirdest thing. It's actually working. I am learning what the difference is and you are really not teaching me other than to say sometimes, 'That doesn't work,' but not telling me what it would be and why."

Good design is starting with all your basics being correct—fine proportion, well-located piercing of the openings for windows and lights and lighting—and then simultaneously having a furniture floor plan that is incorporated into that whole in a sense of balance. Then it doesn't matter how good the art is or how it's hung. A simple piece will do it because the room is in harmony. And good design is therefore very hard up front and very easy at the end, whereas bad design is very, very much harder at the end to make good and very easy in the beginning because there's not much you can do. You have very few choices. I would prefer practicing designing, which is hard up front and easy at the end, and not decorating, which is easy up front and hard at the end.

I think it's better to have good bones and good structure. You hear that in the model world and the theater world and such—good bones and good structure is far more important than camouflage. The movies really expose bones and structure. I have a lot of theater training also, so I'm interested in that too. And it relates to my design.

I think that jury feedback of a specific nature is far better. Part of the design jury process could be a question-and-answer period by the students of the jurors as to why they preferred or selected the projects they did so that the students could hear firsthand their feelings and emotions. [There should be] an explanation beforehand that this is to be absolutely open and that if hurt feelings or pride are to get involved that it will not be a successful discussion.

I could speak all day on what I think is wrong with what we're taught in school. And I think basically we aren't taught structure and logic. If you're taught structure and logic, then it's very easy to couple that with creativity and be brilliant. But if there's no structure and logic, and you are only learning creative attitudes, your ideas scatter to the wind.

The best designers that I have ever seen are usually not the best business people. Their work often doesn't go anywhere. They'd be great if somebody could bring it to the marketplace for them, but because there's nobody else to bring it to the marketplace, they're not successful. It's a different set of skills. And that's why you often find that designers need business managers. The most talented people are not always presented to the public because they don't stay in business.

Design is no different from geometry. You have to accept theorems. You can't get past it without them because there has to be some acceptance of a body of knowledge that has been created which the world recognizes as basically correct. From there you can expand. In design, you have to start with acceptance of basic structure, and from there you have to go out on new tangents. You have to think and design things that have not been designed before. But if you don't have the basic structure of what has been designed before, how do you know if what you're designing is new and different and original? I think you have to steep yourself in basic structure.

I think that apprenticeship is very good. People who don't learn design in books have to learn it in three dimensions so that they can then understand what is basically expected and accepted so that they can then create. You can't break a rule until you know the rules. It's just that simple.

Certainly math is probably more important to the design field than anything else. How do you get a pair of curtains to hang if you don't know how many yards to order and if you don't know how to follow the repeat so that they align and match up? That's all math. It has nothing to do with the fabrics you're using. It's all numbers. It's proper measuring. I have had more errors in design with improper measurements because someone didn't think that that $\frac{1}{16}''$ or that $\frac{1}{8}''$ made a difference. It doesn't work that way. The design world is based in practical application on math to a great extent.

Today's design schools are so concerned with keeping up with each other that they're interested primarily in having their students be on the cutting edge in design, but cutting-edge design is what I do today and five minutes from now it's not cutting edge anymore.

Many design curricula leave out too much of the humanities because they can't quite fit it all into the program, but it's probably then that they should most include it.

It takes time to enter competitions properly, but the rewards and the payoffs are probably better financially and public relations-wise than almost anything else you can do in your field.

[Competitions] are valuable to me as an independent practitioner because I look at what wins design competitions to see what kind of new and inventive use of materials are out there that I hadn't thought of. It's part of an educational process for me. The other educational process is networking with my fellow designers. I spend a great deal of time with professionals and talking about what

PETER EISENMAN

What do I think helped me the most in getting through design school? I suppose my sheer desire to be good.

I didn't think very much of the closed jury system in my student days. The Beaux-Arts system was very strong, and we never had any sense of why we received the grades we did. We would come in after the jury and we just got a grade. So one never knew anything [about the evaluation process], and students were not allowed to present their work. I thought it was a system which denied access to any information as to why you were doing well or not.

Design juries are a unique instrument of architecture schools, and they are a very powerful tool. They have become legend in a sense. In other words, they are the symbolic manifestation of doing and completing a design. I think obviously they can be abused, however. In fact I think there's an enormous abuse of this system. Sometimes jurors are hostile and insulting to students and their work without explaining why. They expect students to know a priori why their work isn't very good. But overall the heat of the jury is very important for the student. It's like facing a client or having an interview. I think the jury is good practice for a student because we all go through it in later life.

I think that we have bad architecture in this world because we have bad architects, not because we have bad clients. We have bad architects because the system of education is obviously not very effective. In fact, I think it's one of the lowest forms of intellectual communication.

When music teachers teach their students, they don't teach them composition by having them compose. Instead, they have them listen to music. In architecture schools very few people listen to the music, as it were. They're thrown right in and asked to design. The real problem with architecture is that students who know very little about design are asked immediately to design buildings. They form habits about what design should be without even knowing what the possibilities are, and understanding what architecture really is.

I think Mies Van Der Rohe was wise when he taught students to draw bricks, and to understand how it feels to draw them. I think it's much better for a student to draw a plan by Palladio, and to understand what it feels like in the hand to draw a Palladian plan compared to a plan by Mies Van Der Rohe. It is important that the hand-eye sensitivity of the student is developed. It's like the ear-mind sensitivity that's necessary in music. You can't design until you understand what architecture is.

I think the emphasis on practice in education is also wrong because the best way to learn about practice is to be in practice. I don't think you need to learn about professional practice in graduate education. It's like the difference between an applied education in a business school or in a Ph.D. in economics. I would much prefer to have a Ph.D. in economics because you really understand the theory of money and currency exchange and value, etc., whereas when you're in business school you learn the application of theories of money. I think architecture schools should be more like Ph.D. programs in economics where you learn what architecture is rather than the application of architecture. We don't have enough of that distinction made in architectural education.

If the faculty isn't going to give you wisdom, you should explore the nature of architecture for yourself. In other words, find out personally what architecture is. I think that what design students need to do is to become [more broadly] educated. You need to know what culture in general is. You need to know what philosophy is. You need to know what history is. You need to know what aesthetics are. You need to know what music, art, and

---

Peter Eisenman (Figure 13-8), partner-in-charge of the firm Eisenman Architects in New York City, received his Bachelor of Architecture degree from Cornell University, Master of Architecture from Columbia University, and an M.A. and a Ph.D. from the University of Cambridge. Mr. Eisenman has received such honors as the John Simon Guggenheim Foundation Fellowship, the Brunner Award from the National Institute of Arts and Letters, fellowships from the National Endowment for the Arts and Columbia University, and the Charles G. Sands Memorial Medal from Cornell. An architect and educator, Mr. Eisenman has authored several books, including House X; Fin d'Ou T HouS; Moving Arrows: Eros and Other Errors; *the award-winning* House of Cards; *and* The Wexner Center for the Visual Arts. *He was the founder and director of the Institute for Architecture and Urban Studies, an international think tank for architecture and architectural criticism.*

Eisenman Architects have received several national and international awards including the 1984 Progressive Architecture *Design Award for the Visual Arts Center at Ohio State University in Columbus, 1987 and 1988* Progressive Architecture *Citations, and the 1988 National Honor Award from the American Institute of Architects (AIA) for a project located at the former site of Checkpoint Charlie along the Berlin Wall. The Berlin project was featured on a postage stamp of the Federal Republic of Germany celebrating the 750th anniversary of the City of Berlin. The firm has also won a number of national and international design competitions.*

Figure 13-8 Peter Eisenman, FAIA. (Photo: Dick Frank)

literature are. You have to become an educated human being. That's why architects mature so late in life because you need to have all those things at your command before you can design. You should get as wide an education as possible, travel, see things, and experience life.

There's no rush to be an architect. This is an old-person's profession. I think that most architects don't get a chance to do really important work until they're at least 40. My advice to students is to take your time, slow down, and get educated.

I believe open design competitions are great for young architects. But, I think professional design competitions are also abusive. I think I would never enter an open competition again because it's too costly. I think that closed competitions abuse architects since they are not paid a realistic fee. However, I think they often produce very exciting buildings because you don't have the client limiting you. So I think competitions are good as long as you have a good jury and you have a proper fee. But they're not very good otherwise.

JOSEPH ESHERICK

How well did I do in school? Not very well. I got A's and B's. I was always too much off to the side. The grading system was "mention," "second medal," "first medal," or something like that. I never got any higher than a mention. Was I seen as a star student? By some people, yes, and by others, no.

What helped me most in getting through design school were the people who made me think. These usually weren't the design instructors. They were people who had a broader view of things than just architectural design.

I think I got more of a design education through a job I had doing anatomical drawings of cadavers than I did as a student in architectural school. But it's probably correct to say that I wouldn't have learned anything in the gross anatomy lab if I hadn't had my design education, that is, if I hadn't been thinking about design-related issues in the lab.

Some argue that the jury is a Rite of Passage. My argument has always been that it should not be anything like that. For a long time I have argued that it is in the jury that adversarial roles are developed between the designer and his client. These adversarial roles are built up by the jury member attacking the project, forcing the student into a position of defense. None of that is real and the original

---

Joseph Esherick (Figure 13-9) received his Bachelor of Architecture degree from the University of Pennsylvania in 1937. He is currently principal and chairman of the board of Esherick Homsey Dodge & Davis of San Francisco. Mr. Esherick received the prestigious 1989 Gold Medal of the American Institute of Architects (AIA) and the 1982 AIA/Association of Collegiate Schools of Architecture (ACSA) Medal of Excellence in Architecture. In 1981 the San Francisco Arts Commission selected him for its Award of Honor for contributions to the Architecture of San Francisco. An architect and educator, Mr. Esherick taught at the University of California, Berkeley, for over 30 years, where he served as chairman of the Department of Architecture and acting dean of the College of Environmental Design. He has served on National Architectural Accrediting Board visits to numerous universities. In 1986-1987 he was awarded the prestigious Plym Distinguished Professorship in Architecture from the School of Architecture at the University of Illinois at Urbana-Champaign. His firm has received over 40 awards, including such honors as the 1986 Architectural Firm of the Year award from the AIA; the 1980 Architectural Firm of the Year Award from the California Council of the American Institute of Architects (CCAIA), a CCAIA Honor Award for Excellence in Design for the Monterey Bay Aquarium on Cannery Row in Monterey, California; an AIA Honor Award for the Cannery in San Francisco and for Adlai E. Stevenson College at the University of California, Santa Cruz; and an Award of Merit from the AIA Northern California Chapter for Wurster Hall on the University of California, Berkeley campus.

Figure 13-9 Joseph Esherick, FAIA.

intent of learning gets lost. Scrimmages and battles and football games may be won by such things, but not an education. I was going to say that nothing's learned from a battle, but that isn't true. What's mainly learned from a battle is how to fight a better battle—I would hope architectural education was more than that.

The focus of design juries is really on the end product. It has nothing to do with how students got to that end product or where they go next.... As a student, you really ought not be concerned about what you just did, except in a critical light, but instead about what you ought to do next.

I never sat in on a jury until I started to teach... if you could call it that... at Berkeley.

It wouldn't surprise me if the move towards open juries was started by Gropius. That's just pure speculation. There was a lot of turmoil in the late 1940s. The Beaux Arts Institute of Design had more or less collapsed and as a result of the GI bill, there were tremendous influxes of students at that time.

Learning how to design takes time and long hours. If your objective is to be a weight lifter, you're not going to get there by lifting weights 20 minutes a day or thinking good thoughts or reading a book on weight lifting. You've got to do it! It's hard work. I don't think there's anything wrong with the notion of long hours.

One objective of design education should be to acquire and develop certain skills to a point that they are beneath your level of consciousness. It's just like any sport. For example, there are many technical issues in sailing; if you're the helmsman, how you direct the sails, how you deal with the wind and the tides, and if you're racing against somebody, there are other tactical issues. If your attention is focused only on the process of steering or sail trimming, then you don't have time to do the other things that are important. The mastery of all these skills is what's important.

If you're designing some absolutely inert object, then you don't have to worry about people. But in architecture, what you're designing is always related to people and their perceptions.

I don't like some professional design juries at all because I think they are done injudiciously. I served on a national jury where we had over 500 entries. The first cut was made after about six hours of deliberation, and some jurors made the cut even sooner than that. That's almost impossible to do.

What's the function of professional awards programs and their juries? They are supposed to bring the meritorious works of designers to the attention of the wider public. What good do they do? They're not really "awards" but rather "rewards" for what you've already done. It seems to me that they would be more valuable if they were a learning mechanism so that we could all learn from what has actually been done.

In professional awards entries, I believe that clarity of intentions, simplicity, and reliability are terribly important. Jurors need to be serious and committed and willing to spend their time. Those administering jurors must discipline the jurors: see to it that they do their homework and that they have a decent foundation for their decisions.

Design competitions in practice are often like telling a joke. The idea of a joke is to set up a scene where everyone can't quite be sure what the outcome will be. Usually the whole purpose is to make the outcome something entirely different, something totally unexpected. I think that with modern design competitions, the objective is to produce the unexpected. I'm all for innovation, but not for innovation at all costs.

RODNEY F. FRIEDMAN

I was in the top of my class in design. I shared that honor with a couple of others. My projects always received praise.

Did other students and professors see me as a "star" student? Yes, most of them did. But there were usually about three stars in the class, and there was very strong competition among us three.

> *Rodney F. Friedman (Figure 13-10) attended the University of California, Berkeley, where he earned his Bachelor of Architecture degree with Honors in 1956. In 1964 he formed the firm Fisher-Friedman Associates based in San Francisco. He served as a visiting professor at the University of California, Berkeley, and has been a visiting critic and lecturer at numerous schools including Berkeley, Stanford, Yale, Harvard, the University of Texas, the University of Southern California, and Massachusetts Institute of Technology. The firm has earned over 160 design awards from the American Institute of Architects (AIA), AIA/House and Home magazine, Federal Housing Administration, U.S. Department of Housing and Urban Development, Architectural Record, Masonry Institute, AIA/Sunset magazine, American Builder magazine, Professional Builder magazine, Gold Nugget, American Plywood Association, American Wood Council Design, Builder's Choice, AIA/Housing magazine, Urban Land Institute, and others. The firm's work includes apartments, combination townhouse/flats, custom homes, duplexes, elderly housing, podiums, single-family detached homes, townhouses, office buildings, retail/commercial shopping centers, restaurants, private clubs and recreational facilities, mixed-use developments, rehabilitation/adaptive reuse, urban planning, office space planning, and interior design and furnishing. Among their more noteworthy projects are Promontory Point Apartments and Recreation Center in Newport Beach, California; Peter Coutts Hill Faculty Housing at Stanford University; Golden Gateway Commons townhouses office and retail, San Francisco; Concord Civic Plaza, Concord, California; Vintage Club, Indian Wells, California; Pleasant Hill City Hall with Charles Moore, Pleasant Hill, California; and master planning for BC Place, Vancouver, British Columbia.*

What did I think of the evaluation process as a student? I liked it. I thought it was fun.

[Getting] a bad review in the jury process is better than not having a review at all. I had some bad reviews in school, but I got terrific grades because [I learned from] the professors. Sometimes with a jury it's very easy to create antagonism. [If a student takes the offensive] jurors are going to find everything wrong.

Familiarizing the jury with a project is the responsibility of the professor. [They should] take the time with the jury and let them know what the issues are and read the program to them. If they don't do it, and if they're lazy, then it's a waste of time. The first three projects that are being reviewed are easily victims of the juror not knowing what's going on.

Some of the really best design students, I think, are now unsung people that have never been heard from and really never get a chance to do good work. Some of them were probably the top students in my class. You never hear from them. They never came forward in the profession.

Design alone isn't enough. So students must go to the "super school." "Super architects," like a Superman, should know more about the construction than the engineers. They should know more about the mechanical systems than the mechanical engineer. They should know more about the finances than the financiers. They should know more about the business than the business people. In addition to all that they've got to be able to communicate, and their design should be the most brilliant designers in the world. Architects should be like a "Renaissance Man."

We've never lost a design competition.

Luck is important in a successful architecture career. One of my friends told me, "I was very lucky. I won one design competition because the secretary at the jury liked my scheme the best. In the exhibit room, the staff took his model and put it in the middle of the room under the

Figure 13-10 Rodney F. Friedman, FAIA.

brightest lights. Everybody else's proposal was somewhat in the dark. As soon as I saw where my project was in the exhibit, I knew I was going to win."

I hate professional design competitions. The bad thing about design competitions is that you're never able to interact with clients. And if you really get sophisticated about it and you know who the jurors are in advance, you can actually tailor a scheme based on your knowledge of the kind of work the jurors may do. You can be pretty cynical about it.

Many design firms have a list of phone numbers of students or employees in other offices [and they will] get them to work on design competitions. If you work on a competition and you don't work for that firm, they often just reimburse gas money. You work for free. So you go through [design school] and then you're victimized by your own profession! You buy into this [myth] that architects do not get paid for their work. Work for free; therefore your work is worthless.

I enjoy design awards juries. They are a way of providing recognition inside the profession for projects that have already been built.

The whole idea of an ungratifying profession and minimum compensation is at the root of the [problem]. When you go to engineering school or law school you're told not to work for free. If you place a value on your services, why would you do such a thing? A painter may work for free, but it's often for recreation. But it's hard to do architecture for recreation. You can knit for free. But at least when you knit a sweater you've got a sweater.

The reason that I'm against design competitions is that the people who sponsor them really are taking the easy way out. They won't get out and do the research to find out what these architects have done. They're very reluctant to make decisions, so they figure, "Bring me your structures and I'll just pick." It's like this great big party that they're hosting but there's no prize. Everybody doesn't get to share. I'd like to stop that. It seems to me that there should be an interview process and the jury should have to go out into the community and visit the office of half a dozen architects and then pay them what it costs to enter the competition.

Jurors need to visit the firms to see whether they indeed have the capacity to do the work, and to make sure that they aren't just smuggling in six or seven students and having them build models feverishly late at night. That's terrific for the sponsor, but not fair for the people doing the work.

MICHAEL GRAVES

As an undergraduate architect major at the University of Cincinnati, I did very well. At Harvard as a graduate student in architecture, I did well during some academic terms and very poorly during others. My doing well or poorly depended greatly on who was the design critic. It really had to do with what I was trying to do and what the critics were trying to do. With some critics, my ideas worked well, but with others they were disasterous.

I guess in undergraduate school other students and professors did see me as a good student.

The issue of juries is important to me, because I had a devastating jury while a graduate student at Harvard. In fact, it's still talked about today—and that was over 30 years ago! Some of us had not wanted to do what was prescribed for our design studio, or, as we called the exercise; "to mix concrete for the rest of the term." I'd already had a lot of building experience during summers

Figure 13-11 Michael Graves, FAIA. (Photo: William Taylor)

as an undergraduate and I really didn't want to spend my graduate time doing this "hands-on" exercise. So the faculty gave a few of us another project to do. But what we didn't know at the time was that this was going to create a very political scene. In fact, we "got dumped on" for having rocked the boat. We certainly did rock the boat. The jury for that project was clearly an awful, awful experience. It was hideous. Fortunately, I was saved by another faculty member, but if it hadn't been for him, I would have probably been a goner.

My students might not agree but, quite frankly, I don't think that the kind of devastation I experienced as a student on that one jury really occurs in universities today, at least ones in which I participate.

Juries are really teaching mechanisms. I always say to my students that we as faculty members are as much on line as they are. The onus is as much on our heads as it is on theirs. We need to have something to say that students can work with relative to their own schemes, especially well before the end of the term. That is really the more important time for reviews.

What helped me the most in getting through design school? I suppose coffee. I didn't mind working hard—and it helped me. In design school, you can't finesse it, but there are always students who try. I, like so many other students, worked extraordinarily hard. I also felt that while my time on any one project was limited, there was always another way to skin the cat, and I tried and tried all kinds of ways to investigate my design projects. That experimentation was very worthwhile for me later on, because as a result, I have continued to see the larger possibilities in every project I've been given to do.

In my beginning years as a faculty member at Princeton, what helped me the most was inviting other academics to

> *Michael Graves (Figure 13-11) received his Bachelor of Science in Architecture in 1958 from the University of Cincinnati. In 1959 he earned his Master of Architecture degree at Harvard University. From 1960 to 1962 he was a fellow at the American Academy in Rome. Since 1964 he has been the president and principal architect of Michael Graves, Architect, in Princeton, New Jersey. He has designed over 100 architectural projects including office buildings, housing, theaters, museums, institutional buildings, retail and other cultural facilities. Mr. Graves has designed the interiors of many of his buildings as well as an extensive collection of furniture and artifacts.*
>
> *Both an architect and educator, he has served on the faculty at Princeton University since 1962, where he is currently the Schirmer Professor of Architecture. He has been a visiting professor and guest juror at numerous schools and has written numerous books, including* Michael Graves: Buildings and Projects 1982-1989; Michael Graves: Buildings and Projects 1966-1981; *and* Michael Graves. *He has also been the subject of a book by Charles Jencks,* Kings of Infinite Space: Michael Graves and Frank Lloyd Wright. *Among the numerous awards to his credit are several American Institute of Architects (AIA) National Honor Awards, New Jersey Society of Architects Awards,* Interiors *magazine awards,* Progressive Architecture *Design Awards and Furniture Design Awards,* Metropolitan Home Magazine *Design 100, and* International Design *awards. Mr. Graves is the 1980 recipient of the Arnold W. Brunner Memorial Prize in Architecture from the American Academy and Institute of Arts and Letters.*
>
> *Among Mr. Graves's landmark projects are the Portland Building in Portland, Oregon; San Juan Capistrano Library in San Juan Capistrano, California; the Humana Building in Louisville, Kentucky; Riverbend Music Center, Cincinnati, Ohio; Michael C. Carlos Hall at Emory University in Atlanta, Georgia; Walt Disney World Swan and Dolphin Hotels, Lake Buena Vista, Florida; the Newark Museum in Newark, New Jersey; and the Aventine, a major hotel and office complex in La Jolla, California.*

serve as visiting critics, people such as Colin Rowe. Listening, working, and teaching with Colin for the first time was truly an educational awakening for me. Although I was now a faculty member, it didn't really matter. Quite frankly, it made me feel as if I had missed a lot as a student. His teaching was like night and day from what I had experienced as a student at Harvard. I decided to promote a level of inquiry that would keep me alive in teaching as well as in practice, and keep my students interested as well.

In selecting a particular school, it is important for prospective graduate students to study the mixture of personalities of their future design faculty as well as the institution as a whole, so that they understand what they're getting into. I never mind at all when students want to transfer to Princeton or, for that matter, transfer out of Princeton because they, or we, have made a mistake. It's better that they get whatever they are really looking for—wherever that is. We've had students who've taken their thesis at Princeton while enrolled elsewhere, or who used one of us for their advisers while going to another university, simply because they would like to broaden their experience.

The design juries at the University of Cincinnati where I was an undergraduate were private, but at Harvard where I was a graduate student, they were public. It was just a difference between the two institutions.

When I came to teach at Princeton in 1962, juries involved public presentations by the students, but no debate. They simply presented their projects and went home. Within a year I helped change that so that juries turned into a public forum.

I believe that juries changed from closed to open because students required it. As soon as somebody reported back to their own school that, say Harvard or Yale held an open jury, they probably asked for the same format to occur at their own institution. And little by little as people were trained at schools like Harvard and Yale and then went on to teach at another institution, which might have had a closed jury system, they would start to use open juries in their own design classes. This pattern then spread throughout their schools, I imagine. I think faculty found great benefits in the open jury system. And once one faculty member started using them, it tended to show up the laziness of the rest of the faculty who relied on the closed system. In fact, closed juries were really maintaining an "old boy system," but that is not what the university is all about. The university is about inquiry and open debate and open juries began to offer that.

When I was an undergraduate at the University of Cincinnati, I applied to four or five different graduate schools and I went to each of them to listen to their juries. I called them in advance to find out their jury schedule and then I just went from one to the other. Since the juries were all at the end of term it was rather easy. I visited Columbia, Yale, and Harvard, all of which had open juries at the time (1958). I think the only jury I missed was at MIT because the timing didn't work out.

I sat in the audience and listened to juries because I thought they were a pretty good barometer for what the school would be like. Whether or not those particular critics would be on the faculty was not the point. Instead, what mattered to me was the kind of people they would invite, the kind of discussion they would initiate, how open it was, and so on. I remember that I was very, very encouraged by a jury that Paul Rudolph had organized at Yale where he had invited some extraordinary people in the profession to serve as critics: Eero Saarinen, Philip Johnson, and others. I felt that that experience was terribly enlightening and encouraging for me.

I believe that juries are essential. However, I do think that in some schools, juries are still rather archaic. I don't know how one can get that to change, but I think it's simply the nature of the school. In most cases, however, I think juries are very, very thoughtful—though difficult for some. However, I think they're more than simply a necessary evil.

Juries are an extraordinary teaching tool because not only can you debate the work, debate the student, but you can debate your colleagues on the faculty as well. And the students can, in turn, debate the faculty. That in itself is a great gift that we have in this field—when the language used by the jurors is understood. The juries that are especially difficult for students, however, are those where jurors speak a private language, where a faculty member might, in all candor, say "I like it" or "I don't, and I can't tell you why." This is not going to do anybody any good. It's really the requirement of whoever is judging students—whether they be students or faculty—to be articulate and to describe what it is about a particular project that is both positive and negative. And I don't mean to simply compliment the work. They must find ways of describing those aspects that are useful to keep and those that are not: why they are worth keeping or not. What are they doing to both the function and character of the composition? And unless you can do that, then for me, you're not really being helpful.

I believe that one way to improve juries is to attempt to break down the students' perceived trauma of the jury situation. And that's not to say that you simply hold the jury in your living room.

The public nature and exposure of juries aren't really satisfactory for some personalities. *We expect every student to adhere to the same kind of standards, but they are not right for everyone.* I know that in the past I have had some students who have been very shy or become very emotional at juries, and it's really, really difficult for them. Yet they had to go through those same routines that someone much more gregarious, much more confident, whether earned or not, can easily sustain.

I had one student who was one of the best in the school, and every time she would get up to present her work to the jury, tears would well up in her eyes. It was simply too traumatic and fearful for her. *It's not up to us as faculty to resolve that issue but it is up to us to be sensitive to it.* We need to find a way for students like that to welcome the debate on a review. It's at the same time very difficult to treat one student very differently than you might treat others. Therefore we ought to be exploring ways of making the debate more palatable to students with all types of personalities. You will never be able to make juries a great experience for everyone, but there ought to be a way to make them more relaxed, so as to make it easier for students who do have a difficult time.

What words of wisdom can I offer to design students? *Read.* I think that students probably are and always will be too interested in the present and the work of contemporary people that they admire. What I think is the biggest problem in education today, and you could say this even if you were in law or in medicine, as well as in architecture, is knowing the language. *You really have to learn to play the scales before you can innovate.* But instead, our students start by wanting to innovate without proper grounding. The American system is set up to encourage individual rather than collective language. However, we work within a discipline that has a long and glorious history and students need to be aware of its many precedents. We're simply not inventing the wheel everytime we design.

If I ask a student to describe a plan of Palladio because he or she wants to use it as a paradigm and part of a critical debate, I expect that after a period of time in the university, the student will know. They learn it in history courses, design analysis courses, and elsewhere. Too many students see this kind of knowledge as old-fashioned and inappropriate. They're more interested in today and technology and being new—but without knowing the fundamentals of the language.

When I say read, I mean look, read, examine, trace, and do whatever it takes to understand the discipline and what it has been. So indeed, if a student wants to revolutionize the discipline he or she can. More than anything else, you must know the craft, you must know the discipline, and what it has been, before you can really understand *what it can be.* This knowledge is the key to making anything new.

One of the reasons why students stay up all night is, in some cases, poor management of time. But on the other hand making an architectural composition takes a sustained period of time to, as a student would say, "just get into it": to unravel the work of the day before and to investigate what is possible in reworking a plan, reworking the character of the space, and continuing to refine whatever you're doing. It's very hard for a lot of people to understand that the design process isn't scientific. But then again, design is not so artsy that it can't be defined either. It's a fine line. Just as you can't pick up a written text on which you might be working and finish writing a sentence without rereading a lot of what you have written before, the same is true in design. It does take time to get into it.

What often happens is that, in some cases, it's so difficult to let your work captivate you to the point where you can truly concentrate. In these instances, those people who are easily distracted and mismanage time have real problems. Because it's at that point that they leave their desk and go do something else. You've got to love that project and stay with it long enough to get into it. Let it engage your thoughts thoroughly. You also have to have some successes at it or you won't like it very much. A student has to experience some success with his or her work through the encouragement of faculty, peers, and so on, to want to stick it out and do it. In fact, we don't do things that we don't like to do on a very regular basis. Instead, we avoid them. We don't like to go to the dentist; therefore we'll do anything to avoid going. If students feel like failures on a project, they won't want to work on it.

Those who administer professional design juries often try to construct a jury that's like a "Chinese menu," with one of each: a designer, a technocrat, a business person, a woman, a man, somebody tall, somebody short. The awards that are given by a group of people like this, all well meaning, generally become a compromise. Or else, a couple of strong individuals on the jury who are skillful and clever enough dominate the event. It's human nature. There's nothing wrong with this system except that you can get a very mixed, mediocre result.

Professional juries are very different from teaching juries. A teaching jury has to do with conversation and debate. It has not to do with results, not to do with selecting a winner. But a design jury for a magazine or for a building project has to deal very clearly with winning and losing. So they're really very different animals.

I think that the award of buildings through competition juries is much, much more political than people ever realize. And this is true for a variety of reasons. For instance, if an architect is young and has good ideas but hasn't built very much, and is up against an architect with lots of built work and also with good ideas, and both schemes are equally good, the jury will probably award the prize to the younger architect because he or she hasn't yet had a chance. Depending upon the nature of the competition, the jury might pair that young architect with someone who has greater experience in the technical field. And this is done with all good intentions. Nevertheless there is definitely a political dimension to it.

I'm not sure that competitions are the best way to select an architect. I really am not. The interview process involves the client selecting an architect—the person as well as the work. And the interview process works both ways: The client interviews the architect and the architect interviews the client. In the end this process is really superior to juries, simply because there is a chance for dialogue.

I certainly have had my successes in entering competitions and winning a few, and they helped enormously in my early practice. But at the same time the way juries for professional design competitions are conducted today is usury to a great extent. The amount of money lost by well-intentioned architects is frightening and immoral. It takes so much money to win because it seems the ante is increased with each successive competition.

One of the problems that occurs when you graduate as a young architect from the university, and you're out in the big world and start to work for another architect or practice architectural design yourself, is that you suddenly lose the debate that you might have had with your peers in the university setting. Together with my colleagues in the classroom and other faculty members, Peter Eisenman and I tried starting a group of young architects that would routinely get together to debate our own design work. We didn't want to lose contact with different ideas and with each other, and we still needed our colleagues to evaluate our work. I think this is essential for practicing architects—to find ways of exchanging thoughtful evaluations among colleagues. It can be very stimulating. It's really what part of the joy of designing is all about. It's too bad that doesn't happen very often.

It would be great for older designers to do that too, but for a well-known architect that happens to a certain extent in the critical press. However, presentations in magazines and newspapers are usually rather descriptive. Magazine and newspaper criticism should not be thought of as a substitute for critical conversations with your peers during the actual process of making a building.

Architecture has to do with how society at large understands the composition relative to its formal construct. It has to convey meaning by virtue of form: whether the making of a room, the making of a building, or the making of a city. Architecture is not in a sense just laid on by some more private languages of design. Instead, an architect has to convey the character of the place by virtue of the language at hand.

Unfortunately too many architects have been very anxious to turn the language on its head, therefore, we tend to see a new language every Monday morning. I don't want to do that. While nobody would call me a traditional designer working in a traditional style, I do need to rely on the traditional context—what has gone before—in order to make the next move. The local context has meaning, and the city has meaning, both positive and negative. The difficulty within our society is to find a consensus of what those meanings are. As architects we direct many actors in the play, but we tend to act individually. I believe that if we act in concert with the prevailing interest of the society, we will be able to say something significant within the context of the existing language. We are then more likely to be heard or understood. I hope that is what others are reading and seeing in my buildings.

CHARLES GWATHMEY

When I was at Yale, the studio system was based on having visiting critics and visiting jurors. Compared to my previous experience at the University of Pennsylvania, I think that was much richer and more animated, much more

> *Charles Gwathmey (Figure 13-12) attended the University of Pennsylvania and received his Master of Architecture from Yale University in 1962. He is a partner in the New York firm Gwathmey Siegal & Associates Architects, founded in 1970. Charles Gwathmey was the only architect named in* Time *magazine's "Leadership in America" issue (1974), and has since been inducted into* The Interior Design *Magazine Hall of Fame. In 1982 he received the Medal of Honor from the New York American Institute of Architects (AIA), and in 1985 he was the first recipient of the Yale Alumni Award from the School of Architecture. He has been a visiting faculty member at several universities and served on numerous design award juries. Gwathmey Siegal & Associates' work has been published widely in magazines, books, and monographs, and featured in major exhibitions. The firm's work covers institutional, corporate, corporate interiors, commercial interiors, private residences, and housing. Selected projects include the International Design Center in Queens, New York; New Town for the Disney Development Corporation in Orlando, Florida; and the Retail Concourse at Lincoln Center for the Performing Arts in New York City. The firm has received over 60 design awards, including three* Progressive Architecture *magazine Design Awards, 12 Record House Awards, and seven Record Interior Awards from* Architectural Record, *five National AIA Honor Awards, the 1982 AIA Firm Award, and the New York AIA's Medal of Honor. He is also the recipient of the Arnold W. Brunner Prize from the American Academy and Institute of Arts and Letters.*

Figure 13-12 Charles Gwathmey, FAIA.

informative and actually more fun to have architects whose work you admired come to the school and participate.

Every project, especially in school, is a measure of both your ability and your growth. You try very hard to exceed everything that you've done before, and you try to grow simultaneously and take risks. I think when that works, you learn a lot and you are recognized. If you don't risk and you get caught by your own preconceptions where you don't try to push yourself, then you don't get the maximum benefit.

Criticism forces you to reevaluate and to confront your work and yourself. On two particular occasions when my design work was judged as a student, even though I was very defensive and outraged emotionally at the criticism I was given, I realized upon reflection that what was said was accurate. The criticism made my work better.

There is generally a more pluralistic atmosphere in schools today than there used to be. I think that when I was in school there was a clear dogma or a manifesto. There was an unquestioned commitment to modernism. I'm not making a value judgment, but I think dogmas are dead ends. I don't think modernism is a dead end, but what has happened to students in the last 15 years is that there's an awful lot more information and different sets of standards. It's a more difficult environment for students right now than it was when I was in school, which makes for both a less specific focus but also a more provocative set of parameters depending on how articulate and how committed both the jury and the students are.

I think there are two kinds of teaching. One type is to teach what you believe and, in a sense, you use your students as surrogate explorers of your personal design ethic. They become, in a sense, your disciples. The other way of teaching is to be more accommodating to a student's position and try to be conscious of both expertises, always asking questions to provoke the student to further investigate and refine his or her ideas. That's the kind of teacher I am. When I'm on a jury, I tend to accept both the problem and the students' proposition and I always give criticism by questioning whether they have been loyal and committed to their set of constraints or parameters on their own terms. If I disagree with their parameters, I say so but *I say why.* I tend not to be subjective, but if I am subjective I say so. I do try to keep it on a more objective level. I think in the end that's more supportive of the students' ideas.

Participation on juries is a very good exercise and very revealing experience for practicing architects. You see what [is being taught] in schools, and you see what students are thinking about. I always think that kind of confrontation is sharpening and incisive. I would encourage more practitioners to participate in juries, if they can't teach full time.

I think that the discovery process in design is a very frustrating and uneven course, and I would advise a younger person who is less informed and naive in the best sense of the word, to maintain the energy and the commitment to discover. I say that students are naive because you learn that the creative discovery process is full of peaks and valleys and plateaus, and the more you know the more difficult it becomes. The less you know the more free-spirited and primitive you are. There's this energy and intuition which overrules, making discovery actually easier. If you understand that as a student, then I think you're ahead of the game. If you don't understand it, you're in for a very frustrating awakening.

I think that European competitions are more accurate than American competitions because basically in Europe that's the primary way that architects get work. There's a different understanding of it and there's a much more objective judging process.

What I would encourage is that when you have a competition the parameters be sincere and real. If the budget is fixed, one of the constraints in the solution is to deal directly and accurately with that constraint. If there's a time schedule, then you have to deal with it as part of the interpretation of the design solution. In other words, there needs to be a clear objective and a moral obligation to writing a program, fulfilling the program, and judging it all on the same terms. What tends to happen is that you lose sight of the objective and you get caught up in the image. It negates both the ethic of the competition and its intended purpose. I wish that the program and the designers who decide to participate and the jurying are all on the same ground.

If you try to cater your design to the jury you're losing your convictions and you tend to compromise. That's an error. You really have to maintain your convictions and design within the parameters of the problem. Once you start trying to adjust your convictions to another person's perception you're going to lose [the uniqueness of your own ideas]. Don't give up your convictions for anything.

DONALD J. HACKL

What helped me most in getting through design school was me—a dedication, a conviction that I knew I wanted to be an architect, I had the ability to be an architect, and I knew I had the desire to become an architect.... I had been raised by an immigrant family who created in me a value system, a sense of drive, a thirst for information and knowledge, a curiosity about the world in which we live, and in large measure that was reinforced by some of my educational experience.

Architecture is both an art and a science. One can deal with the scientific aspects of the practice in a clearer, much more organized, intelligible way. The creative or architectural portion of it is much more frustrating. It brings with it, even to this day, enormous elation when an appropriate solution is found and enormous depression when that solution doesn't come quickly, adequately, or to a degree which is satisfying.

One of the really difficult things about the architectural education experience has to do with the phenomenon of criticism. One learns not by the concept of positive reinforcement, but by negative criticism.... I don't know whether there is in fact a way to teach architecture or to conduct the jury process in a more positive sense—to herald those things about a solution which are good as opposed to what educators, what most jurors, what most practitioners find wrong.... This can create a permanent mindset in the student.

I believe that the primary relationship is between the student and the material taught. The educator is the facilitator, the vehicle by which that information is conveyed. We don't have a system, to my knowledge, which evaluates the educator or educates the educator to educate.... As a result I think we have, in lots of instances, very mediocre quality educators, and that really doesn't bode well for the entire profession.

As a matter of fact, there have been some juries that have been construed to literally poke fun at and abuse students. And I think that's shameful. I think those who do it should be embarrassed. This snide, critical, and negative process really disturbs me. I remember in my days that every student, however poor his or her solution was, worked desperately hard to make a solution, to make a piece of architecture, and to create an idea. Interestingly enough, I know of two instances where people in this firm have served on juries and they have walked out. They have left the jury because other participants on that jury elected to take that kind of tack.

What advice can I offer to improve juries? First is to create a system of evaluating design that prioritizes what students should be saying and helps them with their presentation. Second, the jury should act more like a client in responding to rather than intellectualizing about the solution, because rarely does that intellectualization take place in practice. Clients are dealing with real-world problems of how the architect's solution to their particular project satisfied their program. For the faculty, I strongly suggest approaching the jury process with an open mind, with less prejudice, with a willingness to not only hear but

> *Donald J. Hackl (Figure 13-13) attended the University of Illinois at Urbana-Champaign where he earned his Bachelor of Architecture degree in 1957 and his Master of Architecture in 1958. Mr. Hackl is currently president of the Chicago firm Loebl Schlossman and Hackl. He has held such positions as president of the American Institute of Architects (AIA) in 1987, first vice-president of the International Union of Architects headquartered in Paris, and numerous other positions with the AIA, its Chicago Chapter and Illinois Council, and other architectural and construction industry organizations. The award-winning firm's projects include office buildings, health care facilities, interiors, shopping centers/commercial facilities, educational/recreational, civic and government, planning projects, parking facilities, hotels, restaurants, and religious buildings. Loebl Schlossman and Hackl produced the master plan and architecture for much of Park Forest, Illinois, and regional shopping centers at Old Orchard, Oakbrook, River Oaks, Hawthorn, and Ford City in metropolitan Chicago. Other well-known Chicago projects include Water Tower Place, Two Prudential Center, City Place, various components of Michael Reese Hospital and Medical Center, West Suburban Hospital Medical Center, South Chicago Hospital, Evanston Hospital, and Alexian Brothers. Its university work includes projects at Lake Forest College, Northwestern University, the University of Illinois, Southern Illinois University, the University of Chicago, and Illinois State University. LSH has been the architect for corporate facilities for Household International, Square D, Allstate Insurance, Commerce Clearing House, and Benefit Trust Life. Mr. Hackl has served on numerous juries internationally. One of the firm's mottos by its founder, Jerold Loebl (1900-1978), is "The reasons for buildings are PEOPLE . . . there are people who provide the funds and are responsible for building. There are people who use buildings, and there are people who look at buildings."*

to listen to what the presenter is saying, and then to find techniques to reinforce first what is good about a solution, and secondly how to improve the shortcomings.

Anyone can sit around and criticize. I don't accept that from our own people in the office when they come to me with a problem. They always know that I want them to have identified one or more solutions to that problem so that they're part of making the resolution. One thing I've learned over the years is that the whole process of creation, whether it's another human being or a piece of architecture, involves stake holding and becoming a part of that process. And the more the faculty can be part of finding the solution rather than pointing out the problem, the more helpful it will be for the student, and hopefully the more rewarding for the faculty. It may also separate the great educators from the mediocre.

If you want to be an architect, don't let anyone dissuade you. We've had some very great architects, outstanding practitioners, and award-winning designers who in fact have not made it through school. Do the very best you can. Think hard and work hard, but never veer from the conviction that you can do it, and you will do it if you want to do it.

I'm on record both publicly and privately as being against juried design competitions with rare exception: when a very new and previously unexplored area of practice is undertaken, and the building type is one for which there is very little precedent. In this case a competition has some value in terms of bringing a variety of new ideas to a given subject. . . .

Architects in general have a mindset that says it is a privilege for the architect to serve a client. That's a mindset which in many ways goes back to the educational process. When was the last time your doctors or your lawyers gave you the impression that it was a privilege for them to serve your medical or legal needs, and that they would be willing and honored to do it for free? In my mind, this attitude is terribly unprofessional.

What advice can I offer to help improve juries in professional practice? For practitioners submitting competition entries, first, evaluate very carefully whether or not you should be doing this competition. Set out in your own mind a clear set of reasons why you should participate. Define those reasons. Second, make sure that the client or sponsor of the competition has invested at least enough time to prepare a reasonable program from which a reasonable solution can emerge, and that the client has a professional advisor to make sure that all entries are treated fairly and equally. And third, make sure that a competent jury of professionals decides what the best solution is. What makes one person's judgment in the aesthetic arena more valuable than someone else's? Education, experience, and training. Architecture is a serious business. Fourth, there must be some kind of reward to offset the investment of time by the practitioner—whether it's monetary, it's a commission, or it's recognition. All of those have to be evaluated on an individual basis, but I consider it an insult for a client or a sponsor to conduct a competition just for the sake of garnering to themselves the publicity associated with it.

We're going through some tumultuous times in architecture today. We're experiencing the Vatican II in the profession. All the hard and fast guidelines of prior significant architectural movements . . . have fallen by the wayside.

Figure 13-13 Donald J. Hackl, FAIA.

And so we're left to our own devices today. In one sense, I think this is creating much more exciting architecture, but in the other sense it is filled with showmanship, pastiche, clichés, and historical innuendo. Too frequently we're taking our vision of the future from the rear view mirror of our cars instead of looking directly forward into the future and seeing what it will bring.

In many quarters, architecture is becoming stage-set design and fashion, here today and gone tomorrow. Some of the luminaries, like pop rock stars, are surfacing to do a handful of buildings. They will probably disappear just as quickly from the scene as they have risen to it. Paul Gapp, the *Chicago Tribune* architecture critic, has asked the question: "Where are the people who do background buildings—those buildings which will stand the test of time and fit into their context for a generation or two?"—as opposed to those buildings which fulfill the architect's burning design for his or her building to cry out and scream on the horizon, "I'm different, look at me!" I'm afraid that history will recall these look-at-me buildings with a lot of obscene views. We're doing a lot of X-rated architecture today. I fear that too many architects are losing sight of a moral responsibility that we have to reflect the very best that our culture offers at the close of the twentieth century, not the very worst.

JOHN F. HARTRAY, JR.

Cornell, 1948-1954

How well did I do in architecture school? Not well at all in design, at least from the viewpoint of the faculty, although I learned quite a bit in terms of my own interests. What I did learn wasn't reflected in my grades. At the time I was in school the students and faculty had very different agendas. Many of the design problems were old Beaux Arts exercises that had been repeated for years. They were intended to demonstrate predetermined planning and aesthetic principles, and to culminate in lavish renderings. Most of the students used these programs to investigate other issues with which they were concerned.

When there were projects that coincided with a student's interests it was possible to get a good grade. A few cynical faculty members pointed out that I usually did best on competition projects, but it wasn't greed. The competitions were usually short problems where one could get to the point in a hurry. They were also often sponsored by construction industry organizations or materials suppliers and tended to stress technical issues in which I was interested.

School Juries

The spatial qualities of the designs were not seriously discussed, and it was assumed that materials and the means of construction had little to do with form. An exception to this was site grading. Many of the faculty had worked on the New York throughway system during the depression and were quite sensitive to the niceties of civil engineering and landforms.

I would have preferred open juries. The only time these were held was when visiting critics came to the school. The visiting critics were a valuable subversive influence. Bucky Fuller got us actually building things and Abe Geller was an inspiration and a role model. He still is.

Modernism in the Fifties

I wasn't very happy as an architecture student, largely because of the gap between the goals of the faculty and the students. Most of the students were devout modernists at that time. We were going to save humanity, by eliminating decoration and expressing structure. The faculty at Cornell didn't have a strong enough grasp of history to argue with us. Most of them had been trained in the Beaux Arts system, but they too had accepted the modernist dogma. They didn't teach us what they knew, and they couldn't teach us what we wanted to learn.

The political aspects of modernism were overly optimistic, but I still find that some of our best current

John F. Hartray, Jr., (Figure 13-14) received his Bachelor of Architecture from Cornell University in 1954. Mr. Hartray is principal at the Chicago firm Nagle, Hartray & Associates Ltd. He has served on the National Architectural Accrediting Board and on the boards of both the Chicago Chapter and the national American Institute of Architects (AIA), where he chaired the national Commission on Design in 1975. He currently teaches professional practice at both the Illinois Institute of Technology and the University of Illinois at Chicago and has served on advisory councils for the architecture schools of Princeton and Cornell. He has also served as a visiting critic and design juror at several universities. His teaching, lectures, and writings reflect a critical interest in education, licensing, design, and practice. His articles have been published widely in such places as Inland Architect, Chicago *magazine, the* AIA Journal, Architecture, Architectural Technology, *and the* Journal of Architectural Education.

He has served as a design awards juror for the American Library Association, the U.S. Corps of Engineers, the Mobile, Alabama, Government Complex, as well as for the following AIA Chapters: Ohio, Texas, St. Louis, Northeastern Illinois, Washington, D.C., Western Mountain Region, Northern California, Arizona, and Kentucky. The firm has received approximately 40 design awards, including the Distinguished Building Award from the National AIA and the Chicago Chapter AIA, AIA Housing Awards, Architectural Record *awards, Masonry Awards, and others. Its work has been featured in numerous exhibits and published widely. Projects cover theaters, office buildings, multifamily housing, corporate and commercial, institutional, and single-family housing. Selected projects include the South Campus Student Housing Complex on the Northwestern University campus; the renovation of the Corporate Headquarters and Factory of World's Finest Chocolate; and the Greyhound Bus Terminal in Chicago.*

work grows out of following problems to an unexpected conclusion just as we tried to do in school.

The Army as Continuing Education

Strangely, my architecture school experience put me in a good state of mind to enjoy the army. There was a diverse cross section of humanity. There was travel, and we got to go camping. I also had time to read some of the books that I had heard about in college. Best of all, nobody shot at me.

Serving on Juries

Now that I have graduated from student to juror I am aware of additional problems with the jury system. If you come in at the end of a problem and don't know what has transpired between the students and their studio critic, you can spend hours before you uncover the hidden agenda. You may base your evaluation on issues which were never considered to be part of the problem.

Studio designs are not really buildings. There is no client, and the program is sometimes only a point of departure for the student and the critic. The normal criteria by which we evaluate real buildings usually does not apply.

Most schools must make do with the design standards of their locality. There is little to be gained in hassling students about the fine points of urban design if their school is not in a city. There is also a secondary context of faculty interests which may have little to do with student needs.

The international style, post modernism, and more recent academic styles can be thought of as the remains of the marketing programs of young designers who had to find a way to compete with established practitioners. They did this by promoting the idea that a new historic period had mysteriously come about. There is a market economy in aesthetics which stimulates this kind of stylistic churning.

Deconstruction when applied to architecture is an expression of a critic's mid-life crisis. The students have to pay for this self-indulgence but are in no position to object.

Outside jurors ought to be involved at the beginning of the problem so that the critical criteria can be agreed on with the students and studio critics before any work is done. An interim review is also useful so that the jurors can be informed of any mid-course corrections.

I think that a jury that comes in only at the end of a project is really too late. It will be unlikely to address the same group of issues with which the student and their faculty advisers have been concerned.

Open discussions of student work in which the entire studio participates may be more useful than desk crits, because this is where the group can agree on the critical criteria for the problem. The visiting critics should draw on these sessions rather than bringing their personal criteria to the final review when it is too late for students to respond.

Drexel

I have seen group reviews at Drexel University which seemed to work very well. Drexel had no studios at the time I visited it. The students designed their projects at home and brought them in for reviews which involved an entire class and two or three critics. These discussions were very productive. Students often see design solutions more clearly than critics, and in helping each other they sometimes suggest approaches which also apply to their own work.

Licensing and Education

The profession has an institutional problem in that the state licensing boards have delegated their constitutional responsibility for public safety to schools which are not organized to accept it. Very little is said about public safety in design studios, and except for structures very little academic research is done on it. To compensate for this lack of interest the accreditation board and school administrators tend to load up the curriculum with everything an architect might ever need to know for a lifetime of practice. This leaves little time for a broad education. It also fails in terms of practice, because it's hard to learn from course work that you can't apply immediately.

The Body of Knowledge

It probably required five years for most students to master the classical orders, so there was a justification of the Beaux Arts curriculum. Modernism had much less content, only technological optimism and a lineal design method. The academic styles that have followed are merely superficial fashions. Architecture really isn't based on any specific academic discipline. You can think of it as political science with bricks.

General Education

In the right hands, a design studio can be a pretty good place to get a general education. As an arts and science program, it circumvents the fragmentation of the modern university. Architectural design brings together a number of disciplines which normally have little to say to each other. Building may not be sufficiently abstract to be academically respectable, but as a case study it covers the full spectrum of human knowledge. It also leaves students with the optimistic idea that they need not be stuck with the world as they find it. That kind of optimism is hard to find in the philosophy department.

Licensing in most states is now based on compulsory professional schooling which tries to load up young people with all the information they will need for a lifetime of practice. Any architect who ever thinks that her or his education is complete is ready for a taxidermist, but there should be a great range of choices in how one's continuing education is scheduled within a lifetime.

I've known people who took up ballet as graduate students. They tended to hit the floor a bit heavily. Early education seemed to be an advantage in dance. That is not necessarily the case with architecture. On the other hand, there is little advantage in keeping people in school until they are middle-aged and debt-ridden before they get to work on a real building.

Kids with money and good verbal skills should go to Princeton, educate themselves as poets or philosophers,

Figure 13-14 John F. Hartray, Jr., FAIA. (Photo: Bruce Van Inwegen)

There are, of course, disadvantages in working in isolation, but I'm not sure that Drexel hadn't overcome most of them. Group discussion of projects promotes the idea that there is always more than one solution to an architectural problem, and that it is not necessary, or healthy, to get one's ego mixed up with one's work. The group reviews come closer to the normal interchange with clients and engineers that occurs in practice, than to the isolated acts of artistic creation which is the romantic fiction upon which more traditional architectural education is based.

Students

I feel sorry for the young people today who want to become architects. I was almost completely out of muzzle velocity when I graduated, but the routine now is much more rigid, and the required investment of time and money is scandalous. I doubt that I could bring myself to take out student loans in order to hear lectures on deconstruction from recent graduates who have succumbed to a lust for tenure. The patience and passivity we require from students may disqualify them from dealing with the real world.

and take up architecture in their later lives. But it's not fair to require the same academic routine for youngsters from the ghetto. An early involvement in building may be their best shot at getting an education, and those kids may be the profession's best hope of remaining relevant. Architecture is an urban game, and we ought to let urban youngsters play it.

The Hidden Curriculum

Architecture schools may not be teaching what we want them to. When we give four credit hours for a design studio in which 60 hours of work per week is expected, we are teaching students to undervalue their work and accept low fees. We later lament about the level of compensation in the profession.

At present, schools are faced with a choice of either certifying to the states that their graduates have attained a minimum level of technical competence, or fulfilling an obligation to the university to push back the frontiers of knowledge. These are not compatible objectives. Code compliance is not a proper subject for higher education. We don't teach driver's ed in graduate school. On the other hand there is very little in the architectural application of nihilist literary theories which will lead to a safer environment.

Many of the recent organizational difficulties of the profession reflect, and are probably derived from, the institutional problems of the universities.

The fragmentation of the various design professions grows out of the academic departmental structure which grant their degrees. Engineering and architecture are inseparable in designing actual buildings, but have little to do with each other in most universities.

A current concern of the AIA and state licensing boards has to do with the professional registration of interior designers, yet the only significant difference between architecture and interior design is the name on the degree.

We look back with great admiration to the integrated design of earlier times, when the furniture, landscape, structure, plan, and space formed a seamless whole. The great hotels and public buildings of the nineteenth century are examples of this unity, as are the Olmstead Parks, the Westchester County Highways, and structures like the Michigan Avenue Bridge in Chicago.

By comparison the environment we are now building is the accidental result of isolated economic, legal, engineering, and design activities. I believe that the chaos of suburban sprawl is an outgrowth and reflection of the isolation of the various disciplines within the modern university. I am not sure that the university is a healthy environment in which to study architecture. At the very least we should encourage the development of alternatives.

Design Awards

The AIA has usually assumed that awards programs were a means of stimulating interest in architecture and promoting the idea of its importance. City and regional awards programs may do that, but as in school, it helps if the jury has some background information about the local culture. Jurors from outside the community always run the risk of detaching projects from their context. Local advisers should inform an awards jury about community values and concerns to prevent giving aesthetic prizes to projects which are locally perceived as environmentally rapacious.

It is also unproductive to apply the latest academic design standards to the work of local practitioners who are happily unaware of the last month's cultural advances. I have heard of elite juries which refused to give any awards in local programs. These are the same people who, as studio critics, impose their personal agenda on students.

Architecture is always regional, and so national awards programs are usually detached from the mainstream of practice. They are usually judged on the basis of the current fashions in the academic and media world. These become more irrelevant as one gets farther from New York.

These awards have nothing to offer architects who are secure about their work, but they probably mislead those who are less experienced. They also contribute to an aesthetic class system within the profession which divides design mavins from the peons who are supposed to handle the technical problems. This division results in superficial design and cynical detailing. It will ultimately be more destructive to the profession than an adversary distinction between management and labor.

Competitions

After the Chicago Public Library Competition was over, and the five competing teams had explained their respective schemes to the various users and community groups, and had listened to their reactions, the competitors probably all had a pretty good idea of what they should have designed. The rules of the competition game, however, did not permit them to revise their proposals in accordance with what they had learned.

The library competition generated a good deal of interest. People looked at the various schemes and had to think about how the site and building would work. Also, from what I've read, the jury deliberations were very thorough and fair.

The selection, however, was really decided by the values which the members of the jury brought with them. If spanning over the elevated tracks was considered impractical, a large outdoor plaza was perceived as a maintenance problem, and a recall of the libraries of the nineteenth century was felt to be symbolically appropriate, these preconceptions should have been stated in the program. They are the kind of issues which an architect and client normally discuss and agree upon during the design process.

In the competition format there is no such dialogue, and so we have to hope that at least one of the competitors will guess right on all of the variables. This is statistically unlikely.

STEVEN IZENOUR

I didn't do very well during my first two years of architecture school. I came out of the high-pressure intellectual environment at Swarthmore College. It was the antithesis of a design education. There wasn't even a studio class. By the time I hit architecture school I'd had a lot of art history background. I could write and argue well, but I couldn't do anything with my hands. I had very little practical architectural background. I was thrown in with students who had come out of fairly sophisticated undergraduate architecture programs who were years ahead of me. In fact I just barely got into grad school. I came in through the back door, and had to do a lot of remedial basic design.

My best educational experience was with Bob Venturi and Denise Scott Brown. I never had Bob as a design critic in school. I was afraid of him as a student because he was the most intellectual, tough critic in the school. I found him very scary as a design critic because his theories were so audacious and not appreciated by many of the students and critics in the school, and I felt like I was still just learning my ABCs—the basics of design. What I did was I became his TA in his course and showed all his slides for him and worked for him on the side in the slide library. I felt I could cope with him intellectually but I couldn't cope with him as a design student because I was too naive and inexperienced. I'd come out of a background similar to the kind of education Bob had before he went into architecture. So on that level, working with him was my best experience in school. Later at Yale I dealt with him on

Figure 13-15 Steven Izenour, AIA.

Steven Izenour (Figure 13-15) received a Bachelor of Arts degree in 1962 from Swarthmore College. In 1965 he earned his Bachelor of Architecture degree from the University of Pennsylvania and in 1969 he completed his Master of Environmental Design at Yale University. He is currently senior associate with the Philadelphia firm of Venturi, Scott Brown and Associates. Among his awards are a Fulbright Fellowship; an American Institute of Architects (AIA) National Honor Award for the design of a house on Long Island Sound; the Silver Medal from the Pennsylvania Society of Architects and from the AIA Philadelphia Chapter. The firm, Venturi, Scott Brown and Associates, has received such honors as the AIA Twenty-five Year Award, Merit Award for Urban Design Excellence, AIA Honor Award, AIA Firm Award, Progressive Architecture *Design awards and Record House awards from* Architectural Record.

Mr. Izenour currently serves on the faculty at the University of Pennsylvania and has been a visiting critic and lecturer at a wide variety of colleges and universities. An accomplished writer, Izenour is perhaps best known in academic circles for his book, Learning from Las Vegas, *coauthored with Robert Venturi and Denise Scott Brown. The firm has been featured in over 60 exhibits in the United States and abroad and has received over 80 awards and special recognitions. Its work includes architecture and interior design, planning, urban design, landscape design, exhibition and graphic design, and furniture and decorative arts design. Projects for which Mr. Izenour has had prime design responsibility include the Philadelphia Children's Zoo; Exhibit of the Design for the Sainsbury Wing, The National Gallery, London; Lighting the Benjamin Franklin Bridge, and the Philadelphia Orchestra Hall.*

a design level when I felt capable of coping with his kind of criticism.

When you have to learn the rudimentary skills at the adult age of 22, you feel like, "Well, this is demeaning. I'm a college graduate. What am I doing playing with clay for?"

I didn't revolt. I was too oppressed and felt too insecure to revolt about my design education. Five years after school I totally disagreed with and hated everything I'd done as a design student. That's probably healthy. In fact, it now gives me great pain to look at my design thesis.

It seems to me that design education is at its best when it's more hands-on. I didn't crack a book for three years because I didn't have the energy. In a sense I forgot how to read. I needed to refocus my energies and get from being in first grade to college. Five years after I was out of school I'd begun to read again and reintegrate my intellectual education with my hand and eye practice.

I've taught at Penn [the University of Pennsylvania] for years, and I find there's a group of students that I look for who don't hit their stride until the end of their studies. School is very hard for them, and they keep plugging, and in the end they end up being some of the best students. The students who get patted on the back in first-year design flounder later on. They never take a chance after that because they learn what works and what doesn't. They figure out the path of least resistance. The students that get the A's too soon sometimes stop trying. Very often the work they do in their last year isn't any better than the work they did in their first year. The late bloomers just have to push themselves harder because it is harder for them. They're struggling. I was certainly in the late bloomer category. I didn't get my first commend in school until I was in third year, and then I did very well. But I came totally out of nowhere as far as students and critics were concerned. I certainly wasn't considered a star.

As a teacher, I always try to remind myself that in the end it's the student's project, not mine, and I should help them do what they want to do, irrespective of whether that's exactly what I would do.

I can't say [enough] for [perseverance] in design school. Architecture is a marathon game. Brilliance doesn't get you too far. It's perseverance that makes the difference, which is comforting in a way. I always tell students, "Look, I don't care how good you are, you just have to keep pushing at it 12 hours a day every day and trying to do it better over and over again." Being willing to get knocked down and get up again and being able to withstand harsh criticism is what you need to get the most out of architecture and design school.

The hard thing for a new design student is getting something concrete on paper the first time because you don't have concrete images to put there. You've got words, you've got ideas, but you don't have things that are concrete three-dimensional. The best critics I've had were the ones that weren't afraid to pick up a pencil and draw over what I was doing. That was most valuable because ten minutes of sketching was worth two hours of somebody talking at you. I teach at Penn now, and there are so many more full-time academicians that come out of an academic tradition, not an architectural tradition. They teach architecture, but they talk to the students endlessly, when in five minutes you could draw something for them and it would make your point. In the end the students would get more out of that little doodle than they would out of two hours of talk at them.

Juries didn't bother me as a student because getting up in front of people has never bothered me. It obviously was terrible for some people. I think it's a question of whether or not the criticism comes out of kindness. Teachers ought to spend more effort trying to perceive students as people rather than just design students.

I don't think there's a better system than design juries to evaluate student work. Juries are best for students when there is disagreement amongst the jurors. If one juror hates a project and the other juror loves it, that's more revealing to a student than everybody hating it or everybody loving it. Variety and disagreement and a certain amount of contention amongst the jurors protects the students and it makes it a more educational experience, provided they don't take it too personally.

To improve juries I would suggest that a little bit of humor and kindness go a long way. And disagreement within reason is always healthy. It lets the students know that there isn't only one way of thinking about things.

My advice to students is to not give up. Keep on trucking. It really is an old-person's game in a lot of ways. Look at Bob [Venturi]. He's in his mid-60s and only in the last five years has he gotten any major commissions. It's a game of persistence because you don't stop learning about design. That's the really fascinating aspect [of the profession].

The way we educate people in this country is so one-dimensional and slanted towards book knowledge and not towards experiential and hand knowledge. I think that as we try to make design school more like law school or med school and "raise the intellectual content of architecture," in the process very often we lose the essential idea that design is a very basic physical thing that you do with your hands and your eyes, and it has almost zero intellectual content on that level. You can't talk yourself into a good design. You've got to feel it.

Clients who use design competitions don't understand that by picking the jury you're in effect picking the architect. You've given away the most crucial choice you have to make: What person do I relate to the best and who is going to do the best for me? You've given that choice away to a bunch of people you don't know and who don't know you.

Juries are a sorry way to get ahead in life, but I guess they aren't going to go away. And it certainly has its value in terms of giving the young practitioner that chance to be recognized. I have all the respect in the world for that, so I certainly wouldn't want to eliminate them. But certainly this kind of boutique jury routine, if you could call it that, seems to me to be a terrible thing for architects, architecture, and clients. I just don't see what the up side of it is. And I wish that would go away.

E. FAY JONES

Design was certainly my strongest subject in school. I didn't ever have a design course that I didn't make an A in. But that wasn't true of my other courses. Was I seen as a star student? Probably. I was in a relatively small group—there were only five in our graduating class. I was probably viewed as one who had some talent in design.

I was on the ground floor of a new school that was being started at the University of Arkansas. Of course we had several young instructors here. John Williams came here from Oklahoma A&M to start the new program. Along the way a couple of young fellows who graduated from Yale and Rice came in. They were very wonderful individuals who were enthusiastic about the building of a new school. It was very much an atmosphere that promoted creativity and imagination, one that I feel was very nurturing.

As a student, I accepted juries and really found no fault with them. I can't remember questioning them as a teaching method.

I'd always wanted to be an architect but since they didn't have a school of architecture here in Arkansas prior to World War II, I took civil engineering because it seemed like something fairly close to architecture. The basic background of math and science and technology I felt was a necessary ingredient. Later, after the war, when I enrolled in the new architecture program it was a much more exciting and exhilarating time for me. I felt architecture had a great deal more freedom to it. I felt I was in a field that was exactly what I wanted to do and that I was headed in the right direction.

I somehow feel that the jury system has been a tried and true method over the years. It would be difficult for me to come up with anything that I think is a better method than that. I think this is such a long established method that it's hard for me to offer any advice to help improve it. As a general method in education, I think it's very good. I hope that it will continue. I think it's very likely to.

One key ingredient is for students to have a strong interest in and enthusiasm for what they're doing and to try

---

E. Fay Jones (Figure 13-16) received his Bachelor of Architecture in 1950 from the University of Arkansas. In 1951 he completed his Master of Architecture degree at Rice University, and in 1953 he served an apprenticeship under Frank Lloyd Wright. His Fayetteville, Arkansas-based firm, E. Fay Jones & Maurice Jennings, has received 20 national design awards from the American Institute of Architects (AIA), the Building Stone Institute, the American Wood Council, and elsewhere. In 1990 he received the prestigious Gold Medal Award from the American Institute of Architects. The AIA Honor Award, Tau Sigma Delta Gold Medal, and the Tucker Architectural Award for Design Excellence are among his other awards. In 1985 the Association of Collegiate Schools of Architecture (ACSA) awarded Mr. Jones the title of ACSA Distinguished Professor.

He has taught at the University of Oklahoma and at the University of Arkansas, where he served as both chair and dean of the School of Architecture. He has been a visiting critic and lecturer at numerous colleges and universities. His work has been featured in publications in the United States and abroad. Mr. Jones has designed 200 houses in over 37 years. Among his best-known works are the Thorncrown Chapel in Eureka Springs, Arkansas, and Pinecote, a gathering spot surrounded by nature, in Picayune, Mississippi.

Figure 13-16 E. Fay Jones, FAIA.

to explore different avenues. Be very open and receptive in school to new ideas and approaches, to design literature, and to design professors. Work hard at acquiring as much knowledge and skill as possible in school, a place where there's usually a great deal of freedom to explore.

Those administering juries need to make it as easy as possible for the jurors to review work with a minimum amount of effort.

In professional competitions, some of the entrants are submitting binders with photographs and graphic materials. Some use slide submissions. And I must say there are merits to both ways of doing it. I would not want to try to freeze the process on one type of presentation. What's more important is that everybody's submitting under the same rules.

Try to really make a good presentation with good photographs and try to concentrate on the things that are characteristic and that really show the strength of the project. You're more likely to hold the jury's attention and have it examined more carefully if you do have that initial impact. And the initial attraction has to do with good, clear presentation material.

Professional juries are certainly a very worthwhile enterprise, and they do a lot of good for architecture in the eyes of the public when projects are recognized and published.

RONETTE J. KING

Ronette J. King (Figure 13-17) received a Bachelor of Fine Arts degree in Interior Architecture from Pratt Institute. She has been vice-president of the San Francisco office of Gensler & Associates Architects since 1984. Ms. King is design director of the office and a leading member of the firm's design steering committee. Her work includes corporate and regional headquarters for Fortune 500 companies throughout the country, law firms as well as retail, and special projects. She has produced designs for Price Waterhouse, O'Melveny and Myers, Bear Stearns, Office Pavilion, and others. Since her arrival at Gensler & Associates in 1980, she has helped the firm win a number of national awards from the Institute of Business Designers, the American Society of Interior Designers, the Architectural Woodwork Institute, and other organizations. Ms. King has also been actively involved with the Gensler Art Series and the Gensler Lecture Series. She has taught in the Gensler Lecture Series at the California College of Arts and Crafts in Oakland. Her design work has been recognized in Architectural Record, Modern Office Technology, Interiors, *and other publications.*

I was not a great student, in fact I was a C student until my last year in design. I was an A student in the fine arts, a B student in liberal arts, but in design I was a C student. But in rendering I was an A student.... Some students saw me as a star. In fact, a lot of people say to me now, "You were so talented in school." But I wasn't talented at the things that I thought were important.

When I was in school, I had a teacher who was a Bauhaus student. She was extremely tough, and everyone in school knew it. She assigned a project once to design a boudoir for an aging film star, and after a half hour of working on the project, she failed us all because we actually did the project. Her point was that if you were a serious designer, you shouldn't accept that kind of commission. I remember that incident to this day because it made me realize that I had to think morally about the work that I would do for the rest of my career.

The same instructor also said in class once, in front of everyone, that I would never be a good designer because I knew how to draw and I would always use that as a crutch. I was so devastated by her comment. I remember thinking, "Oh my God, she's absolutely right. This is terrible. What

Figure 13-17 Ronette J. King.

am I going to do? I'll never become a good designer!" I was so convinced by what she said.

A different teacher later recognized the fact that I had grasped basic ideas of concept planning. He encouraged me by giving me a good grade, and telling me that I did a good job. It was wonderful. I can remember that day so clearly. My attitude about my skills did a 180-degree turn. He neutralized my previous teacher's negativity.

When you're a student, you understand only part of the language of design, and you do well in that part of the language that you understand. But there is a whole language that hasn't opened up to you yet. So if all you know is the alphabet, and you don't know how to put words together, you still haven't mastered the language. But someday when you do learn how to put words together, you may be writing novels!

My advice for anyone teaching a studio class is that you don't revamp a student's concept. If you do, you undermine that student's basic thought process. Instead, try to push the edges of the student's concept and have them evaluate it and build upon it.

Our business is very subjective, whether we like to admit it or not. Any art form is extremely subjective. One concept can be just as valid as another. I think that teachers tend to invalidate students' basic premises based on their own limited perspectives. The students' concepts may be completely valid, but they may be ones that teachers just haven't dealt with. I think that invalidating students' concepts can do much harm to a student's self-esteem.

A teacher should motivate students by first acknowledging that they have smart ideas. This is good for their self-esteem, and it motivates them into progressing with more ideas. It's positive reinforcement.

If you impose your own ideas onto the basic parameters of someone else's thinking process, you're not really doing them any good. Instead, you're trying to make little copies of yourself. This is to the detriment of their creativity.

The jury system is very useful. My only recommendation is that it be done more frequently and that it not be reserved for final critiques. Students would learn to become very good salespeople if they got up and formally presented their projects to their colleagues more frequently.... If students were to stand up in front of their classmates and talk about their work for even 15 minutes once a month, by the end of the semester they'd be very good at verbal presentation. They would be forced to learn how to reduce the information succinctly and convey their design ideas quickly and effectively. They could learn how to be entertaining and interesting and learn how to project their voices — and they would gain self-confidence. And when they present their work for an interview, they would have already had lots of practice. That can make a very big difference.

Design instructors are a little bit like Moms and Dads. Studio is like a family structure. After you've been with your family for a long time, you tend to tune them out a bit. But when you have strangers in, you perk up and pay more attention. That's why I believe that visiting critics from the profession can be very helpful.

My advice to students is that they have to become more inquisitive. They must broaden their sense of what design is, and they must become more international in their understanding. If you want to copy someone else's design, go ahead and copy. Just make sure that it's a good design that you're copying. You will learn a lot from that design and you can change it and adapt it to your personal style later on. Study somebody to death that really appeals to you.

I'm a firm believer that all creative people have to broaden their mediums and take the time to delve into other creative artists' work.... Landscape designers can learn from photographers, dancers from musicians, sculptors from painters.... Whether you do it consciously or not, it will affect your design work. In the process, you'll probably develop very strong personal philosophies about why you design the way you do.

In some student design competitions that I've been involved with, students are not a part of the jury's review. The jury talks about the designs after the students have left. That's too bad because students really need to hear the juror's comments. That's how you grow from the experience.

We started a program in our office some time ago and we called it a "design review." It's not unlike the critique sessions in design school. Its purpose is to offer assistance to a project in progress. One designer from a design team presents a project, and he or she and the rest of the team hears comments from other staff members. Altogether anywhere between six and a dozen people participate. The process is long or short depending upon the type of project. The range of projects in our office is so wide—from a 2000-square-foot space to a million-square-foot space. Some of the more difficult projects will come back several times, but everyone benefits from it. The project designer does not have to take the suggestions verbatim. It's up to them to take the suggestions or not. Unfortunately what happened was that people became very defensive and uncomfortable and the sessions became too formal. But by changing the name from "review" to "workshop," the attitudes of the designers as well as the participants changed. The sessions became more like a discussion rather than a formal review process. And since then, they have been very, very helpful.

At Gensler we run a design course in the office. Students come to our office for a series of ten lectures, for which they receive course credit. A different designer teaches each class. I have monitored the entire series as its director, keeping an overview of it. It starts with how to find your client to seeing your job through to the finish. The specifics change from semester to semester. Students get to see jobs in progress. Sometimes the managing principal will lecture, and sometimes the director of marketing will talk. Project managers also give lectures. I try to make it creative, allowing the staff to put together their own outline and format for their particular lecture.

The advantage of this type of course is that instead of having an instructor who works part-time and teaches part-time, students are taught by full-time designers. These are often people who graduated three or four years ago and who have empathy for students. Students suddenly see themselves projected into the role of the instructor because the instructor was a student only recently. And so they see encouragement. They see that if this person can make an impact in one of the largest design firms in the country, then so can they. It gives them a real confidence boost, and they always end our classes with much enthusiasm and excitement.

What design schools often try to do is to pack a lot of information into a short period of time. And sometimes it's too broad because the teachers themselves don't know where the students are going to end up. They may become corporate designers, they may become furniture and decorating people, they may become fabric representatives, they may even become urban planners. By nature, schools try to cover everything. But they often lose specificity in the process. In this course, we tend to focus on what we do best: corporate design with graphics and retailing and architecture. That's our realm. And we offer students very specific information within that realm. We show lots of award-winning projects. We show students how to make models, because we have a model studio. We teach them how to get involved with graphics because we have real graphic designers in the office. It's unlike school where most projects are hypothetical. Students get to see a real project and a real designer sweating over a real job.

Several years after they had been in my class, students would come up and say things to me like, "You really left a great impression on me. Your enthusiasm has really set me in the right direction." They will repeat something to me that I said to them years ago—verbatim! And I think, "Did I really say that?" It's wonderful when they can use my comments to their advantage. But at the same time, I also hope that I didn't say something that was so negative that it may have been to their detriment. The impact of a teacher on a student can be very profound.

Creative people don't often talk philosophically about design. We're too busy designing and running a business. So in juries you have an opportunity for two or three hours to really get into the essence of what design is all about.

Designers don't always use humor. And if you want to diffuse stress, the easiest way is to use humor. You can present criticism with humor easily, and sometimes it's more effective. It is important to use humor without making direct fun of anyone. It's an art form.

RICHARD MEIER

I think that juries are an important and valuable part of the design process. They enable students to hear a variety of opinions about their work and to learn in a way that's perhaps not possible with the normal student/critic system. In addition, I think it's valuable for other students as a learning process to learn not only from their own work but from other students' work and comments that are elicited in the discussion.

Each [student] is different and has to do what he or she is capable of doing. Students are always searching and groping. That's a necessary part of the process. That's why they're in school. The educational process is one of supporting, reacting to, improving, encouraging, and structuring their ideas. That's really the nature of the educational process.

Juries are different from design competitions. Many of the professional juries have their own structure, which is OK in most places. As far as I know, most places try to get people from outside of that area to come in and take part in the jurying. I think that is good to get some nonlocal insight.

There are two types of competitions. One is the open competition and the other is the invited competition. Perhaps the open competition needs to take itself a little more

---

Richard Meier (Figure 13-18) received his Bachelor of Architecture degree from Cornell University in 1957. In 1963 he established his firm, Richard Meier & Partners, Architects, in New York City. He has received several awards including National Honor Awards from the American Institute of Architects (AIA), a Medal of Honor from the New York Chapter of the AIA, the Pritzker Prize for Architecture, and the Royal Gold Medal from the Royal Institute of British Architects. He is an Honorary Fellow of the Royal Institute of British Architects and was elected to the American Academy and the Institute of Arts and Letters.

He has taught at Cooper Union, UCLA, Harvard, and Yale, and he has lectured throughout the United States, Europe, South America, and Japan. Mr. Meier's work has been featured in many international journals and books, including Richard Meier Architect *(1984). His furniture, paintings, collages, and architectural drawings have been exhibited widely.*

Among his best-known completed works and works in progress are the Bronx Developmental Center in Bronx, New York; the Atheneum in New Harmony, Indiana; the High Museum of Art in Atlanta; the Museum for Decorative Arts in Frankfurt, Germany; City Hall and Central Library in The Hague, the Netherlands; and the J. Paul Getty Center in Los Angeles.

Figure 13-18 Richard Meier, FAIA. (Photo: Scott Frances/Esto)

seriously by offering more incentives to those people taking part rather than simply awarding prize money to the first-place winner, which is often the case. The incentive could be to guarantee that the project would be realized, which is less often the case. Most of the time these things are just about making a project and when the competition's over, that's the end of it. Therefore, the open competition lacks a great deal of credibility in terms of it being any realizable situation. That's one thing. The closed competition often is just a means of getting a job rather than being a means for making a building. Often times the invited competition also dies a premature death by the end. That's the end of the project. One of the problems is that these competitions aren't fully thought through. They're not professionally organized in a way that makes them either attractive to the architect or attractive to a young practitioner.

Certainly in France, Holland, and Germany design competitions work much more successfully than here in the United States. It's been a proven method over the past ten years as a valid means for securing work and doing a good building.

CHARLES W. MOORE

In design school, I did very well generally, except at the very beginning of graduate school at Princeton where I had some disastrous juries. My design projects were marked variously, but they were generally A's at Michigan, and they were done on an elaborate 20-point basis at Princeton. After the first couple of low scores, I received good scores. Yes, I think other students and professors saw me as a star student.

I can't think of any serious disasters except my first jury when I went to Princeton. I was just out of the army and new in graduate school, and I was just back from Japan and did some churches that were Japanese in style, things that I thought were very pretty. And I got a particularly terrible grade. They were pavilions on a lake and they didn't look at all like what the jurors thought a church was supposed to look [like]. I just supposed the jurors were misguided and narrow minded. It didn't occur to me that there was anything wrong with me. That's the only [one] that comes immediately to mind.

I remember once at undergraduate school at Michigan, I had gotten a good grade on a sketch problem, and it was marked "pass." Someone had come along and erased the "a" in pass and written "piss poor." And I thought that was serious. I was pretty naive. And I was distressed about that for a minute, but it came out all right.

What helped me the most in getting through design school? I had some very caring teachers whom I was close to and who helped a lot. I also had close friends in the class with whom I was congenial, and we spent a lot of time looking at each other's work and critting it and being helpful. I remember my school experience, undergraduate and graduate both, as being very supportive. It was intensely competitive but not in a negative way.

I guess it's time to say what I've come to feel strongly about: What's wrong with most juries is that even the nomenclature implies that the student is defending his or her project to the jury. This suggests the jury is attacking it. It seems to get students off on the wrong foot. When they try to work with other people later in practice, they so often become defensive. And presenting any project to anybody is seen as "us-versus-them." What one should try to do in presenting a project to clients is to get them into the process so that they end up feeling as though they designed it themselves. But the jury is set up almost always to engender exactly the opposite reactions, where the student is defending his or her personal ideas. And then the students see the jury as a bunch of fast-talking yo-yos usually from New York who are out to attack and have to be

> *Charles W. Moore (Figure 13-19) attended the University of Michigan, Ann Arbor, where he earned a Bachelor of Architecture degree in 1947. He later attended Princeton University, where he earned both a Master of Fine Arts in 1956 and Ph.D. in 1957. He is currently principal of the firm Charles W. Moore, Architect, in Austin, Texas, and holds the O'Neil Ford Centennial Chair in Architecture at the University of Texas at Austin. He has also taught at UCLA, where he served as program head of the School of Architecture; at Yale, where he served as dean of the School of Architecture and chairman of the Department of Architecture; at the University of California, Berkeley, where he served as chairman of the Department of Architecture; at Princeton; and at the University of Utah. Among his best-known designs are various projects at Sea Ranch in Northern California; Kresge College at the University of California, Santa Cruz; and more recently the Alumni Center at the University of California, Irvine; the Piazza d'Italia in New Orleans, winner of a design competition; and the Beverly Hills Civic Center in Beverly Hills, California. His work has been awarded prizes from the American Institute of Architects,* Architectural Record, Progressive Architecture, *and elsewhere. He has authored and coauthored several books, including* Body, Memory and Architecture, Los Angeles: The City Observed, *and* The Place of Houses, *and has been the subject of various journal articles and books. In 1991 he received the prestigious Gold Medal Award from the American Institute of Architects.*

Figure 13-19 Charles W. Moore, FAIA.

fended off. And to adopt that attitude with a client is disastrous.

I think that it's not the juries but the set of attitudes that go with them that seem to me to be in trouble. Part of the trouble, I believe, is that juries are seen as some sort of culmination, as though you do something and then it gets attacked by a set of vicious persons from somewhere. Then you have to defend it and then it's over and you've either won or lost. Yet, in fact, the presentation of any scheme to anybody generally is a step in pushing it ahead. And the important part in practice is what you do after the first presentation and after the second and third and more. Good buildings are the ones that get better and better as they're reacted to, and not-so-good buildings are the ones that stay frozen. I think the timing of juries in architecture schools is at considerable fault. I have to admit, however, that my attempts in my classes to change that have never been altogether successful.

I would push for some continuing experiment in timing and constructing the jury so that it is more useful and more like practice is or should be. My impression is that experimenting in architecture education is not so vigorous in these last 15-20 years as it used to be as late as the 1960s.

I think that two sets of things are often neglected in design education: One, I believe that students come to architecture school with already a couple of decades of experience of being alive and seeing things. And too often architecture schools, or architecture teachers, see their mission as wiping all that clean, brainwashing the student, and getting him or her to think in new ways that don't have anything to do with the student's prior experiences. I think it would be far better to build on the student's experience, on what's familiar and what their beliefs already are, rather than trying to wipe out those experiences and substitute some other, necessarily more spartan ones.

One of the legacies of the Beaux-Arts that we still have with us is that of secrecy, the business of retiring into a room where nobody could see what you were doing.... To keep people from copying each other is presumably why this secrecy was set up. Yet so much of practice is indeed copying each other, building on each other's ideas, and keeping other people interested in what's going on. I think that architectural education could profitably care a good deal more about cooperative efforts. Most of the experiments over the last decades in forming teams among students have been awful. Somebody takes the lead and does it, and the others end up sullenly helping. Encouraging some better ways of acting cooperatively in school is urgent, but obviously difficult.

I would push students toward the courage of their convictions. So many students seem to think that anything they already believe is wrong and wait to be beaten into submission [and so you are forced] to pick up some new and strange ways. I've spent a good deal of my teaching time, especially in courses early in the curriculum, trying to give students the courage of their own convictions. [They need to be able to] stand up to anybody who tries to brainwash them. And there will be somebody who tries to brainwash you.

I go very easy on the grades and don't use them as devices to punish people who don't do what I want. I try to keep that equitable.

I've always enjoyed entering competitions and winning, which happens sometimes but not all that often. And I think it's an encouragement to doing work that one's peers will like. Every jury is different. The chemistry of each jury is dependent on the people that are on it and their points of view. And I've often noted that no matter who's on the jury, the basic reaction to maybe 90% of the entries will be the same. That is, the pile that people have of the ones to save for the final accounting will be shared even among people of very different points of view. But the jury can be swayed by strong personalities or a combination of events so that it shouldn't be taken as by any means the last word.

People are deeply disappointed if they don't win. And one of the things I find myself trying to explain to students after juries that I've been on is that when they say, "I have this wonderful scheme and you didn't give it a prize," that the amount of time that any jury can spend on each entry initially is minuscule. It has to jump out off the boards at them to be retained, to be looked at with any seriousness. I've never won an open competition, though I've entered many, so I don't know how to grab the attention of a juror when it's among a field of hundreds. I've been on many juries that had to look at a field of hundreds.

A recent competition that we lost was won by a scheme that was really vivid. For instance, on a fairly spectacular site, it showed pictures from inside the building looking out onto sunny and compelling landscapes. And our drawings were more serious pictures of the building seen from the outside, which didn't stand up to the visual delights of the other. I knew the minute I saw it that that entry had won. I don't think the building was as thoughtful as ours, and I heard some others on the jury say that. But it was far more compelling.

I always feel guilty and sorry as a juror that people have put in so many thousands and thousands of hours and dollars of effort for such a casual scrutiny by the jury, and I wish it weren't so.

A firm can foster an attitude of healthy client relationships by setting an example, by letting young architects who are going to do some presenting themselves be present while I and the partners do it. They can learn to listen to people and try to accommodate them, and to turn the product into a joint product without losing quality. And that's clearly not easy. It takes a lot of experience with different kinds of people. And some clients don't want to work with their architects. We did a church with a group that said, "We hired you, so don't cheat us. You do it." So I agreed and we did a nice church, although the minister was also responsible for it coming out well because we did pay a great deal of attention to what he wanted.

Rejecting any sort of attitudes of secrecy or doing work in isolation is important. And speaking out against the attitudes in *The Fountainhead* every chance one gets is important. The whole notion that some architect should burn down a building that doesn't meet his personal aesthetic standards is ridiculous as well as criminal.

CESAR PELLI

> Cesar Pelli (Figure 13-20) completed his undergraduate studies in architecture at the University of Tucuman in Argentina and later received his Master of Architecture from the University of Illinois at Urbana-Champaign. He is currently principal at Cesar Pelli & Associates in New Haven, Connecticut, founded in 1977. Both an educator and a designer, Mr. Pelli served as dean of the School of Architecture at Yale University. He has received numerous national and local awards and honors such as the Arnold M. Brunner Memorial Prize, and memberships in the American Academy and Institute of Arts and Letters and the National Academy of Design. He was the first architect to receive a Connecticut State Arts Award. Cesar Pelli & Associates received the AIA Firm Award in 1989. The firm has been widely exhibited and published.
>
> Representative projects include the World Financial Center and Winter Garden at Battery Park City in Lower Manhattan, what some have called "the Rockefeller Center of the '80s"; the Pacific Design Center and its recent addition in Los Angeles; the gallery expansion and residential tower of the Museum of Modern Art and Carnegie Hall Tower in New York City; St. Luke's Medical Tower in Houston; the Norwest Tower in Minneapolis; the Cleveland Clinic and Society Center in Cleveland, Ohio; NCNB Corporate Center and the North Carolina Performing Arts Center in Charlotte, North Carolina; and several buildings at Yale, Rice, and other college and university campuses.

Figure 13-20 Cesar Pelli, FAIA. (Photo: Michael Marstand)

Did other students and professors see me as a star student? Yes, I guess they did.

As a student, I never doubted the jury system. I still think that it is very good. Juries are extraordinary opportunities that students are given to have their designs commented upon by mostly bright, capable professionals. That is something that you don't get when you leave school. It's extremely useful if it's done well. Of course, we all know that some jurors or juries can be destructive. We all get some destructive jurors in our career as students, but when the jurors are reasonably constructive, I think it's very useful.

Having juries in school is excellent training because you do it in an environment where there are teachers there to help you. And you can also see how the very same project can be reinterpreted, reexplained by different students in many different ways.

During my first year as a design student, I remember that my parents wanted to buy me some books on architecture, and I said, "No. Hold on. I'm not sure this is really what I want to do." But after I reached a crucial turning point, I knew that I was going to be an architect forever and that there was nothing else I wanted to do. That was an amazingly exhilarating, uplifting moment for me.

As students, we all go through moments when our work just comes out just right and everybody loves it. Occasionally you do another design that just doesn't quite come out and then everybody hates it. You cannot even defend if for yourself, and you feel just terrible and you think, "How could I have been so stupid?"

When we are sure about the quality of our work, and we know it's good, then when criticism is just off the mark, we become irritated. But it doesn't really hurt or appall. It's just an irritation that goes away.

What helps a design student from the inside is just loving to design and from the outside is having some good, capable, supportive professors.

Students should be clear, have their thoughts organized, go from the general to the particular, and not be too descriptive. Many students make the mistake of repeating what is in their drawings, which is a waste of time. What they need to do is to tell us what's not in the drawings. Otherwise it's just a bore. It's extremely important for the faculty to try to be constructive [jurors], and not to judge the project in terms of how they would design. Instead, try to judge the project in terms of the student's intentions. The important thing is how well the students achieve their intentions. It's irrelevant to figure out how well the students tried to satisfy the faculty's intentions. That serves no purpose.

What practitioners can do on juries is to add their observations about the reality of design practice. Practitioners are very familiar with government regulations, client needs and requirements, users' needs, problems of liability, and other realities of a project. And these types of observations can add another dimension to the jury.

I think it's tempting for practicing jurors to start criticizing the student, saying "I don't like that, so you didn't solve it well." That is of no great use unless these practitioners are experienced teachers too. But if they are not, what the practitioners can do is to add useful observations. The design jury is not really a jury like in law. A jury is not there to judge the student. That is a secondary purpose. One should remember that the jury process is primarily a teaching tool and secondarily a way of measuring the students' abilities.

Students must love architecture. If you are committed to it, everything becomes easier. Even when difficulties are encountered all of the efforts seem worthwhile. If you don't love it, then you have a problem. I cannot tell anybody, "Go ahead and love it." It just happens. For some students, their whole career is a pleasure and the fact that you have little time for dating, sports, or other activities is not a problem because you're having a lot more fun doing your design work. If you don't find that so, then you have a problem and you'll have to find a way of combining both.

Today, architecture has become multifaceted. There are a number of essential activities in architecture that are not design oriented and those other qualities and interests are not necessarily best exposed through the jury system. We all need to understand design because that's what architecture is at its core. But individuals can find very different missions. Design is a mission, but there are many other important missions in the profession, and those appear to be multiplying every day.

I think design education is wonderful for everybody. I could not think of a better education that one can receive because design is all about seeing the world, analyzing it, and reinterpreting it, and also understanding all possible functions in life. Practically all human activities are somehow related to a physical enclosure, even if it's a ball field. We need to know about all human activities so that it puts us in contact with life at all levels, and eventually we end up in a synthesis. I know of no other profession that teaches this combination of analysis and synthesis as well as the tradition of the design studio.

Design competitions have great potential because they open up opportunities to talented architects that may be young and unrecognized to become recognized. But they are always risky. There's no assurance that the best design is going to be chosen. The final pick is always subjective. It's what's in the mind of the jurors, and is affected by personal preferences and momentary fashions. Design competitions offer that great opportunity to unknown or lesser-known architects to come to the fore. However, they have the problem that one is designing in a vacuum. Good, solid designs usually develop through the architect working closely with clients and users. There is a great deal of give and take, where ideas are explored, rejected, or modified to make them properly suit all of the needs of the clients and users. That, to me, makes for a richer, more real project than what one can conceive all alone in a competition.

Figure 13-21 Lawrence B. Perkins, FAIA.

LAWRENCE B. PERKINS

My father, who was a very distinguished architect, when his health was running out, told me if he was going to support my education I'd have to work hard. That discussion I remember vividly, even the time of day. It took about 22 minutes and I never looked back.

The first year and half, after having spent a year in Europe with my family, I thought I knew quite a bit more than I did and [actually] did poorly to the point of a letter or two from home suggesting that I shape up or ship out. Toward the end of sophomore year, I woke up a little bit. I was one of the stronger designers in my last two years, but monumentally, one of the weakest in my first year and a half at Cornell.

I don't know how good Nat Owings of Skidmore, Owings and Merrill was as a student [in general]. He was two years ahead of me, and as a design student he was no better than I—and I wasn't very good. To this day I don't know whether he could draw better with his hands or his feet. But he was one of the most effective human beings that has ever been in our profession.

A generalist is rarely the "hot" specialist in any part of the work. It's his job to assemble enough specialists to add up to one super generalist. It generally takes four or five people to do it.

I was not a star student in the eyes of the faculty or students. I think I ended up with some close friendships [with] faculty members. I was, I think, supremely repulsive to them at first, certainly in the first half of my time there. My partner, Phil Will, was overwhelming the teacher's pet. He worked methodically, intelligently, 60 minutes of each hour. But what I never appreciated until years later was that he was a loner. All his life he was a very presentable loner. I was anything but.

If I was writing a biography of myself, about the only thing I could think to write about is the other people that I've admired. I've had an extraordinarily privileged life that way.

I don't think much of individuality. There's no such thing as a solo act in architecture anyway. It never occurred to me that I would do anything that I wanted to without putting people together.

Too many instructors are individuals training individual star architects. They don't recognize that all you can be is a component of an architect.

During my school education there was a gradual dawning of some of the things I damn well better learn,

> *Lawrence B. Perkins (Figure 13-21) attended Cornell University, where he received his Bachelor of Architecture degree in 1930. He is cofounder of the firm Perkins & Will, established in 1935, based in Chicago, and now with offices also in New York, Washington, D.C., and London. In 1960 Mr. Perkins was named Chicagoan of the Year for his contributions in architecture and engineering. He has served on the advisory board for Cook County Building Codes and is a director of the Adlai Stevenson Institute of International Affairs. His design experience includes commercial and public buildings, urban development, and educational facilities.*
>
> *Under his guidance, Perkins & Will received over 100 awards for elementary, secondary, college, and university buildings. The Crow Island School in Winnetka, Illinois, its first educational project, received the American Institute of Architects' (AIA) 25-Year Award in recognition of its enduring significance. Over the years, Perkins & Will has received numerous honors such as the Silver Masonry Award for Design Excellence, National Honor Awards from the AIA and the Contract Design Award from the Institute of Business Designers/Interior Design magazine. In 1988 President Ronald Reagan awarded to Perkins & Will an Award for Design Excellence for Outstanding Achievement in Design for the Government of the United States of America.*
>
> *The geographical scope of the firm's work has encompassed 48 states and 15 foreign countries, with expertise in planning, architecture, engineering, and interiors. Recent Perkins & Will projects include office buildings at 123 North Wacker Drive, 100 North Riverside Drive, a mixed-use tower at 900 North Michigan Avenue, First National Bank, Amoco Corporation Headquarters in Chicago; Desert View Elementary School, Surlad Park, New Mexico; the Umm Al-Oura University, Makkah Al Mukarramah, Kingdom of Saudi Arabia; Trans World Airlines Redevelopment Program at John F. Kennedy International Airport, Jamaica, New York; International Terminal and Terminal 3/Concourse L at Chicago's O'Hare International Airport; and restoration of the Frank Lloyd Wright home and studio in Oak Park, Illinois.*

and the colossal shame that I would bring on people if I didn't.

[Phil Will, my partner, and I met when we were in school.] As I now look back, nothing of Phil's was thrilling, but it was serenely finished, whereas, on my thesis, half a year later, they got me on some omissions, a failure to specify how the freight elevator was going to work in my building. They never got him on anything like that. They gave him a 99 because they didn't dare give him the other point. They gave me an adequate grade. My good efforts were controversial, incompetent in some ways, but usually exciting. His were not adventurous, but you couldn't trip him up. They were thought out in-depth.

I think [an evaluation of the] jury today depends on whether you are trying to educate or whether you're trying to select a winner. If you're trying to select the best design, then I think it's overwhelming. You better do it in secret.

In a jury in front of an audience, the overwhelming technique by older faculty types is to make a speech to show how smart we are and this is done by downgrading a student.

My job here [at the University of Illinois at Urbana-Champaign, where I occasionally serve as a visitor] is, in a sense, a rebellion. I don't come for the juries. I do what little I can for the students on a one-to-one basis, sitting beside them and working on their designs with them one at a time.

One of the things I hope is that students won't be stupid enough not to wear a necktie and dress shoes when they're presenting. It will make them attach a little more dignity and have some salesmanship to the process of appearing before a jury. It is silly for a kid to come in with blue jeans before a jury and want us to like his work. If you're that much of a slob personally, doesn't that mean your design is also sloppy?

There are basically two kinds of juries in practice. Either to hand out candy or to get a lot of free ideas and defer making a decision, and then from the architect's point of view, to gamble either partially or completely in the hope of getting a job. The reward even for second, third, and fourth place, is reputation, which is also valuable if it's good enough. I give you the Eliel Saarinen second prize Tribune Tower for an example. That second-prize submittal built more buildings for him than the winner ever did.

Competitions where you're simply handing out candy is a self-serving thing on the part of the architectural profession to publicize, hopefully favorably, what architects have done.

The architect, in order to get something written about his work, has to give them something that stands on one ear and flips and turns in the air, or does something extraordinary. But in order for the magazine to be worth anything, it has to go to a layman, and the layman in turn hires the architect on the reassurance that the magazine must know what they're doing to write about it. And it goes round and round and round from the architect to the publicity to the client to the architect. And that little triangle continues.

Incidentally, Frank [Lloyd] Wright talked a wonderful game of integrity. As far as I know, he never did a good building. I didn't say he didn't do great design, but good building. I can take you up and down the North Shore and show you overhangs that have had to be propped up from their limp and underdesigned condition. He and various others built stuff that was a picturesque ruin within five years of being built.

MARTHA SCHWARTZ

When I was a little girl, every Saturday I was taken to art classes at the Philadelphia Museum of Art. I used to wander around the art museum and play hide-and-seek with my friends. Throughout high school, I was taking art lessons at the Philadelphia College of Art. My background in the fine arts and architecture goes back as far as I can remember. It's impossible for me to imagine what it must feel like coming in cold and starting to learn about the visual realm at age 18, 25, or even 30.

How did I learn to develop design concepts? All my life I've been making things. I know I love the act of making things, and I remember back as a little, little girl being dumped at my grandmother's house for her to babysit for me. She'd always save her cardboard boxes, the rolls out of the toilet paper, and crayons, and I'd put this stuff together. I've always loved making something from nothing. It's magic.

I came into landscape architecture wondering, "What is expected of me?" I thought of my career as preordained: You march in step, you graduate, you work for one of the corporate firms; there's a way to draw things, there's a way to design things, there's a methodology. Instead, the more exciting way of looking at it is, "What do you really want to do?" It's such an open profession. You can actually design your own career.

I probably would have dropped out of landscape architecture school had I not been a student of Pete Walker. He was the first teacher I ever heard speak about the relationship between art and landscape architecture. He was brilliant. During the first problem [in his class], Pete just came in and ripped the projects to shreds. He pointed out, "There was no art in them! There was no reason to go and see them! If you haven't pushed anything to its maximum and created something new, then why do it at all? Why waste your time?" To me, that was music to my ears. It was the first time that it occurred to me that art and landscape could be the same. Landscape became a medium, a venue for doing art.

When I had to learn the more mundane, technical aspects of the profession, I had a very solid view of myself as an artist and I truly felt it was beneath me to have to learn how to grade, how to close a section, and how to do a road alignment. My spirit was really provoked because I thought that as an artist, I didn't want to be a designer if this is what it took. I didn't want to be in a position where I was just servicing people by placing shrubs around their

Martha Schwartz (Figure 13-22) attended the University of Michigan, Ann Arbor, where she received her Bachelor of Fine Arts in 1973 and Master of Landscape Architecture degree in 1976. She continued her studies in landscape architecture at Harvard University. She is currently with the firm of Martha Schwartz, Ken Smith, David Meyer, Landscape Architects, Inc., of San Francisco. She has received several honors and awards such as Finalist for the Rome Prize from the American Academy in Rome, and Artist in Residence at Radcliffe College. Ms. Schwartz produced the winning entries as artist/designer for the Marina Linear Park Competition in San Diego, and for the Competition for King County Jail Plaza in Seattle. She has received several art commissions. Among her best-known works are the Swimming Hall of Fame in Fort Lauderdale, Florida, and the Rio Shopping Center in Atlanta, Georgia. Ms. Schwartz has served as a visiting critic and guest juror at Harvard, Rhode Island School of Design, and the University of California at Berkeley. Her work has been published widely and featured in several art shows across the United States.

Figure 13-22 Martha Schwartz, FASLA.

houses. I hated that idea. So at first, I did pretty badly in these aspects.

But in terms of design and presentations, I did great. I usually did well on my design projects. I believe at Michigan during my first year, I received an award for being the most promising student. At Harvard, too, I was probably seen as one of the better designers in the class. In terms of performing, I was pretty nimble on my feet. I rarely "crashed and burned." I wanted to either fail gloriously or get an A on my designs. I tried never to get caught in the middle.

Because I had been involved in doing art all my life, I knew what a magic marker was, I knew how to sharpen a pencil, I knew about proportion, and I knew about design. When I design, I'm dealing with the same fundamental issues of form, balance, composition, texture, etc., which we dealt with in our first art school classes. Those components do not change.

From my point of view, juries in design school were a piece of cake... I thought they were overly polite. In art school, they are far more rigorous. If the jurors didn't like something, and they didn't think that students had worked up to their potential, they said so directly. In art school, I saw some real blood spattered on the walls.... We were scared shitless! Watching somebody's head get chopped off is no easy task. All you can think of is saving your own skin.

I believe that the jury system is a good process. I think you need to get your projects up. You need to have them seen, and you need to hear criticism. Artists need feedback. They don't live all alone in a white room. You must engage the culture. There's no other way of getting that than by holding up your work and seeing what other people think about it.

Juries are very important in teaching. We had a great teacher named Dr. Tom Holmes at Harvard who taught us how to present. He worked for the BBC. He was just fantastic. He would videotape us and then tell us what we were doing—whether or not we were pulling at our hair, mumbling, or being overly seductive. He was brutally honest with us and helped us immensely in sharpening us up. His course has been invaluable in "real life."

I believe that as a design student, you probably have a lot of bad experiences that you inflict upon yourself. Designers are fraught, by and large, with grave self-doubt. At times I was afraid that I didn't really have the courage to be an artist, and there were many, many times when it was painful. But I think that every single time an artist sticks his or her neck out and commits pencil to paper, there can be pain involved.

The final jury is almost always going to be anticlimactic. You've already done 90% of the learning during the design process. You've already been through your struggle, and it's over by the time you present. The real learning process has already happened. Students often think that they're going to get this big kick at the end of all this, but I think that they're looking at juries in the wrong way.

I believe that the most useful jurors are those who give constructive criticism to students. No matter what the problem is, I think you can always find something positive about the scheme. I think you owe it to students to tell them not only where they've failed, but also where they've succeeded. Your job isn't to throw your weight around and be discouraging. You need to be straight to tell what is good and what is bad. You have to balance what you say so that people can go away with something they can work with later on.

One of my relatives just graduated from design school. She almost dropped out because the juries were so destructive and were venues for personal tastes and philosophies. I have found that this is more often the case for juries in architecture than in landscape programs. In architecture, juries are often an opportunity for grandstanding. The star jurors get up on their podiums and if the project is not what they, themselves, would do, they're very unsympathetic. This attitude is a waste of time and harmful to students.

When I was studying landscape architecture at Michigan, my roommate was an architect. The dean told her, "Just forget about becoming an architect! Women never make it in this field!"

My first drawing teacher at college said, "What are you girls doing here? You know, you're going to grow up and have babies. You aren't going to be serious about this. So why don't you leave now!" Our printmaking teacher called all the women "Lulubelle." You got the message loud and clear that you were not taken seriously.

Design, like art, is a subjective medium. It would be great if it were quantifiable, and if there were a method, if you did step A then you could go on to step B, and then on to step C. But I believe that getting where you want to go in design is largely dependent upon how well you are able to learn about the language of design itself. I don't understand how you're expected to teach design to students who don't yet have that basic foundation. It is like asking them to read Dickens when they haven't yet learned their ABCs.

Art history is very important. It teaches you how to look at art and architecture and what the issues were at the time the artist did the work. The first two years in a fine arts school is like boot camp. It's painful and tedious but you need it in order to go on.

One of my big beefs about landscape architecture schools is that they rarely start their students off with the basics: two-dimensional design, cutting out black and white pieces of paper and talking about form, as well as drawing, sketching, and hand-eye coordination.... I believe that you can be taught how to design, and how to see. Schools can teach that stuff; they just can't teach you how to be talented.

So much about juries depends upon the jurors whom you invite. What a faculty member hopes to do is to find people who are equally bright and capable, but who may have different attitudes about design issues. The best juries occur when the jurors are arguing amongst themselves. The more conflict on the jury, the more exciting it is. Those are fun. And they're more useful for students because the students ultimately have to decide for themselves what is appropriate to absorb and what is appropriate to reject. The jury's job is not to tell students whether or not their work is good or bad. Instead, their job is to raise issues and make the students think.

I participated in a jury in "real life" that was much more wild and uncontrollable than juries at school. It was a presentation of my work before a very important architect. He just looked at my work and stuck his tongue out. Then everybody around the room stuck their tongues out. And here I am trying to present my project. It's hard to bounce right back after that.

I believe that juries in practice are absolutely necessary. Our profession is about creating our visual realm, and we have to get people who are sophisticated visually to evaluate our work. These are people who ideally have different points of view, in order to provide a well-rounded perspective. Some jurors are wonderful and others aren't, depending upon the personalities. So much depends upon how people work together. It's really subjective.

In professional competitions, models are extremely powerful tools. We've found that they are able to convey much more than drawings. Doing a convincing model is important. If you're doing landscape, you need to convey the quality of that landscape. A tree is not just any tree. This is our palette we're talking about! You need clear drawings, you need good graphics, good plans, and good sections so that you can see what the relationships are.

In one recent competition where I served as a juror, someone had taken slides of each of the entries—about 1000 of them with three boards each! He put them in the projector and we just sat and watched them for three days, kind of like *Clockwork Orange*. At first we went through every one in about ten seconds. That's awfully fast. But by the time we started getting into it, we realized that we could see whether or not there was any merit in a project in even less time. We actually got it down to about five seconds. We were able to see whether or not we would omit it out or keep it in for the next round. In this case, the visual quality of the entries was crucial. It had to grab you and intrigue you—you had to want to know something more about it; otherwise it didn't survive.

I believe that the sophistication of the jury is very important. It's worth going out and getting really good people if you want to have a successful jury and most importantly, a good choice.

ROBERT A. M. STERN

I would say that I was an indifferent "drawer," a crude model maker, that some of my student projects were horrible, but that some had very provocative ideas. I think my fellow students and some of my teachers thought I was a very interesting student but not slick and accomplished, not the guy who gets the prize.

Regarding whether other students thought I was a star or not, I would say yes and no. I think that there was a sense that I was going to do something big. I already did things when I was at architecture school like edit a magazine. I think my projects were always very interesting to students and faculty. It's not for me to say who was a star or not, but I certainly didn't fall into the gray mass. But then at Yale, all students were stars, or thought they were.

There were many exciting teachers around and guest jurors at the review when I was in school. There were many, many very stimulating moments.

Devastating moments always occur when one's work is not appreciated. I tend to be one of those people who accepts a certain degree of failure or rejection as being not necessarily healthy and not even necessarily well intentioned, but often, in the cool reflection afterwards, as being appropriate. It's hurtful for someone not to like your work, but it's also a part of life.

One summer I had to do an extra project because it was the feeling of some of my teachers that I would never be able to "put together" a building. It was a punishment,

Figure 13-23 Robert A. M. Stern, FAIA. (Photo: Franz Walderdorff)

> *Robert A. M. Stern (Figure 13-23) is a graduate of Columbia University (B.A., 1960) and Yale University (M. Architecture, 1965). He is a practicing architect, teacher, and writer. Mr. Stern, founder and senior partner in the firm of Robert A. M. Stern Architects of New York, is a Fellow of the American Institute of Architects and received the Medal of Honor of its New York Chapter in 1984. Mr. Stern's work has been published widely and exhibited at numerous galleries and universities and is in the permanent collections of the Museum of Modern Art, the Metropolitan Museum of Art, the Deutsches Architekturmuseum, and the Art Institute of Chicago. In 1986, Mr. Stern hosted "Pride of Place: Building the American Dream," an eight-part, eight-hour documentary television series aired on the Public Broadcasting System.*
>
> *His firm has earned international recognition, numerous awards and citations for design excellence, including National Honor Awards of the American Institute of Architects (1980, 1985, and most recently 1990); the distinguished Architecture Award of the New York Chapter of the AIA in 1982, 1984, 1985, and 1990, and a lengthening list of repeat clients.*
>
> *Currently, the firm has projects under way in California, Florida, Hawaii, Massachusetts, Michigan, New Hampshire, New Jersey, New York, South Carolina, Texas, Canada, Japan, France, and Hungary. Among these are: Disney's Yacht and Beach Club Resorts, Orlando; America House, annex to the United States Embassy, Budapest, Hungary; the Center for Jewish Life at Princeton University; 222 Berkeley Street, an office building that is a project of Hines Interests Limited Partnership in Boston; a new library for St. Paul's School in Concord, New Hampshire; the Norman Rockwell Museum in Stockbridge, Massachusetts; the Roger Tory Peterson Institute in Jamestown, New York; golf clubhouses and resort hotels in Japan; and two 1000-room resort hotels near Paris.*
>
> *Among his most noteworthy projects are a wide variety of private residences, offices, showrooms furniture, tableware, and carpets; Observatory Hill Dining Hall and Sprigg Lane Dormitories at the University of Virginia, Charlottesville; Fine Arts Studio IV, University of California, Irvine; Point West Place Office Building, Framington, Massachusetts; Prospect Point Office Building, La Jolla, California; Pasadena Police Building, Pasadena, California; Casting Center Walt Disney World, Lake Buena Vista, Florida; and Mexx International Headquarters, Voorschoten, Netherlands.*

but a punishment deserved and a meaningful one. I've never "put together" another building since except for one little set of working drawings. That doesn't mean I'm not an architect; and the buildings I've designed as a practicing professional since have surely been very well "put together" under my direction. Everybody has different things to do in the profession.

My talent and enthusiasm for architecture and my commitment are what helped me the most getting through school. Architecture is not just something you do at the drawing table, but is also involved in the history and the culture of architecture, changing ideas, lectures, seminars, and so forth. I was determined to be an architect. That's what I wanted to do. And I did it.

We still have juries at Columbia where I now teach. They're not as harsh as they were when I was a student, when the juries frequently reduced students to tears. I'm not saying that's good; I'm just saying it's a fact. We tend to be more gentle in this post-1968 era. Nonetheless I think juries are an essential teaching tool.

I'm not so sure there's anything wrong with the jury system. They should be as open to crosscurrents of discussion as possible. That's all I would say.

I have entered many professional design competitions over the years almost always against my better judgment. I think you stand a better chance of achieving your goals by going to Las Vegas than in entering an open design competition.

Limited competitions, where there are a fixed number of competitors and a more careful process in which the client participates, are more professional. But I prefer working one-to-one with a client. Architecture is not just making pretty pictures. It's about creating a building from a certain set of circumstances. It needs the participation of a client so it doesn't become just a paper exercise.

Often critics on an awards jury look for things that concern their own point of view and they don't look for things that represent quality. They cannot depersonalize themselves. They're not responsible as jurors. You have to say, "This is not what I would do, but it is well done."

Breaking competition rules is worth doing if there's a sense and a reason for it. I think that the rules should be questioned along the way and discussed and balanced in a discourse back and forth among the participating architects, the professional adviser, and in turn, the client body. The best solution is the solution that works with the rules and makes you see them in a new way.

MINORU TAKEYAMA

If I got a bad mark on my drawing, I'd take it to a different teacher to ask for a different point of view.

In Singapore, Hong Kong, Taiwan, architecture students are very carefully selected. In Hong Kong, they say they pick 1 in 100. So these students are very capable.

> *Minoru Takeyama (Figure 13-24) received both his undergraduate and Master of Architecture degree from Waseda University, Tokyo, Japan in 1956 and 1958, respectively. In 1960, he completed a second master's degree at Harvard University. Since 1965 he has served as principal of his firm, Minoru Takeyama Architect and the United Actions in Tokyo. He has also served as a professor at the School of Architecture at Musashino Art University in Tokyo since 1975. His work has been showcased in many exhibitions in Japan, the United States, Italy, the Netherlands, Denmark, Poland, Bulgaria, and elsewhere, and his work has been featured in numerous international publications. Mr. Takeyama has received over 15 design awards for completed projects and international design competitions, including the Annual Design Award from the Osaka Architects Association, among others.*
>
> *Among his best-known projects are the Tokyo International Port Terminal 1 and 2 Ban Kahn, and the Egyptian Embassy in Tokyo; the Hotel Beverly Tom in Tomakomai, Japan; the Pepsi Canning Plant in Mikasa, Japan; and the Osaka Design House in Osaka, Japan.*
>
> *In 1989-1990 he was awarded the prestigious Plym Professorship at the School of Architecture, the University of Illinois at Urbana-Champaign.*

Figure 13-24 Minoru Takeyama. (Photo: Kyle Smith)

Similar situations are occurring at schools of architecture in eastern Europe.

I teach in Tokyo and serve regularly as a jury member for students. Comparing the United States to Japan, I think that here in the United States, juries are much harder on students' work. They are almost like legal procedures here. In Japan, we don't depend on juries as much. Most students in Japan can't take severe criticism of their work. Knowing that, we try to encourage the students to criticize.

I have served as a juror at [the University of California at] Berkeley, Harvard's Graduate School of Design, University of Manitoba, and in Singapore, Hong Kong, Taiwan, the Far East, as well as Rotterdam and Copenhagen. I remember I was a rather quiet juror. I feel that I learn more that way.

In the Far East juries aren't exactly like they are here in the United States. They're more of a presentation. The superior students can teach the others to learn how to present their work. So sometimes the jury even behaves like a client. The professors ask many questions but do not comment as much as I see here in the United States.

One of the problems I see with juries in the United States is that so many different instructors come to the jury that sometimes there is no chance for the students to participate in the discussion with the critics. And if that discussion can go well beyond the student who just presented it, that becomes very interesting. Another problem is that if we jurors try to see student work creatively, it takes time for us to understand it. So our reactions can't come very easily. I can say easily, "Yes, I like it or not." But then I have to spend some more time to think about why it's good or bad.

I think juries are all right, but they're not the most important part of design education. Most important is the *process* used to reach the jury.

I think students need to clearly and immediately communicate their material.

Most of the professional juries on which I have served have been in Japan. The most recent one was an invited competition for the City Hall in Tokyo. And now the building is under construction.

Our firm has won or at least received honorable mention in about a dozen competitions. These include open, international, and invited competitions. The project we are working on now, the Port Terminal, is a competition.

In a professional competition, jurors have to be as fair as possible. And also they have to study a lot in advance.

Once the competition sponsors decide whom to invite to compete, I think we as jurors should have open minds as much as possible. Entries from younger practitioners need just as much attention as those from older ones.

When I enter an open competition, I study the jury. Depending upon who the jury is, I decide whether or not to enter. If I don't like the jury, I don't enter. If you want to win a competition, I think it is important to study the jury.

SUSANA TORRE

> *Susana Torre (Figure 13-25) studied architecture and urban planning at the Argentinian Universities of La Plata and Buenos Aires, receiving her architectural degree in 1967. She continued her postgraduate studies at Columbia University. She is currently principal of Susana Torre and Associates in New York City.*
>
> *Her academic appointments have included positions at Columbia University; Barnard College, where she served as director of the Architecture Program; the University of Sydney, Australia; Florida A&M University, where she served as a Sam Gibbons Distinguished Scholar in Urban Design; Yale; and elsewhere. She has lectured at over 80 colleges and universities in the United States, Canada, Spain, Portugal, England, Australia, and Central and South America. Her research contributions include an edited book and traveling exhibition,* Women in American Architecture: A Historic and Contemporary Perspective, *and* Hispanic Traditions in American Architecture and Urbanism, *an international symposium, traveling exhibition and forthcoming book. Ms. Torre has served on design juries and advisory boards for* Progressive Architecture *Design Awards, the American Institute of Architects, the* Journal of Architectural Education, *and Harvard University. Her work has received Architectural Record Design Awards and other recognition. Ms. Torre has had two solo shows at major museums and galleries and has been exhibited in 35 group shows. She was recently appointed chairperson of the Department of Environmental Design at Parsons School of Design.*

I was educated in Argentina and in the United States in the mid- and late 1960s. Design juries here and there were radically different. At the University of Buenos Aires, juries were held by professors in closed quarters. Students were informed of their grades through posted grade sheets and assumed their work was judged by absolute, if unfathomable, criteria. At Columbia's open, public juries, I learned that the art of judging architecture was of necessity based on arbitrary, evolving, and consensual criteria. The lack of student-faculty interaction in the process of judgment in my early architectural education did not mean that students would not rely on the criticism of professors and peers; if anything, it was even more important than in the States. It was assumed that passing the final, closed jury was more a matter of having a well-executed set of the required drawings. The rare occasion when a student with a good set of final drawings was flunked was cause for student mutiny.

In Argentina, I was educated by committed Modernists; we knew that they would favor plans with clear concrete frame structure, logical circulation, and Corbusian language. A few of us rebelled in our first year, only to find out that the "critical regionalism" we opposed to the International Style could also be absorbed in the Corbusian aesthetic of the Maison Jaoul. Nonetheless, these issues were not debated in the design juries but in student forums and in school governance meetings (where, before the military university takeover of 1968, students had both representative voice and vote).

As a student in the States, I loved the potential—although not always realized—for interaction in design juries, with the opportunity for public defense and argument. I also saw to what extent the public humiliation of students by irresponsible critics could severely undermine the self-confidence that is indispensable to creating designs of great quality.

As a professor, I use juries as teaching contexts. I prefer to call them "reviews" instead, with the connotation of "critical evaluation" rather than that of "verdict." A review also suggests that the interaction may include the students as participants with equal rights to express their opinions rather than as a passive audience. The idea of a jury implies that there is some sort of competition, with a few winners and a majority of losers. In the studio, a student should be only in competition with himself or herself, never with others.

Care and thought should be invested in choreographing and casting a design review. The success of a review is better measured by the level of the discussion and the ideas it inspires than by the performance of individual critics. That is why it is better to present the projects in a sequence that elucidates the major issues, rather than setting up mere comparisons of *partis*. The studio critic should never relinquish the active role of the moderator, who should keep the discussion rigorous and unbiased without claiming excessive time for his or her own opinions.

Tony Desnick, an architect friend from Minneapolis, pointed out to me the influence of reviews in the future professional behavior of students: When the admired visiting critic acts as an arrogant prima donna, or when a student is savaged for the sake of a more dramatic critical performance, the students assimilate the message that this is acceptable, even successful, professional behavior. Because reviews teach about broader values, it makes a great difference whether the invited critics represent different values and are able to debate their positions respectfully without losing sight of the student's project, or whether they are all members of the same ideological party and will judge the student project according to how well it toes the party line.

Sometimes I have staged "silent" reviews, where the students must rely exclusively on their drawings and models to present their projects; critics are then invited to discuss the work without knowing who designed each project, just as in juries for professional design competitions. This type of review introduces the student to a different

Figure 13-25 Susana Torre. (Photo: Max Hilaire)

kind of discussion, where critics do not have access to the student's words as expressive of an intention. As a result the intention is no longer fixed by the author but inferred from the drawings and models by the viewer. This type of review also teaches the students the importance of the visual presentation by itself.

Constructing a successful presentation of a design idea for the first round of judging is like designing a successful television commercial: It has to get ideas across memorably and very briefly. Unlike television commercials, successful competition presentations have to hold the viewer's attention past the first round, revealing more of their substance and complexity with each increasingly critical look.

JOHN C. WALKER

When I was a student, I never was a superstar, but I was never flat-out rejected either.

I liked the system of education when I was in school. I liked the variety of teachers. I couldn't really see how to improve it. And I thought the jury system was a big part of it.

[One of my design instructors] wanted to see lots of paper. He wanted to see a lot of drawing. He could draw very well and he wanted to see many sketches to see that you had gone through everything. He wanted to look at what you thought were good and bad ideas and why you thought that way. If you didn't have a lot of paper there for him to look at, he wasn't very impressed.

Education went through a period in the 1950s where there was a certain amount of turmoil within the faculty, although the students weren't too involved in it. At this time [the schools came up] with the idea of not giving grades. We'd have juries. Everybody would present, and then the jury wouldn't grade them. They thought this was a very liberal method of teaching. But I thought it was just the dumbest thing that they could ever come up with because the student had no idea what the teachers thought about their projects. Then when you had to get your grade at the end of the year you went back to a teacher review board with your three or four projects and they would give you grades. That system didn't work particularly either, because after giving two or three A's then the next student got a B. It seemed like a quota system. But the real problem was not being able to see what the teachers considered good [projects].

I would prefer that students develop great pencil techniques and spend their time on doing presentations in pencil. Magic marker isn't as quick. I think that is what they should develop as a presentation technique for juries or clients because you can't afford the time to do ink presentations. It's too limiting and you can't change the design. It's got you married to the design. I like to use an eraser when I work.

I've gone back to school and been on two juries. I found the unevenness of the work very frustrating. Some students were very confident and very professional, but some students were just being catered to and allowed to

---

John C. (Sandy) Walker (Figure 13-26) studied at the University of California, Berkeley, where he earned his Bachelor of Arts degree in Architecture in 1957. He is currently principal in the San Francisco firm Walker & Moody Architects. His firm has won various awards from the American Institute of Architects (AIA) and has been spotlighted in numerous design publications. It offers services in architecture, planning, and interior design. Representative projects include Pier 39, a major restaurant, shopping, and parking complex in San Francisco; Auberge du Soleil, a restaurant, lodge, and tennis complex in the Napa Valley; San Luis Bay Inn in San Luis Obispo, California; and a variety of mixed-use developments, hotels, restaurants, office buildings, financial institutions, and athletic clubs.

Figure 13-26 John C. Walker.

indulge themselves in fantasies that were never going to work. You can't stand up in a jury and just say, "This is what I did, I like it." I found that the "I like it" argument was being used too much.

I think that jurors generally like models. They may ask for drawings, but if you bring in models, that can make a big difference. My own personal feeling is that I like sketchier presentations. I think it's better not to present a very hard-edge, totally professional [presentation] to show something sketchy that gives the client/jury a sense that they can participate in the design process rather than the sense that it's a [finished] product.

I think that a designer has to be a salesman. I don't know why the school doesn't give courses in salesmanship. One of the best quotes I ever heard was from a designer that explained, "When we've done these type of buildings before we tell our clients that we offer tremendous experience. When we haven't done this type before we tell them that we offer a fresh approach." It was a great line.

PETER WALKER

[Juries are] about personal expression. A teacher must coax out your strength to express yourself. You do this through the studio, little by little. Finally, though, like the old medieval orals, you must go to the town square and explain your ideas to the people. You must develop a sense of conviction and the ability to stand up for your ideas.

I think that, as brutal as the architectural juries can be, the leading architects tend to be more able to stand up for their work and its intellectual content. Artists are even better at this than architects.

I think juries in the hands of someone who is skillful and knowledgeable are a tremendously helpful tool. But I think juries in the hands of people who are either infantile or demeaning can be brutal.

Nobody ever explained to me what education was about. As a student I'd had a little bit of pedagogical awareness because I come from a teaching family; but, basically, my undergraduate education was a wobbly, bumbling process. I can remember taking on one young faculty member because he had at one time given me a D and at another, given me an A, but he couldn't explain to me the difference in my work. I wasn't as angry as I was curious about this.

The studio can be a wonderful place. The act of making decisions is like what happens in a moot court. You take all of your life experience, all of your research experience, all of this, that, and the other thing, and you synthesize them to try to win and to accomplish your goal.

When I taught the first year of the landscape design program, I approached it essentially like football practice, ballet school, or boot camp. It was a physical strengthening and training process.

Early on in my experience I questioned the value of design juries. It was like having a review session every day after football practice, where we all sat around and analyzed what we did: This seemed like nonsense. We were tired. We really should have gone home, gotten some sleep, and started all over again Monday morning. We had played our game. There seemed to be no sense in analyzing it then.

However, over time I've found that juries were useful for two purposes. One is that you may reach a student when he is very receptive to suggestions and new information. A good teacher can sense when to have an interim jury. I've sometimes done pinups the end of the first week during a six-week problem because the students were in trouble. As soon as they're in trouble, and they're really asking questions, they're ripe for new thoughts and information. So that's one of the reasons for having a jury.

The other reason for having a jury is that the students have to be toughened. It's very difficult to take the thing that's in you, this little precious thing, and put it on paper where somebody can see it and criticize it.

In law school, the professors teach you not only the background information about your case, but also how to fight your case before a jury. In design school, we don't sufficiently teach students how to stand up for their ideas.

Very few juries in school accurately simulate the complexity or danger of most juries in practice. For instance, it's

Peter Walker (Figure 13-27) attended the University of California at Berkeley where he earned a Bachelor of Science in Landscape Architecture in 1955. He later pursued graduate studies at the University of Illinois at Urbana-Champaign and received his Master of Landscape Architecture from Harvard University in 1957. He cofounded the firm Sasaki, Walker Associates, the precursor of the SWA Group, and he currently heads the firm Peter Walker and Partners Landscape Architecture, Inc., of San Francisco. His work has been recognized by such organizations as the American Society of Landscape Architects, the American Institute of Architects, the New York Architectural League, and the National Endowment for the Arts (NEA). His work has been published internationally in a variety of publications.

Mr. Walker has served as a juror for the Rome Prize in Landscape Architecture at the American Academy in Rome; Progressive Architecture; *the Prince of Wales Prizes; the American Society of Landscape Architects (ASLA) National Design Awards; and the NEA. He produced winning entries for several design competitions. He has taught for over ten years at Harvard University, where he served as the chairman of the Department of Landscape Architecture, and at the Sasaki, Walker Associates/SWA Group Summer School for Landscape Architecture.*

Among his best-known projects are the designs for the Golden Gateway Redevelopment and ALCOA Plaza in San Francisco; Foothill College in Los Altos, California; Weyerhaeuser Corporate Headquarters in Tacoma, Washington; the Upjohn Corporate Headquarters in Kalamazoo, Michigan; the Orange County Performing Arts Center in Costa Mesa, California; Tanner Fountain at Harvard University; Burnett Park in Fort Worth, Texas; IBM Federal Systems Division, Clearlake, Texas; IBM Solana in Westlake, Texas; and Marina Linear Park, San Diego, California.

Figure 13-27 Peter Walker, FASLA.

very difficult in school to produce a king, but many of our clients are kings.

I always tell my students that their grades are not based on the results of a jury. They are based on my own judgment, not the jury's judgment. But I also tell them that how well they do with the jury is a *part* of my judgment.

Some students can't deal with juries. The minute they're on their feet, they're dead. There are always one or two that are just absolutely petrified.

I think that the key to preparing students for practice is training. You can train. And I do. I don't have a whole semester to do it. I try to do it in the studio rather than in another class.

I try to make the last jury of the term especially frightening by being large and important. That's one of the things you have to deal with in practice. It's like a city council meeting or fine arts commission where there's a lot at stake and a lot of pressure. It is a problem to study in itself and I assign them to this presentation problem.

I have some advice I'd give to researchers. The design professions must keep searching for new ways of living and new ways of seeing. Architecture has benefited from the research branch of engineering, and from some of the sociological research. But architecture is not essentially a research activity—and neither is landscape architecture—so the research that we have is either borrowed or is the work of a gifted practitioner. To put so much emphasis on the normative aspects of the school is to turn away, to deny, and to blunt those few that will produce those visions.

Part of a collegiate atmosphere is being able to talk with colleagues about problems after they happen. In academia, too much pontificating and too little real sharing occurs. If an office staff didn't share experiences with their employees, but just dumped them on a project and said, "Do the best you can," it would be an awful office. Schools do that all the time. There is not enough of a continuous process of colleagues checking back and forth, watching and advising each other.

CYNTHIA WEESE

My freshman year I nearly failed. At the beginning of the midterms I think I had a B, two C's, a D, and an F. The dean called me in. I had a scholarship and I had to be put on

Cynthia Weese (Figure 13-28) received her Bachelor of Science degree from Washington University in St. Louis in 1963. In 1965, she received her Bachelor of Architecture from the same school. She has been principal of the Chicago-based firm Weese Langley Weese Architects LTD since 1977. The firm has won numerous awards from the American Institute of Architects (AIA)/Chicago Chapter. The firm's work encompasses multifamily housing, libraries, churches, schools, commercial projects, and adaptive reuse projects. Representative examples of their work include Coe College Art Museum and library in Cedar Rapids, Iowa; Illinois Wesleyan Chapel on the campus of Illinois Wesleyan University in Bloomington, Illinois; Chicago City Day School in Chicago, Illinois; and over 4000 units of new and rehabilitated housing.

Her work has been published and exhibited both in the United States and abroad.

Ms. Weese served as president of the Chicago Architectural Club and as a board member of the National Institute for Architectural Education. She has been a visiting critic and lecturer at several universities and a Design Awards coordinator for the Chicago Chapter of the AIA. Ms. Weese has served on the National AIA Awards Committee and as president of the Chicago Chapter of the AIA. She has also co-organized a traveling exhibit on Chicago Women Architects: Contemporary Directions.

Figure 13-28 Cynthia Weese, FAIA. (Photo: Norman Phillips of London, Ltd.)

academic probation. And he said, "I know it's hard and I know you'll do better." And the second semester I did much better. When I entered the design curriculum the same thing happened the first semester.

I went straight through architecture school for six years. This was probably too long for one to go without switching around or going to a different school. I should have probably taken a year off after the fourth year and worked in an office. My class was very much a closely knit group; there was lots of peer pressure to go on to finish right away. We were highly competitive.

The school I attended was very good; there were some excellent professors. However, I felt that, with the exception of one or two occasions, the juries were not helpful. They were judgmental, not constructive.

The jury for a final year, semester-long project was ridiculous. It was basically four or five guys trying to outsmart one another. It was a waste of time.

Juries are most useful if they give you an opportunity to interact, but there was very little interaction when I was in school. I was basically very shy so I didn't defend myself. If I was criticized I would just listen. There was very little dialogue.

I do remember some wonderful juries. Aldo van Eyck came and did marvelous critiques one afternoon. As one of the professors said at the end, he proved that the jury system can work. It was just a marvelous kind of energy that he had throughout the whole jury.

One quality that helped me get through school was stubbornness. The attrition rate was very high, going from 70 to (around) 12 or 15. We all wondered if we would make it.

I had tremendous support from faculty members. They were a marvelous, progressive collection of people. They gave a tremendous amount of help.

I think that the key element in the schools is the studio system. I lived in the studio. Our class was not full of talented people, but we were very cohesive and yet competitive at the same time. I think the studio and the building were very much a part of our education because we spent all our time at the school.

The architecture building [at Washington University] was a wonderful place. It's symmetrical with a large airy central stair. On the second floor were the studios with 14-foot ceilings and huge windows. Each studio was divided into two halves by a row of lockers down the center. It was really the best kind of environment—high enough, and the windows were so much a part of the character that the mess that covered the floor wasn't too depressing. You could lift your eyes and see something wonderful. The building environment, both social and physical, was very significant to our state of mind—and to my later work.

I do feel that I was very, very fortunate, particularly as a woman, to have an enlightened group of faculty. They were all very, very supportive. And there was [an almost total absence] of chauvinism. Basically everybody was very straightforward and encouraging.

I have been on a number of juries. There's a wonderful jury system which was introduced to us by Peter Prangnell, a professor in Toronto. It's a matrix jury. You have as many jurors as students and the students pair up into teams of two and each juror talks one-on-one with each team for 20 or 30 minutes until a bell rings, at which time you move to the next team. You make a schedule; by the end of the jury every juror has talked to almost all the students.

It helps to have a jury outside one's own turf. It provides an atmosphere where you realize that you're part of a larger community. Schools get tight and you feel too much a part of a closed community. Juries at the Graham Foundation in Chicago are always positive experiences in very beautiful rooms. The acoustic level is soft and there's natural light, which is very important.

After a jury each student should have something to build on. If you did not come through [successfully], [you should be given a sense of] where you failed or how you failed and what can be done to rectify that. It's terribly counterproductive just to tell people that they've failed and not help them understand how they can improve.

I think that the schools tend to be a little more rigid about pushing an idea or concept than practitioners. They tend to critique the idea and its development rather than the execution. Granted, there are some basic wrong ideas. But many times it's not that the student doesn't have an idea. It's that they are too timid about developing their ideas. They stop too soon.

Students should develop the ability to critique their projects. They very seldom look at a project and say, "What can I do to make this better? Where is this [not working]? What relationships are faulty?" You tend to become too dependent on what other people tell you is wrong, instead of developing your own instincts. You really need to fall back on yourself and really give yourself a critique. You're not going to always have somebody coming to your desk telling you what to do.

Students should learn how to overcome the inevitable infatuation with their solution and to be more objective.

I would like to see more frequent juries or group discussions in school. I think some schools are working toward having frequent times when students hang up their work and talk about it. Never call a jury the "final jury."

Instead, call it "project jury #4" or something similar. They then have a chance to begin expressing themselves about their projects. Architects are more verbal than they were 25 or 30 years ago. In practice you are dealing with multiple clients, multiple owners, and multiple influences. You need to get used to the idea of talking things through.

The architecture profession is becoming a team-oriented profession—although the word *team* is overused. There are multiple influences on the architect. If the architect insists on being by himself or herself as the aloof genius, the whole profession is going to be in trouble. It helps nurture the public perception of architects as being somewhat arrogant.

Students need to learn how to meet people's needs without being thick- or thin-skinned. Otherwise they'll have a tough time.

Architects need to develop leadership capabilities that will enable them to direct building teams; consultants, specialists, clients, and developers. Many projects involve tremendous numbers of special consultants. You need to be able to deal with those people, to coordinate them and to bring out the best in them. Leaders get other people to do wonderful things. Architects need to develop these skills.

Architecture is a highly regarded profession; however, on another level there is a lot of skepticism about architects. I think that they would be much better appreciated if they knew how to be good leaders.

I think that there is developing a tremendous culture of women architects who support each other. One of my chief concerns is a split; either you're a feminist architect or you're a sellout woman architect who deals with men.

There must be a way to help women come together. You spend your life as an architect bringing people together, making things happen—not making them not happen.

I think that young women architects are, on the whole, treated better than they were 10 or 15 years ago. However, I know there are still problems. I would hope that women can join in the profession and strengthen the profession (as a whole); we need as much unity as we can get. I hate to see a woman's separatist movement.

Time is an important issue on awards juries. Sometimes you don't have enough time to really deal with the issues very thoughtfully. Sometimes they're not as carefully structured as a competition jury because they are one-day events.

Ideally in juries you let the jury be by themselves; members of the design committee do not sit in and try to tell them what to do. I've been on juries where the design committee people have been too much a part of the jury, and I have been on juries where they just sat quietly and didn't say anything, and the jury really was free to talk. The latter allows the jury to concentrate much better on the work presented.

I remember one jury in particular where three of us never had met each other, but we were really a very good jury. We argued for things and were able to give and take and make each other see things that the others had missed and appreciate things that we felt were important. That was quite a wonderful experience.

Our firm has not entered any competitions because we feel that it doesn't suit our way of developing projects.

In a competition jury, the adviser's role is critical. The adviser is there to help you as much as they can—but to stay out of your way. I've been on juries where the adviser has been too insistent a part of the jury. In a competition jury, the chairperson is a very critical person who needs to be a strong but not domineering leader; very intelligent, and very articulate.

The first jury I was on was that way; Michael Brill was the chair. He was fantastic. We were there for three days going over 350 projects. It was an exhausting effort, but the synthesis that we were able to come to in the last hours was wonderful. It was a process of joint discussion and discovery.

JEFFREY WERNER

> *Jeffrey Werner's (Figure 13-29) early interest in landscape design led to the study of landscape architecture at the University of California at Berkeley, where he graduated with a Bachelor of Science in Business Administration in 1977. His studies in environmental design continued at the California College of Arts and Crafts, where he received a Bachelor of Fine Arts in 1979. Mr. Werner has been an active California designer for ten years. His firm, Werner Design Associates, in Redwood City, California, practices total-concept design, combining landscape and interior design. Current projects include an expansive Napa Valley retreat, resort homes throughout California, and Silicon Valley executive homes. Mr. Werner's designs have been published in many national magazines and have received the Halo Lighting Award, the California Landscape Award, and several American Society of Interior Designers (ASID) competition awards.*

In my early years as a student, I really don't feel that I did that well in design. Although I was very interested in it, it seems that design education was much more esoteric than applied. I really felt there was nothing objective upon which to judge your success, say, as compared to mathematics where you knew the answer was right or wrong.

In school, I recall that I was always on time and successful with my projects, but I never felt like I was a star. My projects succeeded and they worked. There were always the students who worked for days and nights and had incredible rendering abilities. And then there were others who were so spacy but always came up with a great concept, and whether it applied or not, that more or less put them into the star status. And still others who basically did a good job, and created a project that met all the qualifications. Achieving star status was not necessarily the reward.

I was always anxious to finish school, because I felt that in school you were almost always "put down." There really were no true rewards, because the projects weren't real.

I think what helped me the most in getting through was the studio experience. There was strong comaraderie at Berkeley. You could learn not only from your professors but from the other students who may have had even more skills in certain areas. I think in my case it helped me develop a good team design spirit.

In school, many times you just wanted to get through the educational process, especially in the conceptual phases, so you simply designed what your design professor wanted just to get through the class and avoid a confrontation.

Figure 13-29 Jeffrey Werner.

The evaluation process in design school was, most of the time, very public, whether or not the crits or small groups were in front of the class. Since it was an open studio, even when the professor was just at your desk critting your work, everyone always heard what was being said.

In school I felt that there wasn't enough [evaluation of one's design]. [Perhaps it was a matter of] being in school and not having a great enough sense of self-worth, but I felt that many of the criticisms [of my projects] were unjustified. Many times I felt there wasn't enough background given [as to] why they should criticize my work that way. I think that the evaluation process should be combined with a process that builds self-worth. Think about elementary school. There was always a little starred item on our report cards indicating that the student "accepts constructive criticism." I think that design teachers should be able to give constructive criticism as well.

I really feel that I learned more in the first ten months of actual practice with a design firm than I did in my entire career as a student. While some people enjoy conceptualizing, I enjoy much more the experience of having a real client and knowing that your work is contributing to a definite, real end product.

I believe bringing in professionals from outside the academic realm is always great for a jury situation. But I think juries can work much better if the jurors have a background on the person they are judging, and they really know the project well.

It would be useful to have an evaluation sheet at the end of a jury. You could then critique the students in terms of presentation, the appearance of the presenters, presentation skills, or whether the students clearly presented the concept. I think criticism on these points would be more beneficial than criticisms like, "You're obviously just too safe in your design," or, "You're not searching out the true reality of design." Those are statements that we hear all too often but they don't mean much at all.

I remember one situation where one of my classmates, a good friend of mine, had a project that lacked detail and design completion. But her entire presentation was about how her stairway represented the stairway of life—the evolution of life and the different stages that life progresses through. I really can't remember exactly what she said. But at the time I thought that it was the most ridiculous thing I had ever heard. I really knew that she had no idea at all about what she was doing. She had struggled through the entire project, and was just happy to have something on paper to show. But the jury just ate it up. They just raved about how she really searched for meaning in her design. The key is that she was excited about her work and she communicated her idea in a convincing way. I think that emotion is one of the most important things in presentations. Students should sell with excitement, and a true meaning and emotion in their work. I think the only way to really do that is to feel it in your work, but I don't believe there should have to be a lot of esoteric superficiality in your work either. We see this a lot in school.

In our professional organization, the American Society of Interior Designers (ASID), we have many students who attend chapter meetings. We offer many programs (Career Day, Tag-Along Day, internships within firms), and it seems like there's a very supportive network. I think that these activities are most important in helping students develop a feeling of self-worth. See what happens in a design office. See how designers present their work and how their presentation boards look.

Many firms practice the jury process, almost a crit process, as a way of keeping interaction within the office staff. Luncheon presentations are often given where members of the firm can critique each other's projects. But I think compared to juries in school, they're much more positive. The process is used to improve the design, and to point out issues that you, who may be too close to a project, can't yet see.

One thing I would like to see in professional juries is a selection of a more varied group of judges. In national competitions you often see the same judges used over and over. They're often pulling for big names.

My own work is multidisciplinary, incorporating the fields of lighting, landscape, and interiors. In all these disciplines I've come to realize that the same principles of design apply. Lighting may be more technical, but you're still dealing with scale, with form, with texture. The same is so true in interiors and landscape, in architecture too: You're dealing with how the space works, how it flows, the scale of spaces, how it feels. The plant material is like the fabric. It falls into place. If the design is good, if the space works, it's really hard to ruin it with the furniture and the fabrics. It's the same with a landscape. If it flows, if the terraces are great, the retaining walls all work, and it creates the space you want and the grade levels you want, the plant material falls in. A lot of that applies in lighting also; you're lighting to accentuate texture. If it's done well, it can embody you, it can excite you, it can create drama.

And whenever I've had the chance to design an architectural statement, I'm always thinking: "How is it going to sit on the land?" "How is it going to feel inside as it relates to outside?" "How is the light going to come in?" "How is the light going to feel at night?" "How can I design elements that can be accentuated?" The same principles apply.

APPENDIXES

APPENDIX A
Methodology

This research entailed a series of separate, related studies conducted at a variety of locations over a seven-year period. This section describes each phase in chronological order and provides some summary information about each sample. Figure A-1 shows these phases in chronological order.

My aim was to achieve both breadth and depth in investigating design juries; consequently a strong attempt was made to gather a healthy mix of both qualitative and quantitative information. Figure A-2 shows the research method used in each phase.

Participant-observation, ethnography, and *archives* were three qualitative methods used throughout the duration of this research. As both a participant in and observer of the jury process and the design studio, I have relied

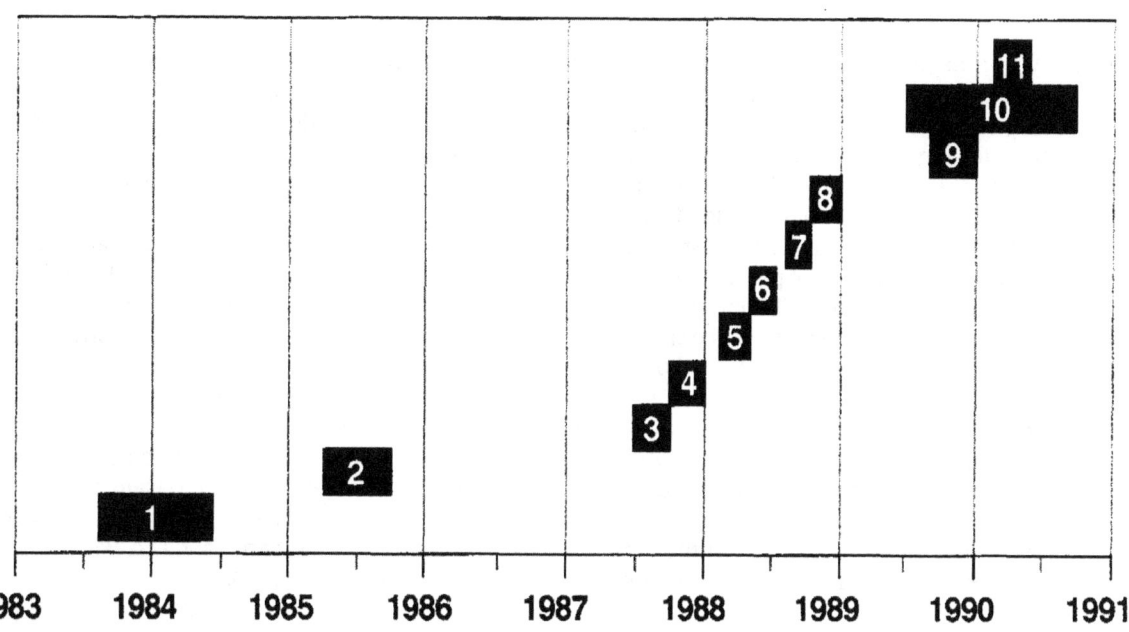

Figure A-1 Research phases when the data was collected. From start to finish, the research took seven years to complete.

RESEARCH METHODS USED IN EACH PHASE

Phase	Sample	Survey	Interview	Observation	Diary	Participant/Observation	Ethnography	Archives
1	California State Polytechnic University, Pomona	X	X	X	X	X	X	X
2	Association of Collegiate Schools of Architecture/ American Institute of Architects (ACSA/AIA) Teachers' Seminar	X				X	X	X
3	American Institute of Architecture Students (AIAS) - 1	X				X	X	X
4	University of Notre Dame	X				X	X	X
5	University of Illinois at Urbana-Champaign (UIUC) - 1	X				X	X	X
6	Georgia Institute of Technology	X				X	X	X
7	Association of Collegiate Schools of Architecture (ACSA) Regional Meeting	X				X	X	X
8	American Institute of Architecture Students (AIAS) - 2	X				X	X	X
9	University of Illinois at Urbana-Champaign (UIUC) - 2	X				X	X	X
10	Prominent designers		X			X		X
11	Design faculty					X	X	X

Figure A-2 Research methods used in each phase. Surveys, interviews, participant-observation, archives, and an ethnographic approach were the primary data-gathering techniques.

heavily on my own experiences and those that students have recounted to me. By using the ethnographic approach, I often relied on students as key informants to learn how they experienced the jury and the studio. My aim was to try to place myself in their shoes and develop a sense of empathy. My experience to date has included over 300 hours worth of "design jury duty" as well as team teaching several design studio courses. For the past seven years, my office has been located across the hall from a large graduate studio, and for the past two years, the office space next to mine has been converted into a graduate studio as well. My own informal observations and listening to random studio conversations have been a valuable source of information. In addition, informal discussions and personal correspondence (in the form of letters and telephone calls) with students, faculty, and visiting critics over the years have been a key source. Many of the insights described in the text are based on my reflections on all these experiences.

Surveys yielded primarily quantitative or numerical data, while *interviews, diaries, behavior observations, participant-observations, and ethnographic discussions* yielded qualitative data. Most of the surveys included a number of open-ended items that also provided qualitative information.

A total of 893 surveys, 113 interviews, and 27 diaries were completed, and 130 student jury presentations were systematically observed; a few individuals participated in more than one research method. A total of 923 individuals were either interviewed or surveyed: 806 students, of whom 725 are in design; 53 faculty, and 64 design practitioners. Figure A-3 shows the breakdown of the samples who were either interviewed or surveyed. The students were drawn from a total of 92 schools, and the faculty were from a total of 30 schools from across the United States (Figures A-4 and A-5). The largest group of design practitioners was from the Los Angeles metropolitan area, and other practitioners were from the San Francisco Bay Area, Chicago, and elsewhere (Figure A-6).

Sample research instruments can be obtained by communicating with the author. Note that unless the specific return rate is mentioned here, the exact return rates of

SAMPLES SURVEYED OR INTERVIEWED   Methodology   227

BREAKDOWN BY DISCIPLINE

Survey

	Phase	Architecture	Landscape Architecture	Urban Planning	Non-Environmental Design	Total
Students	1	189	32	30	81	332
	3	103				103
	4	55				55
	5	114				114
	6	99				99
	8	69				69
	9		34			34
	Total	629	66	30	81	806
Faculty	1	14	5			19
	2	16				16
	7	18				18
	Total	48	5			53
Practitioners	1	34				34
	10					
	Total	34				34
	Grand total	711	71	30	81	893

Interview

Architecture	Landscape Architecture	Interior Design	Total
83			83
83			83
21	4	5	30
21	4	5	30
104	4	5	113

Figure A-3 Breakdown of the samples who were either interviewed or surveyed in each phase, broken down by discipline. The numbers refer to the sample size for each phase.

LOCATION OF STUDENT SURVEY RESPONDENTS*

* plus respondents from Hawaii and Puerto Rico

Figure A-4 A total of 806 students from 92 schools across the United States completed surveys. The map shows the location of the students' schools.

228 Appendix A

LOCATION OF FACULTY SURVEY RESPONDENTS*

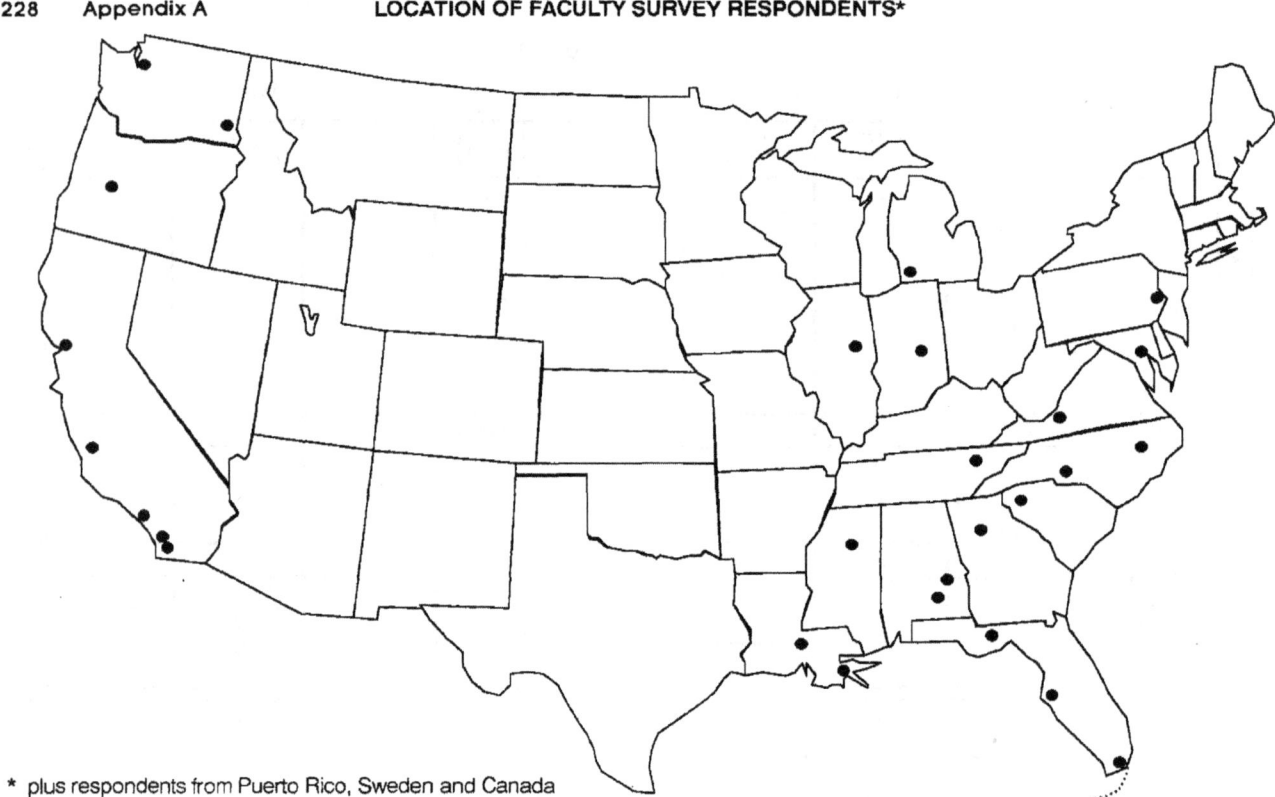

* plus respondents from Puerto Rico, Sweden and Canada

Figure A-5 A total of 53 faculty from 30 schools across the United States completed surveys. The map shows the location of the faculty's schools.

LOCATION OF PRACTITIONERS INTERVIEWED OR SURVEYED *

* plus respondent from Japan

Figure A-6 A total of 64 design practitioners from the greater Los Angeles area, San Francisco, Chicago, and elsewhere participated in surveys or interviews. The map shows the location of their offices in the United States. One was from Japan.

surveys were difficult to assess. In general, the return rates were high; most of those individuals given surveys completed them.

PHASE 1

Phase 1 was an in-depth case study conducted at California State Polytechnic University (Cal Poly), Pomona, where I was on the faculty at the time. The purpose of the study was to begin to seriously explore how students, faculty, and design practitioners perceive the jury process. The study began in *fall 1983* with a literature review, a process that continued throughout the entire duration of this research. Computerized data searches were updated periodically. In addition, we routinely browsed through the library to search for relevant sources. The literature review continued throughout each phase of this research.

Several methods were used to gather information about the jury process from students, faculty, and design practitioners: behavioral observations, interviews, surveys, and diaries (Figure A-2). Phase 1 was completed during spring 1984.

Samples and Procedures

Behavioral observations: Systematic behavioral observations were conducted during nine architectural jury sessions, some of them recorded on videotape, for a total of 130 student presentations. Both verbal and nonverbal behavior of the students presenting their design work, the rest of the class, and the jurors were observed and recorded.

Student interviews: A total of 83 students was interviewed. Forty-three architecture students were interviewed immediately after they finished presenting their projects to the jury. They were asked what they learned and how they reacted to the criticism they had just received. Forty additional architecture students were interviewed on an ongoing basis throughout the academic term.

Student, faculty, and practitioner surveys: One hundred eighty-nine architecture students, 32 landscape architecture students, and 30 urban planning students were administered a four-page, 14-item survey to try to understand how each group viewed the jury evaluation process. Several of the questions had subsections. Eleven questions were fixed-choice and three were open-ended. Students were asked how much they learned from juries compared to other methods such as desk crits; what type of feedback helped them learn the most; what were their best and worst jury experiences—what was the criticism, how was it delivered, and how did they respond emotionally; what were their general opinions of the jury system; and some behavioral questions about their eating, sleeping, and working habits prior to the jury.

To provide a comparison, the same questions, with minor modifications, were posed to 81 students outside the design fields about the ways in which their own work was evaluated. These students were enrolled in a psychology class for nonmajors and were drawn from a wide cross section of majors across the campus.

A separate, short one-page survey following up on some of the issues raised in the prior survey results, asking specifically about alternatives to traditional design juries, was administered to 85 architecture students. All student surveys were anonymous.

Nineteen environmental design faculty (11 in architecture and 5 in landscape architecture and planning at Cal Poly Pomona, and another 3 in architecture at nearby universities) were given a four-page, 10-item survey with all open-ended questions. They were questioned about their own opinions of juries as well as their perceptions of students' attitudes and behaviors toward them. They were asked what criteria they usually used to evaluate a student's design project, what factors influenced their criticism of student work at the jury, and what criteria they use to select visiting critics. They were also asked to compare student presentations to client presentations in practice.

Thirty-four practicing architects, Cal Poly Pomona alumni, completed surveys asking them about their reflections on design juries while they were students. The four-page, 19-item survey contained 12 closed and 7 open-ended questions. Many items were identical to those in the student and faculty surveys. As in the faculty survey, a key question asked alumni to compare juries in academia with client presentations in practice. The alumni addresses were retrieved from Cal Poly Pomona's alumni office. Surveys were sent in the mail along with a cover letter on the dean's stationery. The response rate to this survey was low; while 200 were sent out, only 17% (34) were returned. Financial constraints prohibited any follow-up reminder letter or phone call.

Student diaries: Twenty-seven architecture students were asked to keep diaries of their daily studio experiences whenever they received criticism from their design critic, another student, or anyone else during a desk crit, jury, or casual conversation. They were asked to elaborate on the following questions: "What do I think and feel about my work? What do I feel or think about my instructor's reaction to my work, to what I said, and to me, personally? What do I feel or think about other students' reactions to my work, to what I said, and to me personally? What did I learn?" They kept their diaries for a 10-week period, the duration of the academic term. Students were assured of the confidential nature of the diaries. They were told that although the content of their diaries may eventually be read by others, their names would not be released.

Data Analyses

The behavior observations were coded and plotted into categories of offensive, defensive, and nervous behaviors, based on the categories defined in two classic books,

Julius Fast's *Body Language* and Gerard Nierenberg's *How to Read a Person Like a Book*.[1]

A content analysis was performed on the interviews and diaries. Common themes and trends were noted. The names of specific professors who were mentioned in the diaries were disregarded. Rather than analyzing exactly who said what to whom, the focus was on the content of the interactions among students, design critics, and jurors.

The surveys were analyzed using the Statistical Package for the Social Sciences (SPSS) computer software package. Simple frequencies were tabulated and differences among groups were examined through the use of chi-square and T-tests. Correlations among items were calculated. They were eventually combined with the data from subsequent studies into one large data base and analyzed in greater detail.

Evaluation of the Methodology

The diaries proved to be by far among the most revealing sources of information about students' private feelings and experiences with juries. Fascinating, "juicy" stories and tales of woe surfaced that would never have been found through more traditional research methods. More than any other research technique, they provided an excellent opportunity to get into the shoes of and develop a sense of empathy for the design student. Since Phase 1 was completed and the results disseminated, numerous colleagues have reacted most strongly to the results from the diaries. They seem to have struck a raw nerve. Their open-ended, free-flowing nature and colorful, verbatim quotes are qualities that seem to communicate powerfully to designers. Perhaps this technique relates strongly to individuals who are dominated by the right side of the brain. The emotion elicited by the diaries was what the artistic designers cited most often.

Student surveys were by far the most efficient means of collecting information from large numbers of students. The inclusion of the open-ended items worked well, as many students had a lot to say. The questions asking about the best and worst jury experiences resulted in a wealth of powerful anecdotes. The follow-up, open-ended survey of students that asked specifically for alternatives to design juries was especially revealing.

The low response rate from the alumni surveys can be interpreted in different ways. Perhaps the busy schedules of these practicing architects did not permit them to respond by the deadline. Or maybe they simply were not interested. Or the subject may have been so sensitive that they preferred not to respond. As a result of this low response rate, mail surveys were not used in any subsequent phases of this research. Interested researchers should note that the mail survey method itself is not to blame, but that in order for mail surveys to be most effective they require substantial resources for postage, reminder cards, and extra duplicate surveys to send as further follow-ups. At the time, such financial and staff support resources were simply not available.

Since the completion of Phase 1, many colleagues cautioned that designers—both students and faculty—often feel uncomfortable with mail surveys and thus are unlikely to respond. Consequently, most of the subsequent student and faculty surveys were administered on the spot as part of a lecture, studio, or conference presentation session. Respondents were typically asked to turn in their completed surveys at the start of the session. Practitioners in subsequent research phases were interviewed rather than surveyed.

PHASE 2

The purpose of subsequent phases of research was to determine whether or not some of the issues that students, faculty, and practitioners raised in the initial phase were true elsewhere. Key portions of the study were replicated with additional samples of students and faculty from other colleges and universities as well as with additional practitioners.

The specific purpose of *Phase 2* was to obtain additional information from faculty housed at a variety of schools, and to compare that information with that of the original case-study school.

Sample and Procedures

Phase 2 involved a sample of 16 architecture faculty from 14 different schools who were attending the Association of Collegiate Schools of Architecture/American Institute of Architects (ACSA/AIA) Teachers' Seminar held at the Cranbrook Academy of Art during *summer 1985*. One of the major themes of that year's meeting was design criticism.

The research instrument was an eight-page survey of 23 questions with subparts. Four items were open-ended and the rest were closed. Questions were revised versions of the items asked of faculty in Phase 1. Response formats were more sophisticated and the questions delved into greater detail than had those in Phase 1, for instance, asking about how often written criticism at their schools is delivered in design juries and by whom, how often written schedules for student project presentations are used and maintained, and to what extent jurors are involved in the grading process. Faculty were also asked to describe any new or innovative techniques in use at their schools. The survey was administered on the spot to ensure a high response rate.

The procedures used were as follows: The survey was anonymous, and adding the name of the respondent was optional; many wrote them in. A survey was placed in every conference registration packet and collected at a midpoint during the conference, immediately prior to a keynote address on design juries.

Data Analysis

The data were examined by content analysis. Responses were categorized by type, and frequencies of each type were calculated.

Evaluation of the Method

A few faculty went out of their way to tell me that they refused to participate on the grounds that they simply did not believe in surveys of any kind. But those who did respond were typically quite articulate. The inclusion of open-ended items was essential. Two of the most revealing questions were again: "What is the best jury you have ever had or seen—either as a student or a faculty member?" and "What is the worst jury you have ever had or seen—either as a student or a faculty member?" These items provoked a wide range of responses, especially from some prominent university administrators whose own experiences as students were recounted in the form of horror stories; one in particular recalled the ceremonial burning of his design project after a devastating jury.

PHASES 3-6

The purpose of *Phases 3-6* was to broaden the base of information from students and compare the results with those from Phase 1: Were the problems with juries noted in Phase 1 unique, or were they typical? Another purpose was to explore in greater depth some of the issues that students raised in Phase 1.

Samples and Procedures

Subsequent student surveys were administered during several phases:

- Phase 3, a national cross section of 103 student chapter leaders from 71 schools at the American Institute of Architecture Students (AIAS) national grassroots leadership conference in Washington, D.C., during *summer 1987*
- Phase 4, 55 architecture students at the University of Notre Dame during *fall 1987*
- Phase 5, 114 architecture students at the University of Illinois at Urbana-Champaign during *spring 1988*
- Phase 6, 99 architecture students at Georgia Institute of Technology during *spring 1988*

The research instruments were variations on the original four-page survey used at Cal Poly Pomona. Several items were refined and improved, based on previous findings from survey research and successful item formats used elsewhere.[2] A number of questions went into greater detail than had the earlier version. Surveys used at the AIAS grassroots leadership conference were expanded into 11 pages with 50 items, several of which had lengthy subsections. Six questions were open-ended and the rest were closed. Questions addressed the following issues:

- Students' own levels of satisfaction and the perceived levels of satisfaction of most students at their schools with various aspects of architectural education, including their architectural education in general, design studios, both interim and final juries, lecture and seminar courses, and courses outside the major
- Career goals
- Goals for project evaluations
- How much they learn from juries as compared to desk crits and informal discussions with other students
- Whether or not they believed juries needed improvement and, if so, in what specific areas
- Their own eating and sleeping habits as well as their perceptions of those same habits of most students at their schools
- Ratings of how often students budget their time, prepare for the jury's oral presentation, receive written feedback, and so on
- The shortest, longest, and average jury session at their schools and the minimum and maximum numbers of jurors
- The basis for selecting visiting critics, how students respond to jury criticism, and what criteria are used to evaluate their work
- What new or innovative ways of running juries are used at their schools

The architecture student surveys at Georgia Institute of Technology were abbreviated into six pages. Those administered at the University of Notre Dame and the University of Illinois at Urbana-Champaign were shortened into two pages and only addressed a few of these issues.

The procedure for administering the surveys was as follows: To ensure confidentiality, all student surveys were anonymous. For Phase 3, the survey was administered immediately prior to a conference workshop on design juries. Students were given the surveys while seated altogether in a lecture room and completed them on the spot. AIAS staff members collected the completed surveys and mailed them back to me. For Phase 4, the survey was administered in a similar format. For Phases 5 and 6, surveys were administered through the local AIAS chapter to design studios representing different levels throughout the school. They were distributed to each studio over a period of a few days and were left on individual student desks at the start of class and collected at the end of class. Local AIAS chapter members collected them and returned them to me.

Data Analyses

The data from individual data sets were analyzed using the Statistical Package for the Social Sciences (SPSS-PC) software package on an IBM personal computer. Among the analytic techniques used were the following: simple frequency distributions, T-tests to measure differences between means for various items, chi-square tests to test the association between certain variables, and Pearson correlations to measure the strength of the relationship between variables. Correlations were obtained between a composite measure of satisfaction with architectural education consisting of four survey items and ratings of design juries, satisfaction with design studio courses, satisfaction with architecture lecture courses, and so on. The four satisfaction questions were as follows:

> "If financial considerations and finding a job were of no concern to you, then ideally, how long would you like to study architecture?" (Responses ranged along a 5-point scale from "as long as possible" to "no longer than I have to.")
> "If you were to start your schooling all over again, would you like to study architecture?" (Responses ranged along a 5-point scale from "would be very happy to" to "would be very unhappy to.")
> "Would you recommend studying architecture to one of your friends, if they were looking for a major and interested in the field?" (Responses ranged along a 5-point scale from "I definitely would" to "I definitely would not.")
> "How satisfied or dissatisfied are you with your architectural education?" (Responses ranged from "very satisfied" to "very dissatisfied.")

Responses from the four questions were combined and the total number divided by four to derive an average index of satisfaction. This procedure was based on similar items used to measure housing satisfaction.[3] Further analytic techniques are discussed in Phases 8-9.

Evaluation of the Method

Because so many of the same questions had been used repeatedly, few problems were experienced in obtaining responses to these items. More on some specific problems with the combined data analysis is included in Phases 8-9.

PHASE 7

The specific purpose of *Phase 7* was to determine the extent to which the issues raised by faculty in Phases 1 and 2 were representative of issues at other colleges and universities. The goal was to obtain yet additional data from faculty, thereby broadening the basis of faculty viewpoints represented in this research.

Samples and Procedures

Phase 7 involved a sample of 18 architecture faculty from 14 schools who were attending the ACSA Southeast Regional Meeting at the University of Puerto Rico during *fall 1988*. The instrument used was an abbreviated version of that used in Phases 1 and 2, consisting of 10 open-ended questions.

The procedures used were as follows: The survey was administered on the spot to ensure a high response rate. It was administered orally to a group of 18 faculty who were given time to respond individually in writing. The survey was anonymous; however, it did request the name of the respondent's school. Some respondents chose to fill in their names. The survey was conducted at the beginning of one of the conference sessions.

Data Analysis

The data from Phase 7 were analyzed using SYSTAT, a software package on the Macintosh computer. Frequencies were calculated and the data were examined by content analysis.

Evaluation of the Method

As was the case in previous data sets, two of the most revealing questions continued to be: "What is the best jury you have ever had or seen—either as a student or a faculty member?" and "What is the worst jury you have ever had or seen—either as a student or a faculty member?" Again, some fascinating anecdotes surfaced, both positive and negative. After individual, completed surveys were collected, a lively discussion ensued.

PHASES 8-9

The purpose of *Phases 8-9* was similar to those of Phases 3-6, that is, to obtain additional information from students and to determine the degree to which problems with juries were widespread. In addition, the purpose of Phase 9 was to understand students' responses to various alternative forms of evaluating their work, thus extending some of the issues raised in previous studies.

Samples and Procedures

Subsequent student surveys were administered via:

- Phase 8, a national cross section of 69 architecture students from 48 schools at the American Institute of

Architecture Students (AIAS) Forum in Chicago, Illinois, during *fall 1988*
- Phase 9, 34 landscape architecture students at the University of Illinois at Urbana-Champaign during *fall 1989*

The research instruments were variations on the original four-page survey used at Cal Poly Pomona. The architecture student surveys at the AIAS Forum were abbreviated into two pages.

The final survey of landscape architecture students at Illinois was three pages and slightly different from the others. In addition to asking some of the same questions as the previous surveys, it also asked students to evaluate both traditional jury and innovative evaluation techniques immediately after they had been used in the studio.

The procedure for administering the surveys was as follows: To ensure confidentiality, all student surveys were anonymous. For Phase 8, the survey was placed at the conference registration desk, along with other handouts, and asked to be returned to the same location by the end of the conference. AIAS staff members collected the completed surveys and mailed them back to me. For Phase 9, the same survey was administered on three different occasions during the academic term to the same class of 34 students. It was administered during the next class session following the design jury.

Data Analyses

The data set from Phase 8 was analyzed using the SYSTAT software package on the Macintosh computer. Among the analytic techniques used were the following: simple frequency distributions, T-tests to measure differences between means for various items, chi-square tests to test the association between certain variables, and Pearson correlations to measure the strength of the relationship between variables.

The data from Phase 9 were reviewed but not analyzed in detail. Time and financial constraints precluded additional, more sophisticated analyses for Phase 9.

Data Analyses of Common Core Survey Items

Common items from architecture student surveys in Phases 1, 3-6, and 8 were eventually combined into one large data base for analysis using the LOTUS software package during summer 1989 (Figure A-7). The responses to a number of survey items had to be recoded into a common response format for analysis. Some items that were originally 4-point scale were converted into a 5-point scale, and some response scales were reversed. The SPSS-X package for the mainframe computer was used to analyze the results.

The data were broken down into various subgroups for analyses based on the following demographic characteristics: age, sex, race, year in program, level in program, and number of design studios. Because the variation along

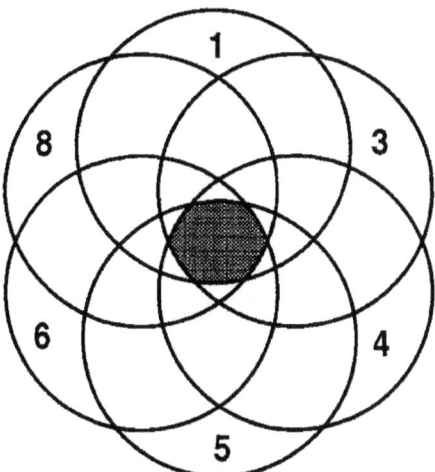

Figure A-7 The data base that was used for the combined data analysis. Core survey items from six separate phases (1, 3-6, and 8) were analyzed altogether.

race was minimal, the same data were also divided into two groups: traditional (white males) versus nontraditional students (women and minorities) for additional analyses.

Frequencies were calculated, and the following analytic techniques were also used: chi-square, T-tests, correlations, analysis of variance, factor analysis and multiple regression. Space limitations prohibit a detailed discussion of these results in this book; however, they may be reported elsewhere at a later date.

Evaluation of the Method

Because so many of the same questions had been used repeatedly, few problems were experienced with any of the surveys. In retrospect, one can always think of questions that could or should have been asked, but time, space, and financial limitations precluded lengthy surveys for most samples. One of the key questions that remains is, To what extent are the students' project or course grades or their grade point averages related to their assessments of design juries? Do students who receive poor grades hate juries, while students with good grades love them? Perhaps future researchers will choose to address this issue.

The combined data analysis was cumbersome. As the surveys had been conducted over several years and since on occasion response scales were reversed from one survey to another, coding and analyzing the combined data set was difficult and required care. In addition, since some questions had been asked repeatedly while others had been asked only of specific samples, the sample sizes responding to specific questions differed. This must be noted in interpreting the results. Finally, because some data has been input using an IBM computer and others in a Macintosh, preparing the data for one large analysis was extremely time consuming. Nonetheless, in retrospect, each study built upon the previous one and the combined data analysis reflects a wide cross section of opinions. The large sample size of the combined data set increases the generalizability of the results.

PHASE 10

Given the strong base of information collected from students, the purpose of *Phase 10* was to better understand how practitioners viewed design juries. Some of the issues that practitioners had raised in Phase 1 were still intriguing, and some key unanswered questions remained. Hence for Phase 10, a series of 30 interviews with prominent practitioners was conducted; 29 agreed to include them in this book.

A natural question to ask is, Why did I interview the "stars"? The answer is complex. First, I felt that my research to date on academic design juries needed to be broadened further to include juries in practice. My purpose was to explore questions like these: Which problems found in education juries in school are also found in professional juries? Which strengths do both systems share? What can the experiences of one setting help teach the other? To what extent do academic juries resemble professional presentations to clients? In seeking out information, it made the most sense to speak with those individuals with success on both sides of the jury experience — both as submitters of design work and as jurors.

Second, I was curious about the academic histories of the "stars." If by chance some of them were not truly "stellar" students, and perhaps had a difficult time with juries themselves, then this could provide some much-needed hope to students currently enrolled in design programs. Third, I was interested to learn whether or not they were in favor of the ways in which juries are currently administered. I thought that perhaps their opinions of juries might shed some new light on the well-publicized gap between academia and professional practice. Could juries be one of the missing links to help bridge that gap? Finally, I was intrigued by the remote possibility that some of the "stars" might share some of the sentiments that the students had expressed. If so, their own voices could lend greater credibility to the students' concerns. Much to my surprise, for the most part, this did turn out to be the case.

Sample and Procedures

A brief description about the sample selection for these interviews: No attempt was made to be overly scientific. However, the overall intention was to try to interview a mix of professions within environmental design, designers of varying ages, both men and women, and to a certain extent, representatives from various geographic regions of the United States. Other than Minoru Takeyama, a distinguished architect from Japan, all designers interviewed are based in the United States. However, a number were educated abroad. Another criterion was that each designer interviewed had played a significant role in the jury process, either as a juror or as a recipient of a design award. I knew nothing about their views on design juries when inviting them to be interviewed.

The sample was also to a certain extent what researchers call a convenience sample; that is, many of the interviewees lived within easy driving range of where I was situated at the time. As my base is in the Champaign-Urbana, Illinois, area, two designers were interviewed while visiting on our campus and a number were interviewed in Chicago. As I spent the summer of 1989 in Berkeley, California, several were also interviewed in San Francisco. Others located elsewhere were interviewed by telephone.

The research instrument used was a one-page cover letter and a three-page list of interview questions. The questions were divided up into three sections: *Your Past as a Design Student* (12 questions), *Your Views of Design Juries in Education Today* (six questions), and *Your Views of Design Juries in Practice Today* (six questions). Each question was open-ended, and the last question in each section asked about any other general comments on the subject. As in prior research instruments, questions were phrased in a general manner, that is, "What is your opinion of, ..." to avoid any potential bias. Because of the nature of the audience, a special effort was undertaken to make the interview form somewhat graphically appealing.

The office of each designer was telephoned and an initial inquiry was made to see whether or not he or she might be interested in participating in this project. Usually the designer's staff assistant requested a letter with more information. After the sending of a more detailed cover letter along with the list of questions, the offices were contacted to schedule an appointment. Once the interview list reached a reasonable size, prospective interviewees were also sent a list of those designers who had already been interviewed. A total of about 35 designers were approached, and 30 agreed to be interviewed.

Nineteen interviews with designers in San Francisco and Chicago were conducted face to face, lasting anywhere from about 45 minutes to 2½ hours. The San Francisco interviews were conducted during *summer 1989*, while the Chicago interviews were conducted during *fall 1989*. Due to financial constraints, nine interviews with designers whose offices are located elsewhere were conducted over the telephone and one was submitted in written form. The phone interviews ranged in length from 15 minutes to approximately one hour and were conducted during *spring and summer of 1990*. Minoru Takeyama and Lawrence B. Perkins were interviewed during their visits to the University of Illinois at Urbana-Champaign in *fall 1989*.

Not all questions were asked of all those interviewed. While in some cases, we went right down the list, asking each question in order, in others, if time was limited, only selected questions were asked. These were highlighted with an asterisk. In a few instances, the questions were used only as a rough guide to evoke a free-flowing conversation on the subject. In all cases, interviewees were given a copy of the questions to refer to throughout the interview.

Each interview was tape-recorded in its entirety. In addition, I also took written notes as a backup. Each person was sent a personal thank-you note following the interview. In all, this interview process took about a year and a half to complete.

Data Analysis

For Phase 10, all designer interviews were tape-recorded and transcribed in their entirety. Selected excerpts were edited for style and sent to each interviewee for revisions and final approvals. In some cases, follow-up reminders were sent or phone calls were made to obtain the final approved copy.

A content analysis was performed on the data.

Evaluation of the Method

In retrospect, the designer interviews were among the most revealing components of this research. The research procedure worked exceptionally well because of its flexible format. Designers appreciated the ability to deviate from the original list of questions as they wished. The only aspect of this part of the research that proved problematic was obtaining the approved, edited copies of the transcripts from the designers' offices. Although they were given a one-month turnaround, one that many of the designers were able to meet, some took as many as five months to return the materials despite repeated letters and phone calls. Fortunately, enough time was available so that all materials were still usable in time for publication.

PHASE 11

The purpose of *Phase 11* was to obtain additional information about what kinds of innovative techniques faculty across the country were using to evaluate student design work.

Sample and Procedure

Archives, in the form of personal correspondence via letters and telephone calls, were the primary data-gathering technique used in Phase 11. An announcement was placed on the conference registration desk at the Association of Collegiate Schools of Architecture (ACSA) annual meeting in San Francisco during *spring 1990*. A similar announcement was placed in the *ACSA News*, the organization's regular newsletter. The newsletter is sent to every architecture faculty member at every ACSA-affiliated college or university in North America. As of January 1990, the total number of architecture faculty in ACSA affiliated schools was 4143.[4] Both announcements briefly described the book and asked for innovative suggestions from faculty, along with some documentation about the process and how students reacted. I asked faculty to write me a letter describing what they had done.

A total of eight faculty responded to my written announcement. In addition, I followed up on various leads that others had told me about throughout the course of this research. I wrote to and telephoned five additional faculty, whose names had been recommended through an informal networking process, and asked them for a written response. Altogether the responses of 13 faculty were received.

Data Analysis

The eight letters received from faculty were reviewed for content analysis. Where necessary, I followed up with phone calls or letters to request additional information.

Evaluation of the Method

Considering the large circulation of the newsletter, a response rate of only eight persons is truly abysmal! My speculation was that (1) some instructors were too busy to reply, (2) all instructors receive the newsletter but few may read it carefully, or (3) few instructors had really been trying anything other than traditional juries, thus substantiating my earlier claims. Further research would be needed to determine the possible reasons for the low response rate.

NOTES

1. Fast, Julius, *Body Language*, New York: Evans, 1970; and Nierenberg, Gerard, *How to Read a Person Like a Book*, New York: Cornerstone Library, 1973.

2. A number of surveys developed by my colleagues James R. Anderson and Sue Weidemann at the University of Illinois at Urbana-Champaign, Housing Research and Development Program, were used as models in constructing survey items for Phase 3 and subsequent research phases.

3. Francescato, Guido, Sue Weidemann, James R. Anderson, and Richard Chenoweth, *Residents' Satisfaction in HUD-Assisted Housing: Design and Management Factors*, report presented for the Office of Policy Development and Research, U.S. Department of Housing and Urban Development, Washington, DC: U.S. Government Printing Office, 1979.

4. Groat, Linda, and Sherry Ahrentzen, *Status of Faculty Women in Architecture Schools: Survey Results and Recommendations*, Washington, DC: Association of Collegiate Schools of Architecture, 1990, p. 11.

APPENDIX B
Selected Results

A summary of the results from Phase 1 has been reported in previous publications.[1] The results from some of the individual studies in Phases 2-8 have also been previously reported.[2] Results from Phases 9-11 are reported throughout this book. Excerpts from the interviews from Phase 10 were provided in Chapter 13 and throughout the text.

In a nutshell, the patterns originally witnessed in Phase 1 tended to be the norm. Many of the problems that students at the case-study school reported experiencing with design juries appear to be true elsewhere.

Some summary demographic data and responses to key core items in the student surveys are presented here. Note that the sample size of minority students was too small to allow for wide enough variability among races; hence no racial differences are reported. Tests comparing nontraditional (women and minority) versus traditional (white male) students were weighted heavily toward females; hence only a few of these results are reported.

Differences are reported here for the data broken up by sex and level (undergraduate versus graduate); space does not permit reporting of breakdown by other groups. Where statistically significant differences between groups were found, they are identified along with the level of significance ($p < .05$, $.01$, etc.). Otherwise the results present general trends found among different groups.

Several correlations among survey items were found to be statistically significant, but space prohibits a detailed discussion of them here. For more information about the results of these tests and others, consult the author.

DEMOGRAPHIC DATA

Who are the respondents? Table B-1 shows a breakdown of their demographic characteristics. Note that not all demographic questions were asked in each phase; these are reflected in the different n's for each item. The percentages have been rounded off; hence not all add up to exactly 100.

The majority of the respondents are male and Caucasian. Relatively few minorities are represented; this is partially attributable to the fact that minorities are underrepresented in architectural programs. On several otherwise completed surveys, students omitted this item. In fact, a few surveys were returned with sharply pointed questions handwritten in the margins about why I wanted this information in the first place. It could be that the sample represents more minority students than Table B-1 actually indicates. Minority responses were not sought out specifically, but perhaps they could be in future studies.

When the data are broken down by traditional (white male) versus nontraditional (women and minority) students, the sample shows just over two-thirds traditional and just under one-third nontraditional students.

Also note that two separate items measured students' status in the architectural program, items "Level" and "Year in architecture program." At some schools fifth-year students are undergraduates, while at others they are graduates. In any case, no matter which item is used, the majority of the sample is undergraduates. This should be

DEMOGRAPHIC CHARACTERISTICS OF THE STUDENT SURVEY SAMPLES

Item	n	Mean	%	Other
Age	409	22.5		range 18–40
Sex	604			
Male	440		73	
Female	164		27	
Race	321			
Caucasian	273		85	
African American	16		5	
Hispanic	9		3	
Asian	14		4	
Other	9		3	
Traditional vs. Non-traditional	627			
White males	431		69	
Women and minorities	196		31	
Level	251			
Undergraduate	213		85	
Graduate	38		15	*(continued)*

Table B-1 Demographic breakdown of the student survey samples.

taken into account in interpreting the results. Finally, note that the average number of design studios students had taken at the time of the survey was 5.5. This indicates that most students had had a fairly extensive exposure to studios and to the jury system; thus one can place substantial credence on their responses.

KEY RESEARCH FINDINGS

Goals of Juries

Figure B-1 shows students' responses to the question, "What should be the goals of design juries?"

Satisfaction with Architectural Education and Design Juries

Figure B-2 shows students' responses to the question, "How satisfied or dissatisfied are you with . . ." various aspects of their architectural education. *Note that students are most dissatisfied with final juries, juries in general, and interim juries. Final juries are the greatest source of student dissatisfaction.*

Compared to undergraduates, *graduate students report slightly higher levels of satisfaction with architectural education, design education, design studios, and juries.*

Figure B-3 shows the responses to some of these same items broken down by sex. *Compared to men, women's levels of satisfaction with each of these aspects of architectural education are markedly lower.* Statistically significant differences ($p < .05$) were found for five out of six items. This trend is confirmed by responses to a number of items throughout the survey.

Results from two other satisfaction items reveal that compared to traditional students, *nontraditional students are less likely to want to continue studying architecture, and less likely to want to study architecture if they had to start their schooling all over again.* On the latter item, the differences were statistically significant ($p < .05$).

Some relatively low correlations were found between

Item	n	Mean	%	Other
Year in architecture program	571	3.6		
First	21		4	
Second	132		23	
Third	93		16	
Fourth	191		33	
Fifth	103		18	
Sixth	28		5	
Seventh	3		1	
Number of design studios taken	192	5.5		
1	3		2	
2	17		9	
3	37		19	
4	15		8	
5	16		8	
6	49		26	
7	12		6	
8	24		13	
9	--		--	
10	13		7	
11	--		--	
12	5		3	
13	1		1	
Number of previous schools attended	103	1.2		range 1-3

Table B-1 Continued.

the composite measure of satisfaction with architectural education computed by the process described in Appendix A, Phases 3-6, Data Analysis and several survey items (Table B-2).

Amount Learned from Juries Relative to Other Methods of Design Evaluation

Figure B-4 shows the answer to the question, "How much do you usually learn from . . ." various methods of design evaluation, including juries, desk critiques, and others. Note that while the amount students report learning from criticism of their own projects at interim juries ranks seventh on the list of 13 items, *all other items relating to design juries (criticism of others' projects at interim juries, criticism of others' projects at final juries, and criticism of their own projects at final juries) are rated at or near the bottom.* This is one of the most striking findings from this research.

For most of these items, *graduate students report learning levels slightly higher than those for undergraduates;* on one item, "negative criticism," the differences approach statistical significance ($p < .10$).

Women report higher levels of learning than men from the final jury ($p < .05$).

Opinions of Juries and Design Studios

Figure B-5 shows students' responses to the question, "Do you think any of the following need improvement?" Note that both design studios and juries in general are tied at 83%.

No significant differences were found between undergraduates and graduates on any of these items.

Women are much more likely than men to respond that design studios need improvement ($p < .001$).

Results from other items asking students' opinions about juries—both interim and final—as well as design

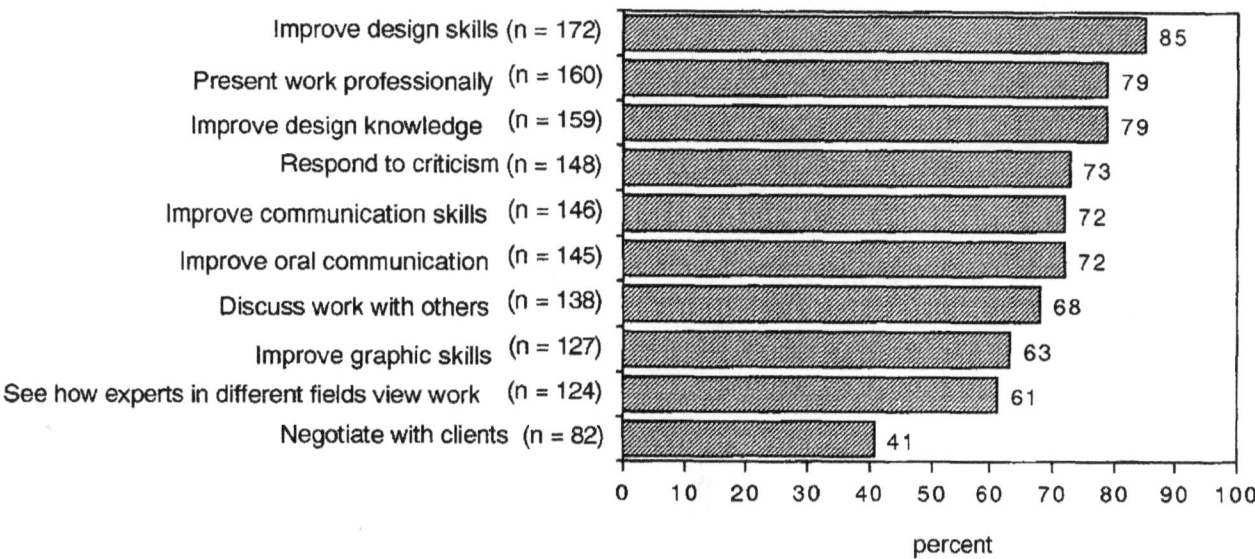

Figure B-1 Students believe that juries should achieve several goals. The data represent 202 respondents from Phases 3 and 6; n represents the number of responses to each question.

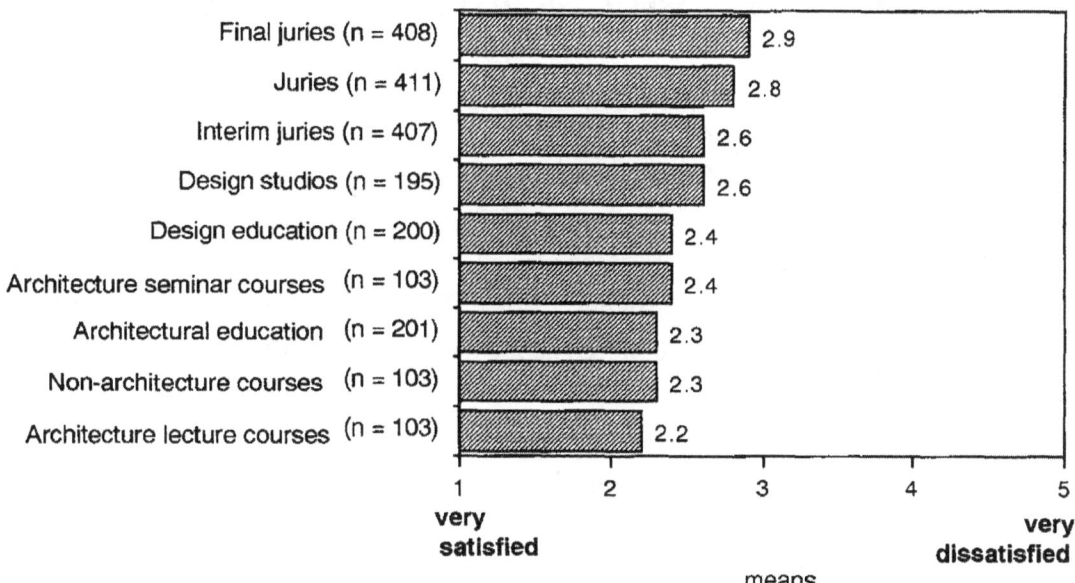

Figure B-2 Compared to other aspects of architectural education, students report the highest levels of dissatisfaction with design juries. Items *ARCHITECTURE SEMINAR COURSES, NON-ARCHITECTURE COURSES,* and *ARCHITECTURE LECTURE COURSES* represent respondents from Phase 3. Items *DESIGN STUDIOS, DESIGN EDUCATION,* and *ARCHITECTURAL EDUCATION* represent respondents from Phases 3 and 8. Items *FINAL JURIES, JURIES,* and *INTERIM JURIES* represent respondents from Phases 3-6 and 8; n represents the number of responses to each question.

STUDENTS' RESPONSES TO: HOW SATISFIED OR DISSATISFIED ARE YOU WITH...?
BREAKDOWN BY SEX

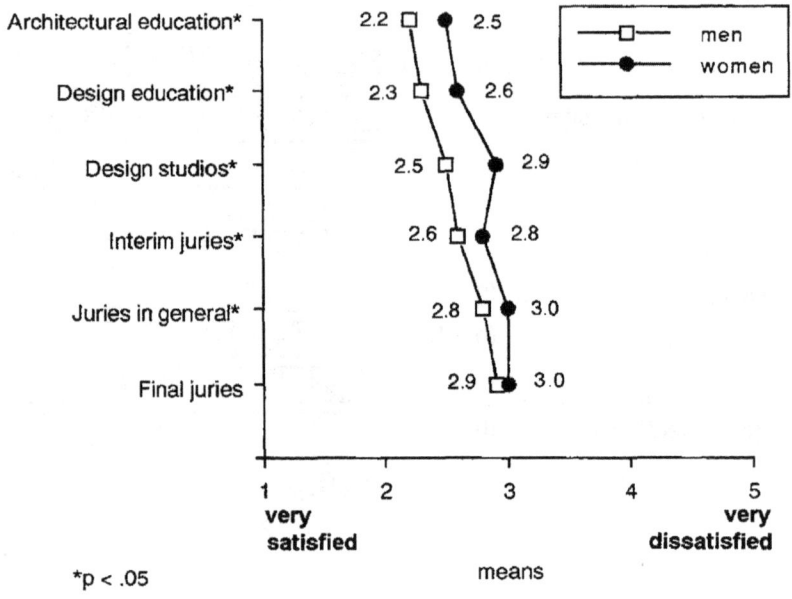

*$p < .05$

Figure B-3 Compared to male students, women students report greater dissatisfaction with each of these aspects of their architectural education. Items *DESIGN STUDIOS, DESIGN EDUCATION,* and *ARCHITECTURAL EDUCATION* represent respondents from Phases 3 and 8. Items *INTERIM JURIES, JURIES IN GENERAL,* and *FINAL JURIES* represent respondents from Phases 3-6 and 8.

STATISTICALLY SIGNIFICANT BIVARIATE CORRELATES OF COMPOSITE MEASURE OF STUDENT SATISFACTION WITH ARCHITECTURAL EDUCATION

Item	n	r
Amount students learn from criticism of their own projects at final juries	187	.32**
Students' satisfaction with final juries	185	.30**
Students' opinions of final juries	184	.27**
Students' opinions of design juries in general	188	.25**
Students' opinions of design studios	191	.25**
Amount students learn from oral feedback	190	.24**
Amount of food students eat the week before the jury	187	.23**
Amount students learn from written feedback	166	.20**
After negative jury criticism, students try to hold back tears	92	-.20*

* $p < .10$
** $p < .01$

Note: Only those correlations with r values > than .20 are reported

Table B-2 Those items from the student survey that correlate with the composite measure of satisfaction with architectural education; *n* refers to the number of responses to each pair of questions, *r* refers to the strength of the correlation on a scale from .00 (no correlation) to 1.0 (perfect correlation).

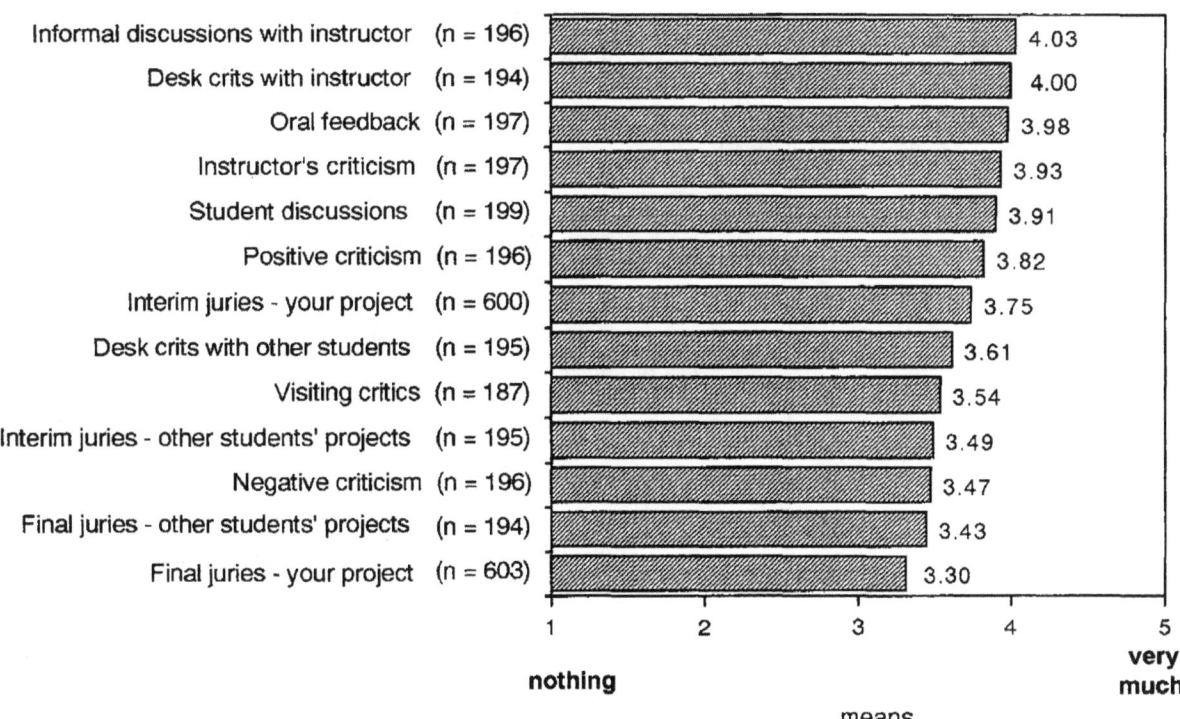

Figure B-4 Students report learning *most* from informal discussions and desk critiques from their instructors, and *least* from criticism of both their own and others' projects at final juries. The data represent 202 respondents from Phases 3 and 8. Items *INTERIM JURIES – YOUR PROJECT* and *FINAL JURIES – YOUR PROJECT* represent a total of 629 respondents from the combined data analyses of Phases 1, 3–6, and 8; *n* represents the number of responses to each question.

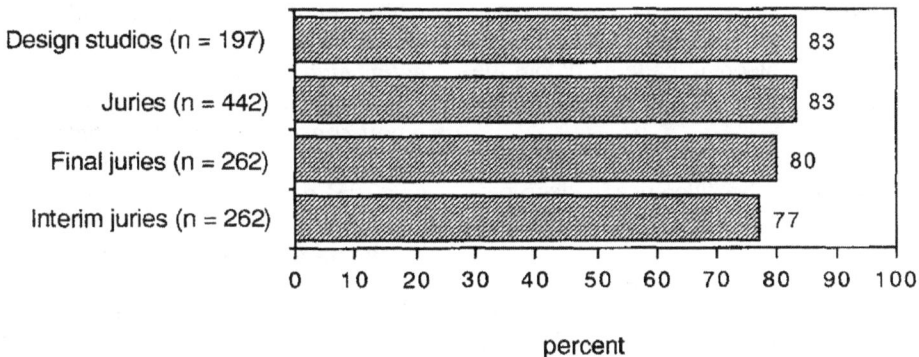

Figure B-5 The vast majority of students believe that juries and design studios need to be improved. Item *DESIGN STUDIOS* represents respondents from Phases 3 and 8. Items *FINAL JURIES* and *INTERIM JURIES* represent respondents from Phases 3, 7, and 8. Item *JURIES* represents respondents from Phases 1, 3, 6, and 8; n represents the number of responses to each question, including "yes" and "no".

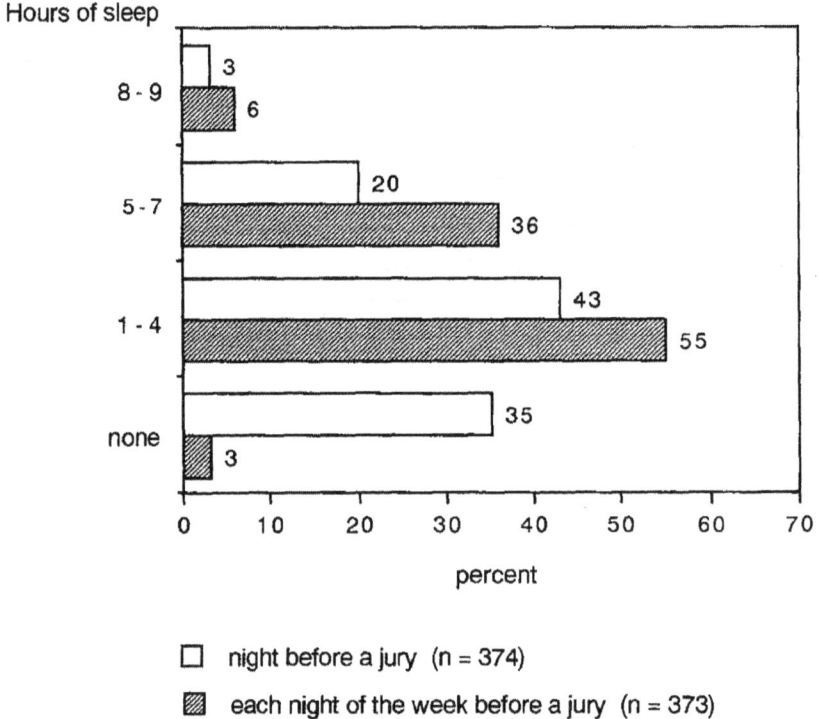

Figure B-6 Most students receive little or no sleep before the jury; n represents the number of responses to each question.

studios indicate that *compared to undergraduates, graduates report slightly more favorable opinions;* on one item, "design studios," these differences approach statistical significance ($p < .10$).

The Studio Subculture

Figure B-6 shows students' sleeping patterns before the jury. Most students sleep very little, if at all, the night before the jury.

Graduates report sleeping slightly more than undergraduates around jury time. The difference in sleep patterns each night during the week before the jury is statistically significant ($p < .05$).

The sleeping patterns around jury time of men versus women are about the same, although *women are more likely to admit that lack of sleep affects their performance* ($p < .001$).

The day before the jury, as well as the week before the jury, most students eat less than usual (means are 1.8 and 2.8, respectively, on a scale of 1-5, where 1 = "much less than usual" and 5 = "much more than usual"). *Women report eating less than men during the week before the jury* ($p < .10$).

Slightly over half (55%) the students report eating mainly junk food on the day of the jury, and just about half (49%) report eating mainly junk food during the week before the jury. *Women are more likely than men to report eating junk food during the week before jury* ($p < .05$).

Graduates are more likely than undergraduates to report consuming junk food before the jury. The differences between the two groups are statistically significant ($p < .05$) during the week before the jury.

Students' Reactions to Negative Criticism

When they receive negative criticism at a jury, compared to undergraduates, *graduates are more likely to become angry and upset after the jury is over.* Women are more likely to become angry and upset after the jury, to try their best to *hold back tears* ($p < .005$), and to *cry after the jury is over* ($p < .005$).

NOTES

1. See, for example, Anthony, Kathryn H., "Private Reactions to Public Criticism: Students, Faculty, and Practicing Architects State Their Views on Design Juries in Architectural Education," *Journal of Architectural Education*, 40:3 (spring 1987), pp. 2-11; Anthony, Kathryn H., "The Need for Creative Criticism at Design Juries: A Study of Architectural Student Diaries," in Warfield, James, (ed.), *Fostering Creativity in Architectural Education. Proceedings of the 1986 Association of Collegiate Schools of Architecture (ACSA) West Central Regional Conference,* Champaign: School of Architecture, University of Illinois at Urbana-Champaign, 1986, pp. 147-155.

2. For a summary of the results from some of these individual studies, consult: Anthony, Kathryn H., "The Influence of the Jury System on Architectural Education," in Enrique Vivoni-Farage, and Luisa Vigo-Cepeda (eds.), *Text and Context in Architectural Education. Proceedings of the 1988 Association of Collegiate Schools of Architecture (ACSA) Southeast Regional Meeting,* Rio Piedras, Puerto Rico: School of Architecture, University of Puerto Rico, 1990, pp. 20-23; Anthony, Kathryn H., "Judging Juries: A Comparative Study of Student and Faculty Reactions to Design Juries in Architectural Education," in McGinty, Tim, and Robert Zwirn (eds.), *Debate and Dialogue: Architectural Design and Pedagogy. Proceedings of the 77th Annual Meeting of the Association of Collegiate Schools of Architecture (ACSA),* Washington, DC: ACSA, 1989, pp. 3-12; Anthony, Kathryn H., "Juries on Trial," *Architectural Record,* (July 1991), pp. 77-78.

APPENDIX C
Sample Jury Forms

This appendix contains some sample forms that can be used to help make juries more effective. Figures C-1 through C-3 show some sample evaluation forms that can be used to establish criteria for reviewing design work at juries. Figures C-1 and C-2 are adaptations of actual forms that have been used in architecture courses, while Figure C-3 is a generic form that can be used for any of the disciplines in environmental design. Figure C-4 shows a form that can be used as a screening process to select projects to discuss at the jury in both large and small groups, based on the model described by Stefani Ledewitz in Chapter 10. Figure C-5 shows how the round-robin technique can be used to divide up jurors among a large class.

Student Design Project Evaluation

Name of School:

Department:

Student's Name: Reviewer's Name:

Rewiew: Interim / Final   Class: Date:

Sketch:

Concept:

| Site Design and Development: | + | 0 | - |

| Architectural Design and Development: | + | 0 | - |

| Interior Design and Development: | + | 0 | - |

| Systems Designs and Integration: | + | 0 | - |

| Graphic Presentation: | + | 0 | - |

| Model(s) | + | 0 | - |

| Oral Presentation: | + | 0 | - |

Additional Remarks:

Figure C-1 Sample jury evaluation form #1. Here is an adaptation of a sample form that has been used to help jurors critique and evaluate student design work in an architecture class. (Courtesy Robert I. Selby.)

Student Design Project Evaluation

Name of School:	Student:
Department:	Project Title:
Class:	

	+				−
Concept					
Integration of research into design					
Site development					
Functional planning					
Spatial quality					
Building form					
Aesthetic design					
Structural system					
Use of materials					
Environmental control systems					
Oral presentation					
Graphic communication					
Presentation model					

Comments:

Reviewer:

Figure C-2 Sample jury evaluation form #2. Here is an adaptation of another sample form that has been used to help jurors critique and evaluate student design work in an architecture class. Both jurors and students are given the glossary in order to use the form effectively. (Courtesy Arthur L. Kaha.)

Evaluation Instructions

For the purposes of this review the terms on the evaluation sheet are defined as follows:

Concept:
  Overall strength, clarity and appropriateness of an *idea*; concern for the *whole*; spatial considerations; desirability of the image.

Integration of research into design:
  Extent to which findings and recommendations from environment-behavior research are incorporated into the design solution.

Site development:
  Building massing and composition on the site; exterior spaces; easy identification of entry; auto driveways; drop offs; parking; service; pedestrian paths; landscaping - all with respect for the existing contours and natural landforms. Contextualism.

Functional planning:
  Circulation; flow; entry; organization; activity zoning; level changes; understanding of functional requirements and relationships; appropriateness of areas and volumes.

Spatial quality:
  The manner in which spaces are arranged to clarify their relative importance and functional or symbolic role in the building organization.

Building form:
  Appropriateness of the building massing and scale to both the function of the building and the context in which it is placed.

Aesthetic design:
  Aesthetics is concerned with what is "good". The concern is to create works that transcend the ordinary and become works of art.

Structural systems:
  Consideration of the structural elements, supports, spans, and relative sizes of members that combine to produce a unified system.

Use of materials:
  Appropriateness of selected materials with respect to context, structure, form, image, cost and maintenance.

Environmental control systems:
  The ability to recognize and resolve situational problems of mechanical and electrical systems including the integration of solar energy concepts.

Oral presentation
  The ability to present in oral form the above aspects of the design solution; proper use of the spoken language; organization of thought processes and the ability to respond effectively to questioning by the jury.

Graphic communication:
  Clarity, quality, completeness and readability of drawings; depth of detail, *vitality*. Display of graphic communication skills.

Presentation model:
  Display of modeling skills appropriate to the design solution and scale of the required model.

Figure C-2 Continued.

Student Design Project Evaluation

Name of School:

Department:

Student's Name: Reviewer's Name:

Rewiew: Interim / Final   Class: Date:

	+	0	−
Identification of Project Goals:			
Achievement of Goals:			
Concept:			
Integration of Research into Design:			
Design Development:			
Graphic Presentation:			
Model(s)			
Oral Presentation:			
Written Presentation:			

Additional Remarks:

Figure C-3 Sample jury evaluation form #3. Here is a generic example of a jury evaluation form that can be used for interior design, architecture, landscape architecture, and urban planning projects.

SUBMISSION REVIEW

PROJECT NAME:
SCHOOL:
DATE:

All reviewers, including students, faculty, and guests, are asked to select three projects that are particularly "commendable". Your judgement should be based on your own criteria. The studio has defined a set of goals that all schemes address. You might find it helpful to consider them in making your selection:

Add goals here as previously agreed upon by studio participants, for example:

> *Is it appropriate to its surroundings?*
> *Does it have an appropriate image?*
> *Does it provide for privacy?*
> *Does it meet the needs of those who will use it?*
> *Can it expand easily?*

In addition, each entry should demonstrate at least one aspect of the problem that has been investigated in some depth, which is to be explained by the presentation.

My selections are:

ENTRY NUMBER ____

ENTRY NUMBER ____

ENTRY NUMBER ____

The three schemes that receive the highest number of "votes" will be reviewed by the group as a whole. Then we will divide into (#:___) smaller groups, each of which will review the remaining (#:___) schemes.

Figure C-4 This form can be used as a screening process to select projects that will be discussed in depth by the jury. (Courtesy Stefani Ledewitz.)

Round Robin Jury

Juror:	Time:	Time:	Time:	Time:
Juror:	Student # 1. 2. 3.	Student # 1. 2. 3.	Student # 1. 2. 3.	Student # 1. 2. 3.
Juror:	Student # 1. 2. 3.	Student # 1. 2. 3.	Student # 1. 2. 3.	Student # 1. 2. 3.
Juror:	Student # 1. 2. 3.	Student # 1. 2. 3.	Student # 1. 2. 3.	Student # 1. 2. 3.
Juror:	Student # 1. 2. 3.	Student # 1. 2. 3.	Student # 1. 2. 3.	Student # 1. 2. 3.
Juror:	Student # 1. 2. 3.	Student # 1. 2. 3.	Student # 1. 2. 3.	Student # 1. 2. 3.

Figure C-5 This chart shows the basic structure of the round-robin jury. By dividing a few jurors among many students, several small-group discussions can occur at once and many students can be reviewed during a short period of time. The format can be modified to accommodate classes and juries of different sizes.

Index

Index

Aalto, Alvar, 157
Active listening, 74, 110, 131
Advice to students from practitioners, 172-174, 176, 178-179, 180-185, 188, 191, 195, 198, 200-201, 204-206, 208, 213, 215-216
  (*See also* Graphic presentation; Presentation, verbal; Time management)
Agenda, hidden, 12, 107, 168, 194
  (*See also* Curriculum, hidden)
All nighter syndrome, 4, 4 fig. 1-2, 45, 97, 99, 165
Alternatives to juries, 125-134, 160-161
  (*See also* Recommendations for improving juries)
  debates, 161
  exhibit, 125-126
  jurors on trial, 129
  portfolio, 131
  postdesign evaluation, 127
  professor as advocate, 130
  round robin, 129
  video review, 130
American Institute of Architects (AIA), 40, 141, 143-145, 163, 166, 169n.15, 196, 230-231
  Gold Medalists, 183, 199, 204
American Institute of Architecture Students (AIAS), 42n.21, 100n.2, 231-233
American Planning Association (APA), 143
American Society of Interior Designers (ASID), 141, 143
American Society of Landscape Architects (ASLA), 141, 143
Amount learned from juries, 238, 241 fig. B-4
Anderson, James, 134n.5, 135n.14
Annotated plan, 59, 60 fig. 5-6, 160, 160 fig. 12-3
Antoniades, Anthony, 127
Anxiety (*See* Stress)
Architect Registration Exam (*See* Professional licensing)
Arendt, Hannah, 22
Assertive behavior, 76-77, 82n.13

Association of Collegiate Schools of Architecture (ACSA), 117, 135, 230, 232
Association of Collegiate Schools of Planning (ACSP), 117
Athletics, 15-16
Attoe, Wayne, 105, 107
Authority, 21-23, 116, 118, 168
  (*See also* Paternalism)
Awards, design, 4-5, 16, 84, 139-140, 164
  (*See also* American Institute of Architects, Gold Medalists; Orchids and Onions Program; Rudy Bruner Award for Excellence in the Urban Environment)
  compared to awards in other media, 151
  pros and cons, 143-145

Bacon, Francis, 43
Bauhaus, 10-11, 24n.24
Baum, L. Frank, 168
Beaux Arts, Ecole des, 6, 23n.3,4,8, 24n.11, 38
  competitive environment, 166-167
  history, 9, 9 fig. 2-1
  influence of, 10-11
  male dominance in, 165
Beaux-Arts Institute of Design (BAID), 9-10, 23n.8, 24n.12
Beaux-Arts Society of Architects, 23n.8
Beaux Arts system, 1, 8, 20, 166-168, 193
  use of closed jury, 182, 204
Beckman, Ronald, 129-130, 135n.14
Bergson, Henri, 103
Bertotto, Juan C., 128
Bill of Rights for design students, 162
Blau, Judith, 161
Bledstein, Burton, 15
Bloodbaths, juries as, 20, 210
Bloom, Benjamin, 133
Blutter, Joan, 65, 74, 84, 140
  interview of, 173

Booth, Laurence, 46, 71, 84
  interview of, 173-175
Boswell, Peyton, 8
Bosworth, Francke Huntington, Jr., 10, 17, 23n.8, 38, 45, 105, 164
Buchanan, Peter, 167
Burnout, 40, 91
  (*See also* Stress)

Calendar, portable, 47
Callaway, William, 31, 38, 46, 65, 74, 84, 107
  interview of, 175-176
Canadian Housing Design Counsil, 145, 151
Carelessness in presentation, 173
Cass, Gilbert, 139
Charisma (*See* Star system)
Charrette, design, 9, 170n.49
Cicero, 65
Circle chart, 77, 78 fig. 6-17
Cocteau, Jean, 75
Colloquia, 160
Comments, written, 113-114, 119n.23, 129, 131, 133
Communication skills, 65-82, 80n.1,2, 81n.1
  (*See also* Graphic presentation; Presentation, verbal; Speaking, public)
  importance of, 65, 130, 168
  nonverbal, 72-73, 114-116
  summary of, 79-80 fig. 6-18
Competition, 4, 15-16, 77, 214, 218
  intergroup, 16, 25n.47
  intragroup, 16, 25n.47
  negative effects of, 163-164
  role in studio, 163-165
Competitions, design, 139-153
  alternative models, 149-150
  evaluations by practitioners, 139, 140, 147, 148, 149, 173, 176-177, 179, 181, 183, 184-185, 189, 191, 192, 196, 198, 200, 202, 203, 205, 207, 208, 211-213
  incorporating public opinion, 149-151
  in Finland, 152, 152 fig. 11-17
  postjury evaluation, 149
  prejury evaluation, 150-151
  presentation techniques for, 84-85
  pros and cons of, 145-149, 153
  reform of juries, 164
  student involvement in, 16, 146, 164
  types of
    closed and open, 141
    invited, 146
    limited, 146
    quasi, 146
Comprehensive exams, 15
Confucius, 27
Congor, Cornelia, 179
Constructive Criticism (*See* Criticism, positive)
Cooperation (*See* Teamwork)
Cooper Marcus, Clare, 150
Coping mechanisms, 92
  (*See also* Stress)
Council of Educators in Landscape Architecture (CELA), 117
Coxe, Welde, 40

Criticism, 105-119
  at professional design awards, 141-143
  definition of, 105
  delivery of, 109-113
  effects of and reaction to, 163, 182, 190-191, 200-201, 242
  hidden agenda of, 107
  negative, 13, 15, 32-35, 34 fig. 3-5, 105-113, 106 fig. 9-1, 109 fig. 9-3, 113 fig. 9-7, 162-163, 182, 190-191, 200-201
  positive, 32-33, 35, 105-113, 109 fig. 9-3, 113 fig. 9-7, 133, 167-168, 210, 220
  power relationship, role of, 116, 118
  private, 12, 113-114, 119n.23, 129, 133
  public, 12, 12 fig. 2-3, 14, 17, 19, 36-38, 112-113, 113 fig. 9-7, 220 (*See also* Humiliation, public)
  types of, 107, 108
  written, 12, 113-114, 119n.23, 129, 131, 133
Critics, visiting, 5, 35, 107-118, 121, 129, 168, 194
  (*See also* Jurors)
  delivering criticism, 108-110
  listening, 109-110
  nonverbal communication, 114-115
  workshops for, 117
Critique
  design (*See* Juries, academic design)
  desk, 12, 115-117, 127, 132, 159, 194
    educational value of, 35-36, 36 fig. 3-7, 121
  peer (*See* Review, peer)
  shared, 116-117, 127, 159-160, 216
Curfew, 124
Curriculum, hidden, 12, 159, 196
  (*See also* Agenda, hidden)

Deadlines, 124, 135n.8
Debate and dialogue, 21, 115-117, 130-132, 158-161, 187
de Cervantes, Miguel, 103
Degenhardt, Christopher, 31, 65, 84, 107
  interview of, 176-177
DeHaan, Norman, R., 31, 84, 95, 144
  interview of, 178-179
Demographic data, 236-238, 237-238 tbl. B-1
Design competitions (*See* Competitions, design)
Design education (*See* Education, design)
Design guidelines, 54, 151
Design juries (*See* Juries, academic design)
Design process, 14, 132
Design studio (*See* Studio, design)
Desk crit (*See* Critique, desk)
Deutsch, Larry N., 67, 83, 140
  interview of, 179-182
Diaries, student, 35, 229
Doctoral dissertation, 15
Double-loop learning, 13
Doubts about design project, 37
Drawings (*See* Graphic presentation)
Dress at presentations, 72, 82n.11, 208
Dutton, Thomas, 107, 118, 129

Education, design, 157-167
  Beaux Arts as model, 9-11, 166-168
  compared to other disciplines and settings, 15-19, 117, 158-159

competition, role of, 163-165
dilemmas, 19-20
evaluation of students, 13-15, 13 fig. 2-4
increased involvement of students, 131-132, 160-161
instructor training, 19
juries, role of, 11, 34-36, 158-159
male dominated, 165-166
professional ethics, 161-162
star system, 20-23, 159, 165-166
Educational value of juries, 34-36
Eisenman, Peter, 76, 84
    interview of, 182-183
Ellis, Victoria J., 39
Emerson, Ralph Waldo, 43
Environmental design, 159, 168
Environmental Design Research Association (EDRA), 63n.9, 134n.4, 143, 150
    definition of, 55-56
Environment and behavior, 6, 55, 62n.2,3,4,8, 63n.11, 135n.12, 151, 158, 160
    definition of, 54-55
Esherick, Joseph, 8, 10, 20, 46, 54, 75, 94, 96, 107, 148
    interview of, 183-184
Ethics, professional, 161-162
Evaluation forms (*See* Forms)
Evaluation of students, 13-14 (*See also* Criticism; Education, design)
Evaluations
    postdesign, 127
    postjury, 149
    postoccupancy (POE), 58-59, 63n.11, 114, 128, 135n.17, 151
        definition, 58
    prejury, 150-151
Exhibits, 125-126, 160

Feedback, 125, 127-128, 131
Festivals, juries as, 20
Final exam, 13 fig. 2-4, 14
Fine arts, 16-17, 95-96, 201, 209-210
Fisher, Roger, 78 fig. 6-17
Fisher, Thomas, 157
Forms
    jury evaluation, 244-249
    round robin, 250
Franklin, James R., 157
Friedman, Rodney, F., 80, 147
    interview of, 184-186

Gans, Herbert, 105, 164
Gapp, Paul, 193
Gender issues (*See* Women)
Ghirardo, Diane, 158, 166
Goals of juries, 29-31, 121-127
Grades
    competition for, 163-164
    influence of jury upon, 100n.2, 121, 129, 131
Grandstanding, 129 (*See also* Star System)
Graphic presentation, 83-89
    advice from practitioners, 83, 84, 85, 179, 211
    clear communication, 86-89, 90n.5
    importance of labels, 87-89
    importance to jury, 83-85, 179
    neatness, 88-89
    setup, 88-89
    summary checklist, 89 fig. 7-4
    text, 88-89
Graphics (*See* Graphic presentation)
Graves, Michael, 24n.26, 46
    interview of, 186-189
Gropius, Walter, 10-11, 22, 22 fig. 2-7, 91, 100n.1, 184
Gutman, Robert, 166-167
Gwathmey, Charles, 31, 85, 140
    interview of, 189-191

Hackl, Donald J., 31, 107, 139, 148-149, 153
    interview of, 191-193
Hartray, John F., Jr., 8, 96, 139, 147, 153
    interview of, 193-197
Hazing ritual, 3, 12
    (*See also* Rite of passage)
Hero worship (*See* Star system)
Hightower, Cullen, 155
History of juries, 9-11
Humiliation, public, 133, 143, 162, 214
    (*See also* Criticism, public; Bill of Rights for design students)

Information
    (*See also* Research, student/practitioner use of)
    documenting and recording of, 56, 61 fig. 5-7
    filing of, 56, 57 fig. 5-3
    gathering of, 55-56, 60-61 fig. 5-7
    summary board, 57, 57 fig. 5-2
    summary checklist, 60-61 fig. 5-7
Interests, broadening of, 179, 182, 188, 201
    leisure activities, 50, 95-96, 99 fig. 8-6, 100n.11
    nonstudio courses, 158-159
Interior design, 3, 82n.22, 159, 166
Interior Design Educators Council (IDEC), 117
Interpersonal relationships, 38
Izenour, Steven, 15, 30, 85, 140, 149
    interview of, 197-199

Jackson, Philip, 12
James, William, 43
Jones, E. Fay, 144
    interview of, 199-200
Jones, Roy Childs, 10, 17, 23n.8, 38, 45, 105, 164
Juries, academic design
    (*See also* Alternatives to juries, Criticism, Recommendations for improvement of juries)
    best, 32-33
        compared to
            other disciplines and settings, 15-19, 121
            other student evaluations, 15-16
            professional design juries, 139, 140 fig. 11-1, 141-143
    cost benefit analysis of, 133
    educational value of, 34-36
    evaluation by practitioners, 31, 105, 107, 172-176, 178, 180-183, 185-186, 190-193, 198-199, 201-204, 206, 208, 210-211, 213-214, 216, 218, 220
    evaluation forms for, 244-250
    evolution from open to closed, 11

Juries, academic design *(continued)*
  goals of, 29-31, 121-127
  history of, 9-11
  parameters affecting, 121-122, 122 fig. 10-2
  professional ethics of, 161-162
  pros and cons of, 158
  public nature of, 188
  research about, 27-42
  student participation in, 111, 127-129, 131-132
  types of
    closed and open, 11, 24n.25, 133
    final, 35, 40, 123-124, 134n.7, 237
    interim, 35, 40, 112, 114, 123, 132, 134n.7, 216, 237
  worst, 32-34
Juries, professional design, 139-153
  (*See also* Criticism at professional design awards)
  compared to academic design juries, 139, 140 fig. 11-1, 141-143
  evaluations compared to public opinion, 149-150
  reforms suggested, 158, 164-165
Jurors
  as stars, 21-22
  briefing ahead of time, 122-123
  consistency of, 123-124
  delivery of criticism, 107-115
  orientation sessions and workshops for, 117
  roles of, 123, 123 fig. 10-2
  skills needed, 109-112, 130
Jury duty, 127, 159

Kahn, Louis, 157
Kaiser, Kay, 144
Kang, Junmo, 149, 151
King, Ronette J., 67, 85, 95, 107, 112, 140
  interview of, 200-202
Kohn, Alfie, 16, 163-164

Lakein, Alan, 45
Landscape architecture, 3, 54, 82n.22, 159, 166, 176, 209, 233
Langdon, Philip, 150
Lawrence, Howard Ray, 128
Lawson, Bryan, 136n.33
Le Corbusier, 22, 26n.84, 157
Ledewitz, Stefani, 116, 124-125, 131, 244, 249
Legal education, 18-19, 158-159
Levy, Robert, 128
Lewis, Roger K., 29
Littlejohn, David, 81n.5

Mastery-mystery phenomenon, 54, 82n.21, 133
Medical education, 17-18, 117, 158-159
Meier, Richard
  interview of, 202-203
Michael, John, 25n.54
Military, 15
Minorities (*See* People of color)
Moore, Charles W., 8, 20, 81n.5, 85
  interview of, 203-205

Nasar, Jack, 149, 151
National Architectural Accrediting Board (NAAB), 20
National Endowment for the Arts, 25, 143
National Institute of Architectural Education, 10
  (*See also* Beaux-Arts Institute of Design)
Negative reinforcement (*See* Criticism, negative)
Negotiation, 75-80, 78 fig. 6-17, 80 fig. 6-18
Nisbet, Robert, 168n.7
Nonverbal behavior, 72-73, 114-116
Numbers, M. Joe, 131
Nutrition
  and performance, 97
  eating patterns, 39, 41n.18, 19
  importance of, 97, 101n.19
  recommendations for improving, 97-99

Ollswang, Jeffrey, 141
Opinions of juries and design studios, 238, 242, 241 fig. B-5
Orchids and Onions Program, 143, 150, 164
Organizational skills (*See* Time Management)
Ostrander, Edward R., 129-130, 135n.14

Panel discussions, 160
Parnall, Ruth, 135n.11
Paternalism, 22-23, 165
  (*See also* Star System)
Pawley, Martin, 1, 16, 157, 167
Pelli, Cesar, 8, 67, 85, 93
  interview of, 205-207
People of color, 15, 36, 40, 166, 236
Perceptions of others' feelings, 75-76, 76 fig. 6-14, 128
Perfectionist syndrome, 52
Perkins, Lawrence B., 8, 65, 83, 107, 140, 234
  interview of, 207-209
Physical exhaustion (*See* Burnout)
Pinups (*See* Critiques, shared)
Plutarch, 137
Portable calendar, 47
Portfolio, 17, 131
Positive reinforcement (*See* Criticism, positive)
Postdesign evaluation, 127
Postjury evaluation, 149
Postoccupancy evaluation (POE) (*See* Evaluations, postoccupancy)
Prangnell, Peter, 129, 218
Prejury evaluation, 150-151
Presentation, verbal, 35, 174
  (*See also* Salesmanship; Speaking, public)
  advice from practitioners, 65, 67, 74, 75, 76
  dress, 72
  key points, importance of, 69-70, 70 fig. 6-7
  negotiation during, 75-80, 78 fig. 6-7, 80 fig. 6-18
  nonverbal behavior, 72
  physical requirements for, 134
  questions, handling of, 74
Procrastination, 50
Professional design juries (*See* Juries, professional design)
Professional education, 17-20
Professional ethics, 161-162
Professional licensing, 19, 141, 142 fig. 11-2, 153n.3, 195-196
Professional registration (*See* Professional licensing)
Pruitt-Igoe, 145
Psychological health, 162

Public chastisement (*See* Criticism, public; Humiliation, public)
Public speaking (*See* Speaking, public)

Quasi-client, 126–127
Quasi-competition, 146

Rand, Ayn, 166
Recommendations for improvement of juries, 123–134, 158–166
  (*See also* Alternatives to juries)
  increase student involvement, 160–161
  limit number of presentations, 124
  peer review, 128–129
Reich, Robert, 170n.50
Registration, professional (*See* Professional licensing)
Research
  (*See also* Environment and behavior; Environmental Design Research Association; Evaluations, postoccupancy)
  methodology, 225–235, 226 fig. A-2
    data analyses, 229, 231–233, 233 fig. A-7, 235
    evaluation of, 230–233, 235
    location of respondents, 227 fig. A-4, 228 fig. A-5, A-6
    phases, 225, 225 fig. A-1
    sample breakdown, 226–227, 227 fig. A-3
    samples and procedures, 229–232, 234–235
  results, 236–243
    amount learned from juries, 238, 241 fig. B-4
    demographic data, 236–238, 237–238 tbl. B-1
    opinions of juries and design studios, 238, 242, 241 fig. B-5
    satisfaction with architectural education and design juries, 237–239, 239 fig. B-2, 240 fig. B-3
    studio subculture, 242, 242 fig. B-6
    students' reaction to negative criticism, 242
  student/practitioner use of, 54–61, 159–160, 179, 195, 217
    (*See also* Information)
    applying findings to design, 59, 60 fig. 5-6, 61 fig. 5-7
    gathering new information, 57–58, 61 fig. 5-7
    presentation of findings, 58–60, 59 fig. 5-5, 60 fig. 5-6, 61 fig. 5-7
    summary, 60–61 fig. 5-7
  tools
    archives, 225–226
    diaries, student, 229
    ethnography, 225–226
    interviews, 5–6, 58, 63n.12, 226, 229, 234
    participant observation, 6, 225–226
    surveys and questionnaires, 4, 58, 63n.12,13, 226, 229–231
Review, 120–121, 134, 134n.3
  (*See also* Juries, academic design)
  peer
    at professional competitions, 149
    in studios, 127–129, 194, 214
  self, 131–132, 219
  shared, 116–117, 127, 159–160, 216
  silent, 214
Rite of passage, 16, 183
  (*See also* Hazing ritual)
Rochefoucauld, Francois de la, 103
Role playing, 160
Ross Barney, Carol, 52
  interview of, 171–173
Round robin, 129, 150

Rudy Bruner Award for Excellence in the Urban Environment, 150, 164
Rules, breaking of in competitions, 84, 141, 179, 212
Russell, Bertrand, 27

Salesmanship, 30, 65–66, 172, 201, 216, 221
San Diego, California's Orchids and Onions Program, 143, 150, 164
Satisfaction with architectural education and design juries, 237–239, 239 fig. B-2, 240 fig. B-3
Schlensker, David, 105
Schools
  Arizona, University of, 179, 180
  Arkansas, University of, 199
  Aukland (New Zealand) University of, 135n.14
  Ball State University, 80n.1, 90n.6
  Barnard College, 214
  Buenos Aires, University of, 214
  California, Berkeley, University of, 175, 183, 185, 204, 215, 217, 220
  California, Los Angeles, University of (UCLA), 202, 204
  California, University of, 214n.12
  California State Polytechnic University, Pomona, 7n.6, 229, 231
  Cambridge, University of, 182
  Carnegie Mellon University, 24n.12, 116, 214
  Catholic University, 24n.12
  Cincinnati, University of, 186, 187
  Columbia University, 24n.12, 182, 212, 214
  Conway School of Landscape Design, 81n.1, 135n.11
  Cooper Union, 202
  Cornell University, 23n.8, 24n.12, 129, 130, 135n.14, 182, 193, 194, 202, 207, 208
  Drexel University, 194
  Florida A & M University, 214
  Georgia Institute of Technology, 231
  Harvard University, 10, 82n.16, 174, 175, 185, 186, 187, 202, 209, 213, 217
  Idaho, University of, 131
  Illinois at Chicago, University of, 194
  Illinois at Urbana-Champaign, University of, 24n.12, 75, 114, 119n.23, 129, 134n.5,7, 135n.14, 171, 183, 192, 205, 217, 231, 233
  Illinois Institute of Technology, 194
  Institute of Environmental Quality in San Francisco, 128
  Kansas, University of, 24n.12
  La Plata, University of (Argentina), 214
  Massachusetts Institute of Technology, 129, 174, 185
  Miami University, 107, 129
  Michigan, University of, 203, 204, 209
  Minnesota, University of, 23n.8, 24n.12
  Musashino Art University (Tokyo), 213
  Newcastle Upon Tyne, University of (England), 177
  New York at Syracuse, State University of, 177
  Notre Dame, University of, 231
  Oklahoma, University of, 199
  Oregon, University of, 24.n12, 129
  Pennsylvania, University of, 23n.8, 24n.12, 54, 81n.1, 90n.6, 183, 189, 190, 197
  Pennsylvania State University, 128
  Philadelphia College of Art, 209

Schools *(continued)*
  Pratt Institute, 200
  Princeton, University of, 186, 187, 194, 203, 204
  Puerto Rico, University of, 232
  Purdue University, 23n.8
  Radcliffe College, 209
  Rice University, 199
  Savannah College of Art and Design, 128
  Southern California, University of, 185
  Stanford University, 174, 185
  Swarthmore College, 197
  Sydney, University of, (Australia), 214
  Texas, University of, 185
  Texas at Arlington, University of, 127
  Texas at Austin, University of, 204
  Toronto, University of, 129
  Tucuman, University of (Argentina), 205
  Utah, University of, 204
  Waseda University (Tokyo), 213
  Washington, University of, 24n.12
  Washington University, 129
  Washington University in St. Louis, 24n.12, 218
  Wye College, University of (London), 177
  Yale University, 145, 185, 189, 190, 197, 202, 204, 205, 211, 212, 214
Schwartz, Martha, 50, 83, 148
  interview of, 209-211
Scott Brown, Denise, 117, 165-166
Selby, Robert, 75, 129, 134n.5, 135n.14, 150
Self confidence, 37-38, 45, 164, 201, 210
  and negative criticism, 15, 40, 112, 113 fig. 9-8, 133, 166
Self critique *(See* Review, self)
Self esteem *(See* Self confidence)
Sennett, Richard, 21-22
Sert, Jose Luis, 22
Sex differences *(See* Women)
Shibley, Robert G., 150, 157
Sleep
  patterns, 39, 41n.16, 17
  recommendations, 97, 99 fig. 8-6
  restrictions, effects of, 39, 96-97, 100n.12
Sommer, Robert, 58, 145, 150
Speaking, public, 65-80
  (See also Presentation, verbal; Salesmanship)
  delivery, 71
  errors to avoid, 71-74
  handling questions, 74-75
  key points, importance of, 69-71, 82n.12
  mastering, importance of, 65-66, 66 fig. 6-1
  negotiating with audience, 75-78
  preparation for, 66-69, 70 fig. 6-7
  summary of recommendations, 79-80 fig. 6-18
Stamps, Art, 128
Star system
  charismatic leaders, 20, 21 fig. 2-6, 26, 164, 165-166, 234
  in design education, 21-22, 159, 166, 207
  jurors as part of, 21-22, 210
State licensing *(See* Professional licensing)
Stern, Robert A. M., 8
  interview of, 211-212

Sternberg, David, 37
Stress, 91-101
  causes of, 39, 91-92, 100n.3
  definition of, 91
  reactions to, 91
  reduction of
    at jury, 92-93, 99 fig. 8-6, 133, 168
    before and after jury, 94-95, 99 fig. 8-6
Student diaries *(See* Diaries, student)
Student participation, 111, 127-129, 131-132, 160-161
Studio, design
  compared to nonstudio courses, 158-159
  competition, role of, 163-166
  evaluation in, 13-15, 13 fig. 2-4, 174, 158-159
  history of, 9-11
  similarities to other settings, 11-12, 15-16
  subculture of, 38-40, 96-98, 99 fig. 8-6, 242
Subculture, studio *(See* Studio, design)
Sullivan, Louis, 157
Summary board, 57, 57 fig. 5-2, 59 fig. 5-5

Takeyama, Minoru, 46, 140, 234
  interview of, 212-213
Tape recording, 69, 74, 114, 116, 130
Tavris, Carol, 112
Teamwork
  in professional offices, 166, 170n.50, 175, 219
  needed in design studios, 16, 161, 164, 167, 220
Term paper, 13 fig. 2-4, 14
Thiel, Philip, 157
Time management, 45-52
  advice from practitioners, 46, 47, 188
  as information management, 46
  as self management, 46, 168, 188
  tips for improvement of, 47-50, 51 fig. 4-5
Torre, Susana
  interview of, 214-215

Universities *(See* Schools)
Urban planning, 3, 26, 166, 82n.22
Ury, William, 78 fig. 6-17

Van der Rohe, Mies, 22, 22 fig. 2-7, 157, 178, 182
Venturi, Robert, 165, 197
Video recording
  jury workshops, 117
  presentation practice, 69, 69 fig. 6-6, 81, 82n.9, 130
Vischer, Jacqueline, 150
Visiting critics *(See* Critics, visiting)
Visual-verbal communication, 88
Vonier, Thomas, 157

Walker, John C., 30, 50
  interview of, 215-216
Walker, Peter, 50
  interview of, 216-217
Ward, Anthony, 127, 135n.14
Ward, William A., 27

Weber, Max, 20
Weese, Cynthia, 129
   interview of 217-219
Welch, Frank, 144
Welch, Polly, 150
Werner, Jeffrey, 67, 84, 95
   interview of, 220-221
Will, Phil, 207, 208
Wilson, Woodrow, 137
Witzling, Lawrence, 141

Wolfe, Tom, 21
Women, 6, 16, 72-73, 110
   demographic data, 236
   evaluation of juries and education, 35, 35 fig. 3-6, 36, 165
   representation in architecture, 26n.94, 40, 82n.10, 165–166, 170n.40,41, 172, 210, 219
Workshops, 117, 121, 134
   with user groups, 160-161
Wright, Frank Lloyd, 21, 21 fig. 2-6, 22, 157, 158, 166, 199, 208, 209

www.ingramcontent.com/pod-product-compliance
Lightning Source LLC
Chambersburg PA
CBHW081218170426
43198CB00017B/2650